Before the Quagmire

Before the Quagmire

*American Intervention in Laos,
1954–1961*

William J. Rust

 UNIVERSITY PRESS OF KENTUCKY

Editorial and Sales Offices: The University Press of Kentucky
663 South Limestone Street, Lexington, Kentucky 40508-4008
www.kentuckypress.com

16 15 14 13 12   5 4 3 2 1

Maps by Richard A. Gilbreath, University of Kentucky Cartography Lab

Library of Congress Cataloging-in-Publication Data

Rust, William J.
  Before the quagmire : American intervention in Laos, 1954–1961 /
William J. Rust.
      pages   cm
  Includes bibliographical references and index.
  ISBN 978-0-8131-3578-6 (hardcover : alk. paper) —
  ISBN 978-0-8131-3579-3 (ebook)
  1. United States—Foreign relations—Laos. 2. Laos—Foreign relations—United
States. 3. United States—Foreign relations—1953–1961. I. Title.
  E183.8.L3R87 2012
  327.73059409'045—dc23
                            2012003860

This book is printed on acid-free recycled paper meeting
the requirements of the American National Standard
for Permanence in Paper for Printed Library Materials.

∞

Manufactured in the United States of America.

  Member of the Association of

ACC LIBRARY SERVICES AUSTIN, TX

Contents

Illustrations follow page 166

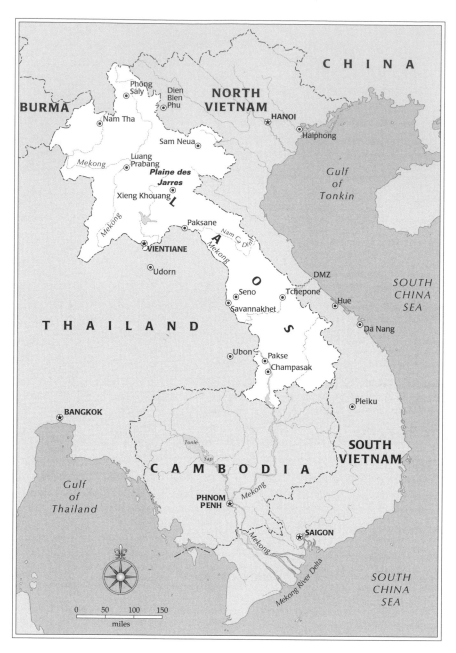

Laos and bordering countries, 1954–1975

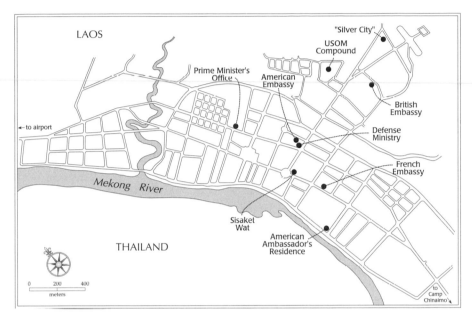

Vientiane, Laos, 1960

Abbreviations

AEC	Atomic Energy Commission
ANL	Armée Nationale du Laos
CAT	Civil Air Transport
CDNI	Committee for the Defense of National Interests
CIA	Central Intelligence Agency
CINCPAC	Commander-in-Chief, Pacific Command
CIP	Commodity Import Program
CNO	Chief of Naval Operations
DCI	Director of Central Intelligence
DCM	Deputy Chief of Mission
DEFCON	Defense Readiness Condition
DRV	Democratic Republic of Vietnam (North Vietnam)
Embtel	embassy telegram
FAL	Forces d'Armée de Laos
FAR	Forces Armée du Royaume
FMM	French Military Mission
HRC	High Revolutionary Command
ICA	International Cooperation Administration
ICC	International Commission for Supervision and Control
ISA	International Security Affairs
JCS	Joint Chiefs of Staff
LHL	Lao Hom Lao (Rally of the Lao People)
MAAG	Military Assistance Advisory Group
NCO	noncommissioned officer
NIE	National Intelligence Estimate

NLHS	Neo Lao Hat Sat (Lao Patriotic Front)
NSC	National Security Council
OCB	Operations Coordinating Board
OSS	Office of Strategic Services
PARU	Police Aerial Reinforcement Unit
PAVN	People's Army of Vietnam
PBCFIA	President's Board of Consultants on Foreign Intelligence Activities
PEO	Programs Evaluation Office
PL	Pathet Lao
PRC	People's Republic of China
RLG	Royal Lao Government
RVN	Republic of Vietnam (South Vietnam)
SEA	Southeast Asia
SIGINT	signals intelligence
SEATO	Southeast Asia Treaty Organization
USAF	United States Air Force
USIS	United States Information Services
USOM	United States Operations Mission

Introduction
Interested Outside Powers

J. Graham Parsons, once a rising star among the career professionals in the US Department of State, was appointed ambassador to the kingdom of Laos in 1956 at the comparatively young age of forty-eight. Senior officials in the department considered him an "outstanding" diplomat whose assignment to the sparsely populated and newly independent Southeast Asian country would prepare him "for more important ambassadorships" in the future. After loyally serving the Eisenhower administration in Vientiane, a town he later called "the administrative capital of the kingdom that no one really administered," Parsons returned to Washington in 1958 to become deputy assistant secretary of state for far eastern affairs, then assistant secretary of state for the region the following year.[1]

When Dwight D. Eisenhower's presidency ended on January 20, 1961, Parsons was the administration official most closely identified with Laos, a country a colleague had characterized as being in a state of "perpetual crisis."[2] Compared to the ideological struggle with the Soviet Union and the People's Republic of China, and to the major cold war battlefields in Europe and Asia, Laos often seemed a small-scale skirmish in the fight against communism. In the last six months of Eisenhower's second term, however, Laos became a priority after a coup d'état, led by an obscure US-trained paratroop captain, evolved into a superpower confrontation that threatened to become another Korean War or worse.

Parsons later acknowledged that his association with Laos had not only earned him professional advancement but also nearly ended his career. To the new officials of the Kennedy administration, he was a symbol of ineffectual anticommunist policies in Laos and other parts of the world. Within a month of Kennedy's inauguration, Parsons learned that he would be the next US ambassador to Sweden. The appointment was not an obvious demotion for the career Foreign Service officer, much less a hardship post. It was, however, geographically and politically remote from the Far East, his primary area of expertise and a region where the new administration was determined to meet the challenge of Soviet premier Nikita Khrushchev's support for "wars of national liberation."[3]

Parsons served in Stockholm for six years, an unusually long assignment for a US ambassador and an indication that he was out of favor with the administration of President Lyndon B. Johnson. With characteristic professionalism, Parsons performed well as ambassador to Sweden, even in the face of angry politicians and citizens whose political neutrality did not preclude angry and sometimes violent denunciations of the Vietnam War. While serving in Stockholm in the summer of 1965, he learned of a book manuscript by historian Arthur Schlesinger Jr., which "unfairly represented" his role in Lao affairs. The source for this information and assessment was Winthrop G. Brown, an old friend who had served as American ambassador to Laos at the end of Eisenhower's presidency and the beginning of Kennedy's. The book was *A Thousand Days: John F. Kennedy in the White House,* a history-memoir based on the Pulitzer Prize–winning author's privileged access as a presidential special assistant.[4]

A Thousand Days was an instant bestseller and well on its way to winning another Pulitzer Prize for Schlesinger when Parsons first read parts of the book in early 1966. In addition to providing a hagiographic portrait of the recently slain president, Schlesinger criticized sharply the foreign policy of President Eisenhower, Secretary of State John Foster Dulles, and the Foreign Service officers who served them, particularly in the Bureau of Far Eastern Affairs. The historian charged that Parsons had "drastically misconceived the situation" in Laos and that his appointment as ambassador to Sweden exemplified a "conspiracy" allowing the Foreign Service to take care of its "worst as well as—sometimes better than—its best."[5]

Parsons thought the Laos portion of the book was "composed of half-truths and highly colored distortions." The volume's specific references to him were relatively few but hurtful. Accustomed to being a target for critics of the Eisenhower administration's policy in Laos, Parsons thought it unfair that someone as sophisticated as Schlesinger refused to recognize that neither ambassadors nor even assistant secretaries of state made US foreign policy. They contributed to policy deliberations, to be sure, but their primary role was carrying out the decisions of the president and the secretary of state. And to use Parsons as an example of the Foreign Service somehow outmaneuvering the president in the appointment of bungling ambassadors seemed to him an "intemperate abuse of my name and reputation."[6]

In fact, Parsons was hardly the incompetent diplomat Schlesinger portrayed, and his advice to senior policymakers often reflected a subtler grasp of Lao realities than the kneejerk views the author attributed to Foreign Service professionals in the Bureau of Far Eastern Affairs. Parsons did, however, share the fundamental policy perspectives of senior Eisenhower administration officials: Communist control of Laos would threaten US security interests in Southeast Asia and around the world; a neutral Royal Laotian Government (RLG) would inevitably succumb to communist subversion; and Prince Souvanna Phouma, the kingdom's leading statesman, was weak, naive, and dangerous. Although regretting aspects of his own performance in Vientiane and Washington, Parsons later wrote in an unpublished memoir that he "would not in the circumstances of the time have been happy with any other policy."[7]

Parsons, who was replaced as ambassador to Sweden by a Johnson administration political appointee, never again served as a US chief of mission. He was prescient in fearing the impact of Schlesinger's book on his reputation. When Parsons died in 1991, at the age of eighty-three, his five-hundred-word obituary in the *New York Times* devoted two paragraphs to quoting Schlesinger and summarizing the historian's views. "As far as is known," the obituary observed, "Mr. Parsons never commented specifically in public about these and other assertions by Mr. Schlesinger involving him."[8]

Parsons was, of course, just one of many US civilian and military officials who helped formulate and execute the Eisenhower administration's Laos policy from 1954, when the Geneva Accords ended the first Indochina war, until January 1961, when John F. Kennedy became president. This book is the story of the decisions these officials made in Washington and the actions they took in Laos. A case study in transforming a small foreign-policy problem into a large one, the American experience in Laos in the 1950s was a key initial misstep on the road to war in Southeast

Asia. Moreover, the political and military "cures" prescribed by the US government sometimes worsened the "disease" of communist subversion in Laos. In his presidential memoir, Eisenhower defended his Laos policy but admitted that his administration had "left a legacy of strife and confusion" there.[9]

Inheriting President Harry S. Truman's commitment to support the French in Indochina, President Eisenhower decided in 1954 to assume direct US responsibility for aiding resistance to communism in Laos, South Vietnam, and Cambodia. In Laos, a constitutional monarchy, the Eisenhower administration's commitment included financing 100 percent of its fledgling armed forces, providing the country's army with covert military trainers, and establishing a US civilian aid mission that Parsons once described as "probably the most unsatisfactory program in the entire world."[10] The cornerstone of Eisenhower administration policy was encouraging the development of a pro-Western, anticommunist Lao government and opposing a coalition government that included the Pathet Lao, a Laotian political-military organization supported by Vietnamese communists and led by members of the Vietnamese Workers' Party.

An important instrument of Eisenhower's policy in Laos was a relatively new government organization established in 1947: the Central Intelligence Agency (CIA). In 1954 policy guidance from the National Security Council (NSC) included the recommendation that the CIA "conduct covert operations on the maximum feasible and productive scale" in Laos. In addition to collecting intelligence, countering subversion, and providing arms to anticommunist guerrillas, the CIA played a key role in the internal political affairs of Laos. The goal of agency political action was straightforward: to support or oppose various noncommunist leaders based almost exclusively on the perceived strength or weakness of their anticommunist convictions. Interference in Lao political affairs, as State Department officials recognized, created a "heavy responsibility" for the US government. There was not, however, an equivalent awareness that manipulating the kingdom's political life had a destabilizing impact on the fragile noncommunist base the United States sought to strengthen and unify. Richard M. Bissell Jr., the agency's deputy director for operations from 1959 to 1962, and an aggressive supporter of political action in Laos, later concluded that the US government's goal of a stable anticommunist, pro-Western government was "unobtainable in the context of that nation's politics."[11]

The Eisenhower administration's efforts to thwart communism in Laos were complicated by the divided views of State Department, Pentagon, and CIA officials, many of whom were prisoners of the parochial views of their agencies. Though united in their aim of preventing a communist takeover, diplomats, military officers, and intelligence operatives often proposed and pursued contradictory actions in the field. The culmination of US disunity occurred in the second half of 1960, when officials in Vientiane, the State Department, and the Pentagon and CIA headquarters held three different viewpoints about policy in Laos. One consequence of the poorly resolved institutional conflict was that the US government found itself providing nominal support to the internationally recognized RLG, while giving "substantial moral and material support" to the Lao general who sought to overthrow it. This latter policy, opposed by Western allies of the United States, placed the Eisenhower administration in an "untenable and exposed position," in Parsons's words.[12] By the time a more defensible policy emerged, covert American military trainers were combatants in Laos, the Soviet Union was directly engaged in the conflict, and the United States was propping up a politically weak, militarily incompetent government.

The lack of unity among Western allies, particularly the sometimes-toxic relations between the United States and France, also hampered the achievement of US objectives in Laos. Although defeated by the communist led Viet Minh in the first Indochina war (1946–1954), the French remained deeply embedded in the ministries of the RLG, and the small French military mission in Laos was the only foreign force permitted by the 1954 Geneva Accords. Constantly at odds with the US government over Lao political leadership and military training, France faced a daunting post-Geneva challenge in Indochina: simultaneously maintaining its influence in Laos, South Vietnam, and Cambodia; avoiding involvement in hostilities with the communists; and preserving a good relationship with the United States. "The fact that these three objectives contain elements of mutual inconsistency poses real problems to French policy," US intelligence analysts concluded. An unacknowledged problem for US policy in Southeast Asia was avoiding a too-close association with the

French, while simultaneously learning from them and from their long experience in the region.[13]

One of the more troubling aspects of the American experience in Laos was the inability of the US government to apply the harsh lessons from that country in the 1950s to neighboring South Vietnam in the early 1960s. In both insurgencies, the primary response to political challenges was a disproportionate emphasis on US military assistance. Both the Eisenhower administration in Laos and the Kennedy administration in South Vietnam failed in their attempts to unite anticommunist leaders, who often demonstrated a greater commitment to gaining or retaining political power than to fighting insurgents. The visible divisions among the US missions in Vientiane and Saigon confused friends, emboldened opportunists, and ultimately undercut American objectives. A particularly ill-considered US policy in both Southeast Asian countries was to encourage the overthrow of sometimes-difficult civilian heads of state— Souvanna Phouma in Laos and Ngo Dinh Diem in South Vietnam—in favor of generals who quickly revealed their political ineptitude. "Everything that occurred in Laos occurred later in South Vietnam [on] a larger scale," recalled Lieutenant General Andrew J. Boyle, who served as one of the chiefs of the US military advisory effort in Laos.[14]

Although its first kingdom dates back to the fourteenth century, Laos was often described as more of a geographic area than a nation, in part because of the arbitrary boundaries created by French colonial administration. Approximately the area of Utah and shaped somewhat like a key, Laos was granted full independence by France in 1953. During the years covered by this book, the population of Laos was approximately 2 million.[15] Within this small population were scores of ethnic groups, each speaking one of four principal languages. The country's rugged terrain and primitive communications further hampered the development of a unified national identity. One of the poorest countries in the world, Laos had high rates of illiteracy, infant mortality, and other social problems associated with poverty. Before World War II, "less than a dozen Lao had received the equivalent of a full college education," and in the 1950s most Lao ministers "had the equivalent of a United States junior high school education."[16]

The kingdom was a cold war pawn largely because of its geography. A landlocked country, Laos had more powerful neighbors that included two communist nations, the People's Republic of China (PRC) and the Democratic Republic of Vietnam (DRV), commonly referred to as North Vietnam, and two pro–United States countries, Thailand and the Republic of Vietnam (RVN), better known as South Vietnam. The governments of all these countries shared a foreign-policy goal that encouraged conflict: each wanted Laos to serve as a friendly, even compliant, buffer state that would enhance its own security. Joel M. Halpern, an anthropologist who first traveled to Laos in late 1956 as a young member of the US economic aid mission, later observed: "Americans, Chinese, French, Japanese, Thai, and Vietnamese have all participated in trying to control and change the lives of the peoples of Laos and, in this endeavor, have received help or 'supervision' from Canadians, English, Indians, Poles, and Russians. It would seem that seldom in world history has such a large and varied company meddled in the lives of so few."[17]

Among the defining documents of modern Laos are the agreements and declarations constituting the July 1954 Geneva Accords, which ended the French colonial era in Indochina and temporarily stopped the fighting in Vietnam, Cambodia, and Laos. Aptly characterized as a "bag full of contradictions" by historian Arthur Dommen, the accords were influenced by the larger geopolitical interests of the Western nations, the Soviet Union, and the PRC. The more powerful countries pressed their smaller Indochinese allies to make concessions they disliked and did not long observe, which ultimately led to an even larger war in Vietnam, Laos, and Cambodia. The United States described its role at Geneva as "an interested nation" that was "neither a belligerent nor a principal in the negotiation." The US government did not sign the Geneva Accords but pledged, in the words of a Dulles press statement, that it "would not seek by force to overthrow the settlement."[18]

Consistent with its subordinate status in French Indochina, Laos received less attention at Geneva than Vietnam. To the Western allies and the RLG, the issue in Laos appeared straightforward: The Viet Minh invaded northern Laos in April 1953 and central Laos the following December. Once these forces were withdrawn, the RLG would be able to settle its own internal affairs. But the communist nations at Geneva claimed there were substantial "local resistance forces" in Laos that should be recognized and accommodated in a political settlement. The primary interest of the PRC was to prevent the United States from establishing any military bases in Laos and to prohibit the kingdom from joining a Western military alliance. A key US goal at Geneva was to block any agreement that "might lead to [a] coalition" government with the Pathet Lao.[19]

The Geneva "Agreement on the Cessation of Hostilities in Laos" ordered all foreign combat units—French and Vietnamese—out of the country, and it recognized the sovereignty of the Western-leaning RLG over the entire kingdom. The "fighting units" of the Pathet Lao were allowed to regroup in two northern provinces adjacent to North Vietnam, Sam Neua and Phong Saly.[20] According to the agreement, all Laotians— whether they had fought for or against the RLG—would be integrated into a single national community through an election in 1955.

The Geneva agreement explicitly prohibited the introduction of foreign troops or military personnel into Laos, but it did allow up to fifteen hundred French officers and noncommissioned officers to remain in the country to train the Armée Nationale du Laos (ANL). The French were also permitted to maintain two military bases in Laos, with personnel totaling no more than thirty-five hundred men. Because the French had sole responsibility for training the Lao army, the US government could not establish a Military Assistance Advisory Group (MAAG) in the kingdom, as it did in South Vietnam and Cambodia. The inability to establish a legal, overt MAAG in Laos turned out to be a chronic military and political headache for the Eisenhower administration.[21]

Lao officials were bitterly disappointed by the Geneva Accords. The agreement created a de facto partitioning of the country and appeared to legitimate the weak territorial claims of the Pathet Lao, which sought to transform a small military presence in Sam Neua and Phong Saly into total administrative control of the two provinces. Many RLG officials felt doubly betrayed by the French, who had not kept their promise to fight the war in Laos to a successful conclusion and who then pressured the kingdom to agree to an unfavorable peace. When each delegation at Geneva was asked to declare its position on the final agreements, the Lao representatives swallowed their objections, saying they "had no observations to make."[22]

For the US government, the Geneva Accords were a discouraging conclusion to four years of increasing support to the French in Indochina. The Eisenhower administration was disappointed not only by the French defeat at the hands of the communist-led Viet Minh, but also by the inability of the Western allies to work together to prevent that defeat. President Eisenhower had demonstrated his willingness to provide US military equipment and money to support France's fight in Indochina. But without allies, he had refused to intervene directly with US military forces. In the spring of 1954, his administration had vainly attempted to enlist the United Kingdom in united diplomatic and, if necessary, military action to prevent a catastrophic French defeat in Indochina, symbolized by the doomed garrison at Dien Bien Phu. Rebuffing an appeal by Secretary of State John Foster Dulles, UK foreign secretary Anthony Eden observed: "Military intervention would be 'terrific business,' a bigger affair than Korea, which could get us nowhere."[23]

On July 30, 1954, a report by the Operations Coordinating Board (OCB), the interagency body overseeing the execution of national security policy, reflected the post-Geneva mood of defeat within the US government. The OCB characterized the accords as "a serious loss for the free world, the psychological and political effects of which will be felt throughout the Far East and around the globe." Days later a National Intelligence Estimate (NIE), a consensus document summarizing the views of analysts in the CIA, the State Department, and the Pentagon, concluded that the Geneva agreements had benefited the communists by providing international recognition of North Vietnam and its military and political power in Indochina. The US intelligence community believed that the communists would continue to seek control of all of Indochina.[24]

The prospects for Laos, according to the NIE, would depend largely on two uncertain future developments: a strong and stable government in neighboring South Vietnam and continued French military assistance to Laos. US intelligence analysts concluded that the current internal situation in Laos was relatively stable but that Pathet Lao "freedom of action" could contribute to the overthrow of the RLG "through subversion or elections." Reflecting a realpolitik view of the future of Laos, Cambodia, and Vietnam, the NIE predicted: "The course of future developments will be determined less by the Geneva agreements than by the relative capabilities and actions of the Communist and non-Communist entities in Indochina, and of interested outside powers."[25]

The Eisenhower administration's policy response to the collapse of French Indochina was to step up the US commitment to the region. After many months of deliberations with his advisers on Indochinese affairs, the president agreed on August 17, 1954, to provide direct US assistance to South Vietnam, Cambodia, and Laos, instead of passing military and economic support through the French. Eisenhower's second far-reaching decision that day was authorizing Dulles to proceed with the collective defense treaty establishing the Southeast Asia Treaty Organization (SEATO). Signed by eight nations* in Manila the following month, the treaty had been influenced by the administration's disappointing pre-Geneva diplomatic maneuvers, which led to the conclusion that "arrangements for collective defense need to be made in advance of aggression, not after it is under way." The former states of Indochina could not join the alliance without violating the Geneva Accords, but a separate SEATO protocol extended the treaty's protection to them.[26]

When seeking presidential approval for the pact, Dulles acknowledged that, on one hand, the SEATO alliance risked US prestige "in an area where we had little control and where the situation was by no means promising." On the other hand, the secretary of state observed, failure to go ahead with the treaty "would mark a total abandonment of the area without a struggle." Extending the treaty's protection to South Vietnam, Cambodia, and Laos, Dulles declared, "was the lesser of two evils."[27]

The only senior Eisenhower administration official to question US strategic interests in Indochina was Secretary of Defense Charles Erwin Wilson, the former president of General Motors. At an October 1954 NSC meeting, he told the president and his advisers that "the only sensible course of action was for the U.S. to get out of Indochina completely and as soon as possible." Eisenhower did not agree with Wilson, who had a reputation for impetuous pronouncements. The president valued Wilson's previous management experience at the enormous industrial enterprise that manufactured vehicles and materiel for the Pentagon. Moreover, he depended on "Engine Charlie" (a nickname that distinguished Wilson from President Truman's chief of the Office of Defense Mobilization, Charles E. "Electric Charlie" Wilson, the former president of General Electric) to help him develop a robust US military capability that would be economically sustainable. Eisenhower did not, however, look to his secretary of defense

---

*Australia, France, New Zealand, Pakistan, the Philippines, Thailand, the United Kingdom, and the United States.

for substantive advice on military or foreign affairs. At the NSC meeting, Eisenhower explained to Wilson that continued retreat in the face of communist advances in Southeast Asia "would lead to a grave situation from the point of view of our national security."[28]

Wilson did not accept this rationale for involving the United States in the former French colonial territory. According to the minutes of the meeting, Wilson said that if the US government "had ever been in control of Indochina, as we had once been in the Philippines, he would feel differently about it. As matters stood, however, he could see nothing but grief in store for us if we remained in this area." Although unprepared to propose a reversal of the NSC recommendation to assist anticommunist governments in Indochina, Wilson presciently observed that US policy was based on an assumption of French and British support, "which, in point of fact, we did not now appear to have."[29]

Engine Charlie's skepticism about US strategic interests in Southeast Asia inevitably leads to the question, Why did virtually all policymakers—from the Truman administration through Kennedy's—believe that resisting communism in the former states of French Indochina was a vital US interest? (During Lyndon B. Johnson's presidency, official dissent began to grow, but in the 1950s and early 1960s there was little high-level disagreement about the necessity of preventing communist takeovers in Indochina.) In the five decades since Eisenhower's presidency ended and Kennedy's began—and particularly since the final collapse of the Soviet Union in 1991—the falling-domino principle, the monolithic communist threat, and other cold war truisms have not aged well.

Contemporary hindsight, however, runs the risk of underestimating the fear and political orthodoxy inspired by the aggressive tendencies of communist leaders in Moscow and Peking in the immediate post–World War II era. Communist advances in Europe and Asia, combined with the Soviet Union's earlier-than-expected development of the atomic bomb, had a profound impact on the foreign policies and domestic politics of the United States, ranging from the enlightened self-interest of the Marshall Plan to help rebuild Western Europe to the destructive excesses of Senator Joseph McCarthy's witch hunt for communists in the US government.

Christian A. Chapman, a career Foreign Service officer who served with Parsons in the embassy in Vientiane and as his Lao desk officer in the State Department, later recalled the mood of the 1950s, particularly its impact on policymaking for the Far East: "Anybody who had said at that time, 'Well, maybe we should talk to the communists,' would have been crucified within the executive branch, in the legislative branch, and in the press. There was a degree of unanimity in this country that created a lot of pressure, and made it virtually impossible to propose alternatives."[30]

In a March 29, 1955, letter to UK prime minister Winston Churchill, President Eisenhower summarized his view of the threat in the Far East, concluding:

> The time to stop any advance of Communism in Asia is here, now. We have come to the point where every additional backward step must be deemed a defeat for the Western world. In fact, it is a triple defeat. First, we lose a potential ally. Next, we give to an implacable enemy another recruit. Beyond this, every such retreat creates in the minds of neutrals the fear that we do not mean what we say when we pledge our support to people who want to remain free. We show ourselves fearful of the Communistic brigands and create the impression that we are slinking along in the shadows, hoping that the beast will finally be satiated and cease his predatory tactics before he finally devours us. So the third result is that the morale of our friends crumbles.[31]

Eisenhower, the last US president born in the nineteenth century, was a leader with a warm public persona that sometimes masked an incisive mind. A national hero for commanding the Allied forces in Europe during World War II, Eisenhower was a popular, reassuring presence in the White House for most Americans. His sometimes-mangled syntax, usually an intentional effort to avoid commenting substantively to the press, and his fondness for golf, a country-club game requiring little physical exertion, contributed to the image of a passive president who deferred to strong-willed subordinates, particularly Secretary of State John Foster Dulles. Declassified documents and statements by former presidential advisers have conclusively refuted this notion. "Eisenhower was always in full charge," recalled C. Douglas Dillon, a diplomat who served as undersecretary of state in the 1950s.[32]

President during a decade of relative domestic and international stability, Eisenhower later declared: "We kept the peace. People ask how it happened—by God, it didn't just happen, I'll tell you that." This comment was made in the 1960s when Eisenhower's reputation as president was at a low point among historians, who in one poll ranked him between Andrew Johnson and Chester Arthur. Until his death in 1969, Eisenhower remained convinced that his underappreciated achievements in foreign affairs were based on good planning, organization, and management, as well as sound judgment honed by his military career and long experience with world leaders such as Franklin D. Roosevelt, Winston Churchill, Charles de Gaulle, and Joseph Stalin. By the mid-1980s, many historians had reached similar conclusions about Eisenhower's presidency. Robert A. Divine, an early and leading member of the "Eisenhower revisionism" movement, observed that his "moderation and prudence served as an enduring model of presidential restraint—one that his successors ignored to their eventual regret."[33]

Eisenhower biographer Stephen E. Ambrose wrote that the president was at his "best" when managing crises—for example, in the Taiwan Straits, the Middle East, Berlin, and other cold war flash points: "Eisenhower managed each one without overreacting, without going to war, without increasing defense spending, without frightening people half out of their wits. He downplayed each one, insisted a solution could be found, and found one."[34]

Absent from Ambrose's list of skillfully managed crises was Laos.

Chapter 1

The Most Difficult Post in the Entire Foreign Service

In 1966, THE YEAR he retired from the Department of State as a career ambassador, the highest professional rank in the Foreign Service, Charles W. Yost sat down for an interview to discuss his diplomatic experiences while serving under John Foster Dulles. When the topic turned to the kingdom of Laos, where he had been appointed minister in 1954 and then ambassador in 1955, Yost mentioned the crowded living quarters and vermin-infested offices of the US mission in Vientiane. Preferring not to dwell on "all the gruesome details," which for him included a case of amoebic dysentery that reduced his already slender frame to a skeletal 115 pounds, Yost characterized the US mission this way: "the most primitive and ill-equipped diplomatic post I have ever encountered."[1]

When Yost arrived in Laos on September 22, 1954, the US government was represented by a "legation," a small suboffice of the larger American embassy in Saigon. US diplomatic business in Vientiane, the administrative capital of Laos, was initially conducted by a handful of Americans in two rooms of a villa facing the muddy Mekong River. A few hundred yards downstream—but not always downwind—was a slaughterhouse. Animals were killed just before dawn for delivery to Vientiane markets the same day. Inedible animal parts were tossed on the riverbank and consumed by vultures that dozed in tall trees near the legation, waiting for the next day's meal.

Previously the home of the head of the French hospital in Vientiane, the villa in which the first American diplomats in Laos worked was a forty-year-old pale green stucco structure with a gravel circular driveway and a patchy grass front yard. Bachelor members of the legation lived in one of three bedrooms, the first-floor water closet doubled as a code room (a note on the exterior of the door indicated who was cleared to enter), and a gasoline-powered generator in the backyard provided a limited amount of electric power. As the US presence in Vientiane expanded, a large army tent in the yard of the house provided additional office space.

Tropical heat, poor sanitation, and a nearly total absence of modern amenities contributed to Vientiane's reputation as "the most difficult post in the entire Foreign Service." Appearing to Western eyes as an overgrown village, where water buffalo shared the streets with pedicabs, scooters, and the occasional automobile, Vientiane had been the capital of Lan Xang ("Million Elephants"), a Lao kingdom that was a political and military force in mainland Southeast Asia in the sixteenth and seventeenth centuries. In 1828 the Siamese destroyed Vientiane, which remained a ruin until the arrival of the French in the late nineteenth century. The French rebuilt Vientiane, but the town's primitive conditions reflected its marginal importance to French colonial interests in Indochina. Vientiane, in the words of a US official who served in the legation with Yost, was "a very small hick town, in a hick civilization."[2]

The grim physical conditions Yost encountered in Vientiane matched the tone of the gloomy briefings on Laos he had received earlier in Washington. According to a military intelligence report prepared specifically for him, the Pathet Lao forces regrouping in the northern provinces of Sam Neua and Phong Saly "pose a real threat to Laotian internal security." The ANL, furthermore, was "not a good army"; it lacked "leadership and spirit." The kingdom's poor military capabilities, according to the report, had been influenced by cultural factors, including Buddhism, the religion of the lowland Lao. The largest ethnic group in Laos, constituting about 50 percent of the population, the lowland Lao lived primarily on the fertile plains of the Mekong River and grew rice in irrigated fields. The intelligence report prepared for Yost declared that the Laotians' "lackadaisical attitude, delightful indolence and generally pacifist outlook do not produce good material for soldiers."[3]

The information Yost received on the military capabilities of the ethnic Lao reflected a mixture of fact, fiction, and condescension that merged into an enduring stereotype. Compared with their neighbors in China and Vietnam, the Lao were mild-mannered, soft-spoken, and less aggressive. However, "the picture of Lao tranquility should not be overdrawn," anthropologist Joel Halpern wrote in a 1960 report for the military-funded RAND Corporation. "Warfare has been rather common in this area. Cities have been sacked and slaves taken. After his defeat by the Thai in the early 19th century, the last King of Vientiane was brought to Bangkok where he was exhibited in a cage like a captured animal. Even now, Lao officials and villagers often show little compunction in conscripting tribal people, including women and children, for hard labor."[4]

Yost received perhaps the most pessimistic assessment of Laos from Undersecretary of State W. Bedell Smith, who had served as Eisenhower's chief of staff during World War II, as ambassador to the Soviet Union from 1946 to 1948, and as director of Central Intelligence (DCI) before his appointment to the State Department. Smith, a demanding and effective administrator whose disposition was "foul at the best times," according to his biographer, had been deeply engaged in the negotiations at Geneva. His public comments on the agreements included the pragmatic observation, "Diplomacy is rarely able to gain at the conference table what cannot be gained or held on the battlefield." Privately, he told Yost that the United States would probably have to settle for the loss of Sam Neua and Phong Saly to the communists.[5]

As an eager, first-time chief of mission, Yost was, in his own words, "shocked and disappointed" by Smith's pessimism, particularly since US policy was to hold the line against communist expansion in South Vietnam, Cambodia, and Laos. Yost was also indignant with the attitude of administrative officials in the State Department who were responsible for providing support to the legation in Vientiane. He later summarized their view as, "Well, there's not any point in our sending a lot of stuff up to you there, because the whole place is going down the drain very shortly."[6]

Before he left for Vientiane, Yost wrote down his understanding of US policy in Laos and submitted the document to Assistant Secretary of State Walter S. Robertson for his concurrence. One of "the earliest objectives," Yost wrote, was assisting the RLG in "recapturing control" of the northern provinces. The US government would continue its public declarations that Sam Neua and Phong Saly were "integral and inalienable parts of Laos"; would "exert pressure" in international bodies to help return control of the northern provinces to the RLG; and would, if necessary, "encourage the Laotian and French Governments to drive out or disarm by force the Communist guerillas."[7]

In the view of his State Department colleagues, "Charlie" Yost was an exemplar of the better traditions of the pre–World War II "old Foreign Service." Born in Watertown, New York—the same upstate town where John Foster Dulles and his siblings were raised—Yost grew up in a well-to-do family, attended a private boarding school (Hotchkiss), and graduated from an Ivy League college (Princeton, class of 1928). He was not, however, the stereotypical diplomatic "cookie pusher" in striped pants and morning coat, whose primary occupation was socializing with equally privileged foreigners. According to Seymour M. "Max" Finger, who served as his political officer in Vientiane, Yost "was a man of great courage and decisiveness, who did not hesitate to speak his mind, gently but firmly. His views would often prevail because of the clarity of his thinking, his mastery of the subject matter, and his eloquence in expressing them."[8]

Yost joined the Foreign Service in 1930, initially serving in Alexandria, Egypt, then in Warsaw, Poland, where he met and married his wife. After briefly pursuing a career as a freelance foreign correspondent, he returned to the State Department and subsequently received assignments to a range of increasingly responsible positions in Washington and abroad. In the late 1940s and early 1950s, Yost served in three countries facing communist pressure: Czechoslovakia, Greece, and Austria. On July 20, 1954, the day before the conclusion of the Geneva conference, President Eisenhower approved Yost's nomination as US minister to Laos.

When he arrived in Vientiane, one of Yost's first unofficial duties (he had not yet officially presented his diplomatic credentials to the king) was paying an informal call on Prince Souvanna Phouma. A nephew of the king, Souvanna was widely recognized as the most able statesman in Laos. He was wealthy and urbane, enjoying bridge, wine, and British pipe tobacco or a good cigar. To the enduring consternation of Eisenhower administration officials, Souvanna refused to view Laos in the absolute terms of cold war ideology. Confident in his ability to balance the competing political forces in Laos, Souvanna was willing to compromise with the Pathet Lao if it would lead to reunification of his country. To his detractors on the right and left, he seemed weak. In reality, he resisted those who pressured him the most. In the 1950s, it was the Americans. In the 1960s, it was the communists.

Souvanna, born in 1901, had received an excellent French education in Hanoi and Paris, earning an engineering degree from an elite *grande école,* the pinnacle of higher education in France. When he returned to his home-land, he married a French-Laotian woman. A nationalist, Souvanna joined Lao Issara (Free Lao), a small, short-lived Lao independence movement formed at the end of World War II. It was not very effective but nonetheless respected. When the French returned to Indochina after the war, they easily defeated Lao Issara, forcing Souvanna and other leaders of the movement into exile in Thailand. A subsequent reconciliation with the French, based on the gradual removal of barriers to Lao independence, enabled Souvanna and most members of the movement to return to the kingdom and partici-pate in its political life. A splinter group of Lao Issara aligned itself with Ho Chi Minh, becoming the leadership of the Pathet Lao.

Like many Lao politicians at that time, Souvanna subscribed to a political point of view that US officials found dangerous: no real Laotian could be a communist. The political challenge, he believed, was to sepa-rate the misguided members of the Pathet Lao from the more dangerous North Vietnamese–controlled communists. If such a viewpoint were not offensive enough to US cold war sensibilities, Souvanna's half-brother, Prince Souphanouvong, was the public face of the Pathet Lao leadership. Souvanna attempted to assure Yost that his brother was not a communist, but he failed to persuade him or virtually any other US official.

Insufficient fervor in the struggle against the Pathet Lao was partially responsible for Souvanna's dwindling political support among the king-dom's elites. Many Laotians blamed him for capitulating to French pres-sure at the Geneva conference and agreeing to recognize the Pathet Lao and its temporary administrative control of Sam Neua and Phong Saly. The royal family, in particular, was disappointed by the performance of Souvanna's representatives at Geneva. Yost later wrote that Crown Prince Savang Vatthana, who had assumed virtually all of the responsibilities his ailing father, the king, "pulled the rug from under" Souvanna for sur-rendering "vital interests" of Laos. In October 1954 Souvanna formally resigned as prime minister.[9]

Prince Souvanna Phouma's resignation triggered one of the most durable institutions of Lao parliamentary democracy in the 1950s: a cabinet crisis that prevented any meaningful government action. The fundamental causes of the recurring episodes of political paralysis were the personal, family, and regional rivalries "of the relatively few influential persons in Lao public life," according to US officials in Vientiane.[10] Nearly all of the kingdom's leaders were either the descendants of royalty who exercised power in a specific region or the offspring of feudal lords, village headmen, and tribal chiefs who could afford a French education and participate in government and politics. Together, they formed an "elite of a few hundred people who run Laos politically and commercially."[11]

Exacerbating the destructive political impact of the small, divided Lao elite were the laws for electing a prime minister. A premier in Laos had to win two-thirds of the votes cast by the thirty-nine deputies in the kingdom's National Assembly; deputies who were nominated for cabinet posts in a new government could not participate in voting for the proposed prime minister. The resulting reduction in both eligible voters and affirmative votes for a particular premier gave small minorities disproportionate power to block the will of the majority and to advance their own political and personal interests. The more general political problem was the parliamentary form of government that Laos and many other developing countries had inherited from their former colonial rulers. Effective parliamentary democracy generally requires a limited number of political parties and a degree of discipline within them. In Laos, however, power was fragmented among many factions, and party discipline was limited.

A political assassination added particular bitterness to the fall 1954 cabinet crisis. Only days before Yost arrived in Vientiane, terrorists had killed Defense Minister Kou Voravong, who favored Souvanna's policy of reconciliation with the Pathet Lao. Although responsibility for the assassination was never clearly established, many RLG officials believed that Thailand was involved in the attack. Sensitive to the possibility of a communist-dominated neighbor, Thailand "seemed determined to stir up trouble in Laos in order to increase its influence and perhaps reduce Laos to vassalage," according to Souvanna Phouma. Thai officials declared that RLG foreign minister Phoui Sananikone was behind the assassination, an allegation accepted at face value by some of the leading families in southern Laos, who historically had closer ties with Thailand. The murder of the Lao defense minister, Yost later wrote, was a "cause célèbre" that "poisoned" the political atmosphere in Vientiane.[12]

After several failed attempts by leading Laotian politicians to resolve the cabinet crisis, Katay Don Sasorith successfully formed a new government on November 24, 1954. His cabinet, largely a reshuffling of the Lao officials who had held power in the post–World War II era (and who were colloquially known within the State Department as "the same old faces"), included Souvanna Phouma as defense minister. Despite the new prime minister's reputation for intrigue and "dabbling in a corruption," Katay initially appeared to US officials as an astute politician, an able leader, and an articulate anticommunist.[13]

Katay, then age fifty, was a former civil servant in the French colonial government. A leader of the Lao Issara movement, he too had gone into exile in Thailand, where he published a newspaper advocating the overthrow of the French in Laos. (His pen name was William Rabbit—in Lao, *katay* means rabbit.) Returning to Laos with other Lao Issara exiles, he was elected to the National Assembly in 1951. In the years following his election as prime minister, the US government alternately extended support to Katay and withdrew it depending on the US need for a proven anticommunist leader in a country with a limited pool of political talent or US recognition of the destructive impact of his dishonest behavior.

Within a week of taking power, Katay informed Yost of his plan to probe the willingness of the Pathet Lao to accept the government's terms for reconciliation: demobilizing Pathet Lao military forces and returning administrative control of the northern provinces in exchange for democratic participation in elections. Katay's optimism about reaching such an understanding with the Pathet Lao seemed unrealistic to Yost. Echoing former and future prime minister Souvanna Phouma, Katay told the American envoy that the Pathet Lao leaders were not really communists. He had known these men well when they were members of Lao Issara. And even if they were communists, Katay said, his countrymen were Laotians "first and Communists afterwards."[14] This declaration confirmed an impression of Katay that Yost had earlier reported to the State Department: "The delusion that [the] Pathet Lao are 'not really Communists' is shared to [a] greater or less degree by all Lao politicos, but Katay has it in [a] peculiarly virulent form."[15]

Yost had no objections to having representatives of the RLG talk with the Pathet Lao—if for no other reason than such discussions might be a source of useful intelligence. What he and other US officials adamantly opposed was the inclusion of the Pathet Lao in the government. The 1948 communist takeover of the coalition government in Czechoslovakia had a profound effect on US views about such power-sharing arrangements. Without any discernible analysis of political, cultural, and historical differences between Czechoslovakia and Laos, Eisenhower administration officials were certain that Pathet Lao participation in the Laotian government could only end in a communist victory.

On January 1, 1955, the United States began providing direct assistance to Laos, instead of passing its support through the French. As a matter of national policy in Southeast Asia, the US government had decided to work "through the French only insofar as necessary."[16] The Geneva restrictions on foreign military assistance to Laos, however, required more US-French cooperation than was necessary in South Vietnam and Cambodia. While the United States could provide Laos with money, equipment, and weapons, only the French Military Mission (FMM) could train and advise the ANL. From a military perspective, this approach to assistance was an unsound arrangement that frustrated the French, the Americans, and the Laotians.

Many French military and civilian officials, dispirited by their defeat in Indochina, resented the Americans in Laos, who presumably sought to ease them out of the country and the region at the first opportunity. Poor French morale led, in turn, to deficient performance in advising and supporting the ANL. A US MAAG team from Vietnam visited Laos in December 1954 and described the maintenance of equipment and the training of soldiers as "deplorable." Such conditions, according to the team's report, were caused by the "complete indifference of the French to the very real problems of the Laotian Army."[17]

The change in role from command to advice was a difficult adjustment for French officers, creating ill will and mistrust between them and the newly independent Laotian army. Lieutenant Colonel Donald B. Gordon, the US Army attaché in Vientiane, reported that the ANL practice of "precipitously replacing their French advisors and instructors with totally unqualified Laotians" had a discouraging impact on the French. Because of such seemingly ungrateful and shortsighted actions, "French noses [are] definitely out of joint," Gordon wrote.[18]

In Washington, the Joint Chiefs of Staff (JCS) disliked the idea of providing military assistance to Laos. The politically fragile kingdom appeared a poor place to invest limited Pentagon resources, and the Geneva

Accords prohibited the introduction of US military personnel who could exercise appropriate control and supervision of American equipment and support. Allowing the French to assume this responsibility would mean no US control at all, and expanding the office of the military attaché in Vientiane would likely be viewed as a violation of the Geneva agreements. One alternative—although "not considered feasible by the Department of Defense"—was hiring US civilians with military backgrounds to supervise military aid. Because of the US policy commitment to Laos, senior Pentagon officials reluctantly agreed to this last option. They also continued to reiterate that such a program was "pointless" from a military perspective and that its results "would be negligible and of doubtful benefit to the U.S."[19]

A reflection of the US military's lack of enthusiasm for assistance to Laos was Defense Department foot-dragging in determining force levels and agreeing on a budget for the ANL. From Vientiane, Yost reported that delays in concluding a military-support agreement had "harmful effects," the most important of which, from a political perspective, was creating doubt among Laotian leaders about the firmness and reliability of the US commitment. The US minister acknowledged that the Laotian army was "far from satisfactory" and that the FMM was "not as effective as it should be." However, Yost wrote in January 1955, the policy of preventing communist expansion in Southeast Asia meant that the United States "must work with such instruments as we have at hand and not sulk because we have no better ones."[20]

In early 1955 the Katay government continued its talks with the Pathet Lao to resolve outstanding disagreements in implementing the Geneva Accords. The negotiations made little progress. Pathet Lao leaders acted as if they had conquered Sam Neua and Phong Saly, when, in fact, their grip on the two provinces was relatively weak. North Vietnamese officials, concerned since Geneva about the Pathet Lao's capacity "to hold on to [Sam Neua and Phong Saly], much less run them," had established a military advisory mission for Laos called Group 100. So named for the initial number of cadres sent to the kingdom, Group 100 indoctrinated, trained, and equipped Pathet Lao forces. The group's immediate goal, according to researcher Christopher E. Goscha, was "to block enemy military moves into these two provinces, as well as protect and consolidate the PL's administrative presence."[21]

Such consolidation seemed to Charles Yost the Pathet Lao's motivation for dragging out negotiations with the RLG. The US minister believed that Lao military action, "a last resort, which should be avoided if possible," could interrupt this process of gradual communist control. He preferred, however, an unequivocal statement from the major Western powers that the de facto partitioning of Laos was a "gross violation" of the Geneva Accords. Yost had concluded that unless the RLG succeeded in regaining control of the northern provinces—an action he characterized as "this first crucial campaign"—all other US efforts to help Laos maintain its independence were "likely to prove useless."[22]

A stimulus for more forceful action in the northern provinces occurred on January 13, 1955, when Pathet Lao forces attacked two small ANL outposts in Sam Neua, approximately twelve miles from the provincial capital. One garrison was abandoned by the ANL; the other remained in government hands. The number of casualties was small, but State Department officials were "seriously concerned" by the incident. A January 19 paper for the Operations Coordinating Board declared that the "combination of a weak government in Laos" and "a determined communist enemy presents a situation of danger." The only "salutary effect" of the Pathet Lao attacks, according to Kenneth T. Young Jr., director of the State Department's Office of Philippine and Southeast Asian Affairs, was "partially awakening the Laotian Government to the true Communist nature of the Pathet Lao, whom it has heretofore regarded as misguided but redeemable Laotian brothers."[23]

ANL commanders, who had been covertly reinforcing Lao garrisons in Sam Neua and Phong Saly, claimed their army was ready and eager to occupy the two provinces. Despite the skepticism of the French military officers, ANL leaders believed that the Pathet Lao could easily be defeated if the North Vietnamese did not intervene. Prime Minister Katay, however, was not yet prepared to support military action in the north. He still wanted to exhaust all possibilities for a negotiated settlement. Crown Prince Savang also opposed immediate military action, but for a different reason: He wanted more specific guarantees of SEATO protection should North Vietnam intervene in any fighting in Sam Neua and Phong Saly.

Strongly pro-Western and anticommunist, the crown prince was, according to the State Department, a "man of great dignity," whose "intelligence and quiet charm have left excellent impressions with those who have met him." Another, subsequent assessment by the department described Savang as "emotional, hypersensitive, and defensive, subject to extreme changes in temper. He considers himself unassuming and democratic, and capable of understanding the desires of his people; actually he insulates himself from his subjects by an aura of semi-divinity."[24]

Born in the royal capital of Luang Prabang in 1907, Savang was educated in France and received a law degree from the École des Sciences Politiques in Paris. His family had ruled over at least some part of Laos for more than five hundred years, and his now-ill father, King Sisavang Vong, had been a reigning sovereign for more than fifty years. Observing the constitutional limits of his position, the crown prince did not involve himself in the day-to-day decision making of government. The royal family was, however, one of the few unifying institutions in Laos, and Savang had significant influence in the formation of Lao governments and in the kingdom's foreign affairs.

The crown prince told Yost on February 12, 1955, that he was "profoundly disturbed" by the indecision of the Katay government. The prime minister had insisted on prolonging negotiations with the Pathet Lao, which Savang believed were doomed to failure. The Lao people, he declared, were getting the impression that the government was "too weak to deal with" the communists. The crown prince said that other members of Katay's cabinet were "fed up" with him and "prepared to overthrow" the government if Savang agreed. Savang, however, was inclined to delay such an action because it would be "unfortunate" if Laos were without a government leader at the SEATO meeting later in the month. At the same time, the crown prince said, further delay and continued indecision would mean the loss of the two provinces.[25]

In a follow-up telegram to the State Department, Yost declared that there was "no doubt" about Katay's "unsatisfactory" performance as prime minister. The Laotian leader had failed to recognize the "true character of [the] Pathet Lao" and had prolonged negotiations with its representatives beyond the "point of diminishing returns." The US diplomat also charged Katay with failing to keep his ministerial colleagues informed of his plans, intriguing "shamelessly" against Foreign Minister Phoui Sananikone and attempting "to outsmart all with whom he has dealt," including US officials. Yost reminded his Washington colleagues that, thus far, the Americans in Vientiane had done everything in their power to prevent the Katay government from falling apart. The envoy now discussed whether Katay's "downfall would be advantageous" to US objectives. Urging scrutiny of alternative leadership, Yost concluded his message by recommending "one more effort to keep this government together and to help it function."[26]

Secretary of State John Foster Dulles, one of the few foreign ministers to set foot in Laos, arrived in Vientiane on February 27, 1955, following a SEATO meeting in Bangkok and a brief visit to Rangoon. The plane carrying Dulles and other State Department officials circled the airfield in Vientiane for twenty minutes—the time required to clear water buffalo from the runway, a World War II–era steel-plank mat. A small wooden control tower transmitted a weak radio signal that provided pilots with limited navigational assistance, and the absence of exterior lighting precluded nighttime operation of the airfield. The combination of Vientiane's primitive air facilities and the town's heat, dust, and flies prompted more than one new employee to the US mission to immediately reconsider his occupational plans and return to Bangkok or Saigon on the next outward-bound flight.

The globe-trotting secretary of state was met at the airstrip by US and Laotian officials and by a Cadillac provided by the king. The automobile had to be flown from Luang Prabang, approximately 150 miles north of Vientiane, because no passable road connected the two towns. Freshening up after his flight, Dulles encountered a malfunctioning toilet at the US legation, which left him ankle deep in water. Despite his stern outward demeanor, Dulles enjoyed recounting this incident to State Department officials who had responsibility for Laotian affairs.[27]

Dulles and the department's career professionals did not enjoy an easy relationship. Assuming office during the McCarthy era, when good Foreign Service officers were falsely blamed for the triumphs of Stalin and Mao, Dulles made an initial demand for "positive loyalty" from department employees that appeared to question their patriotism. He also offended professional diplomats with his tolerance for the extreme anticommunist zeal of State Department security chief Robert Walter Scott McLeod, a former FBI agent whose investigations into department loyalty included suspicions about Soviet experts who read Russian newspapers. As Senator McCarthy and his minions began to self-destruct, and as Dulles developed greater familiarity with the people who represented the United States abroad, the secretary of state established effective, if not warm, working relationships with his D.C.-based and overseas subordinates.

Perhaps the most controversial secretary of state in US history, Dulles was acutely aware of the danger posed by aggressive Soviet moves in Europe but largely blind to the power of nationalism in the developing world. He was a sophisticated student of foreign relations behind closed doors, but he sometimes made simplistic, misleading pronouncements when publicly discussing international affairs. Although Dulles talked boldly about the use of force, he supported President Eisenhower's restraint in the application of US military power. Richard H. Immerman, in his study of Dulles and his diplomacy, concluded that Dulles's "life and career embody the best and worst of U.S. foreign policy."[28]

Dulles, the grandson of one secretary of state and the nephew of another, had a distinguished career as an international lawyer before becoming secretary of state at age sixty-four. Taking numerous leaves of absence from the firm of Sullivan & Cromwell for government work, Dulles had served as an adviser to the US delegations at the Paris peace talks after World War I and at the 1945 conference in San Francisco to establish the United Nations. He represented the bipartisan "cold war consensus" in foreign affairs and was appointed by President Truman in 1950 to negotiate the treaty with Japan that officially ended World War II and the US occupation of the country. A prolific and influential writer whose articles about international affairs appeared in publications as diverse as *Foreign Affairs* and *Life,* Dulles was an adviser to Thomas E. Dewey in his unsuccessful presidential campaigns of 1944 and 1948.

President Eisenhower, who had initial reservations about Dulles's strategic vision and penchant for militant public overstatement, respected his secretary of state as "an intensive student of foreign affairs" who "passionately believes in the United States, in the dignity of man, and in moral values." Although aware that Dulles could be insensitive and arrogant, Eisenhower valued his "wisdom, judgment and integrity." Their frequent formal and informal contact strengthened their mutual admiration and respect. "Dulles never tried to bypass or in any other way trespass on Eisenhower's authority," writes Immerman. "Eisenhower always made the decisions—but always after consulting Dulles."[29]

In his public statements, Dulles was a key proponent of the monolithic view of communism—an efficient, vertically integrated, global conspiracy directed by the Kremlin and executed by its wholly owned subsidiaries around the world. In a 1954 address to the Overseas Press

Club in New York, Dulles described Vietnam's Ho Chi Minh as "the ostensible leader"—a mere Soviet apparatchik—in the fight against French colonialism. A Viet Minh victory in Indochina, Dulles said, would result in a dictatorship that takes "its orders from Peiping and Moscow."[30] Whatever one's views of Ho Chi Minh, he cannot accurately be described as simply a malleable tool of Soviet imperialism.

Although the communist monolith conformed to Lenin's theories and aspirations for global domination, the concept rarely acknowledged the practical difficulties of achieving that end. The Eisenhower administration's "ideological fixation," according to cold war historian John Lewis Gaddis, attributed "to Kremlin leaders a clarity of strategic vision not possible in the Western democracies and, as a consequence, an extraordinary degree of tactical sophistication and flexibility."[31]

This one-size-fits-all view of communism did not accept the idea that Russian and Chinese communists might have differing political and foreign policy goals, based on individual national interests rather than a common Marxist ideology. The so-called Sino-Soviet split, which became evident to some US government specialists in the late 1950s, only gradually became accepted—and politically acceptable—thinking in the 1960s. Most cold warriors of the 1950s would have had difficulty imagining that China would engage in armed conflict with its ideological comrades in the Soviet Union (1969) and Vietnam (1979). The notion that US intelligence agencies would be allowed to build listening posts in China to monitor Soviet missile tests in the 1980s would have seemed implausible.

According to Ambassador U. Alexis Johnson, who began his diplomatic career in Japan in 1935 and ended it as the US negotiator at the 1977 Strategic Arms Limitation Talks, Dulles was "weakest when he attempted to play domestic politics." One such incident occurred at the Geneva conference in 1954, when Chou En-lai, the foreign minister of the People's Republic of China, saw Dulles walking into the lounge during a break in the conference. Smiling, Chou approached Dulles and extended his hand. The secretary of state, noticing the presence of news photographers, brusquely turned his back on Chou. The insulting gesture, which plagued US-China relations for many years, "was not a natural or a normal thing," recalled Johnson, who was chief deputy of the American delegation and standing close to Dulles. "I am sure he was thinking of the impression back here in the United States."[32]

Privately, Dulles expressed views of communism that were more nuanced than his public pronouncements. During a 1954 NSC discussion of US policy in the Far East, Dulles speculated that eventually "China and Russia would split apart because of the pressure of basic historical forces and because the religious fervor of Communism would have died down. The Chinese were very proud of their own history, and Chinese did not like Russians. In the end, therefore, they would split apart." The question for Dulles was: "Could we afford to wait that long for a split between these two enemies?"[33]

Later in the 1950s, during a cordial meeting with Prince Norodom Sihanouk, the neutral prime minister of Cambodia, Dulles compared communism's "mechanistic view of the world" with the US belief that "human beings differ from each other" and do not fit easily into such regimentation. In contrast to his public rhetoric about the power of global communism, Dulles declared: "A world program of trying to make [human beings] act and think alike is not possible." Discussing China, he noted the "individualistic nature" of its people and predicted that "eventually there would be a change to something more independent and less monolithic."[34]

Joseph A. Mendenhall, then the State Department's acting head of Cambodian affairs, attended this meeting and wrote up its minutes. Later recalling how Dulles's "philosophical" remarks that day were at odds with his reputation as "an anti-communist fire-eater," Mendenhall said the secretary of state conveyed a prescient message that "over time [the Russian and Chinese] communist regimes might begin to change, to modify themselves."[35]

The principal purpose of Dulles's visit to Laos was to encourage the kingdom's leaders in their struggle against the Pathet Lao. At the February 1955 SEATO meeting in Bangkok, Dulles had spoken about the prospects for South Vietnam and Cambodia in relatively optimistic terms. The situation in Laos, however, was not as promising. Reminding the treaty partners that communists controlled two northern provinces, Dulles declared: "There is going to be a great need for strengthening and invigorating the forces of the Government of Laos if it is to cope with the difficulties and subversion now threatening it."[36]

In an afternoon of back-to-back meetings in Vientiane, Dulles spoke with the Lao crown prince, as well as the prime minister, the foreign minister, and the defense minister. Because of their political and personal rivalries, the US legation recommended that Dulles meet individually with the Laotian officials, each of whom would "talk much more frankly and substantively alone than he would in [the] company of any of the others."[37]

In each of his conversations, Dulles stressed a common theme: If the Laotian government decided to attack the Pathet Lao in Sam Neua and Phong Saly, US air and naval power would deter intervention by North Vietnam and China. Among the US forces in the Pacific were four hundred navy ships, including the largest US carriers, and thirty air force squadrons with the latest jet fighter bombers and interceptors. Strategic airpower with nuclear weapons was readily available, as were five army divisions. In the unlikely event such a powerful force failed to deter counterattacks from North Vietnam and China, Dulles told Laotian officials, SEATO forces would defeat the communist armies. He also said that, based on his experience, communists used negotiations as a "cloak" for strengthening their military and political position. Therefore, any action against them should be both resolute and prompt.[38]

Crown Prince Savang welcomed the pledge of SEATO support from Dulles. Savang discussed with Dulles the differing opinions within the RLG about tactics to reestablish control in the northern provinces and the threshold for "provoking a massive counterattack" by North Vietnam and China. With the assurances provided by Dulles, the crown prince declared that the government should now move promptly against the Pathet Lao. If some ministers did not agree, Savang said, "there would have to be a change in the government."[39]

Prime Minister Katay was less enthusiastic in his response to Dulles's declarations. Before resorting to force, Katay said, the Laotian people would have to be convinced of the government's good faith and its willingness to exhaust "every possibility for a reasonable settlement." Noting the government's March 15 deadline for concluding negotiations with the Pathet Lao, he hoped that such patience would not be interpreted as weakness. The prime minister told Dulles that many members of the Pathet Lao were unsympathetic to communism. What Katay sought were defections that would "disintegrate" the movement.[40]

Minister Yost, who attended each of the meetings with Dulles and Assistant Secretary of State Walter Robertson, was openly skeptical that Laotian defections would resolve the problem with the Pathet Lao, many of whom were committed communists. The prime minister replied that if negotiations were not successfully concluded by March 15, the government would deal with the situation. Katay was vague, however, about how he planned to cope with the Pathet Lao after the deadline passed. His lack of specificity troubled the Americans, and Dulles reported to President Eisenhower that Katay was a "man of hesitation."[41]

The defense minister, Souvanna Phouma, showed more firmness about eliminating the Pathet Lao threat in his discussion with Dulles. Acknowledging the difficulties the government faced in such an operation, Souvanna "favored prompt action" to recover government control in Sam Neua and Phong Saly. In a transparent effort to urge on the defense minister, Dulles observed that timely action was important. The "danger increased as the situation dragged along." Souvanna said that he "fully agreed."[42] The reason for Souvanna's uncharacteristic militancy during the Dulles visit to Laos is unclear. Because of Prime Minister Katay's opposition to forceful reunification of the kingdom, it is possible that Souvanna told the US secretary of state what he wanted to hear, secure in the knowledge that such an operation would not be carried out.

Dulles left Laos the next day believing he had stiffened the resolve of the kingdom's leaders. His exposure to the difficult conditions under which Americans in Laos worked had a significant impact on him, and he ordered his administrative officials to give prompt attention to requests from Vientiane. If there were any problems meeting these requests, he wanted to know about them. For the officials working in the small but growing legation, Yost recalled, the personal attention of Dulles to their housing and other problems "was a tremendous boost to morale."[43]

The same week as Dulles's visit, the ten-member US legation finally moved out of its villa on the Mekong into a new chancery to conduct diplomatic affairs. Occupying two refurbished buildings formerly used by the French Military Mission, the chancery also provided working space for the eight-person US economic aid mission and the office of the military attaché. The US Information Service (USIS), which produced publications, films, and other media for communicating news and propaganda, kept a separate office in a former shop near the Vientiane marketplace. In its weekly report to the State Department, the legation cheekily observed that the new chancery was "more important than the Secretary's visit."[44]

Prime Minister Katay's March 15 deadline for concluding negotiations came and went without a political settlement with the Pathet Lao. The talks' meager accomplishment was an agreement to continue them on a more formal basis in Vientiane. Yost reported to Washington that extending negotiations to restore RLG control of Sam Neua and Phong Saly would not only prolong the risk that Katay might make "dangerous concessions" to the Pathet Lao but also delay any military action to reestablish government authority in the two northern provinces.[45]

A key question about forceful government action in Sam Neua and Phong Saly was the ability of the ANL to conduct such an operation. Among US government experts, there was a growing realization that without backing from foreign soldiers, neither the ANL nor the Pathet Lao demonstrated any particular zeal for fighting each other. Anthropologist Joel Halpern later wrote that Laotian warfare appeared to resemble the symbolic struggle of primitive combat: "When two groups clash and there are several casualties then the fight is broken off while both sides regroup. This, of course, presupposes that there are two sides remaining to carry on the struggle. If one side, such as the Royal Lao, leaves the scene, it is hard to make contact unless there is direct and vigorous pursuit." Minister Yost's characterization of such fighting was similar, though more sardonic in expression. Reporting on combat in Sam Neua, where the RLG had infiltrated a large number of soldiers to face the encroaching Pathet Lao forces, Yost wrote: "This resulted in [a] tour de force type of action where one side makes it known that it is superior now and would appreciate [the] other side evacuating without shooting."[46]

The most formidable obstacle to reestablishing Lao government control of the northern provinces was the attitude of friendly European governments. The UK and French ambassadors in Vientiane opposed any Lao military action that might restart the recently concluded hostilities in Indochina. Moreover, they sought to refute the assurances of Dulles that SEATO would protect Laos from counterattacks by North Vietnam and China. Yost reported that these diplomatic maneuvers obviously strengthened the position of the seemingly irresolute Katay and undermined the more forceful views of the crown prince and Souvanna Phouma.

In a March 29 letter to Prime Minister Winston Churchill, President Eisenhower cited British opposition to the assurances Dulles had given Laotian leaders as an example of the differing US-UK views of the communist threat in the Far East—a subject that "puzzles us sorely and constantly." In the frank and friendly tone that characterized the personal correspondence between the two wartime allies, Eisenhower wrote that

Dulles had "urged the Government of Laos, while it still has the ability to do so, to clean out" the northern provinces. The British and the French ambassadors in Vientiane, however, had informed the RLG that under no circumstances could Laos expect any SEATO help if external forces responded to such action. The result, Eisenhower wrote, was that the communists in Sam Neua and Phong Saly were growing "stronger and stronger." He added, "We face a possibility of ultimately losing that entire territory to the Communists, just as we lost North Vietnam."[47]

Prime Minister Churchill's immediate reply, dated April 1, was: "Am pondering; will write." Then eighty years old, his health and mental acuity failing, Churchill had a more pressing matter on his mind: his resignation as prime minister just a few days later. The official UK response to Eisenhower later declared that "a precipitate recourse to force" in the northern provinces would be a mistake, with unforeseen international consequences. Questioning the fighting ability of the ANL, officials in the UK Foreign Office believed that even without intervention by North Vietnam, "the outcome of a fight between the Royal Lao Government and the Pathet Lao would be doubtful."[48]

US officials in Washington were reluctantly reaching the same conclusion. The balance of forces in northern Laos did not seem favorable, and there was "growing antipathy" between the ANL and French military advisers, who were essential to planning and directing military operations. Senior State Department officials wired Yost that at "this juncture means other than military must be found [to] restore [the] provinces to Royal control."[49]

Unfortunately for the RLG and US officials, there were few, if any, viable "means" for achieving this objective. The tense negotiations with Pathet Lao representatives—who stridently insisted that the Geneva Accords authorized their control of Sam Neua and Phong Saly—were at a stalemate. Even Prime Minister Katay was losing faith in a negotiated settlement. Laotian appeals to the International Commission for Supervision and Control (ICC), the body responsible for monitoring compliance with the Geneva Accords, had been disappointing. A politically balanced group of anticommunist Canadians, communist Poles, and neutralist Indians, the ICC team in Laos was unable to reach a unanimous decision about the authority of the government to administer the two northern provinces. The Geneva agreement's "insufficient clarity" on this point, the ICC team noted, was "the main source of difficulty" for resolving the issue. On May 3, 1955, Yost advised officials in Washington that "wishful hopes" of eliminating the communist threat through negotiations or the ICC were "dangerously naive."[50]

A long-shot possibility for halting the de facto partitioning of Laos was to continue discreetly reinforcing ANL garrisons in Sam Neua and Phong Saly while covertly arming the loyal civilians there. The crown prince and Defense Minister Souvanna Phouma were particularly interested in encouraging a popular revolt against the Pathet Lao. The Laotian officials assured Yost that such assistance would be entirely covert and involve small sums of money, a limited amount of arms, and perhaps some soldiers in civilian clothes.

Although hardly optimistic that poorly organized irregulars would defeat the Pathet Lao, Yost cabled Washington: "I do not believe we should discourage [the] project." The US envoy explained his reasoning this way: "We simply cannot expect [the] Lao Government to take [the] loss of these provinces lying down." If the ICC could not ensure the recovery of the two provinces, he wrote, the only alternatives left to the Laotian government would either be force or a deal with the communists. The latter would involve "at best neutralism and at worst [the] loss of Laos."[51]

With the recovery of the two northern provinces unlikely in the foreseeable future, Yost urged US policymakers to place a greater emphasis on retaining Laotian government control of the other ten provinces. An essential step toward this goal, he advised, was the formation of a "national front" organization to unite the noncommunist politicians. With elections scheduled for later in the year, a single slate of candidates would ensure the political defeat of Pathet Lao members and sympathizers. Yost recommended that the United States provide "direct but discrete aid"— in other words, covert financial support provided by the CIA—to such a front organization.[52]

A potential barrier to this political scheme was Prime Minister Katay, who continued to inspire ambivalence among US officials. On one hand, his positive attributes included staunch anticommunism and an increasingly hard line toward the Pathet Lao. He was also an accomplished politician with a significant following, particularly in southern Laos. On the other hand, Katay appeared to Yost "interested primarily in his own personal fortunes,"[53] and he had been gradually losing support in the

National Assembly. "If Katay refuses to go along on [with the] national front and continues to display administrative constipation he should be removed," Yost suggested to Washington. In his view, the best political solution would "reshuffle" the current cabinet, with Katay serving as deputy prime minister. Yost doubted, however, that the Lao's "vanity would stand" the demotion. Left unanswered in Yost's analysis was the question of which politician, if any, could provide the dynamic anticommunist leadership sought by the US government.[54]

Throughout the first half of 1955, Pathet Lao forces conducted a campaign of harassing attacks against the small, isolated ANL outposts in Sam Neua, a mountainous jungle area with topography more typically Laotian than the kingdom's tropical plains. The absence of roads in this remote province meant that airdrops were the only way to provide ANL garrisons with food, ammunition, and other supplies. The Pathet Lao used horses and men to move their provisions and equipment along Sam Neua's jungle trails.

The Pathet Lao's low-intensity attacks, combined with antigovernment propaganda, sought to pressure the Lao government into making concessions in the on-and-off negotiations. Yost characterized these maneuvers as "sporadic and desultory shooting, sufficient to keep everyone in bad humor but insufficient to settle anything." On May 30, however, the US envoy reported indications of an "imminent outbreak of guerrilla type warfare" near the government-controlled village of Muong Peun in Sam Neua. In the heights above the village, both the Pathet Lao and the ANL were building up their forces to approximately twelve hundred each, with new fortifications appearing regularly and soldiers moving along the ridges. Although any fighting would "probably peter out within [a] few days," Yost reported, there was a possibility it might spread throughout Sam Neua and Phong Saly.[55]

Nothing much happened in June, but on July 3, the Pathet Lao attacked, driving government troops from their outposts and clearing the hills above Muong Peun. The Pathet Lao force, reported to be three battalions, or approximately eighteen hundred men, controlled a semicircle of high ground above the village. On July 7 the ANL commander in Muong Peun radioed that his post was under attack and requested reinforcements, who parachuted into the area the next day. Three additional ANL infantry battalions were placed on alert for deployment to Sam Neua. In a cable to Washington, Colonel Gordon, the US Army attaché in Vientiane, invoked a powerful image of the French defeat in Indochina, guaranteed to grab the attention of policymakers: the possibility of a "small Dien Bien Phu" that might destroy some of the Laotian army's best units and permit "unimpeded movements" of North Vietnamese forces "into and across Laos, should they so desire."[56]

In Washington, the dire reports from Laos prompted Admiral Arthur W. Radford, chairman of the Joint Chiefs of Staff, to inform the State Department that US forces in the Pacific could provide Marines, air power—whatever military support might be required. Radford, who had been a strong advocate of US military intervention at Dien Bien Phu, did not think the United States should silently tolerate the communist provocation in Laos. "The world should know this situation exists," he told Assistant Secretary Walter Robertson.[57]

Robertson's boss, John Foster Dulles, informed the embassies in Vientiane and Bangkok that this aggression by North Vietnam and the Pathet Lao should be a topic raised for SEATO consideration. Even in the event of inaction, Dulles reasoned, the mere fact of convening SEATO representatives to discuss the matter might have a helpful impact on communist behavior. Like his earlier effort to encourage the RLG to assume control of the northern provinces by force, the Dulles SEATO gambit was thwarted by the UK and France. As cochair of the Geneva conference, the UK government believed that SEATO consideration of the Laos problem would needlessly irritate the ICC and particularly its chair, the government of India. This, in turn, might fatally undermine chances for a solution by the ICC. The French government opposed even an innocuous SEATO communiqué on the grounds that it would appear the alliance was intervening in Laotian internal affairs at a time when there was little evidence of North Vietnamese participation in the fighting.[58]

US officials independently discovered that the scale of combat in Muong Peun reported by the Lao government was "exaggerated," tempering the military planning and diplomatic actions contemplated by the Eisenhower administration. Instead of an aggressive Pathet Lao offensive, the incident turned out to be a smaller probing action, similar to many others aimed at weakening the resolve of the RLG. Total ANL casualties were five killed in action, twelve wounded, and one missing. Moreover, there was no evidence to support the RLG claim that organized North Vietnamese Army units participated in the fighting. A postmortem by intelligence officials from the State Department, the army, and the CIA concluded that the alarming reports from Vientiane represented "a continuation of the Laotian effort to persuade world opinion of Pathet Lao violation of the Geneva Agreement."[59]

A National Intelligence Estimate, dated July 26, 1955, summarized for US policymakers the difficulties facing the RLG: The Laotian army did not have the logistic and command capabilities to conduct large-scale military operations in the northern provinces, and the French were unlikely to provide them. The RLG might be able to develop a covert resistance movement in Pathet Lao territory, but such a movement would not be a significant threat to communist control of Sam Neua and Phong Saly. In the near term, the best the government could hope for was the development of political, police, and military measures to prevent the spread of Pathet Lao influence into the kingdom's ten other provinces. "To retain its independence in the long run," the NIE concluded, "Laos will require strong diplomatic support, technical, economic, and military assistance, and possibly the direct support of foreign armed forces."[60]

The intelligence estimate observed that Katay and Foreign Minister Phoui Sananikone had formed "a 'coalition' of their two parties in order to ensure a solid anti-communist front." With national elections scheduled for December 1955, the Laotian government hoped that a resounding victory by noncommunist candidates would "demonstrate, particularly to the ICC, both the absurdity of Pathet Lao claims to a special status and the government's right to control and administer all of Laos."[61]

In assessing economic conditions in Laos, the NIE noted "a serious shortage of rice," estimated at forty thousand tons. Because of two successive droughts, the rural poor of Laos, who survived on primitive, subsistence farming, had neither rice nor the money to buy it. Max Finger, one of the US officials who investigated the conditions in the Laotian backcountry, later recalled: "We saw plenty of evidence of famine—painfully thin adults and children with distended bellies."[62]

Yost urged the State Department to provide "prompt, massive imports of rice." Free distribution of the dietary staple would both "alleviate suffering" and strengthen popular support for the Laotian government. Although Yost and his colleagues were "raising heaven and earth" to import rice, negotiations among the Laotians and donor governments—

Thailand, Japan, and the United States—delayed delivery of the food. Finally, more than three months after the confirmation of famine conditions, barges from Thailand crossed the Mekong River to distribute rice to the western province of Laos, trucks from Vientiane delivered the food to neighboring villages, and oxcarts carried some of the rest.[63]

Airdrops, however, were the only way to get rice to the people of northern Laos. In mid-September 1955, aircraft of the Civil Air Transport (CAT)—an airline secretly owned by the CIA—began parachuting rice and salt to improvised drop zones hacked out of the jungle. Skillfully weaving through mountains partially hidden by low-hanging monsoon clouds, the CAT pilots and the "kickers" who pushed the supplies out of the C-46 transport planes completed some two hundred missions in the fall of 1955. These relief flights—which also included dropping propaganda leaflets over communist-controlled areas—were one of the first instances of CIA assistance to the mountain tribespeople.

The US mission in Vientiane recognized the political and military potential of the tribal groups. Minorities in Laos constituted approximately 50 percent of the kingdom's population. The two largest, the Hmong and the Khmu, differed from the ethnic Lao and from each other in country of origin, language, religion, customs, and the altitude at which they lived—the Lao in the valleys; the Khmu in the hills, generally at altitudes between 1,000 and 3,000 feet above sea level; and the Hmong on mountaintops and elevations above 3,000 feet. Virtually all RLG officials were ethnic Lao, most of whom considered the tribespeople inferior. Lack of RLG interest in the problems of the minorities increased their susceptibility to recruitment by the Pathet Lao.[64]

Not until years later were there large-scale efforts by the CIA and US Army Special Forces to recruit tribespeople for fighting what some people have referred to as "the secret war in Laos." DCI Richard Helms, who objected to the inaccuracy of that characterization, simply called it "the war we won,"[65] an assessment based on the military successes of the Hmong army against Pathet Lao and North Vietnamese forces. Yet for the Hmong, a minority within a small population, the US war in Southeast Asia was catastrophic: An estimated 30,000 Hmong were killed, and 100,000 fled to refugee camps in Thailand.

On September 13, 1955, Crown Prince Savang discussed internal Laotian politics with Ambassador Yost, who had been promoted from minister earlier that summer when the US legation expanded to a full-fledged embassy. Savang repeated a familiar theme to the American: the disillusionment of his people with the kingdom's politicians and their desire "to throw out the old leaders." The crown prince added that many capable young people were interested in politics, but they were neither united nor well organized. In his report of the conversation, Yost tended to agree with Savang's assessment: "There is probably a strong undercurrent of dissatisfaction with the older political leaders, resulting from their having held power for a number of years and having failed to deal effectively with most of the serious problems confronting Laos."[66]

Concluding that leaders stronger than Katay and Phoui were unlikely to emerge in the immediate future, Yost observed that Laotian politics posed "something of a dilemma" for US policymakers: "which elements, if any, we should discreetly support." He acknowledged that the current leaders were "neither particularly admirable nor particularly effective nor perhaps particularly popular." Moreover, supporting Katay, Phoui, and their parties, as well as encouraging "their collaboration in a loose National Front," prevented new political leadership from emerging naturally. If Laos were "an untroubled part of the world," Yost reasoned, "it would probably be wisest for us to keep our hands off" and allow "discontented elements to disrupt the existing party structure, in the belief that more healthy organizations would eventually emerge." But because of the threat posed by communists, the United States had little choice but to provide "qualified support" to the dominant parties, even though such support might "incidentally slow down the progress of democratic political evolution."[67]

Based on the intermittent negotiations between the RLG and the Pathet Lao, October 10 was the latest deadline for reaching a political settlement concerning Sam Neua and Phong Saly. There was no agreement by that day. Citing the futility of further talks with the Pathet Lao, the RLG announced in November that the election for National Assembly deputies would be held on December 25 in the other ten provinces and those portions of Sam Neua and Phong Saly under government control. The Pathet Lao responded by boycotting the election, claiming that the RLG's unwillingness to recognize its administrative control of the two northern provinces was a violation of the Geneva Accords. When the votes were counted, the kingdom's noncommunist candidates had won a sweeping, if unsurprising, victory.

The election results appeared to have been a great victory for Katay, whose supporters did well at the polls. Nonetheless, the American embassy continued to view him with ambivalence. "We have never been enthusiastic about Katay and consider him shifty and lacking in principle," Yost cabled the State Department. However, the prime minister appeared to be the only leader capable of holding together the kingdom's disparate anticommunist politicians. Yost predicted that Katay, "if handled discreetly, will follow generally pro-western lines as long as aid is forthcoming. His expanding business interests will incline him toward maintenance [of the] status quo."[68]

Despite the prime minister's strong electoral position, a cabinet crisis erupted when Katay attempted to form a government consisting almost exclusively of his political cronies. The combination of personal rivalries, the weak Laotian parliamentary system, and Katay's brusque and cavalier behavior toward deputies prevented him from forming a government acceptable to a two-thirds majority of the National Assembly. To break the political deadlock, the crown prince proposed that Souvanna Phouma form a government, but he too went down to defeat. Phoui Sananikone tried and failed, and so did another attempt by Katay. The bitter political fight, Yost reported to Washington, was a "senseless imbroglio [that] has sown [the] seeds of much future trouble."[69]

After Katay suffered his second parliamentary defeat, it appeared that a leftist candidate might conceivably become prime minister. The crown prince turned again to Souvanna Phouma to form a broadly based anticommunist coalition government. The embassy in Vientiane "strongly urged Katay and other political leaders to throw their full weight behind Souvanna," who seemed to Yost the only candidate for prime minister who was both "acceptable and possible." The ambassador's admission of "discreetly exerting ourselves in support of Souvanna" suggests that the CIA station in Vientiane was using its influence and funds to promote his election. On March 21, 1956, the cabinet crisis ended when Souvanna won overwhelming support from the National Assembly. He told the deputies that a political settlement with the Pathet Lao was the gravest issue facing the kingdom.[70]

In addition to becoming prime minister again, Souvanna led the ministries of foreign affairs, defense, and information. Katay became deputy prime minister but refused any portfolio, telling Ambassador Yost he wanted "to be free to keep an eye on all Ministries." In fact, Katay had little further engagement in Laotian affairs while serving in Souvanna's government. Katay also ended his "close and constant contact" with US embassy officials, who suspected he was responding to criticism that he had become an "American stooge." More troubling reports indicated that Katay's ambition was "unlimited" and his actions were motivated exclusively by "expediency."[71]

When he had served as defense minister in the Katay government, Souvanna appeared to be a proponent of more forceful action in the northern provinces. As prime minister, however, he reverted to a less resolute posture that Yost characterized as "one of those astonishing vagaries which add so much piquancy to dealings with Southeast Asian statesmen." Souvanna's latest "happy solution" to the Pathet Lao problem, the ambassador sarcastically reported, was the return of his "beloved brother" Prince Phetsarath from exile in Thailand.[72]

A respected and authoritarian royal, Phetsarath had been the "supreme chief" of the Lao Issara provisional government. Unlike Souvanna, who reconciled with the French, and Souphanouvong, who aligned himself with the Vietnamese, Phetsarath was a Lao nationalist hostile to both the French and the Viet Minh. Dynamic and more accessible to Laotians than either the king or the crown prince, Phetsarath was said to possess supernatural powers. Some Lao, including Western-educated government officials, believed that Phetsarath could drive away *phi*, a frequently evil animistic spirit, and that he could change his form—for example, into a fish or a fly.[73]

Born in 1890 and educated in France and England, Phetsarath was viceroy and prime minister of the kingdom of Luang Prabang until the end of World War II. Judging the Japanese surrender an opportune moment to declare the kingdom's independence, Phetsarath angered the royal family, who favored the protection provided by the French. Stripped of his titles, Phetsarath remained in Thailand when other members of Lao Issara returned home. In June 1954 he organized an abortive army coup—whether against the Lao government or the monarchy was not clear—and some believed he was behind the assassination of Lao defense minister Kou Voravong. Many members of the ruling elite, including Katay, Phoui, and, particularly, Crown Prince Savang, opposed Phetsarath's return to political power. To US officials, Phetsarath appeared to be an ambitious and "shadowy" intriguer whose political activities "occasionally unsettle the highly personal political alliances in Laos."[74]

Souvanna told Yost that Phetsarath enjoyed the confidence of the vast majority of Pathet Lao. If Phetsarath returned to Laos and made an appeal to them, Souvanna said, the movement would simply dissolve, leaving the few remaining hard-core communists vulnerable to decisive legal or military means. Yost, who was skeptical about such an approach, commented to Washington that Souvanna remained "dangerously naive" about his brothers and the Pathet Lao.[75]

Eighteen months of service in Laos had taken a heavy toll on the health of Charles Yost, who had lost some twenty pounds since his arrival in Vientiane. A Foreign Service inspector who spent three weeks in Laos in September 1955 reported: "Yost is conscientious and hard-working by nature, but presently gives the distinct impression that he is operating under some strain." Acknowledging slow improvements in housing and other areas, the inspector noted "the extremely bad living conditions at this post." When Yost was diagnosed with amoebic dysentery in October 1955, the Department of State granted his request to shorten the planned two-year assignment in Laos to eighteen months.[76]

Before leaving for home in April 1956, Yost wrote a long, perceptive despatch offering some tentative ideas about the prospects for Laos in the years ahead. He reminded his State Department colleagues that 90 percent of the Lao population lived self-sufficiently in remote rural areas. The monarchy, which enjoyed wide acceptance, was "probably too passive" to be called popular. The kingdom's elites were hostile to communism, but this attitude was based more on traditional fear of China and Vietnam rather than ideological conviction. A disturbing tendency among the elites, Yost noted, was a preference for some form of authoritarianism over democracy.[77]

Because of the kingdom's military and economic weakness, not to mention its vulnerability to more powerful neighbors, Yost doubted that Laos could "exist indefinitely as a wholly independent nation." Western military support and subsidies, amounting to "five times national revenues," were "a necessary but temporary expedient, not a viable foundation for permanent national survival." The best hope for the country was participation in some sort of Southeast Asian federation, but, he concluded,

"There is unfortunately no reason to believe such a federation is likely to emerge in the near future."[78]

Ambassador Yost expected that the close and friendly relations between the United States and Laos would continue in the years ahead, but he warned that any US attempt to commit the kingdom "to a military posture which the Lao Government would consider rash and provocative" would damage relations "seriously and perhaps fatally." The Laotians, he explained, wanted to maintain their independence not only from their communist neighbors but also from the United States. For US assistance to be effective, tact and prudence would be necessary. Providing sound advice, some of which he had occasionally found difficult to follow, Yost wrote: "We must give no solid grounds for allegations that we are interfering in Lao internal affairs, are dragooning the Lao Government into military pacts against its better judgment, are blocking 'peaceful coexistence' with her communist neighbors, or are expanding our presence and our numbers to a point beyond reason or necessity."[79]

Yost's paper was warmly received by State Department officials responsible for Laos. Kenneth Young, director of the Office of Philippine and Southeast Asian Affairs, called the despatch "outstanding." William J. Sebald, deputy assistant secretary of state for far eastern affairs, suggested using the paper "as a 'bible' for conducting our affairs in Laos."[80]

There is no record of the reaction to Yost's despatch from more senior members of the Department of State nor any evidence that they read it. What can be said with confidence, however, is that his observations neither influenced nor reflected future US policy in Laos.

Chapter 2

A Frontier Country in the Cold War

By the time Ambassador J. Graham Parsons arrived in Laos on July 27, 1956, the rat-infested legation endured by America's diplomatic pioneers in Vientiane had been transformed into a far more habitable residence for the ambassador. Parsons found the refurbished house "not bad at all, superb in fact" by Laotian standards. Improvements to the structure included electric and telephone service, the unreliability of which still made back-up generators and communications essential. The window air conditioners in the bedrooms and first-floor study were luxuries in Vientiane, where only 20 percent of the houses had electric appliances and kerosene remained a common source of lighting. Parsons and his family were also among the privileged minority served by city water straight from the Mekong River. The pungent, unfiltered water, according to Margaret Parsons, the ambassador's wife, was "so dirty it leaves you feeling you should have a bath because you had a bath."[1]

Ambassador James Graham "Jeff" Parsons, born in Manhattan on October 28, 1907, was a graduate of Groton, a small boarding school in Massachusetts that sought to cultivate "manly Christian character" in its students and groom them for public service. The school's alumni include presidents Theodore and Franklin Roosevelt, Secretary of State Dean Acheson, diplomats W. Averell Harriman and C. Douglas Dillon, CIA deputy director Richard Bissell, and national security adviser McGeorge Bundy. In 1929 Parsons graduated from Yale, where he was a member of Phi Beta Kappa. After college and a year of travel in Europe, Parsons took a job at the banking house of E.H. Rollins & Sons in New York City. Although his father spent his entire career on Wall Street, Parsons had little enthusiasm for the securities business—a career choice that became even less appealing after the stock market crash of October 1929. The younger Parsons, who found work on Wall Street a soul-deadening experience, wryly described his job as trying "to explain to clients why the investment opportunities thrust into their eager hands by our salesman had depreciated in value . . . and why, nonetheless, they should be of good cheer and hang on."[2]

During his year abroad, Parsons's interest in the Foreign Service had been sparked by an Englishman preparing for a career in the UK diplomatic service. After Parsons informed Groton's influential headmaster Endicott Peabody of his interest in international affairs, the "old boy network" eventually connected the young man with Ambassador Joseph C. Grew, a Groton graduate who was looking for an alumnus of the school to serve as his personal secretary at the American embassy in Tokyo. Parsons had an interview with the ambassador and soon found himself aboard the *President Coolidge* sailing for Japan.

Parsons provided Grew with clerical help such as filing the ambassador's personal correspondence, entering engagements in his calendar, and keeping track of his personal stock of wine. Parsons also traveled widely, including a trip to China, and drafted diplomatic despatches for the embassy in Tokyo. While in Japan, he wrote his college classmate and future diplomatic colleague Winthrop G. Brown: "I'd rather be on a desert isle alone with a copy of Pilgrim's Progress than return to E.H. Rollins & Sons."[3]

Parsons typically spent his early morning hours in Tokyo preparing for the Foreign Service examination, a difficult oral and written test aimed at selecting the most capable men—the Foreign Service was then almost exclusively male—to represent the United States in international relations. The examination had been delayed by the Depression, but when it resumed in 1936, Parsons passed and received an appointment as a Foreign Service officer. That same year he married Margaret "Peggy" Boulton, the niece of the Canadian minister in Tokyo.

Parsons's subsequent diplomatic career in Asia included posts in Manchuria, India, and Japan, where he distinguished himself as counselor and then minister at the American embassy in Tokyo. In the two decades preceding his appointment to Laos, he also served in the West in capitals including Havana, Cuba; Ottawa, Canada; and Vatican City, Rome. Assignments in the State Department in Washington, D.C., an obligatory step for career advancement in the Foreign Service, had been an opportunity for Parsons to learn firsthand about the policymaking process. Before his appointment to the American embassy in Tokyo in 1953, Parsons was the deputy director and then acting director of the D.C.-based Office of European Regional Affairs.

Parsons had never served in Southeast Asia before his appointment to Laos, but he did possess a key qualification for the post: the ability to speak French, the working language of government and commerce there. The State Department's decision to recommend him as ambassador surprised Parsons, who thought that such a promotion, "even at a very little embassy," was still a few years away. Writing to his mother and his two teenage daughters, Parsons summarized the political significance of Laos as "a frontier country in the cold war." The country was sufficiently remote that his Letter of Credence from President Eisenhower, which formally requested that the king accept Parsons as the new American ambassador, was sent "not to Laos, but to Lagos, Nigeria—obviously a post much better known to the [State Department] Mail Room," he later recalled.[4]

Parsons arrived in Vientiane, which he described as "dilapidated, yet somehow ingratiating," in the midst of a construction boom that included public buildings, offices, and residences. To house the rising number of employees in the US Mission, which had increased from a handful in 1954 to more than one hundred in 1956, the US government built prefabricated aluminum bungalows in an area of Vientiane that became known as Silver City. In the capital's business district, concrete sidewalks began replacing wooden boards. And according to an embassy report, the first bakery to sell American-style bread opened in Vientiane. A CIA analyst wrote, "[Vientiane] is probably best compared to a small town in the United States some fifty years ago—when electricity had just been brought in, some streets were being paved, and the town was beginning to style itself a city."[5]

Despite physical changes in the capital since Yost's term as minister and ambassador, health risks remained. The greatest single hazard was malaria, and tuberculosis was prevalent. Shortly before Parsons's arrival in Laos, Secretary of State Dulles told the president that Vientiane "was a terrible diplomatic post, with no sanitary facilities, no decent drinking water, or other elementary necessities." Within days of arriving in the Lao capital, Ambassador Parsons and his wife received the first of two plague shots, which were repeated every six months. Later, Margaret Parsons was successfully treated for rabies after caring for the family's dog, which had been bitten by one of Vientiane's many stray dogs.[6]

Ambassador Parsons assumed his diplomatic responsibilities in Laos at a sensitive moment in US relations with the kingdom. To the dismay of the Eisenhower administration, Prime Minister Souvanna Phouma had accepted an invitation from PRC Foreign Minister Chou En-lai to visit Peking. For Souvanna and his ministers, the decision was straightforward: refusing the invitation would be a "gratuitous affront to [a] big neighbor" that "little Laos [could] not afford." Officials of the US government, which did not recognize the PRC and opposed its admission to the United Nations, found Souvanna's prompt reply to the invitation disturbing and disapproved of his failure to consult with his Western allies before accepting it. To State Department officials, it appeared that Souvanna was either "dangerously wobbly" or planning a rapprochement with the Pathet Lao and Chinese communists.[7]

W. Wendell Blancké, who served as chargé d'affaires between Yost's departure and Parsons's arrival, offered an alternative explanation for Souvanna's response to the invitation. Most Lao leaders, Blancké reported, believed that only the Chinese could resolve the problem in the northern provinces. At the Geneva conference, Chou En-lai had met privately with Lao delegates, who objected to "the plan to divide the country." In Blancké's words, Chou's message to the Laotians was: "If the [Pathet Lao] give you any trouble, come to me and we will fix it in no time." The cold war, Blancké informed the State Department, was of secondary importance to the Lao officials. Their primary concern was reuniting the country.[8]

On July 28, 1956, one day after Parsons arrived in Laos, Souvanna hosted a working lunch for JCS chairman Admiral Arthur Radford and the new ambassador. The meal provided an opportunity for the prime minister to explain why his visit to China and similar actions were necessary. The kingdom's exposure to powerful communist countries, Souvanna said, meant that he "would occasionally have to 'maneuver' and do things which might appear incomprehensible" to Americans. He tried to reassure his guests that Lao neutrality would be "armed neutrality," requiring the strength and firm allies advocated by Admiral Radford. "Laos," said Souvanna, "would not forget its old friends nor abandon substance for shadow."[9]

One Souvanna maneuver that seemed incomprehensible to American officials was negotiating with Pathet Lao leader Souphanouvong to resolve outstanding political issues. Like his half brother Souvanna, Prince Souphanouvong was an intelligent, French-educated civil engineer—a "quite attractive and persuasive figure," according to Parsons. The mustachioed "Red Prince," whose wife was a Vietnamese radical, had been a member of Lao Issara, but his temperament and political views differed sharply from those of Souvanna and the movement's other leaders. In his letter of resignation, Souphanouvong denounced the character of his countrymen: "As long as the Lao will not rid themselves of their disastrous inclination to make the least effort, you may be certain that they will never have any other profession, craft, or livelihood than those of the low wage-earner, the artisan, the coolie, and the debtor. In the end, they will not enjoy a single liberty on their own soil."[10]

Souphanouvong joined Ho Chi Minh's cause early in the French–Viet Minh War. A declared neutralist—an assertion Souvanna appeared to accept for many years—Souphanouvong had secretly joined the communist party and publicly declared himself a Marxist-Leninist in 1967. Within the Pathet Lao, Souphanouvong was subordinate to Kaysone Phoumvihan, the general secretary of the clandestine Lao People's Revolutionary Party (LPRP), formally established in 1955. Kaysone, born in Savannakhet to a Lao mother and a Vietnamese father who was a French colonial functionary, received his secondary and university education in Hanoi, where he was recruited by Ho's Indochinese Communist Party. Nouhak Phoumsavan, who was also born in Savannakhet, was the second most powerful member of the LPRP and the Pathet Lao. Both men, like Souphanouvong, married Vietnamese women. Southeast Asian affairs analysts Paul Langer and Joseph Zasloff concluded: "One cannot escape the impression that very early the Vietnamese Communists singled out Souphanouvong as the Lao who combined the qualities they considered desirable in a public representative of a Communist-sponsored movement that wished to mask its true complexion."[11]

In a joint declaration dated August 5, 1956, Souvanna and Souphanouvong reached an agreement in principle between the RLG and the

Pathet Lao. They agreed that Laos should follow a neutral foreign policy, maintain good relations with all countries, particularly its neighbors, and refuse to participate in military alliances. The only military bases in the kingdom would be those permitted by the Geneva Accords. Declaring a cease-fire, the government and Pathet Lao announced the establishment of military and political commissions to develop terms for the truce, the administration of the two northern provinces, and the integration of Pathet Lao forces into the army. On August 10 Souvanna and Souphanouvong further declared their intention to establish a government of national union that would include representatives of the Pathet Lao. The military and political details of the two agreements were to be subjects of further study and negotiation.

The understanding that Souvanna and Souphanouvong had reached set off alarms in both Washington and Vientiane. At a meeting of the National Security Council (NSC)—a venue where Lao affairs had infrequently required the attention of President Eisenhower and his most senior officials—Central Intelligence director Allen Dulles declared that an agreement with the Pathet Lao would "result in substantial gains for the Communists." To Dulles, the younger brother of the secretary of state, it appeared that the declaration "may be the first step in Communist penetration of the Laotian Government." But he said, "The situation may not be lost" if the Lao government effectively built up its security forces.[12]

In Vientiane, Parsons voiced US concerns directly to Souvanna in terms that were diplomatic but unmistakable. The ambassador congratulated the prime minister on his efforts to bring peace and unity to the country but then said he felt obliged to point out that the American public would likely view the agreement as "an accommodation with [the] Commies." Moreover, Souvanna's planned trip to Peking would further inflame US public opinion. The US government, Parsons said, had no desire to interfere in Lao internal affairs, but the prime minister must understand that US aid to Laos required the support of the American people and their representatives in Congress.[13]

Souvanna responded that, on one hand, he understood the strength of American feelings about China, which had been consistently and viciously hostile to the United States. On the other hand, Souvanna said, Americans must understand that he had to go to Peking. He had no intention of capitulating to the communists, but Laos and the United States must face the reality that his small, landlocked country had to find a way to live with its more powerful neighbors. The prime minister attempted to reassure Parsons that the trip to Peking would be a simple courtesy visit, without any commitments. Souvanna said he would stress this point when he announced the trip. Commenting on the proposed announcement, Parsons observed that the visit to Peking would make headlines in the United States; its "courtesy" purpose would not.[14]

In his report to the State Department, Parsons cabled that Souvanna appeared "slightly nettled" by questions raised at the meeting—an indication that the relationship between the two officials had gotten off to a rocky start. The prime minister and Parsons represented two fundamentally different approaches to preserving Lao independence and "developed an active dislike" of each other, recalled Christian Chapman, a political officer in the embassy in Vientiane while Parsons was ambassador. "Unfortunately, there was a personal antagonism between the two men," said Chapman. "It was a clash of policy, but it became personal."[15]

For routine diplomatic reporting, Parsons and other American ambassadors used encrypted embassy communications. More restricted messages—for example, sensitive personnel topics—might be transmitted on the "Roger" channel of the State Department's Bureau of Intelligence and Research. To discuss covert activities, ambassadors typically chose the more secure channels of the Central Intelligence Agency. On August 7, 1956, Parsons communicated with Washington through this channel to recommend a clandestine program—that is, US involvement was supposed to remain hidden—that would strengthen the ability of the Lao government to resist subversion and penetration by the Pathet Lao. The "gravity [of the] situation," Parsons advised, made it "imperative" that the US government act promptly.[16]

A basic requirement, the ambassador suggested, was helping the Lao government screen and process members and sympathizers of the Pathet Lao. The CIA would assist the government in such areas as setting up reception centers and providing training and equipment for taking personal histories and photographing individuals. Specifically, Parsons recommended US support for two planned Lao "re-education" camps to "reindoctrinate selected refugees, PL adherents, and other individuals." Qualified Pathet Lao applicants seeking positions in the government or army would be "isolated and reindoctrinated by appropriate means" before their assignment to particular jobs.[17]

Parsons proposed that the US government assist Lao civilian and military agencies in strengthening their capabilities for propaganda and for countering espionage, sabotage, and guerrilla operations. This support would include helping the Special Branch of the Lao police cope with subversion, assisting the army intelligence agency with internal security within the armed forces, and supporting the Lao civilian intelligence service in activities "deemed appropriate to counteract commie" actions against the government. Parsons also suggested a program for educating key government officials on the "general nature and tactics of international communism designed to subvert and gain control of [a] target government."[18]

Having reported the concurrence of CIA chief of station Milton J. Clark, as well as other US and Lao officials, Ambassador Parsons received approval for this initiative on September 10, 1956. In developing more detailed plans, Clark proposed a Refugee and Relief Rehabilitation program in Sam Neua and Phong Saly. By every appearance a Lao government initiative, the program would provide refugees with blankets, medicine, mosquito nets, clothing, and other necessities. The CIA would also develop a propaganda capability in the provinces, including radios, leaflets, and mobile teams. In his recommendation to the ambassador, Clark wrote: "We feel [that a] bold, dramatic move of this type has not only humanitarian aspects in relieving the suffering of the people, but also should be of immense propaganda value to the government in supporting its position and detracting from the Pathet Lao attacks on the Royal Regime."[19]

In addition to strengthening the countersubversion capabilities of the RLG and funneling covert US funding to anticommunist politicians, the CIA station in Vientiane was providing small arms to villagers in Sam Neua and Phong Saly through the Laotian Auto Defense program, a direct descendant of a clandestine scheme developed at the end of the French–Viet Minh War. The Composite Airborne Commando Group of the French Army, commanded by Major Roger Trinquier, trained tribesmen and villagers in northern Vietnam and Laos for counterguerrilla operations in Viet Minh territory. Interdicting supplies from China and ambushing the enemy's regular units, Trinquier's "maquis" warriors in-

flicted losses on the Viet Minh. After the disastrous defeat at Dien Bien
Phu—"the regrettable Dien Bien Phu incident" in Trinquier's words—the
French ended their support for their Indochinese irregulars, which the
RLG declined to continue out of fear they would become a private army.[20]

In mid-1955 specially trained officers and noncommissioned officers
of the ANL began organizing villagers in the northern provinces to defend against Pathet Lao attacks in areas the army could not protect. As the
Auto Defense program evolved, its mission included "originating small-
scale commando action behind Pathet Lao lines." In addition to conducting combat operations, the Auto Defense forces in the northern provinces
supplied intelligence information to commando and regular ANL units
operating there. General Graves B. Erskine, director of the Pentagon's
Office of Special Operations, reported to DCI Allen Dulles the military's
view that "Central Intelligence Agency progress in supporting the resistance forces is good." Erskine wrote that the secretary of defense and JCS
had concluded: "Increased emphasis on CIA operations can provide a useful and timely mechanism for increasing US efforts to bolster Lao resistance to Communism."[21]

Arming the Auto Defense forces employed a standard tactic for the
clandestine provision of weapons to resistance forces. The ANL supplied
the Auto Defense forces with a diverse collection of small arms, manufactured in France, the United Kingdom, and other countries. Providing
"older, heterogeneous" weapons helped disguise their true source. In return, the ANL received an equal amount of new carbines and submachine
guns from the US government. This arrangement not only provided arms
for the Auto Defense forces but also helped the ANL upgrade and stan-
dardize its weapons. Clark's case officers supplied the Auto Defense forces
with blankets, radio equipment, and a limited amount of training.[22]

By the fall of 1956, the Auto Defense forces comprised some six thousand to eight thousand members, who operated under the supervision
and control of ANL commandoes. Because of the possibility of a peaceful
settlement between the RLG and the Pathet Lao, the Auto Defense forces
planned to shift their mission from attacking enemy forces to demonstrating "to the people that the army is really the 'brother of the people.'" By
assisting villages in such areas as improving roads, repairing bridges, and
building schools, these military forces could improve the lives of the rural

Laotians and strengthen their allegiance to the central government. Such programs helped reduce the threat of subversion and increase reports from villagers about insurgents living among them.[23]

On September 20, 1956, Crown Prince Savang arrived in Washington, D.C., to attend a series of meetings with US officials that he had requested only days before. Savang had spent the previous two months in France with his ill father, and he had not been in Laos when Souvanna reached his agreements in principle with Souphanouvong or when the prime minister visited the PRC later in August. The crown prince told Foster Dulles that he had traveled to Washington at the urging of Souvanna and his ministers, who appeared "anxious, uncertain, and fearful" about the US reaction to their recent policies and actions.[24] A particularly troubling aspect of Souvanna's August trip to China was "a joint Sino-Lao communiqué" stating that the two governments "agree to develop their economic and cultural relations."[25]

This was a "political error," Savang told Dulles. The purpose of his visit to Washington was to see how it "could be remedied." Dulles reassured the crown prince that Laos could count on continued expressions of friendship from the United States, but this support must "be translated into acts." If Laos wished to remain free, the US government could help. Musing that perhaps it would "have been better if the Lao had struck at the Pathet Lao" around the time of his 1955 visit to Vientiane, Dulles acknowledged that "the moment for military action had passed." The secretary of state absolved the RLG of any fault in the matter, blaming British and French officials "who had discouraged the Lao from acting." When Savang expressed his country's commitment to freedom and independence, the secretary agreed, but he added that Laos was pursuing these goals "in a rather weak manner."[26]

After a declaration by the crown prince that his people were opposed to communist dictatorship, Dulles responded with a question: Didn't the Souvanna-Souphanouvong agreements "mean the introduction of the Pathet Lao into the Government?" According to the minutes of the meeting, Savang reminded the secretary that no final agreement had been reached. And even if there were a settlement, "the Lao knew the true Communists among the Pathet Lao." Souphanouvong, he added, was of "no consequence," holding a relatively minor position in the movement's hierarchy. The communists used him, Savang said, "only because he belonged to the Prime Minister's family."[27]

In his meeting with Dulles, Savang twice mentioned "the possibility of having to replace certain leaders," a transparent reference to Souvanna. The crown prince had earlier assured Assistant Secretary Walter Robertson of his willingness to "redress" any "weakness" in the RLG and "stand more firmly" against the communists. State Department official Kenneth Young wrote to Parsons that Savang had "made clear beyond a doubt his displeasure with the Prime Minister." Washington policymakers, Young wrote, "would not be surprised if he undertook a line of action that eventually ended the tenure of the Prime Minister but that is speculation."[28]

Despite the reassurances of the crown prince, whose talk was often tougher than his actions, US officials continued to brood over the "almost inexorable drift" of the Lao government under Souvanna's leadership. To eliminate any possible misunderstanding in Vientiane, US policymakers instructed Ambassador Parsons to inform Souvanna and other Lao leaders that the United States would reappraise its policy toward the kingdom if it allowed the Pathet Lao to participate in a coalition government, accepted economic or technical assistance from communist nations, or took any other steps that would jeopardize the kingdom's independence. A cable to Parsons declared: "Communists must if possible be barred at gate since successful control after their entry [is] doubtful."[29]

On November 13, 1956, Parsons delivered a letter to Souvanna summarizing the US position. In a subsequent meeting, the prime minister insisted that including two or three members of the Pathet Lao in the government was the key to regaining control of the northern provinces. Souvanna repeated to Parsons that his half brother Souphanouvong and other Pathet Lao leaders were neither communists nor under communists' control. And in exchange for a few Pathet Lao leaders entering the government, Souvanna would obtain a written agreement that would unconditionally restore the authority of the RLG in Sam Neua and Phong Saly. The Pathet Lao followers would then be immediately removed from the northern provinces and undergo screening, reindoctrination, and eventual integration into national life.

Souvanna concluded his appeal by telling Parsons that for several months he had worked to the limit of his ability to reunify the kingdom. He had "no material motive" for remaining in power, and, in fact, had told the UK ambassador that same morning of his personal desire to be done with the responsibilities of office. Souvanna did, however, have faith in his proposed solution and wanted the opportunity to try it. All that was required was support from the United States.[30]

Parsons, not wishing to exceed his instructions, agreed to communicate Souvanna's appeal to Washington. In relaying the message, the ambassador recommended a negative reply, and top officials in the Department of State concurred. For the Eisenhower administration, the decision was straightforward: the Pathet Lao was a "Communist appendage" of the North Vietnamese, and "past painful experience with other attempts [to] meet Communists half-way through coalition government" had been failures. The introduction of communists into the cabinet was, therefore, a "potentially dangerous arrangement" that would threaten Lao independence.[31]

Ambassador Parsons delivered Washington's unfavorable reply to Souvanna on November 27. The Lao prime minister said he was "deeply disappointed" but observed that the attempt had been worth making. Without any visible rancor, Souvanna said that he must now deal with other more important problems. In his report of the meeting to the State Department, Parsons wrote that Souvanna had "made no commitment but I would be surprised if [the] coalition idea is not shelved as impractical in [the] present circumstances."[32]

To the consternation of the ambassador and other US officials, a coalition government returned as a viable political idea almost immediately. In December Souvanna presented a proposal to his cabinet that included the addition of two Pathet Lao ministers. The cabinet approved Souvanna's proposal, and on December 28, 1956, Souvanna and Souphanouvong issued a joint communiqué announcing the planned formation of a coalition government and the implementation of the joint declarations of August 5 and 10. "The coalition government," the communiqué noted, would have to be approved by "the National Assembly in accordance with the Constitution."[33]

In the view of US government officials, the December 28 agreement appeared even more favorable to the Pathet Lao than the earlier declarations signed by Souvanna and Souphanouvong. Vague about the obligations of the Pathet Lao, the new communiqué did not provide guarantees in such areas as the restoration of RLG authority in Sam Neua and Phong

Saly and the submission of Pathet Lao soldiers to the national armed forces. Parsons, who assumed the agreement would be quickly ratified by the National Assembly, suggested to the State Department that the "time has come to watch [the] situation from [the] standpoint of Souvanna being forced out of office. If he should show weakness in [the] face of PL non-performance or treachery, [his] RLG colleagues and we might be on common ground in wishing [to] force him out."[34]

In Washington, State Department officials shared Parsons's alarm about the December 28 communiqué. Assistant Secretary Walter Robertson "was obviously very disturbed" about Souvanna's latest agreement with the Pathet Lao, according to Paul A. Bridle, a Canadian diplomat and former ICC commissioner in Laos. At a meeting with Bridle on January 2, 1957, Robertson said there was nothing in the Geneva Accords that required a coalition government or any of the other concessions made by Souvanna. This latest agreement, said Robertson, was a step toward turning the government of Laos over to the Pathet Lao, the North Vietnamese, and ultimately international communism. Responding to a question by Robertson, Bridle said that Souvanna "was fundamentally more of a friend to the West" than the United States believed. When the Canadian asked about the US response to Souvanna's agreement with the Pathet Lao, Robertson said there was a possibility of discontinuing aid. He immediately added, however, that such an action would be the "one sure way of losing the ball game."[35]

Walter Spencer Robertson, a Virginia investment banker and an Eisenhower Democrat, was one of the administration's most influential voices in determining US policy in the Far East. Known for his personal charm, eloquence, and intense anticommunist convictions, Robertson was a trusted associate of the secretary of state and an unbending architect of the administration's China policy. "There was no question in Robertson's mind that we should be 100 percent pro-Nationalist government on Taiwan and 100 percent anti-Communist government in Peking," recalled Joseph Mendenhall, who held a number of Far East posts in the State Department in the 1950s and 1960s. "There was no suggestion that he would be prepared to even consider the possibility of regularizing our relations with the Chinese Communists."[36]

Born in 1893 in Holloway County, Virginia, Robertson dropped out of college to pursue a career in investment banking. During World War

I, he served as a pilot in the Air Corps, and a plane crash caused migraine headaches that he suffered the rest of his life. After the war, Robertson returned to banking and became a partner at the Richmond firm of Scott and Stringfellow. Too old for military duty in World War II, Robertson wanted to contribute to the war effort and accepted an appointment as chief of the Lend-Lease Mission to Australia. In 1944 Secretary of State Cordell Hull asked him to serve in the embassy in China, overseeing all of the US economic programs. Once there, Robertson became more involved in political affairs.

Robertson wished to return home after Japan was defeated, but he reluctantly remained at the embassy during the postwar effort by General George C. Marshall to mediate the civil war between the Chinese nationalists and communists. Robertson recalled thinking that General Marshall had been given an impossible task. "They had been fighting for some twenty years," said Robertson, adding: "Chiang Kai-shek and Mao Tse-tung were mortal enemies, and neither one of them for a moment ever had any desire to join hands to work for China."[37]

At a time when many American diplomats attributed the declining fortunes of the Chinese nationalists to corruption, incompetence, and indifference to social problems, Robertson believed that Chiang Kai-shek and his followers were victims of vacillating US policy and an appalling lack of support. "The U.S. does bear a very large part of the responsibility for the loss of China to the Communists," he said. "If we had applied the policies we used in China to our European allies, we would have lost them too."[38]

Robertson left the State Department in 1946, vowing that he "wouldn't work for the government in peacetime for all the money in the United States Treasury." He returned to investment banking in Richmond but retained a deep interest in the Far East. Robertson's testimony before the House Foreign Affairs Committee in 1948 and his speeches about China attracted the attention of Republicans. When John Foster Dulles asked him to serve as assistant secretary of state for far eastern affairs, Robertson demurred for a few weeks, then accepted the position.[39]

Dulles gave Robertson considerable latitude in managing the State Department's Bureau of Far Eastern Affairs. His China-centric view of the region, however, prompted some officials to question the depth of his engagement in other parts of the Far East. Robertson's "primary interest was Formosa and Chiang Kai-shek. It was difficult to get him to focus very much on other areas, such as Southeast Asia," recalled Charles F. Baldwin, who served as a deputy to Robertson and later as US ambassador to Malaysia.[40]

Elden B. Erickson, who returned to the State Department's Office of Southeast Asian Affairs after serving in the embassy in Vientiane, said of Robertson: "Everything in his eyes was related to China and communism. Laos wasn't pro-West enough for us and their officials weren't pro-West enough for us so therefore we were always kind of at loggerheads with them."[41]

On January 12, 1957, Robertson spoke bluntly to the Laotian ambassador to the United States, Ourot R. Souvannavong, about the December 28 agreement between the RLG and the Pathet Lao. The only concessions made by the Pathet Lao, Robertson said, were those required by the Geneva Accords. The US government, he added, "knew that the Pathet Lao were receiving their instructions from the North Vietnamese, who in turn were directed by Moscow and Peking." Robertson told Ourot that the US government had been making "the most earnest representations" through its ambassador in Vientiane, warning Souvanna against the agreement. "Never in history had there been a successful coalition with the Communists, since the Communists wanted not coalition but control," said Robertson. He concluded the meeting by admitting that he could not predict what the United States would do next in Laos. He did, however, issue a warning: if there was an agreement that "would eventually turn Laos over to the Communists, it was certain the Congress would not continue to support such a regime."[42]

The State Department instructed Ambassador Parsons to exploit the uneasiness that some conservative Laotian officials had expressed about the December 28 communiqué. Embassy and CIA officers set out to delay the adoption of the agreement, create further doubts and reservations about it among Lao leaders, and, if possible, defeat it. National Assembly deputies, cabinet ministers, and ANL leaders were discretely informed that ratification of the agreement would lead to a reevaluation of US economic and military support. Within a week of receiving his instructions, Parsons informed the State Department: "There is no Lao of importance who does not know that this is [a] critical moment in Laos relations with [the] U.S."[43]

A key actor in the American political action campaign was former prime minister Katay, the nominal deputy prime minister in Souvanna's government. Largely absent from Laotian political life, Katay served as chief of the kingdom's delegation to the United Nations. Although Ambassador Yost and others had considered him a dishonest and incompetent administrator when prime minister, Katay had other redeeming qualities, including his anticommunist convictions, his distrust of the Pathet Lao, and his ability as a politician. At his own request, Katay called on John Foster Dulles and other State Department officials three weeks before the December 28 agreement was signed. Undersecretary Herbert Hoover Jr. told Katay that he hoped disturbing reports of the Pathet Lao joining Souvanna's cabinet were untrue. If they were true, Katay replied, "it was the Prime Minister's plan, not the government's."[44]

Katay was in Paris when the Souvanna-Souphanouvong communiqué was issued. Parsons wanted him in Vientiane to lead the resistance to the agreement with the Pathet Lao. Katay delayed his return, however, claiming a "crise de foie," a medically dubious liver malady found almost exclusively in France and its colonial territories. The real reason for his hesitation, US embassy officials in Paris believed, was that Katay doubted his ability "to block the Assembly's approval of a coalition government."[45]

Parsons, who thought Katay's long absence from Laos made him a poor judge of both the political mood in Vientiane and the outcome of the debate in the National Assembly, cabled the State Department:

> Despite [the] current low ebb [of] his political fortunes, we consider [that] Katay's presence would not only be salutary in giving cohesion to political opposition to [the] declaration but also force him [to] face up to [the] realities of [the] moment by adopting [a] clear-cut position, rather than by taking refuge in convenient absenteeism. Katay must realize if [the] agreement goes through in [its] present form, he or any other eventual successor to [the] Prime Minister will be saddled with it. Perhaps it could be intimated to him that what he does at this juncture will undoubtedly be [a] criterion in judging his eligibility for [the] support he angled for so sedulously in Washington.[46]

Katay arrived in Vientiane on January 10 to play his designated role. With covert US financial support, Katay emphasized to Laotian officials the importance of demonstrating the country's commitment to anticommunism. He proposed new laws for banning subversive activities, registering political parties, and regulating propaganda leaflets. And he stressed that any agreement should include guarantees dissolving the Pathet Lao, submitting its forces to ANL control, and restoring government administration of the two northern provinces. In addition to raising local awareness about the agreement, Katay's political maneuvers helped delay a vote on it in the National Assembly.

On March 15, 1957, Parsons triumphantly reported to the State Department that the Lao National Assembly session had come to a close—without the government's presenting the "disastrous" December 28 agreement between Souvanna and Souphanouvong for approval. Because some official records still remain classified more than fifty years after Parsons's political struggle with Souvanna, it is difficult to describe in detail the covert tactics employed by the CIA station in Vientiane. To date, the best available evidence of a significant political action campaign is a letter, dated March 21, 1957, from Parsons to DCI Allen Dulles. In this letter, the ambassador commended CIA chief of station Milton Clark and "two other officers" for "their exceptional service in connection with our efforts to forestall the entry of the Pathet Lao Communists into the Government of Laos." Said Parsons, "I can assure you that Mr. Clark and his subordinates made a most effective, in fact indispensable contribution and reflected great credit on their Service."[47]

Parsons added: "While Mr. Clark was indefatigable and resourceful in reaching those whom we desired to influence, the volume of work coming from his office and the variety of ideas put forward were such that everyone in his office must have contributed a great deal as well." The ambassador concluded his letter to the CIA chief with a prophetic observation: "While the recent phase has passed without disaster from our point of view, there will be new crises in the future and I count very much on the support of your representatives here."[48]

"Milt" Clark was described by one of his subordinates as "very laid back," a man who "loved to puff on his pipe and philosophize about what could or couldn't be done in Laos and with the Lao."[49] Parsons admired Clark's skill as an intelligence professional, but he did not like the high profile that the station chief maintained and his casual view of established policies and regulations. In a memorandum to Clark, who ostensibly served as a second secretary in the embassy's political section, Parsons noted that despite being furnished with quarters in the embassy compound, where officers of comparable rank lived, the CIA officer had moved to a new residence and paid "an exorbitant rental for the premises." The ambassador, who had made a personal visit to Clark's new home, "was struck by the size and scale of [his] new living quarters as compared to other high ranking officers of the Mission." The propriety of such a large expenditure of taxpayers' money concerned Parsons less than the incongruity of Clark's residence and his cover as a midlevel embassy official: "Such accommodations by an officer in the Political Section must immediately raise questions as to your true status, with consequent jeopardy to your cover. The question is already being asked to us why such a house did not go to one of your superiors, for example the DCM [deputy chief of mission]."[50]

Although there were undoubtedly good operational reasons why the CIA chief of station should live outside the embassy compound, Parsons had identified an emerging problem of Lao and international perceptions, which grew over time and created difficulties for the US mission in Vientiane: a highly visible and powerful CIA presence in Laos. "Both the exorbitant rental and the size and luxuriousness of the house," Parsons admonished, "are causing comment among the diplomatic corps and others, who cannot but remark at your apparently unlimited sources of funds."[51]

In the 1950s and early 1960s, CIA involvement in Laos was one of the worst kept secrets in the kingdom. "They had their own airline. All of their cars were marked specially. They had separate nice housing," recalled Elden Erickson, who served as the Vientiane embassy's economic officer from 1956 to 1958. "They stood out, not like a sore thumb but like a sore hand."[52]

The conspicuous CIA presence made a mockery of the NSC directive on covert operations—specifically the recommendation "that any U.S. Government responsibility for them is not evident to unauthorized persons and that if uncovered the U.S. Government can plausibly disclaim any responsibility for them." CIA officers who served in Laos have said, however, that such government boilerplate had little meaning in the kingdom and that strict adherence to that language would have prevented the accomplishment of anything at all. Stuart Methven, a CIA case officer in Laos in the late 1950s, exaggerated only slightly when he later wrote: "We operated in the open, because there was little cover, no place to hide, no secrets that wouldn't come out, no 'plausible denial.'"[53]

The other technically covert but still visible US entity in Laos was the Programs Evaluation Office (PEO). Formally established on December 13, 1955, when its first three officers arrived, the PEO was responsible for overseeing the use of the US military equipment furnished to the ANL and for advising the ambassador on the military needs of the Lao army. To avoid the military-advisory prohibitions of the Geneva Accords, the Department of Defense initially hired retired or reserve military personnel. Wearing civilian clothes, these men usually had some experience in military budgeting and logistics. Ostensibly part of the United States Operations Mission (USOM), which provided civilian economic assistance to Laos, the PEO received funding from the Pentagon and reported to the ambassador in Vientiane. On purely military matters, PEO communications went directly to the commander of US forces in the Pacific and the Pentagon, with information copies to the ambassador.

The PEO was established at a time of declining numbers of ANL and French forces and increasing numbers of Pathet Lao soldiers and their Vietnamese advisers. Should regular units of the North Vietnamese army invade Laos, the ANL could at best delay them for ten days or so and then fight as a scattered guerrilla force in the rear areas of the advancing communists. The French Military Mission, in the view of the PEO, would not directly oppose invading North Vietnamese forces "except in protection of French Nationals or self-defense."[54]

The staff of the PEO, which had increased to twenty-two Americans by June 30, 1956, and for the next three years never rose much higher, had the same low opinion of the French advisory effort as other US military organizations. The vast majority of the declining number of French military advisers served at top-level headquarters, rather than in the field with the troops. Moreover, the French were uninterested in addressing the most critical need in the ANL: top-to-bottom training of Lao officers. "Individual training is grossly inadequate in the ANL," according to a January 1957 PEO report. "Unit commanders are not sufficiently qualified to develop their men. Until these commanders have been trained, no improvement may be expected in this area."[55]

The first PEO chief was Rothwell Hutton Brown, a brigadier general who had retired after twenty-eight years of active duty in the US Army. In the early 1930s, Brown served with the Fifteenth Infantry Regiment in China, where he witnessed the Japanese occupation of Manchuria and became a friend of Chiang Kai-shek. During World War II, Brown commanded the joint Chinese-American First Provisional Tank Group in the China-Burma-India Theater of Operations. After serving in the postwar Marshall Mission to China, Brown was assigned to Korea, where he first encountered communist guerrilla tactics on Cheju Do Island. His final active-duty posting, before retiring and reporting to Laos, was in Pakistan as chief of the US MAAG.

Brown's experience with communism in Asia convinced him that the United States was on a "blundering path to final defeat" in the Far East: "For it is in the East," he later wrote, "that the final great struggle will occur between our Christian-industrial-technological civilization and the explosion of teeming millions who, like lemmings on route to the sea, may burst their present boundaries and attempt to inundate the world." To Brown, Laos appeared to be nothing less than the linchpin of the global communist conspiracy. Dismissing the notion of Lao neutrality, he embraced an extreme version of the domino principle and the communist path to world domination:

> An independent, neutral Laos simply cannot exist because it lies in the direct path of communist expansion and because this southward expansion is a part of the great communist master plan of encirclement. This great master plan, conceived by Lenin and placed in execution by Stalin, prognosticated that the final downfall of the United States could be best accomplished by seizing China, and then by sweeping south through the riches of Southeast Asia and Indonesia, across India, across Africa, and thence to South America. China is communist and the outposts of communism are dotted along the way from China—in northern India, in India itself, in North Africa, in the Congo, in Ghana to Cuba, just 90 miles from our shores. But these outposts cannot be linked up until the communists have direct access to South Asia, and this they cannot obtain until they have taken over Laos.[56]

The gap between Brown's apocalyptic view of the communist threat in Laos and his condescending perceptions of the Laotians' ability to resist it was considerable. Commenting on the morale of the Lao military, Brown declared: "The nature and characteristics of the Lao people make evaluation of morale, as Americans understand it, almost impossible. Their attitude is friendly, however, it is nearly impossible to implant a sense of urgency or desire for hard work or the accomplishment of projects on schedule."[57]

In administering US military aid, which at $40 million per year represented approximately 80 percent of total US assistance to Laos in the mid-1950s, Brown and his fellow PEO officers discovered that "by American standards corruption is high." Lao corruption was inadvertently encouraged by the US Commodity Import Program (CIP), which was designed to prevent the large amounts of military and economic assistance from causing severe inflation in Laos—that is, too much currency chasing too few commodities. The CIP provided US dollars to the RLG treasury, which in turn sold them to local importers, who paid for the dollars in kip, the local currency. Importers "often key government officials," according to a PEO report—were supposed to bring consumer goods and other commodities into the country, which would theoretically absorb the additional currency introduced by US aid and prevent inflation. Importers needed a license approved by a government agency, which "purportedly" assured propriety. Import abuses, which included invoicing phantom commodities from nonexistent companies, led to "gross misuse of U.S. aid funds," according to a 1962 assessment of the CIP by the economic aid mission in Vientiane. The report concluded: "The RLG bureaucracy had neither the will, leadership [nor] discipline to play the system straight."[58]

What made import licenses particularly valuable—and further encouraged graft—was the inflated official value of the kip. The Lao government claimed that only 35 kip equaled the value of one US dollar. Outside of Laos, however, 85 kip was needed to match the purchasing power of a dollar. In other words, an importer who purchased dollars from the RLG treasury with kip could buy a US refrigerator, ship it across the Mekong River for sale in Thailand, and nearly triple his investment. "Any Lao who had a license had money in the bank because licenses could be sold and that led to widespread corruption," recalled Christian Chapman. "A lot of people became very rich through the system."[59]

Parsons considered official Lao corruption "one of our more discouraging problems." He continued to urge the government to adopt import

control and monetary reforms that would reduce opportunities for dishonesty. He was skeptical, however, that Lao ministers would take remedial measures. People "in high places" were profiting from the current
system, he informed the State Department. The business interests of the
kingdom's two leading anticommunists, Katay (the Lao-Vieng Bank) and
Phoui Sananikone (the Lao-Thai trading company), benefited from the
gap between the inflated official value of the kip and its free-market value.
In an unpublished memoir, Parsons recalled that Katay "flew into a rage
and attacked me for interfering in Laos' internal affairs by trying to force
a devaluation of the currency."[60]

Corruption was not confined to imports and exchange rates. Purchasing and contracting for USOM, which administered US aid in such areas
as health, agriculture, and transportation, provided lucrative opportunities
for graft. Parsons reported to Washington allegations of "rigged" bidding
to ensure that a particular American company won the contract for constructing the Vientiane airport. The embassy had on file an affidavit from
an employee of a US contractor who witnessed a bribe passed to a Laotian
official. And Edward T. McNamara, who served as USOM's public works
officer from 1955 to 1957, later admitted to a House subcommittee that
a US construction company "had paid him $10,000 for his assistance in
landing [a] Lao government contract." McNamara subsequently pleaded
guilty to a charge of conspiring to defraud the US government in connection with construction contracts for restoring the road from Vientiane to
Luang Prabang.[61]

Corruption among USOM employees was rare, but the program's ineffectiveness was endemic. N. Carter de Paul Jr., the first USOM director
in Laos, attributed the problems to bureaucratic red tape: "The main difficulty is that Washington requires too much detail and too many justifications by too many different people. This, in turn, results not only
in excessive delay but also in masses of paper work and in frustration on
the part of the technicians. These technicians, who are sent over here to
provide technical assistance and training for their Lao counterparts, find
instead that they have to spend most of their time behind their desks
sending data and justifications to Washington."[62]

The House Subcommittee for Foreign Operations and Monetary Affairs, chaired by Porter Hardy Jr. (D-VA), reached a different conclusion
about USOM's difficulties, charging that neither de Paul nor his successor

"showed any clear awareness of the problems that confronted the program or any expertness in meeting them." The principal organizational weakness, the subcommittee concluded, was a lack of adequate direction: "The staff is estranged from USOM leadership and feels a lack of adequate policy direction and guidance."[63]

De Paul, an economist and former Brown professor who had served as a special USOM representative in Vietnam, is perhaps best known for having a 1947 Cadillac shipped to Laos, a country with few paved roads. (The only other Cadillac in the country belonged to the king.) When de Paul left the country in 1957, according to the House subcommittee, he sold the inoperable car to a US contractor "at an inflated price." The rusting hulk of an automobile remained in front of the contractor's office, a source "of scornful amusement" and a symbol of the discredited US aid program. Eventually, the car was cut into pieces that were dropped into an abandoned well.[64]

Parsons, who believed that his friend de Paul received "no credit for the much good he did," attributed the failings of USOM to what he diplomatically termed "the indifferent quality of many individuals" who worked for the program. Unlike the State Department and the CIA, which assigned career professionals to Laos, the Mutual Security Administration—the agency responsible for foreign aid programs and for staffing USOM—"had great difficulty in recruiting any but opportunists or almost unemployable types for many parts of our end-of-the-line operation," Parsons wrote in his memoir.[65]

Carter de Paul's successor, Carl B. Robbins, was, if anything, an even weaker director of USOM. The most notable characteristic of Robbins's tenure as USOM director was its brevity. After serving only six months in Laos, he announced at a meeting of the leaders of US government agencies in Vientiane that he was seeking reassignment in Washington, D.C. Parsons later characterized Robbins as "a bitter disappointment," who, "to put it charitably, had to have been prematurely senile."[66]

Chapter 3

Behind the Scenes

It was a little after 1:00 p.m. on April 15, 1957, when John Gunther Dean, a junior political officer in Vientiane, arrived at the US embassy and found the first secretary of the French embassy waiting to speak with an American official. The French diplomat had a disturbing message to deliver: Ambassador and Mrs. Parsons, along with some twenty other members of the diplomatic community traveling by convoy from Vientiane to Luang Prabang, had been taken "as hostages by a detachment of Pathet Lao." Handwritten in red pencil on the French report were instructions to "go and see the Americans."[1]

Dean immediately sought out a senior member of the French Military Mission but was unsuccessful. He then went to the residence of French ambassador Olivier Gassouin, who had declined the RLG's invitation to celebrate the restoration of the road to Luang Prabang and the Buddhist New Year. Ambassador Gassouin suggested that Dean go to the airport, where a plane from Luang Prabang may have returned with additional information. A French major at the airport told the American that he had received the same information about the kidnapping and was sending three planes over the area for reconnaissance. Dean requested, and was granted, permission to join the flight. Shortly after takeoff, the control tower radioed the planes, announcing the cancellation of the mission but providing no other details. Unable to find anyone who had additional information about the kidnapping, Dean returned to the American embassy to alert officials there. After he went back to the French embassy, then the airport, the French counselor there finally revealed that the entire story was a hoax.

Dean considered the incident a prank "with no malicious motive." Ambassador Parsons, however, found the elaborate practical joke "anything but funny." When he returned to Vientiane, Parsons called on the French ambassador seeking an explanation. When Parsons received "none that made sense," he later wrote, "my relations with the French Embassy, never as close as they should have been, went into an un-Lao-like deep freeze."[2]

Since the Geneva conference, US-French relations in Laos had been proper but troubled, with little true cooperation. The US military took a dim view of French tactics and training, and the embassy deplored France's openness to a coalition government. The French, for their part, "all too often held a cynical view of the Americans as ill-advised, self-seeking successors in their former colony," according to Parsons.[3]

A measure of the rancor between the two countries was the American belief that French officials were spreading disinformation about US intentions. According to one rumor, the United States, having given up on a satisfactory resolution of the Pathet Lao problem, was supporting a separatist movement in southern Laos that would establish a noncommunist buffer state between neighboring South Vietnam and Thailand. The French were also presumably responsible for spreading the allegation that the United States was more interested in keeping two "Commies" out of government than in helping the kingdom resolve its national problem in the north.[4]

The differing US and French perspectives in Laos were reflected in their respective choices for political backing. The US provided covert support to Deputy Prime Minister Katay primarily because of his anticommunist zeal, a quality intermittently more important to American officials than his dishonesty and the "widespread dislike of him among other Lao politicians." As for Prime Minister Souvanna Phouma, Parsons admitted in an informal letter to Assistant Secretary of State Robertson that his relationship with the prime minister had "deteriorated greatly," adding: "While I do not like to say so bluntly in the cables, I wish that Souvanna were out of office." Most US policymakers shared the same view.[5]

French officials feared Katay's strong anticolonial feelings, which would reduce their influence in Laos should he return to power as prime minister. They favored Souvanna, who received direct assistance from French political advisers and speechwriters. "All the legislation introduced into the Lao National Assembly was drafted in French by French bureaucrats seconded to the Lao government," recalled Daniel O. Newberry, who covered the Lao legislature for the US embassy.[6]

In addition to the Western allies' divided views about him, Souvanna faced dwindling political support in the Lao National Assembly. Some deputies thought he had not taken a tough enough line with the Pathet Lao. Others felt his Western-leaning point of view was not sufficiently neutral. Virtually all were disturbed that it had been nearly three years since the signing of the Geneva Accords and Laos was still not unified. A May 9, 1957, briefing paper for DCI Allen Dulles reported mounting evidence that Souvanna would "resign (or be ousted)" in the next session of the National Assembly, which opened two days hence.[7]

In the previous session of the National Assembly, the US embassy and the CIA station had been instrumental in preventing the approval of the December 28, 1956, Souvanna-Souphanouvong agreement. At the opening of this new session, Parsons requested instructions from the State Department on responding to Lao inquiries seeking his "view as to whether Souvanna should be refused [the] confidence of [the] National Assembly." As a matter of form, the ambassador intended to reply that "this is no affair of ours and that we are interested only in [a] government which will vigorously defend Laos independence." However, Parsons intended to provide "guidance through appropriate channels" of the damaging impact of a coalition government on US-Lao relations.[8]

Souvanna's difficulties with the National Assembly became acute on May 27, 1957, when he outlined to the legislature his views of the kingdom's recent past and its future challenges. Reviewing the history of negotiations with the Pathet Lao, the prime minister declared that his policies could achieve national unity without jeopardizing the security of the country. Phoui Sananikone, a former prime minister and foreign minister who was close to the Americans, was the first deputy to speak. According to a report by Parsons, Phoui suggested that the National Assembly take an "informal vote" to guide Souvanna's Pathet Lao policy.[9]

Two days later, three questions were put before the National Assembly, with Souvanna agreeing to exclude cabinet members from the vote. The first was whether the assembly was satisfied with the agreements signed by the RLG and the Pathet Lao. A show of hands indicated that all of the deputies approved of them. The second question was whether the assembly was satisfied with the implementation of these agreements. Not a single deputy raised his hand. The third vote, which was secret, addressed the question of whether the government should carry on with the policies outlined by the prime minister. Eleven deputies voted "yes," and thirteen voted "no." Although the third question was not a formal vote of confidence, Souvanna and his cabinet resigned the next day.[10]

Parsons, who described the resignation as a "strange and unexpected debacle," reported that although Souvanna probably did not enjoy the confidence of a majority of deputies, the fall of his government "was accidental" and not the result of a calculated Lao political maneuver. Some deputies had voted "no" for policy reasons; others, who agreed with his policies, were motivated by personal rivalries to vote against him. The ambassador admitted that the transparent unhappiness of the US government with "Souvanna's policy of appeasement" played a role in his downfall: "While [the] Lao themselves toppled Souvanna, [the] US had much to do with it as we played upon Lao fears of [the] loss of aid."[11]

Souvanna's resignation triggered another cabinet crisis. The United States supported Katay in his bid to form a government and reclaim the office of prime minister. Like President Ngo Dinh Diem in South Vietnam, Katay represented a single, strong anticommunist figure to whom the US government could give full support. Parsons reported to Washington that the embassy had made an "intensive behind [the] scenes" effort on Katay's behalf and had received "good support" from UK, Thai, and South Vietnamese representatives in Vientiane. Many Lao leaders, however, found Katay "arbitrary, often tactless, always opportunistic," Parsons wrote to the State Department, adding, "Quite a few can recall [a] real or fancied double-cross at his hands."[12]

There was another problem with Katay, which the US government chose to overlook in the summer of 1957. Unlike South Vietnam's Diem, who, whatever his other faults, was personally incorruptible, Katay was one "of the chief culprits" using US aid "for personal and political profit," according to the State Department. The US embassy estimated that Katay and his associates had fraudulently issued import licenses worth some $12 million. Such abuses were a continuing propaganda gift to the Pathet Lao, yet cracking down on them meant that the United States might lose its "meager support for resistance to Souvanna's drive for settlement, any settlement, with the Pathet Lao."[13]

Despite American backing, Katay failed in two bids to form a government and become prime minister. Phoui Sananikone, the "only other promising candidate from our point of view," according to Walter Robertson, failed too. Parsons found Phoui easier to deal with than Katay, but the French opposed both American candidates. Claude Lebel, who was in charge of Lao affairs for the French Foreign Ministry, told US officials in Paris that Katay and Phoui were "regarded in [the] Lao public eye as corrupt and reaping personal profit from the United States aid program." The US defense of the two men was that "few Lao public figures" were immune to charges of corruption.[14]

The seventy-two-day Lao cabinet crisis ended on August 9, when a government led by Souvanna received the necessary two-thirds majority from the Lao National Assembly. Katay was the new minister of the interior and Phoui the minister of foreign affairs. A parliamentary maneuver essential to Souvanna's election was reducing the number of cabinet members from fifteen to six. Because the Lao constitution banned members of a prospective government from participating in voting for prime minister, Souvanna's reduced slate of proposed cabinet members increased the number of deputies eligible to vote for him.

In his investiture speech to the National Assembly, Souvanna said he did not know whether to "be glad or complain" about the honor and responsibilities of leading the country. Reaffirming his commitment to neutrality, he said: "None amongst us nourishes the design of selling his country to foreigners wherever they come from; no one wants to sacrifice our civilization, our religion, our customs, and institutions on the altars of the East or the West." Souvanna noted that the deputies had unanimously supported the December 28 agreement with the Pathet Lao and estimated that "two months will be sufficient to put into application" the agreement and all of its clauses.[15]

Three days *before* Souvanna's investiture speech, the US embassy received a draft of it, presumably from the French advisers who wrote it. The State Department considered the speech "weak," and the time limit on negotiations with the Pathet Lao meant that Souvanna would "again be under self-generated pressure [to] make foolhardy concessions in order [to] achieve settlement as [a] matter [of] personal prestige." From Washington's perspective, the situation in Laos remained "perilously close" to the dire circumstances existing when Parsons first arrived in Vientiane.[16]

Parsons complained to the State Department about French unwillingness to work with the United States and the United Kingdom to achieve common objectives in Laos. Though grateful for the information provided by the French, the American ambassador denounced their work "behind [the] scenes" to return Souvanna to power. Acknowledging the US embassy's vulnerability to similar accusations, Parsons observed that the "French could perhaps equally well reproach [the] United States–United Kingdom with showing [a] marked preference for candidates other than Souvanna but they cannot reproach us with [an] unwillingness to try and patch up our differences."[17]

Souvanna's return as prime minister did little to reduce US-French tensions in Vientiane. Parsons reported to the State Department that a key "French adviser remarked acidly [the] other day 'you Americans must be happy now with Katay and Phoui in power.'"[18] State Department officials were, indeed, hopeful that these two conservative politicians would exert a moderating influence on Souvanna.

An August 20, 1957, NIE, however, took a more pessimistic view, concluding that the "political situation in Laos continues to be dangerously unstable." One reason that Laos had "not disintegrated," the intelligence estimate explained, was "the apathy of the majority of its inhabitants, who live in primitive villages which are largely self-sufficient and who are little dependent on action by a central government." More significant factors holding Laos together were "the receipt of American assistance, continued Western diplomatic support, and the continued presence of French advisors in the government and the army."[19]

The NIE reported strong pressure on the Lao government for a negotiated settlement with the Pathet Lao: "The desire for national union has achieved an almost mystical quality among the Lao leaders and populace." Although the analysts in the CIA's Office of National Estimates had a relatively good record of assessing future developments in Southeast Asia, a key prediction in this NIE—the unlikelihood "that a settlement will be reached during the next six months"—was not borne out by subsequent events.[20]

On October 16—a little over two months after the formation of the latest Lao government—the US embassy in Vientiane reported that Souvanna and Souphanouvong had reached another milestone in their ongoing negotiations. Immediately following a proposed transfer of military and civil authority in Sam Neua and Phong Saly to the RLG, a coalition government that included Pathet Lao representatives would be presented to the National Assembly for approval. Pathet Lao military forces would be integrated into the ANL, and its political arm would be allowed to function legally in the kingdom. Although National Assembly approval could not be guaranteed, the accord reached by the two princes now had the support of virtually every Lao political leader, including former prime minister Katay, whom Parsons now privately called "the little heel." Unlike earlier agreements between Souvanna and Souphanouvong, this accord provided limited opportunities for the US government to delay or alter it.

In Washington, Walter Robertson was once again "deeply disturbed" that Lao leaders had "been taken in" by a "dangerous settlement." Ambassador Parsons, who had been on home leave when the agreement was reached, returned to Vientiane and met with Souvanna on October 24. Despite the contentious topic of conversation and the personal antagonism between the two men, Parsons reported to the State Department that their conversation had been "extremely frank but calm." The prime minister and the ambassador revisited their old quarrel over communist control of the Pathet Lao, agreeing only that they disagreed on this topic. In an attempt to reassure Parsons of his toughness with communists, Souvanna declared that under a new antisubversion law, any rebel would be shot. Acknowledging the prime minister's hard work to bring about national unity, Parsons replied, perhaps with some asperity, that he was quite certain the prime minister would be "pitiless if he found out he had been tricked."[21]

At the end of the conversation, Parsons said that his superiors in Washington would likely be compelled to reappraise US support for Laos, as the embassy's November 13, 1956, letter to Souvanna had been quite specific about the consequences of forming a coalition government that included the Pathet Lao. There was really nothing else left to say, Parsons declared. Admitting his failure to persuade Souvanna of the risks he and his government were running, the ambassador said he would, of course, report Souvanna's explanations to Washington. He could not, however, predict the reaction of the US government or the outcome of any policy reappraisal.[22]

Foreign Minister Phoui Sananikone was one of the few Lao politicians of any stature who opposed the RLG–Pathet Lao agreement. On

October 29, he told Ambassador Parsons that he and the crown prince found the accord "completely unacceptable." Parsons replied that Washington officials referred to the agreement in "even stronger" terms. (It is unclear from his report of this meeting whether Parsons quoted Walter Robertson's "shocked" reaction to the RLG's "irresponsibility" and "stupidity.") Appealing to the economic interests of Laos, not to mention those of Phoui, Parsons said that any serious consideration of the RLG–Pathet Lao agreement "would cause [the] value of the kip to plummet."[23]

Three days later, Phoui made an urgent request to see Ambassador Parsons to deliver a message from Souvanna: The prime minister had ironed out the political and military details of his latest agreement with Souphanouvong the previous evening. More importantly, Souvanna planned to present immediately to the National Assembly an expanded government that included two Pathet Lao representatives—even though the northern provinces had not yet been turned over to the RLG. When Phoui asked whether Parsons had any reply to this message, the ambassador said he did have a brief response that he trusted would be absolutely clear. Paraphrasing a proverb from *Poor Richard's Almanac,* he said that "to act in haste meant to repent at leisure."[24]

Parsons told Phoui: "Any government that acted in such a precipitate way would not enjoy [the] confidence of my government." Having acted in this fashion, it was evident that the RLG "placed no value on U.S. assistance" or advice. Regretting—and likely resenting—the lack of opportunity to speak directly with Souvanna, Parsons said that he disliked speaking "so brutally" about Lao affairs. He ended the conversation by referring to Phoui as both the "Foreign Minister and [a] friend" and by volunteering "his service if [he] could be [of] any help" in the current crisis. Phoui's reliable anticommunism and his future election as prime minister under unusual circumstances suggest that this exchange may have been more significant than a mere diplomatic pleasantry.[25]

Despite some ineffective lobbying by the Americans, Souvanna successfully presented his coalition government to the National Assembly on November 18, 1957. In his remarks to the deputies, which were well received and applauded, Souvanna acknowledged the risks of including the Pathet Lao in the government. "I do not underestimate your apprehension, and I understand your uncertainties," he said. Turning to foreign affairs, the prime minister declared his intention to "keep Laos out of all political adventures" and pursue "vigilant neutrality," while maintaining good relations with all our neighbors and "having the best relations with our traditional friends." Parsons thought this last remark was aimed at placating the US and reassuring the UK and France.[26]

US officials were unimpressed by Souvanna's words or deeds. When reporting to Foster Dulles the formation of a coalition government, Walter Robertson wrote: "This 'settlement' is clearly of the dangerous type we have been trying to prevent." On November 26 Robertson informed Sir Harold Caccia, the British ambassador to the United States, that the US government would be reexamining its policy toward Laos. UK officials generally supported the US position in Laos, but they considered it unwise to oppose a settlement that had widespread Lao support. Sir Harold, a diplomat with considerable experience in the Far East, observed that Laos presented a dilemma for US policymakers: withdrawing aid "would drive Laos into the arms of the Communists," yet the absence of a response to the coalition government risked "subsidizing" a communist "satellite." Robertson assured the UK ambassador there would be no hasty withdrawal of US aid. He did not, however, expect the Pathet Lao to abide by its agreement with the RLG. Why would it? Communists never keep their agreements, he complained, and they "always won." In Laos, the Pathet Lao had ignored the Geneva Accords for three years, and they "ended up with cabinet portfolios" they had not even asked for at the conference.[27]

The formation of a coalition government in Laos prompted an even stronger reaction from Admiral Felix B. Stump, the commander-in-chief of US forces in the Pacific (CINCPAC). In a January 7, 1958, "limited distribution" top-secret cable to Chief of Naval Operations (CNO) Admiral Arleigh Burke, with PEO chief Brown the only other addressee, Stump recommended that the US government prepare to encourage a "take-over in Laos by a strong anti-Communist leader." In Admiral Stump's view, Souvanna lacked the ability, desire, and leadership "to ruthlessly oppose the Communist threat." Although the United States had to work with the prime minister for the time being, Stump acknowledged, the ANL was "the ultimate source of strength" in Laos, and Colonel Ouan Ratrikoun, the chief of staff of the army, appeared to be the best choice for effective political and military leadership. Reporting his plans to coordinate an examination of possible alternative leaders, Stump concluded: "While I do not advocate any action at this time to promote a military dictatorship under Ouan, I do believe such a course of action should be recognized and we should be prepared to promote and support it whenever necessary or [the] opportunity so indicates."[28]

Stump also agreed with an observation by Brown that the only way to make "real military progress" in strengthening the ANL was to establish a full-fledged US MAAG in Laos. Such a step would mean a sharp increase in the number of uniformed, active-duty US military personnel. Acknowledging that the Geneva Accords presented a problem, Stump wrote that the prohibition against foreign military advisers would somehow have to be "removed." The admiral, who thought the PEO represented the nucleus of a regular MAAG, recommended that General Brown return to active duty as the head of the new MAAG and receive a promotion to major general "to reflect the increased stature of the organization."[29]

The CNO, which at that time was still in the operational chain of military command, forwarded Stump's message to Walter Robertson, commenting that it "merits careful consideration." No record has been found of Robertson's reaction either to the substance of the policy and political recommendations or to the absence of any coordination with embassy officials responsible for these matters. What is known is that Ambassador Parsons considered the message "a serious problem" and "objected vigorously" to CINCPAC. Exclusive communications between the PEO chief and Admiral Stump were fine for purely military matters, but Parsons insisted that Brown coordinate policy recommendations with him, as required by executive order. If the message had been shown to him in advance, Parsons wrote Stump, he and Brown "would either have reconciled our views or I would have given you my own views simultaneously in a separate message." The ambassador's message to the PEO chief was more pointed: any more uncoordinated policy recommendations to military superiors, said Parsons, would result in an immediate request for Brown's removal from Laos.[30]

Parsons officially concluded his own service in Laos on January 15, 1958. Assistant Secretary Robertson had asked him to return to Washington as his deputy. In his memoir, Parsons wrote that he was flattered by the new assignment and disappointed by leaving the job in Vientiane unfinished. He had served in Laos about as long as Charles Yost and had executed his instructions to the satisfaction of his superiors. Later faulting himself for inexperience and immaturity, Parsons admitted that he had done "some things, mostly small, which I would do differently another time." Vague about specific regrets as ambassador, Parsons may have been referring to his inability to develop friendly, influential relations with French ambassador Olivier Gassouin and, in particular, with Prime Minister Souvanna Phouma. The latter "easily contained his regret" when Parsons mentioned his transfer to Washington.[31]

In mid-January 1958, Souvanna Phouma traveled to Washington to defend his coalition government before US policymakers and to correct any misunderstandings they might have about it. The previous month the Lao Ministry of Foreign Affairs had released a statement about the Pathet Lao, acknowledging that the movement received support from North Vietnam and other communist nations and that it "was subject to Communist indoctrination." But the statement also declared that the people of Laos were "neither by temperament, civilization, nor social traditions predisposed toward communism." The absence of a "dissatisfied peasantry or urban proletariat," Souvanna's government claimed, would make it difficult for Marxist-Leninist ideology to take root in Laos.[32]

Top Eisenhower administration officials simply did not accept this line of reasoning, placing far greater emphasis on the global threat posed by communism than on the national factors that might encourage or discourage subversion. At the State Department, Walter Robertson predicted to Foster Dulles that Souvanna would "assert that his policy was the only one possible, that it corresponded to the national will, and that it had the unanimous support of the National Assembly." Repeating Parsons's assessment that Souvanna was "vain," Robertson noted that the prime minister's visit posed a diplomatic challenge: "One of our problems will be to reconcile our giving him red-carpet treatment—which he is due and which will very likely determine his satisfaction or dissatisfaction with the visit and his future attitude toward the United States—with our desire not to appear to endorse his hazardous policy of coalition with the Communist Pathet Lao."[33]

At a January 13 meeting at the State Department, Dulles attempted to persuade Souvanna of the danger posed by communist ideology and tactics. Deliberately skirting the divisive issue of communist control of the Pathet Lao, Dulles acknowledged that the prime minister possessed an "intimate knowledge of the situation in Laos." However, said Dulles, the US government had global "experience in the way international

Communism operates, in the subtlety of its means and the disguising of its purposes until too late." Suspecting that Souvanna needed education on the tactics of communists, Dulles had earlier requested the preparation of a paper on their techniques for subverting governments in Eastern Europe. Handing the document to Souvanna, Dulles said that it "might provide useful ideas of the kind of thing the Prime Minister and his associates should be on guard against."[34]

Agreeing with Dulles that Laos faced "problems," Souvanna said he "did not misunderstand the Communist danger." Just as Dulles had felt compelled to discuss the dangers of international communism, the Lao prime minister thought it important to remind Dulles and other US officials about the recent history of his country. Reunification, for example, was important because of the loss of Lao territory to Thailand and Cambodia during French rule of the kingdom. And while Dulles may have preferred to avoid a debate about communist control of the Pathet Lao, Souvanna raised the topic, estimating that only a few hundred of its followers were communists. He also disputed the comparison of Laos with other countries. It was Souvanna's impression that Romania, Hungary, and Czechoslovakia were under communist control not because of the subversive power of ideology but because of the presence of the Soviet Army. He thought a better comparison with Laos was Finland, where the Red Army had withdrawn and the country remained free.[35]

Dulles, an advocate within the Eisenhower administration for the "Finlandization" of Eastern Europe—that is, domestic autonomy for countries within the Soviet sphere of influence—replied disingenuously to Souvanna: Finland was the exception, not the rule. Laos should take little comfort in the small number of communists in the kingdom, Dulles said, since "they always preferred to operate from a minority position. Stalin, in his discussions of Leninism, had stated the revolutionary party must always remain a minority because only a minority could be highly trained, disciplined, and efficient. A majority group became incompetent and the slave of mass opinion."[36]

Souvanna and Dulles spoke with—or, more precisely, past—each other for ninety minutes. There is no evidence that either man was at all persuaded by the arguments of the other.

A topic on which Lao and US officials did reach at least partial agreement was the importance of establishing a realistic exchange rate for the Lao kip, which would sharply reduce opportunities for corruption. What they disagreed on was the timing of monetary reform. The Americans sought immediate change, but Souvanna wanted to wait until after the spring supplementary elections for the National Assembly. The Lao prime minister argued that a sudden devaluation of the kip would increase the cost of living and give the Pathet Lao an invaluable propaganda opportunity. Robertson and Souvanna agreed to a subsequent meeting of US and Lao experts to develop a monetary reform program that would not be politically harmful. Robertson, who was under congressional pressure to make US aid in Laos more effective, "could not believe that we lacked the resourcefulness and wisdom to find a solution which took care of both points of view."[37]

On January 15, 1958, the last day of his visit to Washington, Souvanna attended a special luncheon meeting at the Alibi Club, located a few blocks from the White House at 1806 Eye Street, N.W. The club's three-story townhouse was unprepossessing, but its exclusive membership comprised a powerful group of elected and appointed officials, military officers, and private citizens. The host for the meeting with Souvanna was one of the club's fifty members: DCI Allen Dulles, whose officers in Laos recruited agents and gathered intelligence on friends and foes, operated clandestine "nation building" programs on behalf of the RLG in rural areas, and supplied arms to Auto Defense forces in the northern provinces. Whenever possible, Dulles's operatives had also tried to thwart the formation of a coalition government and put Souvanna's conservative political rivals in power.

Once harboring his own aspirations to become secretary of state, Allen Dulles, like his brother Foster, had pursued a career that mixed diplomacy and international law. He established himself in the field of intelligence during World War II, when he successfully ran European agents for the Office of Strategic Services (OSS), the wartime predecessor of the Central Intelligence Agency, from his base in Bern, Switzerland. Appointed CIA's deputy director of operations in 1951, and then deputy director of Central Intelligence that same year, Dulles was tapped by President Eisenhower to be the first civilian CIA chief in 1953.

Unlike his older brother, who was known for moralizing, Allen had a reputation for womanizing. The secretary of state had done little to defend the Foreign Service against McCarthyism, while the DCI told McCarthy that only he, not his subordinates, "would answer to the senator." Foster was a confidant of President Eisenhower; Allen was not. The DCI had, however, earned the professional respect of the president, who repeatedly deflected criticism of Dulles's leadership of the CIA. In 1954 a small presidential study group, led by air force general James H. Doolittle, reviewed the covert activities of the CIA and concluded that Dulles's "principal strength" was his unique knowledge of intelligence. The agency he led, however, had grown too fast—"like topsy"—and suffered from "sloppy" management. Dulles inspired and returned loyalty, according to the Doolittle group's assessment, but surrounded himself with subordinates who lacked competence and discipline. James R. Killian Jr., the first chairman of the President's Board of Consultants on Foreign Intelligence Activities (PBCFIA), established in February 1956, later wrote that Eisenhower "failed to recognize the administrative inadequacies of Allen Dulles as director of Central Intelligence."[38]

Defending Dulles, Eisenhower observed that an intelligence agency was "one of the most peculiar types of operation any government can have, and that it probably takes a strange kind of genius to run it." To Killian's complaints about Dulles's limited abilities as an administrator, Eisenhower replied: "Whom could I get as a replacement whose competence would approach that of Dulles as an *intelligence officer*?"[39] When questioned about the advisability of brothers' simultaneously leading the State Department and the CIA, Eisenhower responded that the arrangement "did not disturb him because part of CIA's work is an extension of the work of State Department." In fact, Eisenhower said, "the confidential relationship between the two brothers is a good thing."[40]

A major criticism of the CIA under Allen Dulles's leadership was an excessive emphasis on covert action, which the Eisenhower administration confidently embraced as a means of containing communism and advancing US interests. Notable operations early in the Eisenhower administration were the overthrow of Iranian prime minister Mohammad Mosaddegh and the coup toppling Guatemalan president Jacobo Árbenz Guzmán. Policy approval for such clandestine political, psychological, and paramilitary activities was provided by the 5412 committee, the name of which was derived from the Eisenhower-era NSC directives outlining control of CIA covert operations. Its members included undersecretaries from the state and defense departments, the president's national security adviser, and Dulles himself.

Members of Eisenhower's intelligence advisory board viewed covert operations skeptically. In the fall of 1956, a PBCFIA report observed: "The CIA, busy, monied and privileged, likes its 'King Making' (the intrigue is fascinating—considerable self-satisfaction, sometimes with applause, derives from 'successes'—no charge is made for 'failures'—and the whole business is very much simpler than collecting covert intelligence on the USSR through the usual CIA methods!)." The board never changed its mind—nor the minds of the president and Dulles—about the overall efficacy of covert operations. In January 1961 PBCFIA chairman John E. Hull, a retired lieutenant general and former vice chief of staff of the army, reported to Eisenhower: "We have been unable to conclude that, on balance, all of the covert action programs undertaken by CIA up to this time have been worth the risk or the great expenditure of manpower, money and other resources involved," according to the minutes of their meeting. "In addition, we believe that CIA's concentration on political, psychological and related covert action activities have [sic] tended to detract substantially from the execution of its primary intelligence gathering mission."[41]

Regrettably, there appear to be no minutes for the luncheon meeting that Allen Dulles hosted in Souvanna's honor. About half of the guests were senior officials of the CIA. Although Dulles was likely discrete about the specific titles and responsibilities of at least some of his associates, Souvanna had an opportunity that day to speak with

- Robert Amory, deputy director of Central Intelligence
- Milton Clark, former chief of the CIA station in Vientiane
- General Graves Erskine, the director of the Pentagon's Office of Special Operations
- Desmond FitzGerald, head of the agency's psychological and paramilitary warfare staff
- Richard Helms, the number-two man in CIA's operations directorate
- Robert Jantzen, the new chief of station in Bangkok
- Sherman Kent, head of CIA's Office of National Estimates
- Alfred Ulmer, chief of the agency's Far East Division

The only agenda item for the meeting was a "briefing on Communist tactics and strategy." Considering Parsons's warnings in Vientiane, Foster

Dulles's exhortations in Washington, and the paper specially prepared by the State Department, Souvanna could easily have concluded that his hosts considered him, at best, a dim bulb when it came to the dangers of communism. Perhaps Allen Dulles intended the gathering at the Alibi Club to be an informal opportunity for agency professionals to discuss with Lao officials the civic action program, Operation Brotherhood, and other CIA-supported initiatives to identify insurgents and promote villagers' loyalty to the RLG. But one wonders whether such a meeting might have been either intended or perceived as a not-too-subtle message—the covert action equivalent of "gunboat diplomacy"—concerning the possible consequences of insufficient anticommunist ardor in an area of interest to the US government.[42]

On the same day as the Dulles-hosted luncheon for Souvanna, President Eisenhower held a press conference—his first since suffering a mild stroke on November 25, 1957. Neither reporters nor the president mentioned Laos or any other country in Southeast Asia. The questions posed to Eisenhower focused on the federal budget, the economy, and the president's own health. The discussion of foreign affairs was limited largely to the president's recent exchange of letters with Soviet Premier Nikolai Bulganin concerning a possible summit meeting of world leaders. A question about Foster Dulles, a lightning rod for critics of the administration's foreign policy, prompted a robust presidential defense of the secretary of state: "I think he is the wisest, most dedicated man that I know."[43]

Although a country of professional interest to selected officials in the national security bureaucracy, Laos in the mid-1950s seemed a relatively small problem to the president, not to mention the press and the public. Eisenhower had spoken briefly with Souvanna during his visit to Washington, but the meeting was merely a courtesy call, with little substantive conversation. Souvanna told the president that he and his ministers "had been truly touched by the warmth of the welcome they had received in the United States." Reciprocating the pleasantries, Eisenhower assured the Lao prime minister that the United States was "extremely interested" in Southeast Asia. "The United States," he said, "stood ready to help Laos within the limits of its capabilities."[44]

In early 1958 US policy in Laos focused on the upcoming supplementary National Assembly elections scheduled for May of that year. As part of the negotiations with the Pathet Lao, the National Assembly had passed a law increasing the number of deputies in each province by 50 percent. Approximately one-third of the seats in the expanded assembly would be decided by the May election. Should candidates of the recently legalized political arm of the Pathet Lao, the Lao Patriotic Front (Neo Lao Hak Sat, or NLHS), win a significant number of National Assembly seats, Walter Robertson predicted, "the Communists would be well on the way toward achieving their objective of taking over the entire country; if, on the other hand, the Government is victorious in the great majority of districts, the Communists would suffer a setback from which they would require a long time to recover."[45]

As in the 1955 election, the United States provided covert financial support to bring together the members of the two anticommunist Laotian parties—the Nationalists and the Independents—into a United Conservative Front. By February 1958, 85 conservative candidates had registered for the 21 seats at stake. The more disciplined NLHS and other leftists had registered precisely 21 candidates. To encourage a reduction in the number of conservative candidates, the US government turned over 2.1 million kip—or 100,000 kip per candidate—to the front organization. More US funds would be available after the number of candidates was reduced.[46]

Embassy second secretary John Gunther Dean was one of the financial intermediaries between the US government and the Laotian conservative front. The State Department prohibited Foreign Service officers from passing covert funds to organizations and politicians, which was a traditional function of the CIA. But Dean, who "felt my job was always to be helpful to my colleagues," later recalled requests from the CIA to assist the agency "from time to time." For his cooperation, Dean said, he "received an official reprimand from the Secretary of State that I had abused my functions as a Foreign Service Officer, since a State Department Officer is not allowed 'to pass funds.'"[47]

To assist conservatives further in the supplementary election, the US government approved a crash program to provide aid to rural Lao villages. The goals of the program, called Booster Shot, were to demonstrate RLG concern with the rural population and the reality of US aid. Examples of projects envisioned for Booster Shot included drilling wells in drought-stricken areas, bulldozing roads to link villages together, and constructing schools and repairing pagodas. The criteria for selecting projects would be "immediate and tangible political benefits" for conservative politicians.[48]

Ordinarily, a program like Booster Shot would be the responsibility of USOM, the agency specializing in agricultural, health, and other forms of nonmilitary assistance. The Eisenhower administration, however, turned to the CIA to play the leading role in the village-aid program. One reason was to prevent the possibility of obstruction by Souphanouvong, now a member of his half brother's government and responsible for the Commission of the Plan and Reconstruction, a ministry that worked closely with USOM in carrying out economic aid programs. Other reasons for CIA responsibility for Booster Shot included the operation's explicitly political objective and USOM's demonstrated inability to organize and manage such an operation.

In a memorandum to Allen Dulles, C. Douglas Dillon of the State Department said that five hundred thousand dollars would be dedicated to Booster Shot "for handling through your covert mechanisms." The CIA station in Vientiane would work with the ambassador or his deputy to select projects that "maintain or promote political or economic stability in Laos." CIA officers in Laos would also be responsible for "channeling the funds securely to their intended destination." Proposed projects requiring more than ten thousand dollars "would be referred to the Department of State, through [CIA] cable channels, for approval."[49]

The CIA officer responsible for helping manage the Lao side of Booster Shot was Rufus C. Phillips, a broad shouldered young man not yet thirty, who literally stood head and shoulders above the Laotians with whom he worked. Phillips had been recruited to the CIA from Yale (class of 1951), and he was one of the earliest graduates of "the Farm," the CIA paramilitary training center near Williamsburg, Virginia. His formative experience in political action was serving in the Saigon Military Mission, a special CIA project in the immediate post-Geneva years that sought to prevent a North Vietnamese takeover of South Vietnam. Phillips's boss in Saigon was Colonel Edward G. Lansdale, a controversial and unorthodox intelligence officer revered by many Asian leaders for his empathy and loathed by perhaps even more US officials for his freewheeling approach to political action and psychological warfare operations. Like Lansdale, Phillips was a charismatic optimist who approached the Lao with respect and couched his appeals to them in democratic terms. Lucien Conein, a

CIA operative who served with Phillips in the Saigon Military Mission and later in South Vietnam after Phillips left the agency, called him "the boy scout."[50]

Working under USOM cover, Phillips was originally assigned to Laos in February 1957 to develop a civic action program similar to the one he had supervised in South Vietnam under Lansdale, who had originally developed the concept in the Philippines to help the government successfully suppress the "Huk" insurgency. A countersubversion initiative with an ostensibly humanitarian purpose, civic action sought to engage soldiers and civil servants in improving the living standards in villages contested by insurgents. The initial reason for civic action was elementary, according to Lansdale: "to win over the people to help the Army in finding and fighting an enemy who hid among the population."[51]

The overall goal of civic action was to win the allegiance of rural people to the central government, which, in Laos, had thus far failed to provide assistance to the villages. "The Lao villager has a great deal of common sense but is ignorant of the outside world including the rest of his own country," Phillips told officials of the Pentagon's Office of Special Operations. "He is confronted with the choice of believing in a government which has never done anything for him and whose representatives in many cases he has never seen, or believing in a Pathet Lao propaganda agent who lives with him, shares his poverty, and promises him better times if he will only cast his vote in support of the Pathet Lao."[52]

With CIA providing funding and USOM supplying tools, construction materials, and other supplies, Phillips worked with the Lao to develop ten-man civic action teams, each having two specialists in education, health, agriculture, public works, and information. Typically, a Lao team would arrive at a rural village, establish a medical dispensary, and attempt to organize local self-help projects—for example, repairing roads, digging drainage ditches, and building bridges. While the civic action team engaged in community projects and spoke positively about the central government, Lao intelligence agents, "disguised as farmers" and cooperating closely with the team, "employed negative propaganda" about enemies of the government. From the perspective of some US intelligence operatives, an additional benefit of the civic action program was the opportunity for younger, more dynamic Lao leaders to demonstrate their ability and rise to power within the RLG.[53]

Civic action's use of community self-help to advance countersubversion and political objectives confused many officials in Washington. At an April 2, 1957, working group meeting of the Operations Coordinating Board, officials from various US agencies sought "to clarify the possible relation, if any," between civic action and the rural aid programs of the International Cooperation Administration (ICA). A memorandum summarizing the meeting reported a consensus of views: Civic action was "primarily" a short-term security and propaganda program that involved several US agencies, promoted political objectives, and operated only in Indochina.[54]

In contrast, the community development activities of ICA, the parent organization of USOM in Laos and other countries, were managed by a single agency, worldwide in scope, and "concerned with improving the living conditions of villagers." The memorandum noted that civic action and community development varied in the personnel they employed; presumably this was a stereotypical reference to CIA "knuckle draggers" and ICA social scientists. For a committee responsible for coordinating the work of multiple agencies to achieve a common national security objective, the OCB working group reached a dubious conclusion: "There is not and should not be any planned relationship between the two types of programs."[55]

Although Parsons and some other officials in Vientiane considered civic action one of the most promising programs in Laos, this form of political warfare had little success against the Pathet Lao. One problem with the program was that it did not fit neatly into any of the bureaucratic silos of US and Lao agencies. A largely overt activity, civic action was an atypical program for the CIA, and many of the USOM employees in Vientiane did not like cooperating with "spooks." Although the army was the largest and most effective government organization in Laos, there was resistance within the ANL to working on projects that were more civilian than military in nature. Such jurisdictional arguments, Phillips once wrote Parsons, are "where the Communists are beginning to make us seem foolish."[56]

Booster Shot had some of the elements of civic action—and all the limitations of a short-term, crash program. To finance Booster Shot, the CIA purchased Lao kip in Hong Kong and flew the money to Vientiane, where it was stored in an agency vault within the US compound. With authorization from CIA chief of station Henry Hecksher, who had replaced Milton Clark, Phillips withdrew kip to buy tin roofing, tools, and other supplies in Thailand. Because large-denomination Lao currency did not exist, and the market rate of exchange was 85 kip for one US dollar, transporting significant amounts of Lao cash was unwieldy. Using large cardboard boxes from the embassy PX, Phillips would load up his Nissan jeep "with as much money as it could hold" and delivered the cash to Lieutenant Colonel Oudone Sananikone, the Lao chief of civic action. His teams purchased the supplies in Thailand and stored them at the civic action training center. ANL trucks or US airdrops made most of the deliveries to the villages.[57]

A key difference between civic action and Booster Shot was that the former kept US involvement as far out of sight as possible. This not only allowed the program's benefits to accrue to the RLG but also helped avoid the taint of colonialism, limiting the propaganda opportunities associated with overt US programs. Booster Shot, in contrast, became a transparently American undertaking, complete with publicity provided by the USIS in Vientiane. There were disputes between officials in Washington and Laos, and within the US mission in Vientiane, over the visibility of US involvement in Booster Shot operations. When asked by President Kennedy in 1961 to name the worst mistake the United States had made in Laos, Parsons cited Booster Shot, with the sky "raining supplies" from US Air Force planes, as an example of "the American hand" becoming "far too prominent." It was, he said, "counterproductive."[58]

Chapter 4

Dangerously Unstable

IN LATE MARCH 1958, as the campaign for the Lao supplementary election entered its final six weeks, and as Booster Shot deliveries to rural villages were about to begin, the new American ambassador to Laos, Horace Smith, arrived in Vientiane. Like Yost and Parsons, Smith was a career Foreign Service officer whose first appointment as an ambassador was to Laos. But unlike his predecessors, Smith never received another assignment as a chief of mission. His term as ambassador was marred by policy disagreements with his superiors in Washington, D.C., and personality conflicts with other American officials in Vientiane. In a 1966 monograph about Laos for the US government, Smith wrote that he had been "instructed to resign" from his post in Vientiane.[1]

A stocky man with a black belt in jujitsu, Horace Harrison Smith was in his early fifties when he was appointed ambassador to Laos. Born in Xenia, Ohio, and a graduate of Swarthmore College, Smith passed the Foreign Service exam and accepted an assignment in China as a language officer in 1929. This appointment meant two years of full-time study of Mandarin Chinese in Peking, followed by five years of diplomatic service in China. "He had never studied a word of Chinese," recalled Ruth Little, who married Smith two months after meeting him and just before they left for the Far East. "And languages were not his favorite sport. So it was very difficult for him."[2]

After serving four years in Canton and less than one in Tsinan, Smith returned to the United States in 1936 for a year at Harvard, where he studied international commerce. Returning to China in 1937, Smith was interned by the Japanese after Pearl Harbor and returned to the United

States in 1942 on the *Gripsholm*, a Red Cross exchange and repatriation ship. After World War II, Smith served in Moscow, Athens, and Washington, D.C., where he worked for the assistant secretary of state for congressional relations. He served as deputy chief of mission in the Manila embassy prior to his assignment in Vientiane. Smith did not speak French well and always brought along an embassy translator for official business in Laos.

"The Ambassador's inability to speak French made it difficult for him to communicate with the leading personalities of the Kingdom," recalled John Gunther Dean. Dean's wife, Martine, was French, and she had known Souvanna in France, where his children attended school and spent summers at her family's estate. In Vientiane, Dean handled some of the translating duties for Smith and, with Martine's assistance, helped entertain Lao, French, and other officials at the ambassador's residence.[3]

Ambassador Smith wanted the US mission in Vientiane to make a fresh start in its relationships with the RLG and the French. Based on his briefings, Smith concluded that it should be possible to establish a new type of cooperation with Souvanna and the other older noncommunist politicians. Moreover, French culture, history, and political influence in the kingdom persuaded the new US ambassador that the French "knew the Lao and Laos best." In his monograph, Smith acknowledged "the extreme pessimism" of State Department and Pentagon officials about the possibility of unifying conservative politicians and working effectively with the French. But just before departing for Vientiane, at a March 1958 SEATO conference in Manila, Foster Dulles and Admiral Stump "informally, personally approved," in Smith's words, his proposed new approach to Lao and French officials. After reading this assertion in Smith's monograph some years later, J. Graham Parsons requested a search of State Department files but could find no record of the "Dulles-Stump-Smith agreement." He concluded that Smith was trying "to cover" positions he had taken in Vientiane that were "at variance" with his instructions from the State Department.[4]

There were documented discussions at Manila between Stump and Vice Admiral d'Escadre Ortoli, France's military adviser to SEATO, to improve US-French military relations. The two admirals agreed that they would promptly remove officers in Laos who "refused to get along" with those of the other country. From the State Department perspective, US policy in Laos had "shifted from the negative one of seeking to prevent a sell-out to the positive one of helping the Lao Government succeed in executing the settlement already reached."[5]

One of Smith's first decisions in Vientiane was to take personal charge of Booster Shot. Until his arrival, Smith later wrote, planning for the operation was disorganized, and the country team—the leaders of the US agencies in Laos—had "major differences of opinion" about its execution. By "establishing more unified control," according to Smith, "the operation was carried out less inefficiently than might have been expected." Parsons later noted sarcastically: "This account reflects how Amb[assador] Smith brought order out [of the] chaos he found on arrival."[6]

As part of his approach to more unified control, Smith wanted Rufus Phillips to report directly to him about Booster Shot, rather than receive information or transmit instructions through Chief of Station Henry Hecksher. Phillips quickly formed "a rather poor opinion" of Smith. "I found him to be a sort of pompous individual," Phillips recalled. "He could be quite charming, but he wanted to take the credit for what happened." A substantive disagreement between the CIA station and the ambassador was the visibility of the US government in Booster Shot. Hecksher wanted unmarked planes to airdrop supplies to the villages, ensuring that maximum credit for the program went to the RLG. Smith, however, sought recognition for the US government and clear identification of the aircraft as US Air Force (USAF).[7]

On March 31, 1958, the USAF's 483rd Troop Carrier Wing began delivering Booster Shot cargo to rural Laos, particularly in provinces where Pathet Lao propaganda was most intense. Flying at the end of the dry season, when cumulus clouds caused severe turbulence, twin-engine C-119 Flying Boxcars air-dropped sheet roofing, tools, and other supplies to the villages. "Some of the roofing bundles came loose, sending sheets spinning like large snowflakes through the air then slicing into the ground, while errant cement bags burst, dusting the landside," Phillips wrote in his memoir. "Close calls were recorded, but fortunately no one was killed."[8]

USAF crews received assistance from pilots of the CIA-owned Civil Air Transport Corporation, which had established a permanent presence in Laos on July 1, 1957. The CAT pilots—virtually all former US military personnel—helped the USAF identify the precise locations of proposed drop zones. An Air Force history of air operations in Laos called the CAT pilots the "most fertile source of information for the Booster Shot crews." CAT airmen also flew Booster Shot missions with older, smaller C-46 transports for "light drops" of rice, salt, and medicine. The most impressive Booster Shot missions were flown by four-engine C-130 Hercules transports, which air-dropped bulldozers in Sam Neua, Phong Saly, and three other remote areas.[9]

Ambassador Smith reported to the State Department that Booster Shot was "a spectacular success," citing the "very favorable impressions" created by the air-dropping of bulldozers into the countryside by massive C-130s. Smith had insisted that each piece of equipment be "prominently labeled with large USOM handshake signs on all sides, top and bottom, and American and Lao flag symbols attached to [the bull]dozers."[10]

Policymakers in Washington did not share Smith's excitement. They were "greatly concerned" by the use of aircraft clearly marked as USAF and by US officials' in Vientiane "openly taking credit for [the] airlift." Fearing charges of large-scale US intervention in the Lao elections, the State Department informed Smith: "We at no time contemplated [the] open use of such aircraft and assumed [that the] airlift [was] being accomplished by commercial planes and sanitized military aircraft. We have repeatedly expressed [our] concern [that the] elections efforts not assume such [an] overt character as to damage [the] conservative cause."[11]

Smith replied with a robust defense of the execution of Booster Shot, arguing that the United States "would lose [a] great psychological advantage if [the] USAF had not participated in these peaceful missions or if its participation [was] unknown." He continued, "Perhaps [the best] proof is [the] latest Communist propaganda in [the] northern provinces, namely that heavy drop equipment and materials are Chinese and dropped by Red Chinese planes."[12]

The State Department reluctantly acceded to Smith's request for continued use of USAF planes, rather than relying exclusively on "sanitized" military or commercial aircraft. But department officials did want the US role in Booster Shot minimized to avoid offending "Asian sensitivities" and arousing nationalist "resentment to Communist advantage." There was also concern in Washington about possible protests from the ICC about the use of foreign military aircraft in Laos, in violation of the Geneva Accords.[13]

Unlike Booster Shot, the US political program to strengthen the chances of conservative candidates in the supplementary elections caused little dispute among the country team in Laos: all agreed that the effort to merge the Nationalist and Independent parties into a united anticommunist front was "coming apart at the seams." Ignoring their commitment to promote a single slate of candidates, the two parties were "coveting [the] same seats," in the words of one cable to Washington, and the split among conservative candidates was "directly benefiting" the NLHS and other leftists. Ambassador Smith shared the view of his embassy colleagues that although the US-designed national front "still exists in name and some Lao render it lip service, it is actually [a] dead letter."[14]

On May 4, 1958, the failure of the Lao conservative parties to back a restricted slate of candidates led to an election-day debacle. Although conservatives won a large majority of all votes cast, the more disciplined NLHS party won nine of the twenty-one contested National Assembly seats. Four more seats went to other leftist candidates. The supplementary election had demonstrated to US intelligence officials that the NLHS was the "most dynamic political force" in Laos—one that would be a formidable opponent in the December 1959 general election.[15] After listening to a summary of the supplementary election results, President Eisenhower observed to the NSC that it would be "a serious matter" if Laos, or any other developing country, "went Communist by the legal vote of its people."[16]

Angered by the election results, Parsons drafted an emotional cable to the embassy in Vientiane, condemning the "lamentable performance [of] Lao conservatives" and denouncing them as "negligent, self-seeking, or worse." Former prime minister Katay, once a politician favored by Parsons and the US government, had opposed a unified slate of candidates in the supplementary election. The resulting conservative defeat in Katay's home province prompted Parsons to point out that the Lao politician had an "almost unbroken record as [a] political liability since mid-1956." As the head of the government, Prince Souvanna Phouma bore a particular responsibility for the election catastrophe. Souvanna's "vain assurances" during his earlier trip to Washington were "well remembered and he is discredited here," Parsons wrote. Above all, the election demonstrated to Parsons and other officials the need for "new faces" in the government—people who had the "energy and courage to carry [the] struggle into remote villages and minority tribal areas." A subsequent State Department communication informed Smith: "The necessity of developing new young leaders appears to us more urgent than ever."[17]

Despite the electoral calamity, all was not lost, in the view of Parsons and other US officials. Conservative candidates received a solid popular majority in the election and held a majority of seats in the enlarged National Assembly. If disciplined, they might be able to form a broadly conservative government that excluded the NLHS. Operating under instructions from the State Department, Ambassador Smith informed "selected Lao leaders" that US support would be "jeopardized" unless there were a merger of conservative parties, formation of an anticommunist government, and monetary reform.[18] The American threat encouraged action by conservative Lao leaders, who were shocked by the strong NLHS showing. On June 13, 1958, the two major conservative parties were dissolved, and their members formed a new party called Lao Hom Lao (LHL), or Rally of the Lao People. The president of the LHL was Souvanna Phouma.

Blame for the supplementary election fiasco was not limited to Lao politicians. In a private message to CINCPAC, PEO chief Rothwell Brown attacked the performance of every US agency in Laos, with the notable exception of the one he led. He denounced the "ineptitude" of USOM programs, which supported Pathet Lao propaganda that US aid enriched the few in Vientiane at the expense of the rural poor. The activities of the USIS started "much too late and were confused" and failed to develop a firm and effective village-level propaganda campaign, promoting either US or RLG identification with Booster Shot. In his political assessment, Brown estimated that the Pathet Lao was now strong enough to overthrow the government in the National Assembly and suggested that Prince Phetsarath, who had returned from exile in Thailand but was not politically active, "might be trusted" to form a government. The only two officials praised by Brown were his civilian and military bosses: Ambassador Smith, who had made "a superhuman effort" in the preelection program, and Admiral Stump, whose support had been "magnificent" and undoubtedly "the strongest factor in preventing an even more overwhelming victory by the Pathet Lao."[19]

Brown's personal message to Admiral Stump was circulated at top levels of the Pentagon. Assistant Secretary of Defense Mansfield Sprague gave the cable further distribution by sending it to Undersecretary of

State Christian Herter, chairman of the Operations Coordinating Board. Sprague suggested that the OCB might want to discuss Brown's observations. The high-level dissemination of a political assessment that clearly had not been coordinated with Ambassador Smith brought a swift reaction from Herter, who advised Sprague that closer attention to the executive order requiring coordination of political messages with the embassy "might well have cleared up certain misunderstandings of the U.S. aid program." Picking apart Brown's analysis in a three-page, top-secret memorandum, Herter concluded that an OCB discussion of an uncoordinated field report would not serve "any useful purpose."[20]

Despite the flattering characterization of his efforts, Ambassador Smith was "astonished and distressed" by Brown's message. It was a direct violation of the understanding about policy cables that Ambassador Parsons had reached with Admiral Stump earlier that year. Thus far, Smith wrote Washington, he and Brown had enjoyed a frank and friendly relationship. Their cordial relations did not, however, preclude Smith from reporting to Parsons, in an "eyes only" letter, that the PEO was "by far the weakest of the elements" of the US mission in Laos.[21]

Smith's official assessment of the PEO was unsparing. Although the majority of its essential personnel had military experience, none had a substantial background in logistics, the PEO's primary mission. Few of its members spoke French, much less Lao; the air adviser was not an aviator; and the engineering adviser lacked a degree in engineering. Because "most of the key personnel are at or beyond retirement age," Smith doubted "that a young and vigorous army could be created by a group who have had no recent military experience and whose professional careers in the military have been completed."[22]

The differences between the ambassador and Brown and the PEO were minor, however, compared to Smith's growing problem with Henry Hecksher and the CIA station. The conflict between the two men was both professional and personal. Hecksher, who referred to Smith as "the great white whale," thought the ambassador was in over his head in Laos and provided him with minimal information about the station's activities. Unlike his affable predecessor, Milt Clark, Hecksher was an intense, dynamic chief of station whose "piercing eyes warned against trifling," according to CIA case officer Stuart Methven. Rufus Phillips described Hecksher's personality as "peppery, impatient and sometimes peremptory." Phillips also found the chief of station "very down to earth." A veteran intelligence operative who was close to DCI Allen Dulles, Hecksher was sufficiently self-confident to reply to CIA guidance that he didn't like by reportedly asking: "Is headquarters still in friendly hands?"[23]

Born in Hamburg, Germany, Hecksher was trained as a lawyer and immigrated to the United States in 1938. During World War II, he enlisted in the US Army, participated in the D-Day invasion of France, and received a Purple Heart for a wound sustained in Antwerp. As a member of the OSS and its successor organizations, Hecksher was appointed chief of counterintelligence in Berlin. As deputy chief of the CIA's Berlin Operations Base, known as BOB, Hecksher was involved with the development of the Berlin tunnel, which tapped into Soviet military communications in East Berlin. Another significant CIA operation in which he participated was PBSuccess, the 1954 coup d'état in Guatemala.

As chief of station in Vientiane, Hecksher's mission "was keeping the Pathet Lao from taking over the Lao Government either through subversion, the elections or a combination of both." Hecksher was instrumental in harnessing the disaffection of younger Lao elites and army officers to the US policy goal of developing a new generation of anticommunist political leaders. Disgusted with the "Francophile gerontocracy," the younger, better-educated Lao conservatives considered the older politicians a national liability because of their self-indulgence and inability to work together. Hecksher provided the emerging Lao leaders with encouragement, organizational ideas, and money. He also held evening seminars for young army officers, government officials, and private businessmen, according to Methven, "lashing out at communism and corruption, extolling freedom and democracy. He told his audience that they were tomorrow's leaders and should start thinking about what they could do for their country."[24]

The combination of discontent among the young Lao elites and of CIA support and encouragement produced the Committee for the Defense of National Interests (CDNI), which formally announced its establishment on June 15, 1958. The organization included younger civilians, but its strength was based on the participation of ANL officers. Claiming it was not a political party, the CDNI said it was committed to stamping out communism and corruption and to rehabilitating the nation. Left unsaid was the group's hunger for power and its hostile view of the prime minister. The CDNI "didn't believe in Souvanna Phouma," recalled Rufus Phillips, who introduced Hecksher to many of its young military officers. "They really didn't want him in charge."[25]

To the embassy in Vientiane, it initially appeared that the CDNI members were "motivated by a growing sense of nationalism, by an awareness of the unsatisfactory state of the nation, by a certain disillusionment with the older political leadership, and by a desire to assume greater responsibilities in the direction of the affairs of the country."[26] Before long, however, Ambassador Smith formed a much more negative view of both the CDNI and the support it received from the CIA.

In early July 1958, Souvanna Phouma faced competing diplomatic and political forces that threatened his position as prime minister. The US government continued to press for devaluation of the kip, which would not only reduce the opportunities for corruption but also have an adverse financial impact on many LHL deputies in the National Assembly. Their votes would be necessary for a new anticommunist government that could meet the challenge posed by the NLHS and include the "new faccs" sought by the United States. Souvanna was also under pressure from CDNI members, who bluntly told him that the army and young elites would not stand by idly and watch the country collapse.

On July 9 Souvanna met with Ambassador Smith, who handed him a letter stating that the United States had cut off financial aid to Laos as of July 1. US assistance would not be resumed until there was a final agreement on monetary reform. Smith reminded the prime minister of the many warnings by the US government that Laos must adopt a realistic exchange rate by June 30, or US financial assistance would cease. But if Souvanna's government acted promptly, the monetary problem could be resolved by the end of month, and the United States would immediately resume its aid. The prime minister said he was disappointed that the US felt compelled to take such "drastic action" at this particular moment. The political situation was "delicate," and "a brutal" devaluation would jeopardize the popular and legislative support needed for his new government.[27]

The US government, however, was indifferent, at best, to Souvanna's political problems. Since the April publication of a *Wall Street Journal* article on aid abuses, "Living It Up in Laos" (reprinted in the August 1958 issue of *Reader's Digest* as "Chaos in Laos"), the Eisenhower administration faced mounting congressional pressure to end the monetary practices that made corruption in Laos all but inevitable. In a meeting at the State Department, Parsons told the counselor of the French embassy that opponents of US aid in Congress "were using Laos as Exhibit A in order to oppose the program as a whole."[28]

A more fundamental reason for Washington's lack of sympathy for Souvanna's difficulties was its disgust with him and the other older Lao politicians who constituted the leadership of the LHL. In the State Department's view, a new "government of the same old faces [would be] useless; we would like [a] clean sweep and all new faces." As for Souvanna, the "ideal" solution would be replacing the prime minister with a "younger and less politically equivocal personality." But department officials also recognized that an all-new government of young, politically inexperienced Laotians was neither practical nor entirely desirable. The most realistic hope appeared to be a new "cabinet headed by Souvanna containing [an] indispensable minimum [of] old faces with some key ministries under young new leaders."[29]

With the ratification of the May election results, Souvanna declared that his government had fulfilled its purpose of reunifying the country. When he resigned on July 22, the crown prince immediately asked Souvanna to form a new government. According to the CIA, the prime minister–designate faced a formidable challenge from the CDNI, which planned to counter his resistance to a younger, "reform" cabinet with a royal proclamation to close the National Assembly and "impose [an] anti-Communist government." Souvanna also received plenty of advice from Ambassador Smith on such issues as the proportion of "old" and "new" faces, the portfolios they would hold, and the unacceptability of Katay's participation in the cabinet. The State Department acknowledged that by "seeking [to] force Souvanna [to] mold" his cabinet to US specifications, the United States was "not only carrying intervention to great lengths, but also assuming [a] heavy responsibility."[30]

DCI Allen Dulles was unimpressed with the government likely to emerge from the internal deals among Lao politicians and the inducements of the US mission in Vientiane. On July 31, 1958, he bluntly expressed his contempt for LHL leaders, telling the NSC: "Most of the Cabinet members would probably be the same old political hacks, whose continued rule will probably result in an eventual Communist take-over."[31]

In early August Ambassador Smith reported that the reluctance of CDNI members to participate in a Souvanna-led government was the "major obstacle" to ending the latest cabinet crisis. Smith could not understand how these inexperienced men, who lacked any visible popular support, could draw back from national service at a dangerous time for their country. Indicating a less than full knowledge of US intentions, and perhaps the activities of the Vientiane CIA station, Smith wondered: "Is it really U.S. policy to encourage younger elements to refuse to participate" in a Souvanna government? More pointedly, he asked his State Department superiors whether the US government intended to "encourage younger elements to attempt [a] coup at this time rather than enter [the] government as now suggested by Souvanna."[32]

The State Department replied that it did not intend to encourage a coup. Its goal was to "obtain [a] new government of maximum effectiveness and avoid either weakening potential young elements or lessening their confidence in [the] U.S." Since the most recent government "proposed by Souvanna seems [the] best parliamentary solution obtainable," Smith was instructed to "encourage but not press young elements into joining."[33]

On August 6 Souvanna informed the crown prince that he had been unable to form a government. A key reason for this failure had been the unwillingness of CDNI members to join his government. At the time, Ambassador Smith thought it significant that Souvanna had "acted persistently in accord with Embassy views that young elements must be included, if possible, [and] Katay excluded." Smith later wrote that when Souvanna was ready to announce a preliminary slate of cabinet ministers, the CDNI "backed out on him, against Ambassador Smith's strongly worded advice, in a manner and with a timing which dealt a humiliating blow to the prestige of Souvanna [and] which might well have been expected to embitter him permanently against the United States."[34]

The continued classification of key documents makes it difficult to establish the precise role of the US government in Souvanna's downfall in the summer of 1958. A recently released, but still sanitized, CIA history of the agency's "surrogate warfare" in Laos mentions that the CDNI had insufficient political influence in the National Assembly "to remove Souvanna, *and Washington decided to intervene directly.*" Unfortunately for anyone seeking amplification of this last statement, the quotation ends page six of the publication *Undercover Armies,* and page seven is excluded altogether from the document.[35]

Further evidence that policymakers in Washington were behind Souvanna's downfall is found in an unpublished manuscript by PEO chief

Rothwell Brown. In the early 1960s, when the Kennedy administration tried to make Laotian neutrality work, Brown wrote that it was precisely this policy that "in 1958, caused the United States to use every means available to overthrow his [Souvanna's] government and force him out as prime minister." A 1962 State Department memorandum prepared for President Kennedy reported that Souvanna "held the United States largely responsible (with good reason) for the overthrow of his government in 1958 and again in 1960."[36]

It seems likely that CIA chief of station Henry Hecksher—probably acting under orders from CIA headquarters and with the concurrence of the State Department—encouraged the CDNI to withhold its participation in a Souvanna government, thereby removing his troubling presence from the political scene. John Gunther Dean, who later became ambassador to Cambodia and Thailand, among other countries, recalled: "Henry Hecksher was committed to opposing the neutralist Prime Minister and perhaps bring about his downfall. That is what happened in 1958."[37]

With Souvanna Phouma stopped from forming a new government—he later became the Lao ambassador to France—the US mission in Vientiane used its influence to promote Phoui Sananikone as his successor. Anticommunist and pro-American, Phoui was a short, portly man in his midfifties. State Department official Christian Chapman described him as "genial, roly-poly, easy-going," and "shrewd and intelligent." A member of one of the preeminent families in Laos, Phoui had entered government service in 1926 and had held virtually every top position in the Lao cabinet. To the Americans, he seemed neither as ideologically unreliable as Souvanna nor as duplicitous as Katay. Phoui, in Ambassador Smith's words, had "proven himself the Lao leader with whom we can most easily and frankly discuss matters."[38]

The diplomatic "task" for Smith, according to his monograph, was to persuade Phoui "to form a government that would include enough of the CDNI in significant numbers to win Washington approval," while maintaining sufficient support from the LHL in the National Assembly. Another aspect of Smith's diplomacy was to prevent the CDNI from overreaching in its demands for cabinet portfolios. Presumably using Henry Hecksher as an intermediary, Smith made it clear that any repetition of CDNI's blocking tactics against a cabinet "approved by the U.S. government" would result in an immediate recommendation by the ambassador to cease "all U.S. pressure to include any of 'The Young' in the government."[39]

On August 18, 1958, the Lao National Assembly narrowly approved a Phoui-led government, which included six members of the LHL, four representatives of the CDNI, and no members of the NLHS. Katay, who was recovering from a stroke, still had sufficient influence to be appointed vice premier. Because of the many compromises required for its formation, the new government inspired little enthusiasm among the Laotians or the Americans. According to the minutes of the August 21 NSC meeting, this was Allen Dulles's view: "While there had been no Communist penetration of the new Cabinet, it contained many old figures like Katay who were notoriously corrupt. There were also four representatives of the younger and more progressive politicians whose influence, unhappily, Mr. Dulles thought would not amount to much. The new Cabinet constituted neither a victory nor a defeat for our side."[40]

Among Phoui's early decisions as prime minister was approving the establishment of a nationalist Chinese consulate in Vientiane and the expansion of South Vietnam's consulate to a legation. These moves antagonized the PRC, which had unsuccessfully sought diplomatic representation in Laos. Phoui's right-wing diplomacy and exclusion of any NLHS representation in the cabinet represented a sharp break with Souvanna's neutralist juggling act.

A decision by Phoui that disturbed some of his Lao supporters was a September 30 agreement with the US government on monetary reform. This agreement changed the official Lao exchange rate of 35 kip per dollar to a much more realistic 80 kip per dollar. Although gratifying to US officials, the new exchange rate exacerbated hostility toward the prime minister in the National Assembly, particularly among corrupt LHL deputies who had profited handsomely from the old system. Because of the slim majority held by Phoui's party, the defection of even a few disgruntled deputies could trigger a new cabinet crisis.

Crown Prince Savang reacted to the possibility of such a crisis with a display of royal equanimity. In a meeting with Ambassador Smith, Savang said he "felt certain that if crisis occurred it would not be long." Moreover, the government that emerged from it "might actually be an improved one." Smith asked the crown prince to explain his reasoning, but he declined, saying he was being "intentionally cryptic." The ambassador reported to Washington that Savang was apparently willing to accept the risks of an "extra-constitutional" solution—that is, a military coup dissolving the National Assembly and political parties, with political and military authority reverting to the royal family, which in turn would appoint members of the new government. Smith was also "struck" both by the crown prince's low opinion of most LHL deputies in the National Assembly and "by his warm endorsement of the 'new elements' in the government."[41]

In early October 1958 the CIA prepared an intelligence evaluation for the Operations Coordinating Board that was a remarkably blunt appraisal of the political situation in Laos. The conservative politicians "continued to be paralyzed by disunity and ineffectiveness." The past success of the old-guard leaders, who had "one hand on the reins of power and the other in the till," tended to make them complacent about the threat from the NLHS. The communists had improved their organization, exploited the weakness and corruption of conservative leaders, and increased their popular following. The agency further reported that NLHS success in associating itself with nationalism, peace, neutralism, and reform was leading to strong political gains in almost every sector of Lao society.[42]

The CIA evaluation also noted increasing pro-NLHS sentiment among the kingdom's thirteen thousand Buddhist monks, a consequence at least partially attributable to Pathet Lao leader Phoumi Vongvichit, who had been in charge of the Ministry of Religion and Fine Arts during the earlier Souvanna Phouma coalition government. A member of both the Vietnamese and Lao communist parties, Phoumi Vongvichit was one of the most important NLHS officials. A former civil servant who had joined the Lao Issara independence movement, he served as the Pathet Lao's lead negotiator with the RLG between late 1954 and 1957. A State Department biography described his external manner as "gentle, amiable and almost shy—he is reportedly fond of poetry, but underneath is extremely energetic, clever, resolute and patient in serving the communist cause."[43]

Historian Martin Stuart-Fox notes not only the irony that Phoumi Vongvichit, a dedicated Marxist, headed the RLG's religion ministry, but also the political opportunities provided by the position, which included "a ready-made communication network from the administrative capital, Vientiane, spreading out to the remotest villages. Also, the ministry could arrange, at government expense, discussion meetings for monks during which social criticism could be introduced. This technique was so effective that even though the first coalition government collapsed within three months, Phoumi Vongvichit reportedly succeeded in convincing a number of young bonzes of the justness of the communist cause."[44]

At an October 8 meeting of the OCB, Parsons disagreed with the CIA conclusion that the prospects for Laos were "dim." He believed that the "failures" of the May supplementary elections were now "well understood" by conservative political leaders in Laos. The situation in Laos, while "precarious," reflected "substantial achievement" by the US government. According to minutes of the OCB meeting, Parsons did, however, note "that the government is in danger of being overthrown by a conjunction of the Communists and corrupt politicians."[45]

This point of view was echoed in the November 6, 1958, edition of CIA's *Current Intelligence Weekly Review,* which reported to senior policymakers that Phoui questioned "the viability of his government" and described himself "as fighting a two-front war" against the NLHS and his own party. Some "unreconstructed" LHL deputies had bitterly resisted monetary reform and other changes he had championed. Exacerbating Phoui's political difficulties were CDNI members of his cabinet who "needlessly" attacked the LHL, further dividing the anticommunist politicians. Analysts in the CIA's Office of Current Intelligence wrote, "[Phoui] feels that time is working against the constitutional regime and that the only real alternative may be radical suppression" of the NLHS.[46]

In his monograph, Ambassador Smith wrote that Colonel Phoumi Nosavan, a CDNI member, "approached Phoui with detailed plans for a military coup to overthrow the [National] Assembly, with the expressed intent of simply placing Phoui and his government back in power with a mandate from the army and the King rather than the Parliament." To Colonel Phoumi and others in the CDNI, it appeared that the NLHS was effectively using the National Assembly as a platform for communist propaganda. Phoumi offered his military services to the prime minister "to relieve Phoui of the need to retain Assembly support."[47]

Phoumi Nosavan, who eventually received support from the Eisenhower administration to seize power in the fall of 1960, was an appealing figure to CIA and Pentagon officials seeking a single, strong anticommunist to run the Laotian government. John F. Hasey, a CIA operative and the American closest to him, characterized the Lao officer as a "complex character." In an official January 1961 "character sketch," Hasey described Phoumi as intelligent, ambitious, insecure, unscrupulous, and subject to sharp mood swings.[48]

The son of a low-ranking civil servant, Phoumi was born in 1920 in Savannakhet in southern Laos, a region that was a separate kingdom until the French unified Laos in 1946 under the sovereignty of the royal house in Luang Prabang. Phoumi received a diploma from the Lycée Pavie in Vientiane, the school attended by virtually all of the kingdom's elites, where classes were conducted almost entirely in French. During World War II, he served in the Special French Police in Laos and fought against the Japanese. The military chief of Lao Issara, Phoumi was primarily a staff officer in the ANL. He was attending the French Command and General Staff College when the CDNI was formed, and he returned to Laos in mid-August 1958.

The CIA actively promoted Phoumi Nosavan's career. According to former defense secretary Robert S. McNamara, Allen Dulles "discovered" Phoumi in France. Whether McNamara meant that Phoumi was a personal discovery of the DCI or an institutional one by the agency he led is unclear. What is clear is that CIA case officer John Hasey became very close to Phoumi during the Lao officer's military training in France. According to historian and longtime foreign correspondent Stanley Karnow, Hasey told him that Phoumi was a fully recruited agent who had signed a secret CIA contract.[49]

Despite his favor with certain US officials, Phoumi was not popular with the Lao prime minister and other older politicians, who "distrusted his ruthlessness, his cleverness, and his driving ambition," according to Smith. Deputy Chief of Mission John Holt reported to the State Department that embassy officers believed Phoumi's defining personal characteristics were "his genius for organization, his personal political ambition and his deceptiveness." Holt further reported that French officials thought Phoumi, who had turned violently anti-French since his return to Laos, was "the most dangerous, unreliable officer in the Lao Armed Forces."[50]

The prime minister and Ambassador Smith did not give their approval for Colonel Phoumi's proposed coup. In his monograph, Smith wrote that in December 1958 his decision was "overruled" by unnamed "proponents" of a coup in Washington. These same US officials, however, would withdraw their support for a coup if Phoui were able to secure a legislative mandate that would allow him to rule by decree for one year—a year during which noncommunists would hopefully coalesce into a united movement for the December 1959 general elections. Such a mandate seemed a remote possibility to Washington, and Parsons "ordered" Smith to leave the country in the ten days preceding a special session of the National Assembly. Smith's absence from Vientiane was intended to foster the impression that any coup d'état would be a purely Lao affair. But the "real reason" for the ambassador's forced absence, according to Rufus Phillips, who had left Vientiane and was then serving as the Laos desk officer at CIA headquarters, "was to keep him from interfering on Phoui's behalf."[51]

The threat of a military coup, combined with the possibility of a NLHS victory in the general election, persuaded the National Assembly to consider granting extraordinary powers to the prime minister. They included governing for one year without consulting the National Assembly and selecting a new cabinet that did not require legislative approval. In a special session of the National Assembly on January 12, 1959, Phoui described the threats facing Laos, summarized his government's accomplishments, and declared that the kingdom stood with its "friends" in the "great ideological combat" dividing the world. Referring to North Vietnamese troops in the Tchepone area of Laos near the Demilitarized Zone separating North and South Vietnam, the prime minister said that his current government was "no longer equal to this situation of national danger."[52]

Two days later, Phoui received the special powers he sought from the National Assembly, "thereby eliminating the necessity at the moment for a military coup," in the words of an intelligence summary written for President Eisenhower. The prime minister appointed a new fourteen-member cabinet that included seven representatives of the CDNI and the army. Among the new appointments was Colonel Phoumi Nosavan, who was named secretary of state for national defense. The CIA had asked Ambassador Smith to persuade the prime minister to include the military officer in his cabinet.[53]

One of the first public statements by Phoui's new government was that Laos had "completely fulfilled" its obligations under the Geneva Accords. The declaration repeated a similar statement that Souvanna Phouma made after the May 1958 supplementary elections. With US encouragement, France, the United Kingdom, and Canada had convinced the ICC to suspend indefinitely its activities in Laos the following July.

Now Phoui faced NLHS allegations of violating the Geneva agreements and communist demands for the ICC to return to Laos. At a February 11, 1959, press conference, Phoui replied: As a sovereign nation and a member state of the United Nations since 1955, Laos "only recognizes arbitration originating from that high international body."[54]

Such diplomatic declarations did not mean that the RLG and the US government could ignore overtly the Geneva agreements without paying a high price. In May 1958 Souvanna had also pledged to the ICC that Laos would continue to abide by the terms of the accords, specifically the articles that prohibited external military assistance. Moreover, the ICC still remained active in Vietnam and could return to Laos with the mutual consent of the Geneva cochairmen, the Soviet Union and the United Kingdom. In other words, the US government had to consider the views and sensibilities of its European allies, whose "continued cooperation," according to the State Department, was "necessary for the achievement of our broader foreign policy objectives not only in Laos but throughout the world."[55]

Although US officials considered Phoui's enhanced executive power an encouraging development, the prime minister complained to Ambassador Smith that he had "not been able to work freely" in executing the political program that the two of them "had devised together." At a February 17, 1959, meeting with Smith and in a follow-up memorandum, Phoui discussed the obstacles he faced, which included conflicting pressures from the LHL, the CDNI, and the crown prince. For example, to persuade LHL deputies to vote themselves out of office for a year, Phoui had promised to appoint them to administrative and diplomatic positions. The crown prince and the CDNI, however, opposed such appointments. The prime minister told Smith of his fear that Savang had favored a military coup and did not want his government to succeed. Appealing for assistance from "the Higher Authorities who worked with me in the formulation of the present program," Phoui informed Smith that if the obstacles to his government were not removed, he would "regretfully be obliged to resign."[56]

After his meeting with the prime minister, Smith reported to Washington on the various noncommunist groups vying for power in Laos. One conclusion was obvious: the "accumulated distrust and misunderstandings among groups are creating pressures on Phoui which may seriously endanger [the] life of [his] government."[57]

Chapter 5

Drawing the Line

JOHN HEINTGES, AN active-duty US Army brigadier general, arrived in Vientiane in mid-November 1958, wearing civilian clothes and bearing a civilian passport. Ostensibly a member of a group traveling with Deputy Assistant Secretary of Defense Charles H. Shuff, Heintges had been ordered to the kingdom by Admiral Harry D. Felt, the recently appointed commander-in-chief of US Forces in the Pacific. Felt, who considered the PEO "a terrible organization," wanted Heintges to develop a plan for improving US military assistance to Laos. Among the officials at the airport greeting Shuff and his party was Major General Jean d'Arrivere, commander of the French Military Mission. Heintges thought he had met d'Arrivere before but could not recall where or when. He had a feeling that the French general recognized him too.[1]

Heintges finally remembered meeting General d'Arrivere during World War II, after the 1945 Battle of the Colmar Pocket on the frozen fields of eastern France. Heintges was then a regimental commander in the Third Infantry Division, which received the Croix de Guerre for bravery in combat. At a party following the award ceremony, Heintges met d'Arrivere, who had been a battalion commander in an adjacent sector. Suspecting that his short-lived civilian cover in Laos was blown, Heintges later introduced himself to d'Arrivere, who had indeed remembered him. The two generals "hit it off real well," Heintges recalled.[2]

John A. "Johnny" Heintges was born in Coblenz, Germany, in 1912. Although he never knew his father, a German army officer who was killed in World War I by Russian forces at Tannenberg, Heintges did remember the postwar breadlines and other hardships of the Weimar Republic. In

1920 his family immigrated to the United States, sponsored by an American uncle of Heintges who was a major in the US Army Medical Corps. His mother, whom Heintges described as "a sweet lady" but a "very strict" disciplinarian, married a US Army infantry officer. Young Heintges, who changed primary and secondary schools often as his family moved from one army post to another, graduated from high school in Haines, Alaska.[3]

Heintges won an appointment to West Point and graduated from the academy in 1936. In World War II, he served as commander of the Third Battalion, Seventh Infantry Regiment, then as commander of the Seventh Infantry, Third Division. This regiment had a distinguished combat record dating back to the War of 1812. During World War II, it engaged in as much combat as any other regiment in the US Army. Heintges and his men fought battles in Sicily, mainland Italy, France, and Germany—some of which were among the bloodiest in Europe. On May 4, 1945, his regiment won the race to capture Hitler's mountaintop retreat at Berchtesgaden, the infamous Eagle's Nest.

After the war Heintges served as a professor of foreign languages at West Point. His own ongoing military education included attending the airborne school at Fort Benning, where at the relatively advanced age of thirty-eight he underwent the strenuous training to qualify as a parachutist, and he attended the US Army War College, whose handpicked military and civilian students received training for senior national security assignments. Heintges returned to Germany in 1954 as chief of the army section of the US Military Assistance Advisory Group. From 1957 to 1958, he was deputy commander of the Army Infantry Training Center at Fort Dix, New Jersey.

It was near the end of his tour at Fort Dix when Heintges received a phone call from the Pentagon informing him that his orders for a planned Korean posting had been canceled. When he asked where he was going, the reply was: "We can't tell you. When can you get down here?" The next day Heintges reported to the Pentagon, where he learned about a possible assignment in Laos, a country with which he—like most other Americans—was only vaguely familiar. A condition of this posting was Heintges's willingness to appear to resign from the army and go to Laos as a civilian. He would be dropped from the *Army Register* listing active-duty officers, and his entry in the *West Point Register* of academy graduates would end in 1958. Surprised and intrigued, Heintges listened to a brief summary of recent military and political events in Laos. The briefing included the observation that the retired and reserve officers of the PEO—characterized as "a bunch of old-timers"—had been ineffective and that US military assistance to Laos required a new approach.[4]

Before his formal appointment as the new PEO chief, Heintges was ordered by Admiral Felt to go to Laos, survey the military program there, and develop a plan to improve US assistance to the ANL. In Washington, the State Department and the CIA provided Heintges with detailed information about Laos and its political and military environment. The general received additional briefings at CINCPAC headquarters and in Tokyo.

Between November 19 and December 6, 1958, Heintges traveled all over the kingdom to observe and question Laotian and US officials. After initial discussions in Vientiane, he flew to the Plaine des Jarres, a strategically located plateau in the center of northern Laos, midway between Vientiane and the North Vietnamese border. The French named the plain for its clusters of ancient stone jars, some of which are ten feet high. Surrounded by jungle-covered mountains, the Plaine des Jarres was the only area in northern Laos suitable for military bases and large airfields.

Heintges was accompanied on this trip by Robert "Bob" Bodroghy, an army intelligence officer who spent much of his career assigned to the CIA and who was currently operating in Laos under USOM-PEO cover. The commander of the ANL battalion stationed at the Plaine des Jarres greeted Heintges and Bodroghy at a primitive, steel-mesh airstrip. The Lao officer, wearing a black overcoat, khaki pants, sandals, and no hat, walked the Americans to his jeep, which would not start because of a dead battery. Jump-starting the vehicle, the men rode over miles of dusty dirt roads to an area with mud huts and a long, low structure that looked to Heintges like a World War I–era cantonment building. Whitewashed rocks encircled a flagpole flying the Lao colors, and ANL soldiers in various states of undress practiced martial arts in a field. Heintges noticed a fence, where a variety of clothes were hanging. "I found out later that each soldier had one uniform," he recalled.[5]

As Heintges inspected the camp, he picked up a rifle so badly rusted that he could not open the bolt. Soldiers on guard duty kept ammunition in their pockets, despite the neatly folded web belts in the supply room. Some of the ammunition was green with corrosion. Even in battalions where the equipment was maintained adequately, Heintges found neither discipline nor such basic military courtesies as saluting. It was also evident that Lao soldiers disliked the "French military very much and would have nothing to do with them," he said.[6]

During his survey Heintges learned that the Vientiane CIA station was furnishing weapons, radios, and other equipment to the Auto Defense forces in the northern provinces and the ANL's elite Second Parachute Battalion, commanded by Captain Kong Le and advised by a CIA paramilitary officer operating under USOM-PEO cover. Informing Henry Hecksher that he had seen new military equipment in Laos that had not been furnished by the PEO, Heintges said that he had to know what the CIA was up to and what it was bringing into the country. "Oh, don't worry, Johnny," Hecksher replied, "You'll know everything," adding, "but I can't tell the ambassador."

"I don't give a damn whether you tell the ambassador or not, but I want to know," responded Heintges.[7]

Returning to CINCPAC headquarters, Heintges wrote a harsh appraisal of the ANL. Its weapons and equipment were, for the most part, poorly maintained, obsolete materiel that had been "dumped into Laos" after the French–Viet Minh War. With few exceptions, Lao soldiers were disorganized, untrained, and ill clothed, and their illiteracy rate was very high. Heintges was optimistic about the fighting potential of the typical Lao soldier, but "his morale and esprit are at a very low ebb." Like other US military officials who had visited Laos, Heintges attributed much of the ANL's problems to poor French training, which had been gradually deteriorating since the Geneva conference. A key conclusion of his report was a "great need for a training program at the 'grass-roots' level, in basic military subjects and recruit training."[8]

The so-called Heintges plan for improving US military assistance to Laos included recommendations for strengthening the PEO and increasing its number of active-duty US military personnel; improving the logistical system for providing materiel to the Lao army; and introducing a US training force to work in the field with each of the twelve regular ANL battalions. Operating in civilian clothes on a six-month temporary duty assignment, each of the twelve US training teams would be supplemented by French officers or noncommissioned officers (NCOs), an arrangement that Heintges had worked out with General d'Arrivere. "I knew right away that it was absolutely useless to organize training teams without the French because they were so firmly embedded in Laos," Heintges recalled.[9]

When discussing his plan in Washington in December 1958, Heintges urged that the mobile training teams be made up primarily of US Army Special Forces—a recommendation that may have been influenced by Bodroghy, who was an unconventional warfare pioneer during the Korean War. Trained to operate behind enemy lines and organize guerrilla forces, Special Forces were not the obvious first choice for instructing the conventional forces of the ANL. Yet senior military and civilian officials in the Pentagon concluded that these elite warriors possessed unique qualifications for the mission in Laos: They were already organized in small teams to operate autonomously in remote areas and train indigenous forces. Moreover, their specialized capabilities in such areas as light and heavy weapons, field communications, and medicine closely matched the training needs of the ANL.

At the State Department, Assistant Secretary of State Robertson "enthusiastically" supported the Heintges plan. He appeared ready to approve it immediately, "letting the chips fall where they may," according to a Pentagon official. Robertson was, however, persuaded by colleagues at the Department of State to seek French concurrence for the plan and then inform the UK and Canadian governments. The Defense Department warned Heintges that from "Parsons down the State boys are extremely skittish about making a big military splash in Laos."[10]

Within the Pentagon, one of the few officers who had doubts about the Heintges plan was Colonel Edward Lansdale, now deputy director of the Office of Special Operations. Lansdale, who had battled with the French in Saigon in the mid-1950s, warned his colleagues: "A combined U.S.-French effort will have unfortunate, Communist-exploitable political features." By teaming up with a former colonial power defeated by an Asian "people's army," Lansdale argued, the United States would be vulnerable to the charge of helping European imperialists: "The concept of a second honeymoon with the French needs some further thought. The blushing French bride might well bring some mature and prejudiced children along on the honeymoon, who would not only embarrass bridegroom Uncle Sam but also wreck the marriage."[11]

Lansdale's minority view did not prevail. The US and Lao governments, as well as the French embassy and military in Vientiane, approved the Heintges plan. French officials in Paris, however, raised strong objections, basing them on the provision of the Geneva Accords that allowed the French—and only the French—to provide training to the ANL. The

Foreign Ministry of Charles de Gaulle's recently founded French Fifth Republic informed the State Department: "France intends to maintain the whole of its responsibilities" in Laos. To the American embassy in Paris, the rejection of the Heintges plan appeared "primarily political and only incidentally jurisdictional." The French desire to maintain its position in Laos "goes beyond mere prestige or *présence* and becomes an element in 'the grandeur of France.'"[12]

The French rejection of the Heintges plan in early 1959 was followed by months of negotiations with the United States to find a compromise solution. In many respects, the French position was weak. The US government had been underwriting 100 percent of the Lao military budget, Phoui's government did not want the French to train the ANL, and the number and quality of French forces in Laos were declining because of the Algerian War. However, a public charge by France that the United States was violating the Geneva Accords would generate international condemnation, not only from communist countries but also from ICC members India and Canada and from the United Kingdom, cochair of the Geneva conference. Such a reaction would, at the very least, undermine the US effort in Laos.

The French government eventually softened its flat rejection of the Heintges plan but refused to accept the idea of US field training for ANL battalions. Moreover, de Gaulle himself insisted that the FMM maintain exclusive control of combat training, concentrating the instruction at the French base in Seno. In the course of the negotiations, Olivier Gassouin, the French ambassador in Vientiane, spoke contemptuously of Lao military officers, dividing them into three groups: the "incapable," the "corrupt," and the "pro-dictators." The only officer in the last group specifically named was Colonel Phoumi. Gassouin told DCM John Holt that "the dictatorship tendencies of some of the army officers were being promoted by the 'special services,'" an unsubtle reference to the CIA. When Holt pointedly asked what the ambassador meant by "special services," Gassouin retreated into generalities, replying "of all countries."[13]

To resolve Franco-American differences over ANL training, the French proposed diplomatic and military talks in Paris. In the last week of May 1959, Ambassador Horace Smith and PEO chief Heintges led a delegation of State Department and Pentagon officials to the French Foreign Ministry on the Quai d'Orsay, a street name that was also diplomatic shorthand for the ministry. French officials would not budge from their insistence on exclusive responsibility for combat training. "The French took terrific exception to my plan of allowing General d'Arrivere and myself to make the decision of who was to do what training," Heintges recalled.[14]

The French were, however, prepared to permit US "logistic" instruction in such areas as communications, demolition, and the operation of American weapons. What this meant was that US trainers could show Lao soldiers how the materiel worked but could not provide "advice in small unit infantry tactics best suited [to the] use of U.S. equipment and weapons." The distinction between tactical and logistical training was sometimes carried to absurd lengths, according to an analysis of military operations in Laos, funded by the Department of the Army: "U.S. personnel could conduct range firing using bull's-eye targets, but when pop-up targets were used, it became tactical training and fell under French jurisdiction."[15]

The original Heintges concept of field training for each of the ANL's twelve battalions could not be revived during the negotiations with the French. French diplomat Pierre Millet argued that spreading American instructors throughout the country would be "courting disaster." Ambassador Smith replied that centralized training at Seno, an airbase near Savannakhet, might be even more "provocative" by creating an impression that the United States was replacing the French. The negotiators finally agreed that US and French instructors would work together at training centers in each of the kingdom's four military regions (a fifth was established in December 1959). Moreover, the US training program would be temporary—no more than one year.[16]

The training agreement reached in Paris was the basis of a formal Franco-American offer of joint military assistance to the RLG in June 1959. In Washington, Deputy Assistant Secretary of State Parsons met with representatives of the French, UK, and Laotian embassies to discuss a coordinated approach to reassuring the Indian government that the new training program complied with the Geneva Accords. In the last week of July, twelve eight-man Special Forces teams and a control detachment, totaling 107 officers and NCOs, arrived in Laos, commanded by Lieutenant Colonel Arthur D. "Bull" Simons. This clandestine operation had many names, including Molecular, Disallow, Ambidextrous, and others, but the one that stuck was Hotfoot. Dressed in civilian clothes, the Special Forces teams generally flew in small planes from Bangkok to training sites in the interior of the country. Once the Hotfoot teams were there, Heintges was under orders from Admiral Felt to arrange some "clandestine" combat training for the ANL. "General d'Arrivere knew I was doing it but didn't say anything ever," he recalled.[17]

General d'Arrivere's friendship with Heintges and his tolerance for US violations of the Franco-American training agreement were the likely reasons that he was relieved as commander of the French Military Mission in Laos. The American embassy suspected that Ambassador Gassouin was responsible for the general's recall to France. When Gassouin told Madame d'Arrivere how sorry he was they were leaving, she replied that both of them knew that "he personally had engineered her husband's transfer." To her friends in the US community in Vientiane, she said: "This [is the] price we pay for being friendly to Americans."[18]

The early spring of 1959 was perhaps the high-water mark of official optimism about the future of Laos and the effectiveness of US programs there. A reliable anticommunist was the prime minister of the kingdom; there were no NLHS members in the cabinet; and the US military would soon be training the ANL. Even the thorny problem of monetary reform had been solved. "At long last we appear to be on the threshold of meeting our minimum national objectives in Laos," Parsons declared to Assistant Secretary of State Walter Robertson.[19]

Publicly, State Department pronouncements of progress in Laos were even more optimistic. In response to a congressional report of abuses and incompetence in the US aid program there, the department released a lengthy rebuttal that declared: "Despite the deficiencies and shortcomings in the administration of the program in Laos, its major objectives have been and are being achieved with signal success." In testimony before Congress, Robertson made the somewhat more cautious observation: "In my opinion the prospects for that country have clearly improved in the past year and our policy objectives have been furthered."[20]

Robertson, who had sought to retire for the past year, had informed Dulles and President Eisenhower of his decision to resign, effective July 1, 1959. He was sixty-five years old and suffering from a debilitating ulcer and migraine headaches. In his final year as assistant secretary, he was often either absent from the department or arrived too late to attend the secretary of state's 8:45 A.M. staff meetings. Robertson later described himself as "sort of hanging on by my fingertips, as far as my health was concerned."[21]

Robertson recommended to Dulles that Parsons succeed him as assistant secretary of state for far eastern affairs. Dulles's only reservation about the recommendation was the fairness of putting a Foreign Service officer "in a position that was so hot politically." The administration's policy of nonrecognition of communist China was controversial, and the assistant secretary's responsibility to advocate and defend that policy before Congress could jeopardize the future of a State Department career professional. President Eisenhower did not know Parsons, but he appointed him assistant secretary of state based on the recommendations of Robertson and Dulles.[22]

The appointment was one of the last senior personnel decisions made by Dulles, a seemingly indestructible administration presence whose health was failing rapidly. Abdominal surgery in February 1959 revealed a recurrence of colon cancer that had initially been treated three years earlier. Dulles sought a leave of absence that same month, officially retired on April 15, and died on May 24 at Walter Reed Hospital in Washington, D.C. The president's "sense of loss was personal and painful," according to Eisenhower biographer Stephen Ambrose.[23]

Dulles's successor was Undersecretary of State Christian A. Herter, an invariably gracious man who was "as easy to feel at home with as Foster Dulles was not," according to Parsons. A tall man (six feet four and a half inches) but stooped in posture because of arthritic hip joints that required his use of aluminum elbow crutches, Herter had a diverse diplomatic and political career before joining the administration at the beginning of Eisenhower's second term. By the time it was clear that Dulles could no longer carry on as secretary of state, the president questioned Herter's physical ability to fulfill the responsibilities of the office, insisting that he undergo a thorough physical examination. "I never thought he would pass," Eisenhower said later.[24]

Herter was born to well-to-do parents who were expatriate artists in Paris; he and his family returned to the United States when "Chris" was nine years old. He attended the Browning preparatory school in New York City and graduated from Harvard in 1915. He began his diplomatic career the following year in the US embassy in Berlin and served in Brussels reporting on the German deportation of Belgians. After the United States declared war on the Central Powers, Herter was rejected for military service because of his bad hips and low weight. He continued to work at the State Department on problems related to prisoners of war and interned enemy aliens.

Herter's older brother Everit, a member of the American Expeditionary Force, was killed by shrapnel at Chateau-Thierry, strengthening Christian's resolve to work for peace. He served as an assistant to members of the US delegation at the 1919 Paris Peace Conference and participated in the drafting of the League of Nations statute. During the immediate postwar years, Herter assisted Herbert Hoover with US relief efforts in Europe and served under him in the Department of Commerce. He left government to write about foreign affairs and lecture at Harvard, then entered Massachusetts politics in 1930 and was elected to the US House of Representatives in 1942. Focusing on international affairs, he played a key role in creating public awareness of the dangerous economic conditions in postwar Europe and framing the legislative debate for the European Recovery Program, better known as the Marshall Plan. Before joining the Eisenhower administration, Herter served two terms as the governor of Massachusetts.

As undersecretary of state, Herter's major responsibilities were serving as acting secretary when Dulles traveled abroad, chairing the Operations Coordinating Board, and serving on the 5412 committee monitoring covert operations. His views on Laos echoed those of Dulles and Robertson. At an OCB meeting on May 22, 1957, a time when the US government was casting around for alternatives to Souvanna, Herter declared that the kingdom was a strategically important buffer state, observing: "For a little country, Laos presented one of our toughest problems." Almost exactly one year later, after the disappointing May 1958 supplementary elections and before Souvanna was prevented from forming a new government, Herter informed the Pentagon: "We may find ourselves having to take some drastic action in the next few weeks."[25]

Despite solid credentials to serve as secretary of state, Herter later admitted that he never developed Dulles's "extraordinarily close" relationship with Eisenhower. Secretary of Defense Thomas S. Gates characterized relations between Herter and the president as "distant." In contrast to the intimate one-on-one meetings between Dulles and Eisenhower, Herter's private conferences with the president invariably included a note-taker—either Brigadier General Andrew J. Goodpaster, the White House coordinator for military and intelligence affairs; or Colonel John S.D. Eisenhower, son of the president and Goodpaster's assistant. In his memoir, John Eisenhower described this practice as an "experiment" that contributed to a more complete historical record of the Eisenhower administration. It also seems likely that President Eisenhower was not entirely certain that his new secretary of state would always grasp the precise meaning and intent of his instructions and therefore wanted an independent witness to, and record of, their conversations. What is certain is that miscommunication between Eisenhower and Herter's State Department over Soviet Premier Nikita Khrushchev's 1959 visit to the United States triggered an outburst of presidential anger and an unflattering comparison with John Foster Dulles.[26]

In sum, Christian Herter lacked Dulles's policy influence and his force of personality. The same could also be said of Parsons in comparison to Walter Robertson. An obvious question raised by the change in leadership in the State Department and its Bureau of Far Eastern Affairs is whether US policy in Laos would have evolved any differently had both Dulles and Robertson been healthy enough to serve until January 20, 1961. Given their beliefs and convictions, it seems highly unlikely that either official would have developed a greater appreciation for Souvanna's leadership or a neutral solution in Laos. What does seem likely is that Dulles and Robertson would have been able to maintain the State Department's preeminence in formulating policy for the Far East.

With the bureaucratically weaker team of Herter and Parsons in charge of Lao affairs, authority and responsibility became more widely diffused through the national security bureaucracy. Unity of purpose and action in Laos suffered, and each agency active in the country tended to follow its own institutional predilections. By late 1959 the ambassador and the CIA chief of station in Vientiane were in open conflict about how best to execute instructions from Washington. And in the second half of 1960, the country team in Vientiane, the State Department, and the Pentagon and CIA headquarters had developed three distinct viewpoints about Lao policy, which were resolved only after months of drift and increasing danger. Referring to these divisions, Parsons later wrote Winthrop Brown, "Horace [Smith] had his troubles of coordination, but they were as nothing compared to mine at home."[27]

In May 1959 the government of Prime Minister Phoui Sananikone believed it was strong enough to conclude a long-delayed agreement to integrate the first and second Pathet Lao battalions into the ANL. The integration and demobilization of Pathet Lao forces had been an explicit provision of the November 1957 agreement between the RLG and the Pathet Lao. By January 15, 1958, only 4,000 of the estimated 7,500 Pathet Lao forces had reported for processing. The relatively few weapons turned in were old, and some were inoperable. It was assumed that the modern arms of the Pathet Lao had been shipped to North Vietnam rather than surrendered to the RLG. In a ceremony the following month, additional Pathet Lao soldiers turned in weapons and swore an oath of allegiance to the RLG; they then returned to their homes. But the integration of the 1,500 officers and men of the first and second Pathet Lao battalions had been stymied by protracted negotiations on such issues as how many officers would be allowed, how much back pay was owed their troops, and whether the battalions would stay together as units or have their soldiers dispersed throughout the ANL.

On May 14, 1959, the RLG issued an ultimatum, demanding that the two Pathet Lao battalions either accept integration into the ANL or resign from military service. Initially, the two battalions—each faced by two ANL battalions—barricaded themselves within their respective compounds. On May 17 the First Pathet Lao Battalion, which was garrisoned near the royal capital of Luang Prabang, complied with the ultimatum. Six hundred soldiers began the process of integration into the ANL, and 150 others were demobilized. The Second Battalion, bivouacked at a former French Foreign Legion camp on the Plaine des Jarres, promised to reply to the ultimatum on May 19. But during monsoon rains on the night of May 18, the battalion's approximately 750 soldiers and their dependents walked out of camp undetected, heading toward the North Vietnamese border.

Discovering the escape the next morning, the ANL tried to block the routes to North Vietnam with four battalions, including paratroopers. The operation, hampered by rugged terrain and the rainy season, was unsuccessful. In early June, the ANL attempted to encircle the outnumbered Pathet Lao battalion in mountainous territory near North Vietnam. Escaping again, the battalion fled through a gap in the ANL units and traveled east along the Nam Mo River, a short distance from the Laotian border with North Vietnam. According to a PEO report, the ANL "abandoned pursuit at this point and issued a communique that the operation was finished and [the] PL dispersed." The RLG later referred to the escape of the Second Pathet Lao Battalion as the beginning of "open rebellion" in Laos.[28]

The American embassy in Vientiane considered the incident a "serious setback" for the kingdom, which lowered the people's confidence in both the RLG and the armed forces. Before the incident, DCM Holt reported to Washington, the ANL had been a source of respect in Laos and, in some areas, even feared. Unfortunately, the failure of the army to either integrate or disarm the Pathet Lao had exposed to "friend and foe [the] glaring weaknesses of [the] ANL."[29]

The RLG responded to the escape of the Pathet Lao battalion by declaring the troops traitors and placing Souphanouvong and other NLHS party leaders under house arrest. Phoui's cabinet also appealed to the US government for more assistance, requesting budget support for increases in the ANL and Auto Defense forces. For the moment, however, the US government was unwilling to finance any military expansion beyond the authorized levels of twenty-five thousand and sixteen thousand, respectively. North Vietnam and China characterized the incident as an alarming threat to peace and urged the ICC to reconvene and investigate the matter. On June 27, the Pathet Lao battalion crossed the frontier into North Vietnam, which the PEO characterized as "a more favorable position to receive support from NVN [North Vietnam] in that it was near [the] old Ho Chin [sic] Minh trail."[30]

At that time, the Ho Chi Minh Trail was still a simple set of footpaths and mountain trails through Laos that allowed infiltration of materiel and men from North Vietnam to South Vietnam. In the 1940s and 1950s, the journey could take as long as three months. Improving this network of trails was one of several important decisions ratified by the leadership of the Vietnamese Worker's Party in May of 1959. Others included strengthening and organizing the revolutionary forces in South Vietnam, as well as stepping up support to the semisecret Lao Communist Party and its front organization, the NLHS. Significantly, the Vietnamese communists viewed South Vietnam, Laos, and Cambodia as a single area of operations and considered support for the Pathet Lao "as vital in aiding the liberation struggle in southern Vietnam." By the middle of 1959, according to a National Security Agency history, a new North Vietnamese–controlled military radio network had been established, "with many of its stations located inside Laos."[31]

Like many ANL soldiers, some Pathet Lao forces had hazy notions about the cause for which they were fighting. A Pathet Lao captain, whose battalion had been integrated into the ANL, admitted to American embassy officials his complete ignorance of Laotian politics. Appearing frank and sincere, the captain said that government accusations of communist control of Pathet Lao forces contributed to the reluctance of these units to be integrated into the ANL. When asked to discuss the communist influence on the Pathet Lao, the captain was unable to describe the meaning of the word "communist."[32]

Prince Souphanouvong, a Laotian leader with a firmer grasp on communist ideology, had been released from house arrest when the government declared the end of the renegade battalion incident. In early July 1959, he denounced the "repression" of the NLHS. According to a CIA report to senior policymakers, Souphanouvong "asserted that he has solid foreign backing and has threatened a return to guerrilla warfare unless the government ceases its alleged persecutions."[33]

At 4:00 A.M. on July 18, a new phase in the Laotian insurgency started when a small ANL outpost of 20 men in northern Sam Neua was attacked by a force that reportedly included both Pathet Lao and North Vietnamese soldiers. The ANL force—members of a local volunteer battalion—offered token resistance, then withdrew from their positions. In the early hours of the next day, a 32-man ANL post in western Sam Neua repulsed a platoon-sized Pathet Lao attack. Five days later, the enemy returned in force, killing 2 ANL officers, 2 NCOs, and 8 soldiers. The remaining men escaped on foot to the provincial capital. Additional small-scale attacks in July were reported in Phong Saly, as well as two provinces in the Laotian panhandle. By August 3, insurgents had established a fifty-mile salient that stretched from the North Vietnamese border into western Sam Neua.

The following day Prime Minister Phoui Sananikone declared a state of emergency in five of the twelve Laotian provinces and instructed the military to maintain internal peace and order. He also locked up Souphanouvong and other NLHS leaders—this time in a jail guarded by soldiers—and cabled UN Secretary General Dag Hammarskjöld, charging that North Vietnam had armed and supplied the insurgents, encouraged former Pathet Lao soldiers to rebel, and offered refuge and assistance to ANL deserters. Phoui sought no specific action from the United Nations at this time, but he did want this statement of facts to be circulated to other member states.

A key challenge for the US government was accurately assessing the reports from the remote northern provinces. Lao officials, who were known to accept uncritically field reports exaggerating enemy strength, emphasized that North Vietnamese combat troops had participated in the July attacks. The absence of Western observers in Sam Neua and Phong Saly, however, made verification of these claims difficult.

Under instructions from their governments, the US, UK, and French military attachés in Vientiane investigated the fighting in Sam Neua and reached identical conclusions about the situation: Most of the information reported by Laotian officials was "manifestly exaggerated." The active participation of regular units of the People's Army of Vietnam (PAVN) could not be proven. And although the communists had substantial potential for reinforcing the Pathet Lao, the actual number of armed guerrillas in Sam Neua "probably does not exceed a few hundred." The Western attachés concluded: "If the disturbances spread, which is very possible, it is to be feared that the ANL will not be capable of countering them effectively."[34]

On August 9 a four-man PEO-CIA team flew from Vientiane to Sam Neua, landing on a rough, muddy airstrip surrounded by jungle and mountains. It was the rainy season, and approximately one hundred workers hand-carried broken rocks to fill in the airstrip's muddy holes. The military situation was quiet, and it appeared that the Pathet Lao attackers had pulled back in many parts of the province: "No evidence was observed to prove participation of uniformed or regular North Vietnamese military personnel; however, general opinion was definite to the effect that the North Vietnamese had undoubtedly instigated the action, provided some cadre personnel (perhaps later withdrawn), and organized and equipped the irregular (Pathet Lao and other) forces involved."[35]

The provincial governor of Sam Neua told the PEO-CIA team that the central government must demonstrate its ability to protect the area, observing: "The people in general will support whatever side is stronger."

Catholic missionaries in Sam Neua said that obtaining the cooperation of the Hmong and other tribal groups, who constituted an estimated one-third of the province's population, was the key to defeating the insurgency. One of the missionaries recalled the many airdrops of rice and salt during Operation Booster Shot, which the Hmong had witnessed, but no food "was given to starving tribesmen."[36]

At the August 18 NSC meeting, Allen Dulles reported that there was "firm evidence" of North Vietnamese "direction and supply of operations in Laos" but nothing "definite" about the presence of PAVN troops. North Vietnamese aircraft had been delivering supplies to a base at Dien Bien Phu, but the small number of flights did "not indicate an all-out effort." Two PAVN regiments north of the demilitarized zone in Vietnam had moved to the Laotian border. Discussing the hit-and-run tactics of the Lao military, Dulles made a sardonic reference to the much-maligned fighting ability of the ANL, observing that it was unclear "whether there was more hit or more run."[37]

On August 30 the Pathet Lao launched their second offensive of the summer of 1959 with coordinated attacks in northeastern Sam Neua. An estimated force of three battalions, totaling approximately fifteen hundred men, overran five lightly garrisoned ANL outposts on the Nam Mo River that were located between seven and twelve miles from the North Vietnamese border. The attacks, supported by heavy artillery, mortars, and recoilless rifles, according to the RLG, were "carried out with greater tactical precision and strength than any since the beginning of the conflict." The government forces fell back to defensive positions northeast of the provincial capital and its airport. In the days that followed, small bands of Pathet Lao guerrillas ambushed ANL forces and executed village headmen to intimidate the population.[38]

The renewed guerrilla warfare in northeastern Laos prompted serious concern in Washington. There was evidence of participation by North Vietnam in the attacks, including reports of howitzers and other equipment that could only have come from that country. The details were sketchy, though, and the State Department wanted reliable answers quickly. Were there any prisoners for interrogation or shell fragments for analysis? "What we need of course are facts and hard evidence, not opinions," the State Department cabled Smith on September 3. Informing the ambassador that the United States "may be faced with very serious decisions in [the] next few days," the State Department sought Smith's help in determining whether the crisis had reached the "proportions of [a] major Communist aggression against [a] free world country."[39]

Ambassador Smith's reply that same day left no doubt about the seriousness with which he viewed the situation. His military advisers had concluded that the ANL could likely contain, and perhaps even eventually throw back, the enemy forces in Sam Neua, but further large-scale communist incursions there might lead to a "second Dien Bien Phu tragedy." Smith recommended a public warning that further North Vietnamese attacks in Laos "may force a major change in nature and magnitude [of] US aid to Laos." He also suggested the deployment of US military forces to Luang Prabang and Vientiane, which would free the ANL battalions stationed there to fight insurgents in the countryside. It was Smith's "deepest personal conviction" that the United States must draw the line in Laos or face the loss of part or all of the country as well as the "entire US position and prestige in SE Asia if not all [of the] Far East." The ambassador added: "Like Quemoy or Berlin, I think the time is now come when we have to take our stand."[40]

The Joint Chiefs of Staff generally agreed with Smith's assessment and recommendations but felt additional action was required "to prevent the loss to communism of the entire country." The chiefs wanted the US government to remove "all restrictions on its actions in Laos, whether taken unilaterally or in conjunction with Allies." The United States, the chiefs argued, should modify its positions on the Geneva Accords and the recently negotiated agreement with France. Citing the difficulty of disguising the presence of US military personnel, whose apparent status as civilians reduced their effectiveness as trainers, the JCS recommended an increase in US training and support troops and the establishment of a MAAG in Laos. They further urged that Admiral Felt, the US commander in the Pacific, alert his forces and prepare to execute existing US military plans for defending Laos.[41]

The State Department had several objections to the JCS proposals: The US government still lacked basic facts about North Vietnamese participation in the fighting. The creation of a MAAG in Laos could not be reconciled with the military restrictions of the Geneva Accords. And it seemed premature to abandon the laboriously negotiated US-French training agreement, which had been in effect for one month. The State Department wanted any intervention to be conducted under the banner of SEATO. The JCS, however, had proposed that the United States "go it alone," if necessary. To Acting Secretary of State C. Douglas Dillon, it seemed that accepting "the JCS proposals would be tantamount to agreeing to no control by the State Department."[42]

In addition to substituting for Herter when he was out of town or ailing, Undersecretary of State Dillon was responsible for coordinating the economic and military aspects of US foreign aid. Dillon, born in 1909, was a schoolmate of Parsons at Groton and a graduate of Harvard. An investment banker, Dillon had been an early backer of Eisenhower's run for the presidency. In 1953 Dillon was appointed ambassador to France and served there at the end of the first Indochina war and during the immediate post-Geneva years. He later recalled that many people in France felt "let down" by the US unwillingness to intervene at Dien Bien Phu. "It was at times unpleasant," he said. "It didn't last too long, but for awhile, you'd go to dinner and get in an elevator to go to some apartment, and other people in the elevator would turn their back!"[43]

Dillon returned to Washington in 1958 to become undersecretary of state for economic affairs, and he moved up to undersecretary of state the following year when Herter replaced Dulles. Dillon's intelligence and judgment, evident to Democrats as well as Republicans, led to his appointment as secretary of treasury under John F. Kennedy, who had been advised that he was "far and away" one of the most able and energetic of the younger officials in the Eisenhower administration.[44]

It was Dillon who, on September 5, 1959, informed President Eisenhower of the recent "grave" developments in Laos and the consensus recommendations of his top diplomatic, military, and intelligence advisers. In a cable to the president, who was in Scotland for a brief golfing holiday following a series of meetings with European allies, Dillon reported that the Pathet Lao, "with probable North Vietnamese support," was pushing toward the provincial capital of Sam Neua, an area where a large proportion of the Lao armed forces were now concentrated. If the town fell and the Lao troops were overrun, the Pathet Lao would establish a "puppet government with international Communist support."[45]

On the diplomatic front, Dillon informed President Eisenhower that the RLG, without consulting any Western allies, had made an appeal to the United Nations for "an emergency force" to halt the North Vietnamese aggression and "prevent it from spreading." Although the Soviet Union would undoubtedly veto the dispatch of any UN-sponsored force, Secretary General Dag Hammarskjöld scheduled an urgent meeting of the Security Council to discuss this threat to international peace. Dillon also reported a planned meeting with representatives of SEATO, whose initial reaction to events in Laos was "not consonant with [the] gravity of situation."[46]

The key request in Dillon's cable was seeking President Eisenhower's "urgent approval" of preparatory steps for US military action. The Pentagon, Dillon reported, believed that the situation might "deteriorate rapidly over [the] next few days" and that US military action might "be required." If the president approved military operations, the Pentagon wanted to be able to "move very rapidly." The preparatory steps the military sought included instructing Admiral Felt to alert his forces, bringing transport aircraft and selected US forces to airfields for embarkation, and sailing elements of the Seventh Fleet to the South China Sea. "I am concerned that Communists may be conducting another serious probe of our fortitude and may seriously underrate our will to respect our SEATO obligations," Dillon concluded to Eisenhower. "Therefore I feel [the] action desired by Defense would be helpful background to UN action which should be our first hope."[47]

General Goodpaster, the White House assistant for military and intelligence affairs, replied the same day, reporting the president's approval of the proposed recommendations. No public announcements of these preparations, however, should be made without further consultation with the president. Goodpaster, an aide the president valued for his intelligence and crisp presentation of national security information and options, reported Eisenhower's comment: "If action is to be taken, it is important that it be taken with great swiftness once [the] decision is made." Moreover, if the crisis required US military operations, the president preferred that "preventive action" should be "taken before the physical situation in Laos has gone against the West."[48]

In the days that followed, US military forces prepared for battle, with initial elements of two Marine battalions in Okinawa and Japan ready to board transport aircraft on two hours' notice. A third Marine battalion, with supporting equipment and Seabee engineer forces, was ordered onto amphibious transport to sail for Bangkok, then a planned movement by rail to the Mekong and Vientiane. In Japan, the assault helicopter aircraft carrier *Thetis Bay* was loaded with helicopters and proceeding to Okinawa. The mission for US forces deployed to Laos would be to secure the Vientiane and Seno airfields and nearby river crossings, which would theoretically free the FAL (Forces d'Armée de Laos) to deal with the Pathet Lao.* If necessary, the Marines planned to conduct further operations "to ensure friendly control of Laos." Three carrier groups from the Seventh Fleet would support the operation: the *Lexington,* operating in the South China Sea; the *Shangri La,* off of Taiwan; and the *Hancock,* arriving soon near the Philippines. On September 7 Vice Admiral Wallace M. Beakley, deputy CNO, informed Admiral Burke: "Seventh Fleet ready for either general war or support of Laos."[49]

US diplomatic action included consultations with SEATO representatives, who now viewed the situation in Laos more seriously. The exception was the French government, which "disparaged" the US conclusion of a threatening military crisis. Emphasizing the ability of North Vietnam and China to reinforce troops in Laos faster than the Western allies, the French appeared "especially fearful of any free world reaction that might provoke increased Communist intervention," according to the State Department. Both France and the United Kingdom wanted to work through the United Nations before invoking the SEATO treaty.[50]

On September 7 Secretary General Hammarskjöld formally reported the Laotian crisis to the Security Council. Henry Cabot Lodge, the US ambassador to the United Nations, introduced a resolution to appoint a subcommittee that would conduct an inquiry into the conflict in Laos. The United States and the resolution's cosponsors, France and the United Kingdom, took the position that simply gathering information, rather than judging what should be done to preserve peace in Laos, was a "procedural" rather than "substantive" matter—a semantic distinction that would preclude a veto by the Soviet Union. The Security Council passed the resolution by a vote of 10–1, with the Soviet Union casting the only dissenting vote. By the end of the week, a subcommittee of the Security Council, with representatives from Argentina, Italy, Japan, and Tunisia, was on its way to Laos.[51]

---

* In 1959 the designation FAL replaced ANL (Armée Nationale du Laos). The abbreviation FAL refers to all Laotian armed forces, and ANL refers specifically to the army. In September 1961 both designations were replaced by FAR (Forces Armée du Royaume).

At a September 8 White House meeting, Acting Secretary of State Dillon briefed President Eisenhower on the UN fact-finding mission, which he said was intended to deter further communist military advances. Dillon warned that if the UN deterrent was ineffective, the United States would have to take additional military steps. According to Dillon's notes of the meeting, Eisenhower agreed, saying: "If new developments occurred which indicated the necessity for additional action by the United States, we should seriously consider an effort to educate the American people to the facts of the situation so that they would begin to be prepared for any action the United States might find it necessary to take." National Security Advisor Gordon Gray summarized the president's view more succinctly a few days later: "This situation may develop into another Korea."[52]

On September 11, as the crisis in Laos appeared to be abating, Eisenhower's senior foreign policy, military, and intelligence advisers met at the White House to clarify the US military commitment to the kingdom. "Under NSC policy it is clear that we would intervene with our own forces to defend the country," said Dillon.[53] Secretary of Defense Neil H. McElroy, however, wanted reassurance on this matter, asking whether the role of the US military was simply to train the FAL, or whether the United States was prepared to back Laos with combat forces? The president, reminding McElroy that the SEATO treaty provided protection for Laos, said he assumed US policy was to fulfill its military obligations under SEATO, adding, "We should not do anything completely by ourselves."[54]

Indirectly critical of advisers urging the United States to "go it alone" in Laos, Eisenhower said that if "we acted unilaterally, then he did not see why we should have Collective Security Pacts," according to the minutes of the meeting. Although the United States would provide the major combat strength of any SEATO force, Eisenhower wanted it led by a commander from another member of the alliance—perhaps Australia or New Zealand. To ensure there was no mistaking his intentions, Eisenhower concluded the meeting by making it "very clear that he desired SEATO planning to be firmed up quickly and said we would insist that all the members should be prepared to do their part."[55]

Despite its military advantage, the Pathet Lao did not seize the provincial capital of Sam Neua. US officials, who concluded that the attacks were a reaction to the strong anticommunist measures of the RLG and the increasing American presence in Laos, speculated that the appointment of a UN fact-finding team had deterred the Pathet Lao from further military advances. According to analysts Langer and Zasloff, the rebel "attacks served as a warning to the RLG that the Pathet Lao commanded powerful outside support that could be swiftly brought to bear in case of future threats."[56]

In September 1959 North Vietnam secretly increased its military presence in Laos by establishing Group 959, which recruited, armed, and trained Pathet Lao forces. With headquarters near Hanoi and a forward command post in Sam Neua, Group 959 was the "main Vietnamese instrument for coordinating the military operations in Laos." Like many in the US military, the North Vietnamese had a low opinion of their allies' fighting ability and "typically viewed the Lao troops as virtually incapable of operating without their advice and the stiffening presence of Vietnamese forces." To the battle-tested North Vietnamese, their Lao comrades appeared "afraid of military fire and hand-to-hand combat, slow in rushing to the attack, and fast to retreat."[57]

Both the US and the Lao governments were disturbed by the open skepticism of French officials about the participation of North Vietnamese forces in the summer attacks in Sam Neua and Phong Saly. The French military attaché told a member of the UN fact-finding team, "There has been no real foreign military intervention in Laos" and said the kingdom's appeal to the United Nations "was possibly inspired by [the] policy aims of [a] 'certain large power.'" To the French, the problems in Laos seemed primarily political and economic, and the Pathet Lao's ability to recruit tribespeople was a consequence of RLG indifference to their needs. In sum, the French believed the current crisis was due to the shortcomings of Phoui Sananikone's government.[58] French diplomats, as well as UK officials, were also worried by the growing American presence in Laos, which they considered "unnecessarily provocative."[59] Between mid-July and mid-October 1959, the number of official US personnel in Laos doubled from approximately 250 to 500. Such increases seemed essential to Pentagon officials, who believed that many of the problems in Laos were "a direct outgrowth" of earlier PEO deficiencies "in both numbers and quality of personnel."[60]

State Department officials, however, were concerned by the "mushrooming U.S. presence in Laos." Robert D. Murphy, undersecretary for political affairs, informed the Pentagon that a proposed increase in PEO personnel "very much alarmed" the department. With world attention focused on Laos and UN fact-finders on the ground, a visible increase in military assistance officials would be an obvious violation of the Geneva Accords. Murphy warned: "Great circumspection is required on our part to avoid forcing the British, French, and Indians into a position where, because of their obligations as participants in the Geneva machinery, they must take cognizance of US military aid to Laos as contravening the spirit of the Agreement on Laos."[61]

On September 15, 1959, the UN fact-finding subcommittee—the more passive sounding term "fact-gathering" was preferred by Hammarskjöld—arrived in Vientiane with a narrow mission: to receive testimony, documents, and other evidence from the Lao government, as opposed to seeking out information and witnesses on its own initiative. If a government other than the RLG—that is, North Vietnam—wanted to provide information, the subcommittee could accept it. The subcommittee's task was to prepare a factual account of events mentioned in the RLG's appeal to the UN but not make any judgment about its charge of aggression by North Vietnam.

During a nearly month-long stay in Laos, the subcommittee received briefings from RLG officials and members of the kingdom's armed forces and met with Savang Vatthana, now the kingdom's prince regent and the certain successor to the throne. Some of the UN fact-finders traveled to Sam Neua, where they studied the terrain and interviewed eyewitnesses, including Pathet Lao prisoners and refugees from areas of fighting. Other subcommittee delegates spoke with wounded men at hospitals in Vientiane and Luang Prabang. The director of the Provincial Hospital of Luang Prabang showed subcommittee members fragments of shells and bullets extracted from the wounded. Also inspected were weapons and other physical evidence captured during the fighting in the northern provinces, including rifles, submachine guns, hand grenades, ammunition, portions of uniforms, medical supplies, and personal papers. The rifles were a mix of Chinese, Czechoslovakian, French, and American arms, all of which were manufactured between 1917 and 1953. The submachine guns were French, and new, wooden-handled hand grenades came from China.[62]

In separate meetings with Prime Minister Phoui Sananikone, the chiefs of the Italian and Japanese delegations agreed that the RLG had "furnished considerable evidence of North Vietnamese participation in [the] recent military operations in Laos." It was, however, the personal opinion of both diplomats that "Laos should make the best of a bad situation and seek closer relations with communist China and North Vietnam." The Japanese delegate said China was certain that the US intended to establish military bases in Laos. The only way to convince them otherwise would be for Laos to establish diplomatic relations with the PRC and allow its representatives see for themselves. The Italian and Japanese delegates doubted that there was much the UN could do in Laos because neither communist China nor North Vietnam was a member state of the world body.[63]

Such views, according to Ambassador Smith, were a "surprising blow" to Phoui, who had expected help from the UN and now feared that it would pressure Laos to negotiate with North Vietnam. Phoui immediately made arrangements to travel to New York and personally argue the Laotian case in any UN discussion of the kingdom. A trip to the United States would also permit Phoui to speak directly with top-level Eisenhower administration officials and to receive medical attention for a range of health problems, including shortness of breath at night, high blood pressure, and back pain.

The prospect of the Lao prime minister's trip to New York appalled Secretary General Hammarskjöld, who believed the visit would be perceived as lobbying the world body during the subcommittee's preparation of its report. The actual findings of the subcommittee's report, released on November 5, were inconclusive, essentially splitting the difference on opposing views of the summer fighting in Laos. The subcommittee concluded that the attacking forces "must have had a centralized co-ordination" and received support from North Vietnam, "consisting mainly of equipment, arms, ammunition, supplies, and the help of political cadres." The subcommittee further declared that the evidence it had received "did not clearly establish whether there were crossings of the frontier by regular [North Vietnamese] troops."[64]

Hammarskjöld initially believed that the United States was behind Phoui's planned trip to the United Nations. The secretary general, who had visited Laos earlier in the year, told Henry Cabot Lodge of his fears that US military and intelligence officers in Laos were encouraging a coup d'état. Referring to Graham Greene's 1955 novel about an American secret agent who meddled dangerously in Vietnam, Hammarskjöld was particularly concerned by the presence of "quiet Americans" in Laos. When Lodge reported to the State Department that he had informed Hammarskjöld "there were no 'quiet Americans' in Laos," the falsehood was of sufficient size that an unidentified State Department official placed two exclamation points by the comment in the telegram.[65]

Discouraged by the State Department and the United Nations from traveling to New York, Phoui flew directly to Washington, D.C., where he arrived on October 22 and was admitted to Walter Reed Army Hospital the next day. The doctors there determined that Phoui had a heart condition, and they wanted him to stay at the hospital for a few days. On October 24 Christian Chapman, the State Department officer in charge of Lao affairs, visited Phoui in the hospital to deliver a letter from Secretary of State Herter expressing US support for the prime minister and his government. When Chapman asked what he wished to discuss with the department, Phoui said that the only problem he wished to discuss in detail was the US aid program. The USOM projects in Laos developed too slowly, and they lacked demonstrable impact. Phoui hoped to have an extended conversation with Assistant Secretary Parsons about these and other matters.[66]

At a meeting with Parsons on October 29, Phoui declared that the principal problem in Laos, and the one uppermost in his mind, was a road network, particularly one that would link Sam Neua and Phong Saly with the rest of the country. His government, he said, was often criticized for its indifference to the tribal minorities in northern Laos, but without a network of roads it was impossible to reach them. Parsons agreed with Phoui about the importance of roads, indicating that the US government would give the matter "maximum attention." The problem, said Parsons, was that the US government allocated funds to "first priority objectives," which for Laos meant "security." With across-the-board reductions in US foreign aid, Parsons said, "it was becoming increasingly difficult to obtain sufficient funds for both security and all other projects."[67]

Among the Lao officials who accompanied Phoui to Washington was Colonel Phoumi Nosavan, the secretary of state for defense and a CDNI leader. The prime minister had included Colonel Phoumi on the trip to demonstrate to the CDNI and the prince regent that his discussions with the US government conformed to their view of Lao interests. Phoui also hoped that the visit might help him win the confidence of the colonel and his CDNI colleagues.

At an informal gathering at the Pentagon, Colonel Phoumi's presentation on the military situation in Laos made a favorable impression on some seventy-five senior officers and Department of Defense civilians. Informative and well organized, the presentation was considered noteworthy by the audience because of Phoumi's frank discussion of the weaknesses and mistakes of both the FAL and the PEO. His enthusiasm for correcting them seemed "heartening though possibly unrealistic" to at least one officer in attendance. According to a Defense Department message to CINCPAC, the interest and enthusiasm of Pentagon officials appeared to make a "considerable impression on Phoumi. At [the] same time[,] his sophistication, self confidence, frankness and open and friendly manner made [a] favorable impression here."[68]

Prime Minister Phoui's trip to Washington was cut short by the October 29 death of King Sisavang Vong, who had ruled for fifty-four years. Phoui immediately returned to Laos to pay his respects to the late king and meet with the new one. Before leaving Vientiane for Luang Prabang on November 3, Phoui had a long conversation with Ambassador Smith, who reported that the prime minister was "profoundly disheartened" both by the Secretary General's negative reaction to his trip to New York and by his reception in Washington. Phoui regretted the lack of time for extended conversations with Parsons and felt that ICA officials lacked any understanding of the political, economic, and social realities in Laos. The prime minister believed that Western support for Laos was "wavering," Smith reported, and feared that his country would be "sold down the river" by UN efforts to placate the communist bloc.[69]

Phoui also told Smith that he was disturbed by political maneuvers of the CDNI, which had never really cooperated in developing a constructive reform program. The prime minister had been reluctant to use his full powers to counter CDNI obstructionism because it would trigger a government crisis, which the US government sought to avoid. Phoui was "certain" that the US mission would back the CDNI in any showdown with the RLG, and he believed that the new king had been "egging [the] CDNI on and that some of [the] younger army officers were just looking for [an] excuse for [a] coup."[70]

Phoui and the CDNI were now locked in a political struggle over principles and power. Both the four-year term of the National Assembly and the prime minister's special powers were due to expire at the end of 1959. Since the outbreak of guerrilla warfare in July, many Laotians—particularly Phoui and LHL deputies in the legislature—favored pushing back the national elections until late 1960 and extending the prime minister's powers for one more year. The justification for these measures was that anticommunist politicians needed the additional time to build popular support, implement economic aid programs, and compete successfully against NLHS candidates in the elections. Of course, Phoui and his party would be the principal beneficiaries of these changes.

The CDNI adamantly opposed extending the legislature's legal mandate and Phoui's special powers. According to CIA officer Don Ropa, who served in Vientiane in the mid-1950s on a full-time basis and subsequently in a temporary capacity, CDNI members were "convinced that a large number of the deputies have lost popular favor, could never be reelected, and deserve political retirement." Another CDNI target was the Lao system of parliamentary government, which many of the younger Lao perceived as giving too much power to feckless National Assembly deputies. Recent political upheavals in France, Pakistan, and Thailand, where national armies helped establish governments with stronger executive authority, had made a strong impression on the CDNI. Its members sought constitutional revisions that would enable the king to appoint a strong government that would stay in office until the time was ripe for general elections. This so-called modified democracy seemed to LHL deputies "a smokescreen" to force them out of politics.[71]

Exacerbating the internal Laotian political struggle in the fall of 1959 were deep divisions within the US mission in Vientiane. In accordance with State Department policy and instructions from CIA headquarters, Henry Hecksher and his subordinates continued to support the CDNI and help build up its organizational strength. Ambassador Smith, who had concluded that the CDNI was playing a destructive role in Lao political life, was a strong partisan for Phoui and a harsh critic of Hecksher. This "dichotomy" in US policy was well and widely known in Vientiane, and top officials in Washington were about to discover, in the words of a CIA postmortem, that "the Agency and the Chief of Station on the one hand and the Ambassador on the other have very different views" on implementing US policy.[72]

Chapter 6

Dichotomy

THE CABLE THAT MARKED the beginning of the end of Horace Smith's diplomatic career was Embassy Telegram (Embtel) 1300, a top-secret, "eyes only" message to Assistant Secretary of State J. Graham Parsons and James W. Riddleberger, director of ICA. Dated November 8, 1959, the telegram was a long assessment of US aid to Laos, cowritten with the new USOM director, John Tobler, who had arrived in Vientiane six weeks earlier. A former news correspondent in his early forties, Tobler had worked as a government information officer, graduated from the National War College, and served at ICA headquarters and on the Operations Coordinating Board. His instructions from Washington were to take a fresh look at the US aid program in Laos. Ambassador Smith found Tobler a keen observer of Lao affairs and an astute judge of the political significance of US actions. The two men engaged in "soul-searching" discussions, in Smith's words, which helped crystallize their view of the "basic problems that beset our effort."[1]

The first part of the telegram, written by Tobler and "fully supported" by Smith, estimated that "the chances are far better than even that this country will go down the drain" unless the US government made a much greater effort. If it was not prepared to make such an effort, the United States "should consider cutting our losses" in Laos and withdraw from the country as gracefully as possible. Acknowledging that such an action might appear "cowardly," Tobler believed it preferable to "having Laos go down in history as a US defeat or, conversely, risk[ing] all-out war over [the] wrong place at [the] wrong time."[2]

Tobler described a "state of siege" in Laos, with travel outside of the

132

larger towns severely restricted and large areas of the country beyond government control. He believed that the US government was ill equipped to deal with Pathet Lao terror in the villages, yet America was closely identified with that effort. The US aid program was "built on quicksand," Tobler declared, and the multiple, uncoordinated programs tended "to defeat each other." Observing the contradictory courses of political action pursued by the embassy and the CIA station, he agreed with Ambassador Smith that agency support for the CDNI was "destroying the effectiveness of the Phoui regime, undermining U.S. prestige and opening the way to the most dangerous and potentially disastrous course of events."[3]

The second part of the telegram was Smith's political assessment, which called the CDNI the "greatest thorn in Phoui's side." Lacking political experience and unlikely to win at the polls, the CDNI had followed a "course of obstructionism" in the cabinet, with the expectation that its members would "come into full power one way or another." Instead of supporting Phoui's wish to extend the National Assembly's mandate for a year, the CDNI apparently intended a "royal solution," with the king naming an authoritarian, unconstitutional government. Such an outcome, Smith predicted, would cost Laos the international advantage of being the "only nation of the area with [a] democratic government."[4]

The major problems facing Phoui, according to Smith, were the inaccessibility of remote areas in Laos, with no major road programs in sight; the likelihood that he would leave office after December 25 because of "unrealistic opposition" by the CDNI and "perhaps" the king; and the less-than-complete support from the US government, even though the prime minister had followed its advice. Smith reported, "[Phoui] has been especially confused and disheartened by what he considers a dichotomy in [the] US approach to Laos. He is convinced [that] blind [CIA] support and guidance to [the] CDNI has hobbled him to [the] point where to use his full powers would bring disaster to the country."[5]

Smith elaborated on the "dichotomy" theme in a follow-up telegram to the State Department: Phoui, he cabled, "maintains that he personally knows beyond [a] doubt that [the] most influential members of CDNI [are] guided step-by-step by [the CIA] and that without continuous step-by-step planning[,] guidance[,] ghost writing[,] and financial and other support[, the] CDNI would never have been able to conceive and execute their blocking tactics or to organize and pay for political rallies and agents in principal centers throughout [the] country." The ambassador wrote that he had accepted the assurances of Allen Dulles and other senior CIA officials that the agency and the State Department were following the same policy in Laos. However, Smith observed, Phoui could "hardly be accused of being oversensitive or indulging in unsupported flights of imagination."[6]

In the joint recommendations of Embtel 1300, Smith and Tobler proposed that the administration prepare the US public for the "very real possibility of failure" in Laos. Within the kingdom, the message to the country's elites should be that without a constitutional, legal government, the United States could not justify continued support at the current levels, much less consider contributing at the larger levels required to preserve the country's independence. There must also be an end to the division in US policy in Vientiane. The embassy and the CIA should present a united front to the Lao, indicating clearly that the US government would not support an authoritarian government established by a CDNI coup or royal decree. The CDNI must subordinate its views to Phoui's guidance, and the prime minister must recognize that he can no longer delay in providing the leadership implicit in his full powers and US support. Smith and Tobler proposed backing up this last recommendation with an ominous-sounding threat: If the CDNI, the king, or any other Lao faction "fails to cooperate reasonably or attempts treacherously to defeat Phoui's effort[,] it must be cast aside or neutralized to the maximum extent we can help arrange it."[7]

In the economic field, Embtel 1300 recommended "an all out effort" to accelerate the road-building program in Laos. A national road network had been a US and Lao objective for years, but US military and political programs had taken precedence over roads and related economic-development programs: "There is little likelihood the United States will achieve its objective of putting Laos on even a moderately sound political, military, or economic footing unless, at a minimum, the core of a transportation and communications network is created as a matter of urgency."[8]

Smith and Tobler urged that a similar priority be assigned to staffing USOM with public-administration and economic experts who spoke French, with the goal of "cleaning up the sins of the past and laying a solid foundation for the future." There should also be a significant diplomatic initiative indicating that the US government would no longer continue "footing the bill and risking its prestige for a country that is unwilling or unable to undertake more specific action to help itself fiscally and administratively." The RLG had to take greater risks in the areas of taxation and enforcement of administrative discipline. In a subsequent telegram to Riddleberger, Tobler wrote that Laos was collecting about $1.40 in revenue per person, whereas the US government provided "the equivalent of $16.50 per person." Unless Laos established "a more effective and more honest governmental machinery[,] and thus contribute more substantially to its own support, no program will succeed in the long run."[9]

Whatever individual decisions Washington made on specific issues that Embtel 1300 raised, Smith and Tobler urged the State Department to make a forceful approach to friendly countries to encourage more UN support for Laos "before it goes under." They declared that the US government could not "continue to carry so much of this free world load alone" and that the nature of the communist threat in Laos could only be met effectively with UN action, protection, and assistance. The "turning point is upon us," Smith and Tobler concluded, and unless the US government was prepared to "grasp the nettle of much greater aid, we should not place US prestige further in jeopardy. We consider this matter of extreme urgency. Situation could well blow up in a matter of weeks or even days."[10]

Washington's initial reaction to Embtel 1300 was shock. The telegram's overall assessment of the situation and the impact of US aid was the most pessimistic report on Laos ever received by policymakers. Moreover, the telegram's recommendations seemed extreme, not to mention inconsistent with US objectives. When summarizing the message to Secretary of State Herter, Assistant Secretary Parsons warned in a cover note: "I believe I should express the early opinion that much of this report should be treated with reserve although we agree that the situation in Laos is indeed serious."[11]

Despite his restrained language, Parsons heartily disliked Embtel 1300, which he characterized as "unfortunate" and "unorthodox." Having specialized in Lao affairs himself for more than three years, Parsons tended to emphasize in his own reports the progress that had been made since the dark days of 1954. In a subsequent message to Herter, he acknowledged, "The situation in Laos is perilous" but the problems were "manageable." Parsons believed that adjustments to the political, economic, and security programs offered "the promise of continued progress in strengthening the country against the Communist threat." He also commented to Herter that the difficulties in Laos had "been portrayed in recent telegrams in an overdrawn and somewhat emotional manner."[12]

Leonard J. Saccio, the acting director of ICA, made a similar point to Undersecretary of State Dillon: "The sweeping negative assessment of the accomplishments of project activities made by the USOM Director is not viewed as accurately reflecting the record of accomplishments. Though it is true that developmental projects have been clearly subordinated to overriding security objectives and have of necessity been limited in scope, nonetheless an impressive and heartening variety of accomplishments can be identified. They comprehend solid, if modest, achievements in the major activity sectors of agriculture, public health, education, public administration and rural development."[13]

Saccio was skeptical about the accelerated road program proposed by Smith and Tobler. Acknowledging the importance of a national network of roads, as well as its "disappointingly slow" progress to date, Saccio questioned whether completing the road system was the most pressing *political* need in Laos. In his view, there were many problems deserving equal or more attention—for example, assisting the tribal minorities, ending corruption in government, and establishing "more harmonious relations" among Phoui's ministers. "None of these would appear resolved by an expanded road program," Saccio wrote.[14]

In a personal message to Ambassador Smith, Parsons cabled that the problems raised in Embtel 1300 were receiving intensive, top-level attention at all US agencies. Moreover, Saccio would be traveling to Vientiane to spend several days with Smith and Tobler reviewing the economic aid program. Parsons, who sympathized with the frustrations and difficulties of achieving US goals in Laos, criticized the Smith-Tobler telegram as "sweeping, imprecisely stated and therefore extremely difficult to assess." More specifically, Parsons refused to accept the "thesis that we should prepare the ground for informing [the] American people of [the] failure of our mission in Laos."[15]

Refuting the telegram's overall evaluation of US aid, the assistant secretary wrote: "Progress reports to date while not glowing had at least been encouraging. To revise totally this program or produce [a] substitute would in our opinion be [a] practical impossibility. Remedial efforts and improvements certainly are required but we cannot accept characterization as 'built on quicksand' and 'programming for failure' as [a] justifiable estimate." Addressing the "dichotomy" of US views in Laos, Parsons reported that the Department of State shared Smith's concerns, encouraging the ambassador and his staff to do everything possible to correct this impression. The ambassador, Parsons instructed, should act as the spokesman for US policy to all Lao factions: the king, Phoui, LHL, CDNI, and the army. Moreover, the CIA's relationship with the CDNI should be confined "to appropriate operational measures fully coordinated by you."[16]

Like many others in Washington, Parsons disagreed with Ambassador Smith's wholly negative appraisal of the CDNI. (Smith had recently charged that the CDNI had "authoritarian 'Nazi' tendencies.")[17] State Department officials, in contrast, approved of the organization's political pressure on older politicians and welcomed the inclusion of CDNI members in the RLG cabinet. Although appreciating the "difficulties inherent in manipulating any power group," Parsons wrote to Smith that the CDNI, with the apparent support of the king, was "in ascendancy" and represented a "vital future asset" in the struggle against the Pathet Lao. "To eliminate our support [to] this organization now would result in [a] serious loss of confidence in [the] US among [the] Lao."[18]

As for Phoui, the State Department still viewed him as the "only Lao political figure at present able to unite all factions under his leadership." But the prime minister was an "astute politician," rather than a "dynamic leader," according to Parsons. To avoid friction in the cabinet, Phoui had to work harder to communicate his views directly and clearly to the CDNI. Parsons informed Smith of the department's "impression" that Phoui sought to "manipulate all elements favorable to him and may even view you in this context."[19]

Parsons followed up his telegram to Smith with a personal letter that questioned the ambassador's leadership of the US mission. Smith's references to the "dichotomy" of US views in Laos had contributed to an impression in Washington of poor coordination among the various US agencies. "As ambassador, you, of course, are the coordinator of the country team," Parsons observed, reminding Smith of the procedures for referring disputes to Washington. The assistant secretary added that he and other officials had not been aware of the seriousness of the ambassador's difficulty with Hecksher.[20]

Another issue that bothered Parsons was "the propriety" of the ambassador joining one member of the country team (Tobler) in criticism of another (Hecksher). This was "likely to be damaging to your position." Moreover, siding with one agency representative against another "creates problems here for us," Parsons wrote, adding: "It is our view that the Ambassador must maintain his prestige and position as the President's representative and must in no way imply that he himself is merely a member—not the leader—of the country team."[21]

In an odd conclusion to a letter devoted to important affairs of state, Parsons admonished the ambassador for the length of his telegrams. Perhaps the State Department's limited capacity for simultaneously processing highly classified, priority cables was the reason for the reproach, but the tone of Parsons's message reflected his irritation with Smith. Sounding like a prep-school prefect scolding an underclassman for a minor infraction, Parsons urged Smith to "enjoin upon [your] drafting officers the importance of brevity and clarity as well as careful organization of content. Excessively long telegrams place an inordinate strain on our resources and it is essential that you review draft messages carefully from the standpoint of economy of language."[22]

Ambassador Smith's initial response to Parsons was nearly as emotionally charged as Embtel 1300 itself. Smith began by challenging Washington's benign view of the CDNI. He recognized the importance of young people gaining experience in government and the reform and anticommunist principles of the CDNI. The organization itself, however, had "contributed little or nothing" that could not have been achieved by appointing talented young individuals to positions of increasing responsibility. The "chief troublemakers" of the CDNI, particularly Foreign Minister Khamphan Panya, had "not demonstrated the character, ability, force or patriotic spirit that would have at least partially justified their demand for key roles in the government," Smith wrote. He added: "I cannot see how the CDNI can be allowed to continue its wrecking policy."[23]

Contrary to the accusations made by the CDNI, Ambassador Smith reported, Phoui had tried to discuss issues and "speak frankly with young colleagues far beyond traditional Lao limits in such relationships." He had even included Khamphan on his October trip to Washington. Yet for all the prime minister's efforts, the ambassador cabled, Phoui had generally "come up against [a] stone wall with [the] young[,] especially Khamphan," whom Smith described as "notoriously sulky, obstinate and uncooperative unless his particular and frequently ill-considered views are immediately accepted."[24]

Ambassador Smith also defended his partisanship on behalf of Phoui, which he characterized as a necessary counterbalance to Henry Hecksher's clear favoritism toward the CDNI. Noting that US support for the CDNI far surpassed its assistance to the LHL, the ambassador observed: "Phoui might well question our sincerity in repeatedly stating our confidence in him while at [the] same time [the] bulk [of] our material backing goes to those who undermine his government." The ambassador shared Phoui's belief that CDNI leaders saw no need to cooperate with him as long as the army backed them. Removing the FAL from politics would deprive the CDNI of its "major anti-constitutional prop," wrote Smith. Because it had become "nothing less than an opposition political party," which frustrated the RLG's reform program, the CDNI should agree to a full and fair merger with the LHL, uniting the kingdom's anticommunist politicians.[25]

There was one particular aspect of the State Department view of the CDNI that "puzzled" the ambassador: What precisely were the "unique or unselfish contributions" the organization had made? Taking a rhetorical swing at Hecksher's support of the CDNI and Parsons's earlier instructions, Smith declared that it would be "much easier to neutralize" the friction between the young and old in Laos if CIA "activities here were confined to 'appropriate operational measures fully coordinated' by me."[26]

In a subsequent, more conciliatory telegram to Parsons, Smith sought to "correct certain misapprehensions" that Embtel 1300 had created in Washington. Possibly recognizing the threat to his career posed by the telegram and questions about his leadership, Smith wrote that it was neither his nor Tobler's intention to level a "wholesale indictment on our entire effort to date." The ambassador also agreed that Embtel 1300 might have been "somewhat imprecise and sweeping." What Smith wanted to reiterate was that the US effort in Laos had "not been nearly successful enough." Without significant changes, American aid to the kingdom would likely prove to be "too little and too late."[27]

The ambassador reminded Parsons that the previous summer Pathet Lao attacks had easily undermined all of the preceding US support for the RLG. "With all due respect," Smith wrote, neither the Laotian government nor the US mission "pulled us out of [that] hole." It was the "rumblings in SEATO," the public statements from governments in Washington, Paris, and London, and the "lightning action" of the United Nations that stopped the communist advance: "We were not prepared then nor are we now to cope internally with a repeat performance."[28]

The ambassador believed that the US government should look to the United Nations for a solution to the problems in Laos. In a second long telegram, Embtel 1500, dated November 30, Smith amplified his thinking, recommending that a neutral UN delegation should play the leading role in coordinating and managing all foreign aid programs in Laos, which would be "transferred fully into U.N. hands." If the views of diplomats in Vientiane reflected those of their governments, Smith reported, US allies in Europe, SEATO, and the United Nations appeared to accept that the United States had no aggressive intention in Laos. They also believed, however, that the PRC and North Vietnam would not permit the "development of Laos under US dominance." These same allies were convinced that the Lao national security effort, including the joint US-French training program, should be brought "under [the] UN umbrella" as soon as practicable. US allies would also welcome an economic development program "under [a] UN flag." Some Western governments, Smith predicted, might even be willing to share a greater part of the financial burden in Laos.[29]

In his analysis, the ambassador noted that the US government supplied 90 percent of the total foreign aid received by Laos, and most of it was military assistance. Such an unbalanced aid program had many undesirable consequences, which included creating both a propaganda opportunity and a pretext for intervention by the PRC and North Vietnam; enabling Lao leaders to assume that the strategic value of their country justified almost unlimited demands for political guarantees and economic aid; and allowing groups in power to ignore the need for improvements in civil administration, better services for the population, and "more modesty in using public funds for [the] benefit of military, political and administrative leaders."[30]

Smith also saw many advantages to channeling US aid to Laos through the United Nations. They included proving the peaceful objectives of the United States and counteracting communist propaganda; stabilizing political life in Laos, in part because UN activities would lead to a reduction in the role and influence of the army; and strengthening the

Lao administration of assistance. Officials of the United Nations, a body that most Laotians revered, would not engender the "outright hostility" faced by US officials who made "unpalatable" economic, administrative, and political demands of the RLG.[31]

Leaders of the State Department were appalled by Smith's latest long telegram, which further undermined their confidence in his judgment and fitness as an ambassador. Although Washington welcomed a continued and expanded UN presence in Laos, "consistent with its capabilities and US interests," Smith's proposal to turn over the bulk of US programs to that organization seemed neither "desirable" nor "feasible." Perhaps the greatest weakness of Smith's approach was the obvious fact that the United Nations could not support programs that were explicitly anticommunist—the precise purpose of the US effort in Laos. Other shortcomings of the proposal, from Washington's perspective, were the United Nations's inability to assume "responsibility for Laos in any such sweeping manner"; the telegram's inattention to the certainty of congressional demands for US control of its foreign aid; and Smith's apparent obliviousness to the repercussions of disengaging from a "vital security area." Handing Laos off to the United Nations, according to the State Department, would indicate that the US government was backing away from regional collective security agreements, which in turn would weaken confidence in American commitments in other parts of the world.[32]

There was another problem with Embtel 1500, in the view of senior State Department officials. Smith's earlier long telegram, Embtel 1300, had a very restricted distribution. His UN proposal, however, was sent not only to the State Department, with instructions to "please pass [to] all agencies urgently," but also to embassies in London, Paris, Bangkok, Saigon, Phnom Penh, New Delhi, Ottawa, Canberra, Manila, Karachi, Wellington, Taipei, Tokyo, Hong Kong, and the United Nations. Smith apparently believed he had articulated an important approach to foreign aid in Asia and that others should know about it.

During the drafting of the State Department's reply to Smith, Undersecretary Dillon told Parsons that the ambassador should be asked "not to circulate telegrams such as No. 1500 so widely." Parsons was reluctant to be the bearer of this particular message, as he had "had several occasions recently to take issue with Ambassador Smith." Parsons wanted a more senior official—specifically, Livingston T. Merchant, undersecretary of state for political affairs—to sign such a communication. "The subject matter," he explained, "has a broader significance[,] and I believe that it would be helpful for the Ambassador to realize that his recent messages have been of concern to the top officers in the Department."[33]

As early as November 28, 1959—ten days after Smith sent Embtel 1300 and three days before the receipt of Embtel 1500—State Department officials discussed removing the ambassador from Laos. Loy Henderson, deputy undersecretary for administration, spoke with Parsons that day, asking for copies of letters from former assistant secretary Robertson that indicated his displeasure with aspects of Smith's performance as ambassador. Parsons complied with the request, adding: "While Mr. Robertson was dealing with official matters in these letters, he almost certainly had not thought of placing them in Mr. Smith's Personal file. It is therefore with some reluctance that I have to send them to you ex post facto without my predecessor's knowledge and in the context of current developments about which he knows nothing. Rather than seeming to attempt to document a 'case,' I would much prefer to treat the subject of our talk within its current context."[34]

On December 3, Henderson suggested to Parsons the possibility of sending Smith to Sydney, Australia, as consul general—an obvious demotion from his position as ambassador. Parsons urged that such an appointment should be to another geographic region, presumably to spare Smith the embarrassment of working with former peers in the area.

In December 1959 officials in Washington sought to restore unity in the US mission in Vientiane by sending a joint State Department–CIA telegram that still remains classified. At the very least, it seems likely that the cable reaffirmed to the embassy and the CIA station the ambassador's role both as the leader of the country team and the sole spokesman for US policy. Whatever their views of Smith's leadership ability, senior State Department officials opposed any "dichotomy" in US policy or agency actions that undermined an ambassador's authority.

On December 15, Smith replied to the joint State Department–CIA message with a long top-secret, "eyes only" letter to Parsons, writing that he was "greatly relieved" to learn that top officials in Washington were "deeply disturbed by the continuing evidence of a CDNI-Phoui split." The ambassador also welcomed the department's recognition "that the

CDNI is actively competing for political power and is assuming the role of an opposition party." Although parts of Smith's letter remain classified, a CIA summary of the document reported the ambassador's claim that his support for Phoui was implementing US policy, "while the Agency and Mr. Hecksher have acted in violation of that policy."[35]

Smith discussed embassy-CIA relations with ICA deputy director Saccio, who traveled to Laos in mid-December with John O. "Jack" Bell, a Dillon deputy for coordinating economic and security foreign aid. A lawyer and a political appointee, Saccio later recalled a meeting with Smith and Tobler that he found "very disturbing." The two men said "Laos was finished," presumably referring to the system of noncommunist government supported by the United States. Moreover, "the CIA was running" the American effort in Laos, and neither the ambassador nor the USOM director knew "what the hell was going on." Smith and Tobler appeared to be "in a state of almost panic," according to Saccio. He and Bell, who also attended the meeting, declared that the United States was committed to preserving the independence of Laos. "Jack, as the policy man, you know, laid it on," Saccio recalled. "And we left the room, shook our heads, and said, 'My gosh. These fellows are absolutely scared.'"[36]

The primary purpose of Saccio's visit to Laos was to review the problem-plagued economic aid program. The Washington and Vientiane officials reached an agreement to accelerate road-building, although not on the scale recommended in Embtel 1300. The second major area of agreement was the importance of an integrated economic assistance program for villagers, including the tribal minorities, which was critical to improving political stability and military security in Laos. USOM, CIA, and PEO each provided supplies and commodities to rural areas, but Saccio and Bell reported that there was little agreement on methods to accomplish US objectives and "a seeming lack of coordinated effort in which each U.S. agency is clear as to its job and how it fits with what other agencies are doing."[37]

On December 17, two days after Saccio and Bell left Vientiane, Ambassador Smith wrote another top-secret, "eyes only" letter to Parsons, charging Hecksher with insubordination and lying to the ambassador. The specific incident involved Phoui's nemesis Foreign Affairs Minister Khamphan Panya, who had been favored by Savang and who had served in local or national Lao government for his entire career. He was the CDNI leader whom Phoui and Smith considered the most arrogant and difficult member of the cabinet. In early December, Phoui decided to shift Khamphan to a less significant cabinet post and to assume personal control of the foreign affairs portfolio.

Khamphan wrote a letter of resignation, but Henry Hecksher, "without consulting the ambassador, prevailed upon Khamphan not to resign and upon the CDNI leaders to maintain solidarity against the Prime Minister," DCM John Holt later wrote to the State Department. "The result was that contrary to U.S. wishes, they pulled out of the Cabinet as a group, weakening instead of strengthening it at the critical moment."[38] According to a CIA inquiry into the incident, Hecksher indicated to Smith and two other embassy officials that he had persuaded Khamphan not to resign. After Hecksher discovered that Ambassador Smith considered his action a violation of US policy, the station chief flatly denied exercising any influence on the foreign minister's decision.

Smith seized upon this incident as concrete proof of Hecksher's "duplicity and untrustworthiness." The Department of State took these charges very seriously. In a memorandum otherwise sharply critical of Smith, Parsons's deputy, John M. Steeves, wrote: "I think we can agree with him [Smith] that we cannot and do not condone the manner in which Hecksher seemingly took matters into his own hands." Parsons wanted Allen Dulles to look into the matter further.[39]

Dulles and Richard Bissell, CIA's deputy director of plans (operations), selected Daniel DeBardeleben, the agency's chief of Operational Services, to conduct a thorough investigation of Smith's charges. During his inquiry, DeBardeleben reviewed the records of the CIA's Far East Division and a "White Paper" on the dispute prepared by its staff. He interviewed the division's chief, Desmond FitzGerald, as well as Henry Hecksher, who wrote up his version of events. DeBardeleben also traveled to Vientiane to provide Ambassador Smith with an opportunity for expanding on his charges and to discuss the matter with members of the CIA station. In a memorandum to Bissell, DeBardeleben concluded that the agency's support for the "CDNI was approved by the Department of State but was contrary to the plans and wishes of Ambassador Smith." This put the agency and Hecksher in an untenable position. The State Department contributed to the problem, according to DeBardeleben, by "not specifically instruct[ing] Ambassador Smith to modify his program to conform with the steps that were advocated by the Agency and approved by the Department."[40]

In discussing his interview with Smith, DeBardeleben wrote that the ambassador "appeared to be ill at ease" and "had some difficulty putting his thoughts into words." Repeating certain statements, with only slight variations in language, Smith charged that Hecksher "had not kept him informed of what the Station was doing in political action." Whenever the CIA in Laos engaged in such activities, Smith said, "it should be consistent with policy as interpreted by him." Put simply, Hecksher "should have kept him informed in detail and accepted his guidance" to avoid any conflict. On one hand, DeBardeleben did conclude that "Ambassador Smith was not kept as fully informed of action taken by the Station as an ambassador should usually be." On the other hand, his investigation revealed that some of Smith's charges were "really a question of his word against Hecksher's." It also seemed to DeBardeleben that the ambassador's two letters to Parsons "manifest a pettiness and vindictiveness which indicate that he would be a most difficult person with whom to work."[41]

But what about the Khamphan Panya incident? Did Hecksher discourage the foreign minister from resigning? DeBardeleben volunteered a "deduction" that inspires little confidence, if for no other reason than that all of the principals agreed it was a *possible* explanation—one that would resolve an unpleasant interagency conflict. "The key to this riddle," DeBardeleben suggested, was Hecksher's belief that Khamphan's resignation would be a "calamity." In addition, the station chief assumed that Khamphan's decision not to resign would please the ambassador because a political crisis had been avoided.[42]

DeBardeleben was "inclined to believe" that Hecksher "consciously exaggerated his influence on this event, thus claiming more credit" than he deserved. "This misrepresentation was not entirely honest but it was human and somewhat supportable since Hecksher felt a responsibility for Khamphan," DeBardeleben wrote. When the station chief learned, "to his surprise," that Ambassador Smith did not agree that Khamphan's withdrawing "his resignation was a good thing," Hecksher "truthfully disclaimed responsibility for the event."[43]

The ugly dispute between Smith and Hecksher ended in late December 1959, when Hecksher was recalled to CIA headquarters a few months before his scheduled rotation to another assignment. Deputy Chief of Sta tion Gerald "Jerry" Steiner became the acting chief in Vientiane, and, for a few months, the ambassador judged that the CIA was performing well. This brief honeymoon ended when Smith submitted new complaints related to the CIA's political action activities. "It appears most probable that any Chief of Station serving under Ambassador Smith would find it difficult to deal with the Ambassador and would be criticized by Mr. Smith regardless of how honestly our representatives tried to cooperate," DeBardeleben concluded. "Ambassador Smith wants to run the show but how he runs it is subject to unpredictable and often surprising changes of direction."[44]

After the mass resignations of CDNI members from his cabinet, and because he was unable to reach agreement with them on the composition of a new one, Phoui formed an all-LHL government on December 15—ten days before the scheduled expiration of the National Assembly's term. A special session of the assembly enacted legislation postponing the general election until late 1960 and extending the terms of the incumbent deputies. Although the Lao constitution empowered the National Assembly to interpret that document, the CDNI claimed that the legislature was acting unconstitutionally.

On December 19 the Department of State requested Ambassador Smith's "best personal judgment" of likely reactions to Phoui's new government. Although the department authorized Smith to consult with his immediate embassy staff, he was to "give no hint" to members of the US mission, and particularly their Laotian contacts, that such an assessment was under way. Among the key questions posed to Smith: Was it not likely that the CDNI might soon retaliate against an all-LHL cabinet with some form of coup? Did the king's calm approval of a cabinet composed largely of deputies he "despises" indicate plans to remove them in the near future? Perhaps the question that revealed the most about Washington's attitude was, "In view [of the] fact [that the] CDNI and FAL contain elements of future strength we cannot and should not disregard, do you believe our best role may be to stand discreetly aloof and let nature take [its] course in order [to] preserve our influence and freedom of action?"[45]

Ambassador Smith replied promptly. He thought a CDNI coup was possible but unlikely. He viewed the king's placid acceptance of the new cabinet as "frank recognition" of Phoui's right to change his government.

And he did not want the US government to "stand aloof and 'and let nature take its course' in a coup." In fact, the ambassador sought specific authority to inform the army, the CDNI, and the king that any attempt to overthrow the legally constituted government of Laos would prompt an "immediate drastic reconsideration" of US support for the country.[46]

The ambassador received no such authorization from Washington. What Smith did receive was a December 21 response of less than fifty words, classified top secret, with "no distribution outside [the] department." Thanking Smith for his prompt reply, Deputy Assistant Secretary of State John M. Steeves informed the ambassador: "Seems we have gone as far as we can with prudence without seeming to 'Mother' Lao domestic affairs." Further comments, Steeves wrote, would follow. The following day Smith cabled that he concurred fully with his latest instructions but felt it "prudent to be in a position to discourage authoritatively [an] army coup" if it became necessary. He also noted that there were currently no indications of a coup d'état.[47]

Three hours later, however, Smith sent another telegram to the State Department reporting that the CDNI and the army planned a coup. Earlier that day, Brigadier General Ouan Ratrikoun, commander of the FAL, had informed PEO chief Heintges of his plan to tell Phoui that he and his government must go to the royal capital and resign on December 26. If the prime minister attempted to extend the term of his government, there would be a "bloodless" coup—perhaps by a walkout of government employees or "direct action" by the CDNI and army to take over government premises. General Ouan, who had generally been candid with Heintges, said he was certain the king would insist that Phoui form a new government. What the CDNI would demand were seven specific ministries out of fourteen in the new cabinet. In his report of Heintges's meeting with Ouan, Ambassador Smith sought authorization to notify leaders of the CDNI and FAL of US opposition to a coup. If such authority were not granted, Smith wrote, the State Department's guidance was "most urgently sought."[48]

State Department officials reacted to Smith's latest report by noting that the planned coup confirmed their earlier analysis that the CDNI and FAL, "probably with [the] King's active encouragement," would not allow Phoui's government to continue beyond December 25. In a striking departure from past directives about influencing politics in the kingdom, the department informed Smith of its increasing concern about "becoming involved ever more deeply [in] internal Lao affairs." This new stated willingness to "step aside and permit [the] Lao to work out [a] new relationship among themselves" seemed disingenuous to embassy officials in Vientiane. A "decision not to intervene," Smith later wrote, proved "to be the most drastic form of intervention."[49]

Perhaps because of their loss of confidence in Smith, State Department officials seemed incapable of simply telling the ambassador that since there appeared to be irreconcilable differences between Phoui and the LHL, on the one hand, and the CDNI, the army, and the king, on the other, the best interests of the US government would seem to be better served by the latter group. Therefore, he must neither warn Phoui of any impending coup nor discourage the CDNI from attempting one. Instead, the department pointedly declared that Phoui must share the responsibility for the political divisions in Laos. The planned coup, according to the ambassador's instructions, might even help the kingdom achieve a "degree of unity [among] anti-communist elements," a political test that Phoui had "failed." How a coup d'état could promote political unity was not explained in the telegram.[50]

On December 23, 1959, Acting Secretary Dillon, CIA chief Dulles, and Assistant Secretary Parsons went to the White House to brief the president on "a fast-moving situation [that] might lead to a coup d'état." Dillon began the discussion by summarizing developments in Laos since Phoui had been elected prime minister in August 1958. Dillon spoke about his achievements and the friction between the older politicians and the CDNI and the army. "In this dispute," according to notes prepared for Dillon for this meeting, "the King has always sided with the CDNI and the Army and has been most critical of the [LHL]."[51]

The rift between the two groups, Dillon said, had grown more serious over the recent formation of an all-LHL government, the interpretation of the Lao constitution, and the extension of terms of National Assembly deputies until the next election, scheduled for April 1960. He told the president that the US government had information indicating that the CDNI and the army would present Phoui with an ultimatum to resign on December 26. If he did not, the army would take the necessary action. The king would support a coup, US officials believed, and it would probably not "result in bloodshed."

President Eisenhower commented that it seemed desirable to get Phoui's reaction to the ultimatum as soon as possible. Dillon replied that the State Department "expected to get further word" that same day. The president asked whether the king could move up the date for elections, resolving the basic conflict between the young and the old. There was little support for this idea among Eisenhower's advisers: there would be practical difficulties with advancing the election date, said Dillon; the dangerous situation in the countryside currently made the Lao shy about voting, said Parsons; and the CDNI and the army would not want Phoui's government "to count the votes," said Dulles. The director of Central Intelligence added that he was not "happy" about the idea of elections when the anticommunist politicians were divided.[52]

Dillon told the president, "Faced with this delicate internal situation we had thought it best not to intervene but rather to stand aside and let the Lao work out their own relationships." The US government would, however, use its influence to avoid violence and any action that might provoke outside intervention. This seemed sensible to Eisenhower, who "approved the line we had been following," according to minutes prepared by Parsons.

After Dulles and Parsons left the meeting, Dillon met with just the president and Brigadier General Andrew J. Goodpaster, his military and intelligence coordinator. Dillon informed Eisenhower of the difficulties the State Department was having with Ambassador Smith, who was close to Phoui but "had no contact with the King and the Army." The next line in Goodpaster's minutes of this meeting remains classified, but it likely refers to Smith's difficulties with Hecksher. Dillon said if there were a change of government in Vientiane, Smith would be recalled for consultations with the State Department. "We would probably recommend that he not go back," he said. Eisenhower approved this action, observing: "We should not be too slow about removing the Ambassador if we think he should be pulled out." Dillon, damning Smith with the faintest of praise, said, "The ambassador has not done a poor job. He is a reasonably average man but is very tired."[53]

Unaware that the president of the United States had just approved his recall, Ambassador Smith continued to urge support for Phoui and opposition to any effort by the CDNI, the army, and the king "to achieve by threat [of] force what they have been unable to accomplish by legitimate

its threatening actions, the prime minister "began to sleep in a different place every night to avoid assassination," Smith wrote in his monograph.[59]

The rumors sweeping Vientiane included a plot by Phoui and South Vietnamese agents to overthrow the Laotian monarchy and establish a republic. The man behind this particular falsehood, the prime minister believed, was General Phoumi. Should King Savang credit this allegation, Laos would likely distance itself further from South Vietnamese President Diem, whom Savang disliked, and move closer to Thailand's Marshal Sarit Thanarat, a cousin once removed of Phoumi's. The Lao general called Sarit "uncle" out of respect and received substantial financial and moral support from the Thai leader, who had seized power with his own coup d'état in 1958. Sarit believed firmly that the military should direct political affairs in less developed countries—particularly in neighboring Laos.

During the year-end political standoff, Prime Minister Phoui and Ambassador Smith found it difficult to overcome palace barriers to meeting with the king. General Phoumi, however, appeared to have free access to the royal residence in Vientiane. In a transparent reference to the CIA, Phoui commented to an American embassy official that it was "unfortunate" that in 1958 US authorities "other than [the] ambassador" had insisted on Phoumi's recall from the French war college to participate in government. On December 27, Phoui finally arranged to see the king, who claimed that he had expected to hear from the prime minister sooner and said that he had no knowledge of any coup plotting. When Phoui mentioned that the American ambassador had also been seeking an audience, the king wondered aloud why *he* had to meet with Smith. The ambassador's instructions came from the US secretary of state, Savang said. Shouldn't Smith meet with the Laotian foreign minister instead of the king? In a subsequent meeting with Phoui, Savang ordered that any messages to him from Secretary of State Herter should be transmitted through the Laotian prime minister or foreign minister.[60]

The key issue between Phoui and the king was not whether the prime minister would relinquish his position—by now, that was a forgone conclusion. The more important question for the two men was which one of them would bear public responsibility for an extraconstitutional change in government. The prime minister proposed that Savang simply issue a royal ordinance dissolving the National Assembly, paving the way for the provisional government that he and the CDNI so clearly desired. The king resisted such a crass political maneuver. It would compromise the status of the monarchy, he believed, reducing it to just another power group in Laos and increasing his vulnerability to the country's political infighting. What Savang wanted was for the prime minister and the National Assembly to sign a document admitting their "erroneous" interpretation of the constitution, declaring actions approved by the special session of the legislature illegal, and apologizing to the nation for their mistakes. The king would then restore order to the country by appointing a provisional government, which would include several CDNI members. An alternative equally acceptable to the monarch was the resignation of all members of Phoui's government because of fear for their "physical safety as a result of military pressure."[61]

The prime minister, his cabinet, and the National Assembly were unwilling to follow either of the king's proposed courses of action. To Smith, the king's attitude seemed "fantastic, unrealistic" and his proposals an "unprecedented humbling of LHL deputies to royal whim."[62] An unexpected plot twist in the unfolding drama occurred on December 29, when former prime minister Katay died suddenly from embolism. The death of this crooked but influential LHL politician—particularly in southern Laos, a region that was General Phoumi's sole source of political support—ended any possibility that the anticommunist factions in Laos would achieve reconciliation.

On December 30 the king requested, and accepted the following day, the resignations of Phoui and his ministers, who had decided that it was no longer possible to conduct the affairs of state. When the prime minister asked the king how he intended to form a new government that was consistent with the constitution, Savang flew into a "towering rage," telling Phoui: "That [is] no concern of yours; it is solely mine." Then, in one of his characteristically cryptic comments, the king said: "Were I to tell you my plans[,] you would say [that] under those conditions you could not resign."[63]

Once Savang accepted the resignations of Phoui and his ministers, the army took over key public buildings in Vientiane and surrounded the residence of the king, ostensibly for his protection. The FAL announced to the public that the military would run the country until the formation of an elected government at some indefinite date in the future. The ruling junta comprised the army's five generals. General Phoumi reportedly received 25 million Lao kip from Uncle Sarit in Thailand and gave 1 million kip to each of the other four generals "to name him as first among them." The military government promptly issued a communiqué that nullified the actions of the National Assembly's special session, specifically the extension of the deputies' mandate beyond December 25.[64]

Stripped of position and power, Phoui met with Ambassador Smith on December 31, pouring out his bitterness. He spoke at length about the "Lao-French conviction that [the] CDNI-military would never have dared [to] execute [a] coup had CDNI-army elements not been encouraged by certain US groups in Laos"—that is, the CIA. Moreover, the CDNI planned to avenge Smith's "dismissal" of Hecksher by having the ambassador removed from Laos once a new CDNI-army government was formed. Smith replied that Hecksher had not been dismissed but had left the country as part of the normal rotation of US personnel. The prime minister said that Phoumi had told the other generals that he had "solemn assurances" from US authorities other than the ambassador— another transparent reference to the CIA—that American aid to Laos would continue no matter what Smith recommended. A top secret State Department review of US-Laos relations reached a similar conclusion in 1962, observing: "It seems clear that Phoumi felt confident that he would ultimately get the backing of the US and this confidence could only have been gathered from the CIA officers with whom he was in contact."[65]

As the army consolidated its power, there were rumors that the junta intended to make radical changes in domestic and foreign policy, turning the kingdom away from its traditional posture of peace, neutrality, and moderation. For example, the military made no secret of its desire for a summary trial and execution of Souphanouvong and the other imprisoned NLHS leaders. Troublesome National Assembly deputies could expect to be jailed. State Department officials, sensitive to the international repercussions of such acts, quickly abandoned their stated new policy of nonintervention in Lao political affairs. They instructed Smith to warn CDNI and FAL leaders that drastic policy changes would produce a "most severe" US reaction and "might well destroy" the basis for American support.[66]

A similar message was communicated to King Savang, who had been surprised by Phoumi's rapid assumption of power and by his apparent intention to hold on to it for more than a brief transitional period. On January 4, 1960, the king had scheduled a meeting with Olivier Gassouin to say farewell to the departing French ambassador. Fifteen minutes before the appointment, Savang invited Ambassador Smith and diplomatic representatives from the United Kingdom and Australia to join the audience. The Western diplomats, who had earlier prepared a joint démarche, reminded the king of the intimate connection between internal affairs in Laos and external support from the United Nations and SEATO. Repressive actions and human rights violations would adversely impact public and parliamentary opinion in the West and among uncommitted countries in the United Nations. Even before the current political crisis ended, Smith urged Savang to reaffirm publicly the kingdom's traditional commitment to peaceful, moderate policies.

The four chiefs of mission asked the king if he would share his views on the status of the generals who claimed responsibility for conducting the business of the Lao government. This question, stripped of its diplomatic embroidery, was both intended and perceived as a sharp protest of the army's unconstitutional seizure of the government. The king replied that the generals had "de facto but illegal control" of his government. With majestic detachment, Savang said the Crown had no part in the dispute between the army and Phoui's government, which was also illegal. He characterized the disagreement as "beneath the Sovereign." By the end of the meeting, however, the Western diplomats had made their point. The king declared his personal commitment to resolving the political crisis, even at the risk of losing his throne. The four diplomats later agreed that the king had been grateful for their advice and counsel but that "the audience would not have been granted had the coup not already taken place."[67]

On January 7 the king appointed a caretaker government that would oversee the April 1960 general elections to establish a more durable, constitutional government. Savang named Kou Abhay prime minister. A sixty-seven-year-old adviser to the monarch, Kou was the president of the King's Council, a consultative body that he had been a member of since 1949. Three of the newly appointed cabinet ministers were members of the CDNI, three were from the LIIL, and four were unaffiliated. The king appointed General Phoumi, the real power in the new cabinet, minister of defense and named Khamphan Panya minister of foreign affairs. There had been talk of Phoui's return as prime minister as a moderating influence on the CDNI "hotheads," but his rift with the king precluded an appointment to any cabinet position. "On [the] whole, [the] Cabinet is able, honest, and one we can work with," the State Department commented to Ambassador Smith. "[The] Prime Minister is not forceful but respected and well liked."[68]

The American embassy in Vientiane had a less optimistic view of the new political order in Laos. The ambassador reported "profound" divisions among the anticommunists, and DCM John Holt wrote to the department: "I am not sanguine that the personal ambition of either Khamphan or Phoumi has been bent in favor of preserving democratic government in Laos."[69]

Decades after Phoui Sananikone's overthrow, Richard Bissell, the CIA deputy director of operations from 1959 to 1962, admitted in his posthumously published memoir that Washington policymakers and his agency had made a mistake in shifting their support from the prime minister to General Phoumi. Candid in describing the CDNI as a "CIA-sponsored political front" (and cryptic when discussing a political "covert operation" in 1958), Bissell remained an unreconstructed cold warrior who neither apologized for political-action programs targeting Souvanna nor considered "pro-Western neutrality" an oxymoron. What Bissell regretted was Washington's failure to recognize that General Phoumi's "staunch anticommunism and pro-Western stance" reflected goals for Laos that were "unobtainable in the context of that nation's politics." Put another way, in a neutrally inclined country, promoting the political career of a military officer primarily because of his strong anticommunist convictions—rather than his competence, honesty, wisdom, or popular support—turned out to be a very bad idea both for Laos and for the United States.

Bissell, a Yale graduate who earned a Ph.D. there, was a brilliant technocrat who shared many of the strengths and limitations of Robert S. McNamara, the secretary of defense under presidents Kennedy and Johnson. Each man possessed an intimidating intellect drawn to abstractions. Bissell's discipline was economics; McNamara's specialty was systems analysis. Both achieved spectacular management success in the production of hardware: Bissell in the development of the U-2 spy plane and other overhead reconnaissance systems, and McNamara in the revival of the moribund Ford Motor Company. Both men's careers were ended by strategically and tactically flawed applications of force to check the spread of communism. In Bissell's case, it was the quick defeat at the Bay of Pigs. For McNamara, it was, of course, the prolonged agony of the Vietnam War.

As with McNamara's belated apology for American policy in Vietnam, Bissell blamed poor decision making in Laos on senior US officials' limited understanding of Southeast Asia. In *Reflections of a Cold Warrior,* Bissell wrote that if he and other responsible officials had "shown more open-mindedness (which is not often compatible with crisis management), the advice and perceptions of experts on Laotian politics, history, and culture might have received more attention." He also believed that the differing perspectives among agencies in Washington and between US- and Lao-based officials were "not helpful to the cause."[70]

Chapter 7

Normal Dishonesty

On Thursday, March 17, 1960, the National Security Council gathered at the White House for its weekly meeting. For President Eisenhower, who highly valued organization and order in managing the complexity of foreign affairs, the NSC was a mechanism for long-range planning and interdepartmental coordination. He viewed the NSC as a critically important advisory body for making recommendations to him and encouraging frank discussion of national security issues. Foreign-policy problems requiring immediate decisions, however, were generally reserved for smaller groups in the Oval Office. Each NSC meeting had specific topics scheduled for discussion, with background papers prepared and circulated to the principals in advance.[1]

On this day Southeast Asia was the main topic of discussion, which began with an extended briefing on developments in the region from Central Intelligence director Allen Dulles. The first country discussed was Laos. Dulles reported that although overt Pathet Lao attacks had been reduced in number and intensity since the previous summer, the insurgents had expanded their influence in the country. The communists, he said, were effectively exploiting the grievances of the tribespeople, who constituted approximately 50 percent of the Lao population. The Pathet Lao no longer controlled completely the two northern provinces, as it did before the November 1957 Vientiane agreement, but it now had pockets of control in all twelve provinces. "Real security exists only in towns, is considerably less in adjacent villages, and is virtually nonexistent in most of the rest of the country," according to a CIA summary prepared for Dulles's NSC briefing.[2]

To illustrate this last point, Dulles told the president and his advisers about the recent experience of a US Information Service team that had attempted to tour the mountain villages of Xieng Khouang, a province in northeast Laos with a large minority population. Although the RLG had assured the USIS team that the area was fully secure, Dulles said, uniformed Pathet Lao forces appeared, interrogated the Americans, and turned them back. The team observed that the insurgents exercised considerable influence over the villagers.

Dulles discussed briefly the election for a new National Assembly, scheduled for April 24, 1960. The conservative politicians, he said, "could be persuaded" to agree on a single slate of candidates, which should prevent a repetition of the 1958 election fiasco. Whether the NLHS intended to participate, boycott, or disrupt the April election was still unknown. No matter what course of action the communists pursued, Dulles warned that the problem in Laos "would continue to be a difficult one for a long time and was not susceptible [to a] quick or easy solution."[3]

The DCI informed the NSC that in Laos the communists preferred to achieve their goals through subversion, guerrilla warfare, and legal means rather than open aggression. Perhaps seeking to end his Laos presentation on an upbeat note, or maybe tossing a bureaucratic bouquet to his colleagues at the Pentagon, Dulles concluded his remarks on Laos with a non sequitur that was not part of his prepared briefing material: "Our military mission in the country was doing an excellent job in combating Communism."

Secretary of State Herter elaborated on this positive theme, reporting that the United Nations planned to send more representatives into Lao villages and to appoint advisers to various departments of government. Herter believed that a partial shift of responsibility to the United Nations in such fields as public health and agriculture would be a favorable development for the US government. According to the minutes of the meeting, Dulles replied to Herter's observation, agreeing that UN representatives "watching over the situation in Laos is important."[4]

After Dulles reported on South Vietnam—"Communist terrorism and guerrilla activity designed to undermine Diem was on the increase"—and each of the other countries of Southeast Asia, he discussed recent developments in South Korea and Cuba.[5] With the intelligence briefing concluded, President Eisenhower raised a straightforward issue that could have stimulated a thoughtful, far-reaching discussion among his most senior advisers: What is the appeal of communism? How many people had been won over by poor living conditions, and how many by the hope of power? Western ideology, he said, seemed incapable of appealing to people in the same way communism did. Virtually none of the underdeveloped countries in the world appeared to be "completely antagonistic" to communism. If the US government could discover why people embrace communism, Eisenhower said, "we could perhaps operate more effectively" against it.

As secretary of state, Herter traditionally offered the initial reply to a presidential question put to the NSC. This day he made the bureaucratically low-risk observation that he agreed with the president, who had identified the two main factors influencing the appeal of communism: a hunger for power among ambitious individuals and the ability of the ideology to tap into people's desire for better living conditions. Admiral Arleigh Burke, the JCS representative, added that there were always a large number of people who were "against everything" and would follow "any aggressive[,] forceful[,] ruthless leader." This was a point of view with which John McCone, chairman of the Atomic Energy Commission (AEC), wished to associate himself. McCone pointed out that during Hitler's years in power, Latin American admirers of the führer's ruthlessness established Nazi enclaves in the region.

Dulles said he "believed that nationalism played a part in the growth of communism." President Eisenhower disagreed. Nationalism, he declared, was not compatible with communism. "Communists would always bow to Moscow," he said. The president then cited the example of the communist coup in Czechoslovakia, wondering aloud to his advisers how often Czech "nationalism could find expression now?"[6]

Eisenhower's belief in the mutual exclusivity of nationalism and communism and in the communist monolith were conceptual barriers to developing more effective means of combating insurgency in Southeast Asia. The European frame of reference of the president and his senior advisers was an obstacle to a more nuanced understanding of anticolonial fervor in the developing world and its implications. And the perception of communism as a worldwide conspiracy micromanaged from Moscow was a point of view that required little knowledge of the history, people, and politics of the area and great faith in the "falling domino principle," which Eisenhower had first mentioned at an April 1954 press conference in response to a question about the strategic importance of Indochina.

Although the late John Foster Dulles had been an adherent of the domino principle, one wonders how he would have responded to Eisenhower's question about the appeal of communism had he lived long enough to complete his full term as secretary of state? Dulles had been as ardent an anticommunist as any member of Eisenhower's NSC, but he was also a particularly well-informed official, with a deep interest in Indochina and an ability to reexamine his own views. At the very least, it seems likely that Dulles would have offered the president something more substantial than the thin gruel provided by his advisers at this NSC meeting.

The upcoming April 1960 Lao election was a source of anxiety for many US officials, whose worst fear was a debacle similar to the one in 1958. Although Operation Booster Shot could hardly be blamed for the poor results in the earlier election, the 1960 contest was not going to feature a similar crash program of US rural aid. The operation had been discredited in the eyes of many officials, including USOM director John Tobler, who dismissed civic action as a CIA effort "to train political experts." Tobler informed ICA's Leonard Saccio that he would "strongly resist any instruction" to participate in a preelection operation similar to Booster Shot. The USOM director also reported that Acting CIA Chief of Station Jerry Steiner shared his view of that operation, calling it "a dismal failure." Even Ambassador Smith, who was still chief of mission in Vientiane because the State Department did not want the CDNI to assume for a moment that it could influence the length of an American ambassador's appointment, had concluded: "This type of activity is counter-productive."[7]

The provisional RLG, however, sought to strengthen the chances of conservative candidates in the 1960 election with a controversial FAL military operation, called Clean Up. Primarily targeting the three southernmost provinces, Clean Up employed some five thousand FAL troops and Auto Defense forces in military sweeps designed to destroy or capture Pathet Lao forces. After the initial military phase, six-man rural security teams and other officials would then establish self-help, propaganda, and other programs to complete the pacification effort in specific areas. PEO chief Heintges was an enthusiastic supporter of Clean Up, which he considered a well-devised plan demonstrating Lao initiative: "I feel it is mandatory that the U.S. provide the full measure of support required."[8]

The civilian members of the US mission were skeptical, however; the operation was essentially regional, chiefly affecting only one-quarter of the kingdom's provinces. Funding for Clean Up was another problem. For a country with the highest per capita US aid in the world, it seemed inexcusable to embassy and USOM officials that the costs of the FAL operation were neither estimated nor submitted in advance to the US government. Even though—or, more likely, because—the United States paid 100 percent of the military budget, the defense ministry had never learned "to live within established levels of expenditure."[9]

Finally, there were civilian concerns about the efficacy of intermittent military "sweeps" and the staying power of the government in remote villages. Based on embassy contacts with the RLG, Operation Clean Up appeared to be an "almost purely military show," without the essential follow-up civilian services and administration. As experience had shown, episodic, short-term military operations sometimes made rural villages more vulnerable to Pathet Lao reprisals. If Operation Clean Up were unable to establish a lasting government presence in the villages, DCM Holt warned, "the broom will be sweeping into [the] wind and [the] litter will be blown back."[10]

Although FAL military operations aimed at influencing the elections were of questionable utility, the political efforts of the RLG and the US government appeared more promising. As in the 1955 general election and the 1958 supplementary election, a key concern was the ability of the kingdom's anticommunist politicians to "rise above narrow factionalism in a time of crisis," in Parsons's words. To promote unity, the US mission in Vientiane once again offered encouragement and covert financial support to conservative candidates, which this time produced a single list of government candidates for most electoral districts. The gerrymandering of these districts by the RLG also increased the likelihood of a substantial conservative victory.[11]

In the weeks preceding the 1960 election, French officials were relieved to discover only the "normal dishonesty" in Lao politics. They hoped that the CDNI and the army would limit their electoral interference "to traditional bribery"—that is, granting gifts and favors to villagers to win their support and other nonviolent types of voter influence practiced by most

Laotian candidates. What disturbed the French were reports that five of General Phoumi's relatives were running for office in the province of Savannakhet and that Thailand's Marshal Sarit had provided the money to bribe other candidates to withdraw. The US embassy in Paris informed the State Department of the French hope that Souvanna Phouma, who was returning to electoral politics and running for a safe seat in Luang Prabang, would be the next prime minister. These same French officials, the embassy reported, "shudder" at the idea of General Phoumi or Foreign Minister Khamphan Panya leading the RLG.[12]

One week before the election, the CIA station in Vientiane reported that conservative candidates appeared to be "assured of a clear victory" in a minimum of forty-two of the fifty-nine contested National Assembly seats. The government that would emerge from this victory was harder to predict. The most likely candidates for prime minister were General Phoumi, who appeared to have the support of the CDNI and the army, and Prince Somsanith Vongkotrattana, a member of the royal family whom the CIA described as "not a particularly able executive or a strong leader." Somsanith was, however, liked and trusted by most political factions. Both the king and General Phoumi were opposed to a government headed by either Souvanna Phouma or Phoui Sananikone.[13]

The results of the 1960 election were a crushing defeat for the leftist candidates and a literally incredible victory for the RLG—a win so lopsided that it could only be explained by fraud. The conservative slate won every seat in the National Assembly; leftist candidates won none. In the Pathet Lao strongholds of Sam Neua and Phong Saly, NLHS candidates won less than 5 percent of the vote. When CIA case officer Stuart Methven visited RLG election headquarters and saw the early returns, he angrily left and protested to Major Siho Lamphoutacoul, an intelligence officer and Phoumi loyalist who was in charge of election security. Methven told Siho the election results were a farce. The Lao officer, whom longtime foreign affairs official William P. Bundy later characterized as "a real thug and very bad news," seemed pleased with the results and apparently thought that Methven would be, too. As the CIA operative was leaving, Siho inquired about the date of his birth, which was September 3, 1927. When Methven returned to election headquarters, he observed that the NLHS candidate in Khammouane Province had made an unexpectedly strong showing with a number of votes that matched exactly the

CIA officer's birthday in the European system of abbreviating dates. The candidate's 3,927 votes were not, however, enough to win.[14]

By the time the early returns—and the news stories reporting them—reached Washington, State Department officials were "seriously concerned" that the Lao elections had "been so rigged as to invalidate them in [the] eyes of world opinion." The only way of "salvaging [a] shred" of electoral credibility, the department cabled the embassy, would be a fair count in districts where the returns had not yet been made public. It was, however, too late to change anyone's mind about the legitimacy of the election. Khamphan Panya did little to inspire confidence in its fairness when he blandly observed to Western reporters: "Sometimes the truth appears to be untrue."[15]

The RLG election committee, which included General Phoumi, had rejected the advice of Ambassador Smith and the CIA station to avoid eliminating leftist opposition entirely. A subsequent State Department summary of Phoumi's "Sins and Blunders," reported that the 1960 election included "innumerable examples of intimidation, bribery, illegal voting by proxy, fraudulent counting of ballots in certain districts, etc." Despite the voting irregularities, the US government concluded that election results would have to be accepted by Laotians and the international community. A new election would be expensive and involve a "serious loss of face" for the RLG. Although there was obvious vote rigging in some districts, State Department officials argued that the extent of the fraud across the entire country was "not at all clear." Perhaps the new National Assembly, they suggested to the embassy, could call for elections in certain districts to counter the impression the entire body was "unrepresentative." The more urgent problem for the United States, however, was preventing the formation of a Lao government "dominated by hotheads."[16]

Such a government was the clear goal of General Phoumi and the newly established CDNI political party, which had chosen the Orwellian name Party of Democracy and Social Progress. Phoumi wanted not only to become prime minister but also to exclude Souvanna Phouma and Phoui Sananikone from the cabinet. State Department officials believed that a new Lao government should not appear to be dominated by the army—in other words, neither too many generals in the cabinet nor one serving as either prime minister or deputy prime minister. A broadly representative cabinet, which included such well-known figures as Souvanna and Phoui, would help persuade the international community of the government's legitimacy.

The UK and French governments agreed with this advice to Lao leaders and, in fact, wanted to back this recommendation with a threat of cutting off all aid to the kingdom if it was ignored. The UN representative to Laos, Edouard Zellweger, approved of this tough line. Calling the election results "disastrous," Zellweger believed they had allowed the Lao military to obtain objectives of a coup d'état, with the appearance of legality. US policymakers, however, were not prepared to issue such an ultimatum, if for no other reason than the self-knowledge that they would not likely carry out such a threat.[17]

On May 12, 1960, Ambassador Smith met with King Savang to communicate US views of the desirable characteristics of the next Lao government. As anticipated, the king's reaction was initially one of irritation. His mouth trembling, Savang replied in the polite language of diplomacy, thanking Smith for the support of the US government and its constant interest in Lao affairs. The king did, however, want to point out his deep desire for the United States "to treat [the] Lao as adults" who were capable of judging national events and their international impact in a responsible manner. "We can nevertheless assure [the] U.S. that regardless of its direct interference in [the] national affairs of Laos[,] there would be no military [government] here," he said.[18]

Smith emphasized to Savang that he was not recommending the inclusion of particular individuals in the cabinet, he was merely suggesting that one dominated by the military would provoke an undesirable international reaction. The king, his temper now under control, said he knew that the basic US attitude was one of friendship, otherwise such "intervention" in Lao affairs "would be impossible [to] explain." In an assessment of Lao internal security that was much more optimistic than any US estimate, Savang predicted that within six months it would be possible to travel safely anywhere, even to the most inaccessible provinces. Laos was on the "road to recovery," the king declared. The population, including the tribespeople, felt encouraged by an increasing sense of security, for which the Lao army was largely responsible. For these reasons, Savang said, Laos would adhere to its anticommunist policies and would keep Souphanouvong and the other NLHS leaders locked up.[19]

The imprisoned NLHS leaders had other ideas. During a rainstorm in the early hours of May 24—almost exactly one year since the embarrassing escape of the Second Pathet Lao Battalion—Souphanouvong and fifteen other NLHS prisoners fled on foot from a jail surrounded by two barbed-wire fences. Eight guards on duty that night disappeared with the prisoners. With assistance from Buddhist monks from a nearby pagoda, the escapees passed through "the forests to a rendezvous with a platoon of thirty-six PL troops north of Vientiane," according to Brown and Zasloff. "Several months later, Souphanouvong reached PL headquarters in Sam Neua by foot, after organizing supporters in several provinces along the way."[20]

The CIA concluded that the escape would "give the Pathet Lao insurgency a strong boost, as well as constitute a serious loss of face for the Laotian Government." On May 24 General Phoumi seemed to US officials visibly disturbed and agitated by a "dressing down" he had received from the king for the army's failure to ensure the prisoners' captivity. The Lao general observed that the "escape was a most unfortunate break for the government." At an NSC meeting that same day, Allen Dulles reported to the president and his senior advisers that the escape "would probably be the signal for increased anti-government activity by the Communists and their sympathizers."[21]

The ultimate responsibility for the escape of Souphanouvong and the other NLHS prisoners was never clearly established. Moderate RLG officials, including Kou Abhay and Somsanith, were embarrassed by the confinement of the NLHS leaders, who were unlikely to be convicted in a court of law for attempting to overthrow the government. However, the rigged election results probably indicated to the Pathet Lao that a fair trial for the treason charges was highly unlikely. "It has never been conclusively proven whether the prisoners were allowed to escape by the RLG or whether the escape was purely a machination of the [NLHS]," State Department officials later observed.[22]

Despite clearly indicating to all Lao officials its disapproval of a military-led cabinet, the United States faced the likely prospect that General Phoumi would be selected to form a new government and serve as prime minister. The CDNI had chosen him to be the head of its new political party, and the king had asked Phoumi to evaluate the possibility of forming a new government. To help answer that question, the general

(*Above*) President Dwight D. Eisenhower at a May 1956 press conference. (National Archives and Records Administration)
(*Below*) A French officer addressing a Laotian NCO in 1954. (U.S. Army Military History Institute)

(*Above*) Secretary of State John Foster Dulles making a statement to the press at the 1954 Manila conference establishing SEATO. (National Archives and Records Administration)
(*Below*) Hauling teak in Laos, "the land of a million elephants." (Joel M. Halpern Laotian Slide Collection, University of Wisconsin)

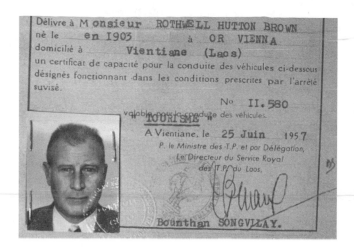

(*Above*) The Laotian driver's license of Rothwell H. Brown, the first chief of the Programs Evaluation Office (PEO), the semicovert U.S. military assistance effort. (U.S. Army Military History Institute)

(*Below*) President Eisenhower meeting with Prime Minister Souvanna Phouma in January 1958. Back row, left to right: Ambassador J. Graham Parsons; Tiao Souk, minister of public works; Leuam Insisiengmay, minister of finance; Ngon Sananikone, minister of national defense; Ouret Souvannavong, ambassador to the United States; and Assistant Secretary of State Robertson. (Dwight D. Eisenhower Library)

Allen W. Dulles, director of Central Intelligence and the brother of the secretary of state. (National Archives and Records Administration)

Laotian Foreign Minister Phoui Sananikone with U.S. Minister Charles W. Yost, John Foster Dulles, and Janet Dulles on the steel-plank airstrip outside of Vientianc. (Charles W. Yost Papers, Princeton University Library)

A Lao military camp with uniforms drying on a fence. (Joel M. Halpern Collection, University of Wisconsin)

(*Above*) Yost and Prime Minister Katay Don Sasorith in July 1955. (Charles W. Yost Papers, Princeton University Library)
(*Below*) Assistant Secretary of State Walter S. Robertson at the United Nations, opposing the admission of the People's Republic of China to the world body. (National Archives and Records Administration)

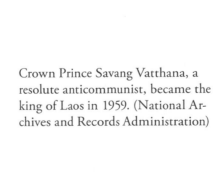

Crown Prince Savang Vatthana, a resolute anticommunist, became the king of Laos in 1959. (National Archives and Records Administration)

Prince Souphanouvong, the half-brother of Prime Minister Souvanna Phouma and the public face of the Pathet Lao leadership. (National Archives and Records Administration)

Lao paratroopers in Luang Prabang. (Joel M. Halpern Laotian Slide Collection, University of Wisconsin)

Horace H. Smith, American ambassador to Laos, 1958–1960. (National Archives and Records Administration)

Hmong hunters posing with their muskets. (Joel M. Halpern Laotian
Slide Collection, University of Wisconsin)

J. Graham Parsons, the Eisenhower administration official
most closely identified with
Laos, served as assistant secretary of state for far eastern
affairs from 1959 until 1961.
(J. Graham Parsons Papers,
Georgetown University Special
Collections)

Brigadier General John A.
Heintges, chief of the PEO,
1959–1960. (National Archives
and Records Administration)

Pathet Lao forces in 1959. (Library of Congress)

A Lao general pointing out terrain features to a UN fact-finding team in October 1959. (National Archives and Records Administration)

With Undersecretary of State Livingston T. Merchant looking on, Winthrop G. Brown is sworn in as American ambassador to Laos. (National Archives and Records Administration)

General Phoumi Nosavan.
(Getty Images)

The formal investiture of the Boun Oum–Phoumi Nosavan government at Sisaket
Wat in January 1961. (National Archives and Records Administration)

Admiral Harry D. Felt, commander-in-chief of U.S. forces in the Pacific, 1958–1964. (National Archives and Record Administration)

Secretary of State–designate Dean Rusk, Secretary of State Christian A. Herter, President-elect John F. Kennedy, and President Eisenhower on January 19, 1961. (John F. Kennedy Library)

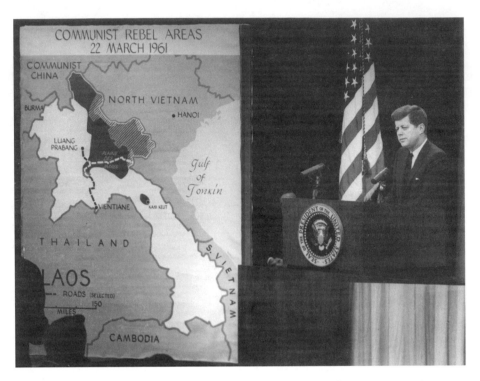

President Kennedy discussing the crisis in Laos at a press conference on March 23, 1961. (John F. Kennedy Library)

requested a "precise redefinition" from the US government of its
toward his leadership of the RLG.[23]

On May 29, 1960, Ambassador Smith delivered to Phot
State Department's precisely scripted reply, which warned the
against overreaching politically. Smith's first substantive point v
the security situation in Laos was unsatisfactory. From every pa:
country, the US government had received reports of skirmishes
ism, and propaganda involving the Pathet Lao. Although the F
improved over the past year, US officials continued to hear abou
arm military tactics that were "deeply resented by the village
humanitarian efforts of the army's six-man rural security teams w
a sufficient answer to this problem," Smith said. The FAL as
needed to "develop a sense of responsibility" for the well-bein
rural population.[24]

Complicating the security problem in Laos was the damage
on the kingdom's reputation by the recent election, Smith sai
next Lao government appeared to be led or dominated by the F
communists "might intensify their armed insurgency." The excl
all NLHS and leftist deputies in the National Assembly had p
them from carrying out legal political activities and deprived L:
safety valve" for their dissent. The escape of the NLHS leaders l
exacerbated matters.

Reaching the central point of his message to Phoumi, Smith
the long-held US desire for a united front of anticommunist pc
The interests of Laos, he said, would best be served "by the forma
predominantly civilian government composed of all these elemen
a government "could be most effective in obtaining the service
men among the older leaders whose experience should not be lo
nation." Officials from the United Kingdom, France, Australia,
United Nations shared this point of view and had "expressed conc
the situation."

Should responsible Laotian officials ignore this advice, tha
course, their own affair, Smith said. But the US government c
predict the effect of such a position on the friends of Laos and tl
ingness to support the country—an unsubtle reference to the p
that Western allies would withdraw their military and econon
tance if Phoumi became prime minister. Smith reassured the gen

the US position was not personal. This was something the ambassador would be instructed to tell any Lao leader.[25]

The US message to Phoumi—and the indirect one to the king and others—was partially effective. On June 3 Prince Somsanith was presented to the National Assembly as the king's designated candidate for prime minister, and his proposed government received overwhelming support from the legislature. General Phoumi was minister of defense and Khamphan Panya minister of foreign affairs, but neither Souvanna nor Phoui were appointed to cabinet positions.

The American embassy reported that Somsanith was "clearly handpicked by Phoumi in advance and must thereby suffer at least initially from suspicion [that] he [is] considered [a] front man to be manipulated by Phoumi." One modestly encouraging sign was the selection of Hmong leader Touby Lyfoung as secretary of state for information and social welfare, a political appointment that suggested greater RLG interest in the needs of the kingdom's minorities. In their overall assessment of the new government, US embassy officials concluded that the cabinet would be less likely to seek counsel from them or any other outside group, would "welcome it less when volunteered, and [would] be less responsive to such guidance after it [was] received."[26]

The Western country least likely to influence the new Lao government was France. Souvanna had often agreed with the views of the French, Phoui had tolerated them, and Phoumi and his followers detested them. Yet at almost the exact moment when the Somsanith government assumed power, Etienne M. Manac'h, the director of Asian affairs for the French Foreign Ministry, visited the US State Department to announce his country's intention to resume full responsibility for military training in Laos. On June 2, 1960, he told Assistant Secretary Parsons and his subordinates that President de Gaulle had recently taken a direct personal interest in Indochinese affairs. Manac'h reminded Parsons that the Geneva Accords explicitly recognized France's military training role in Laos. He added that French training would be less provocative to the communists than the current arrangement.[27]

American, French, and Lao officials in Vientiane had discussed the withdrawal of US training teams the previous March. The US government had a clear commitment to complete its training by September 1, 1960, but

deteriorating security in the country and other factors had thwarted this ambitious goal. Ambassador Smith and PEO chief Heintges proposed an extension of the US program until June 30, 1961, a recommendation with which CINCPAC and the Pentagon concurred. The State Department, attempting to demonstrate "good faith" while abrogating an agreement, proposed the new withdrawal date to the French government.[28]

The delayed, unwelcome response from Manac'h surprised US officials. Parsons told the French diplomat that the cooperation in training between their countries had been excellent. And hadn't the legal difficulty with the Geneva Accords been resolved by the May 1959 Franco-American training agreement? Speaking on behalf of his Pentagon colleagues, Parsons reported their belief that not all of the benefits of the training program had been achieved. He ended his comments by saying that he would immediately discuss the French proposal with his government but could not provide even an interim reply in the immediate future.[29]

US military officials were horrified by the French training proposal. On June 7, 1960, PEO chief Heintges, the architect of the US-French program, warned his superiors at CINCPAC and the Pentagon that removing US training teams "could well result in disaster" in Southeast Asia. Suspecting French intentions to eliminate American trainers ever since the recall of General d'Arrivere, Heintges observed that the FAL, though greatly improved, was still inadequately trained in weapons, communications, logistics, and medical procedures. The FAL "training in anti-guerrilla and anti-terrorist tactics [is] especially inadequate," he wrote. Heintges declared that it was not possible to forecast accurately when the training mission would be completed, and he had "grave doubts as to whether the Lao would accept a purely French training mission if the Americans withdrew from this field."[30]

The following day Admiral Felt, commander of US forces in the Pacific, sent an equally harsh appraisal of the French training proposal to his superiors in the Department of Defense. In his view, the plan was "obviously unrealistic"; the French military's "lack of success" in Indochina hardly recommended an exclusive training role for the FMM; and the division of US logistic support and French tactical training was "clearly unworkable." The withdrawal of US training teams, Felt warned, would cause the FAL to revert quickly to a "low state [of] combat readiness at [a] particularly critical time."[31]

Officials in the French Foreign Ministry, however, would not budge, insisting on US adherence to the previous year's agreement. State Department officials were "embarrassed" by the unambiguous US commitment to finish FAL training no later than September 1, 1960, then withdraw the Special Forces teams. Appeals by the US government to extend the deadline by at least four months to January 1, 1961—"by which time we would hope [the] main objectives of [the] program would be attained"— fell on deaf ears at the Quai d'Orsay. On June 30, 1960, the French ambassador to the United States, Herve Alphand, confirmed to Secretary of State Herter that the withdrawal of US military trainers "should take place by September 1."[32]

The training dispute with the French was part of an overall discussion of US policy in Southeast Asia at the July 21, 1960, NSC meeting. Herter said that the French had agreed to increase their training mission in Laos but had not done so yet. The State Department was attempting to negotiate a more gradual phase-out of US trainers until the size of the French mission matched the American program. Allen Dulles observed that the French position did "not accord with Laotian Government views. The Laotians want the French out and the U.S. in." Dulles added that "the resolution" of the training "problem may be the key to developments in Laos."[33]

The jurisdictional disagreement between US and French officials tended to mask a more fundamental problem within the FAL: the military incompetence of most officers and their unwillingness to remedy this deficiency. Predominantly political appointees, Lao officers believed that military rank was a measure of status and ability and that participation in training would cause a loss of face. FAL field-grade officers were reluctant to take advice from lower ranking, but far more experienced, US Army captains and lieutenants. "We were teaching too many subordinates over there when we should have been teaching the superiors," said one Special Forces trainer. Another wrote of the futility of training Laotian enlisted men because the "lack of technical knowledge" among FAL officers negated instruction in US weapons and tactics.[34]

Although some Hotfoot teams, as well as subsequent White Star Special Forces detachments,* resolved such problems through indirection

---

* In April 1961, when the PEO was converted to an overt, uniformed MAAG, Hotfoot was renamed White Star.

and circumlocution with their counterparts, profound cultural barriers between the US and Lao military remained. Highly motivated Special Forces officers and NCOs, all volunteers committed to repulsing the communist threat, often had difficulty comprehending the lack of aggressiveness among FAL soldiers, many of whom had enlisted because of relatively high military pay. According to a US Army-sponsored study of cross-cultural problems encountered by Special Forces in Laos, many freshly recruited Laotian soldiers had "no understanding of the nature of the struggle going on in their country. Some were even unaware of the existence of Laos as a country. Their identification was with their family, their tribe, or their village, not with their army or their country. They were not particularly interested in fighting anyone and therefore had no particular motivation to learn how to fight."[35]

US military policy also contributed to the problem of training the FAL. Hotfoot and White Star teams rotated out of Laos after six months. One reason for the relatively short tours was the hardship of living in the jungle. Another was a military desire to maximize the number of Special Forces who received operational experience in Southeast Asia. As with the Vietnam War practice of rotating US Army officers from command to staff positions after six months, these brief tours provided little time for learning about the country and the insurgency, building relationships of mutual confidence with foreign officers and NCOs, and maintaining continuity in training.

In a 1974 oral history for the US Army, PEO chief Heintges, then a retired lieutenant general who had served as deputy commander of US forces in Vietnam in the mid-1960s, praised the "absolutely fantastic" job performed by Special Forces training teams in Laos. His overall assessment of the counterinsurgency effort, however, was less complimentary. Without assigning specific responsibility, Heintges observed that upon his arrival in the kingdom, "Laos was all loused up, and when I left, it was still loused up. As far as I can see, it's still loused up."[36]

Horace Smith's term as American Ambassador to Laos ended in June 1960. He officially learned of his recall directly from Assistant Secretary Parsons at the State Department's Far Eastern Chiefs of Mission Conference, held in the Philippines the previous March. In a memorandum to Parsons before the conference, John Steeves wrote that there was no need to discuss Smith's stewardship as ambassador. He had completed his two-year assignment in Vientiane, and it "would be better to let bygones be by-gones." However, should Smith not accept the news "gracefully," Steeves prepared for Parsons a long list of State Department complaints, which included the ambassador's management of the US mission, his partisan relations with Lao officials, and his tendency to act "precipitously" and make official recommendations with "immature reflection."[37]

Based on the subject matter of the conversation, as well as Smith's later admission that he had been instructed to resign, it seems likely that the meeting with Parsons in the Philippines did not go well. It went un-mentioned in both Smith's monograph and Parsons's memoir. (In fact, despite scores of pages devoted to Laos, Parsons never mentioned Smith by name in his manuscript.) Smith's next post was in Montgomery, Ala-bama, where he served as an adviser at the Air War College at Maxwell Air Force Base. He never again served overseas as a Foreign Service officer. He did, however, remain popular with at least some of the elected offi-cials he had met earlier in his career as a State Department liaison officer with the US Senate. In 1961 Smith traveled with Lyndon B. Johnson to Southeast Asia, serving as an observer and adviser to the vice president. By the mid-1960s, Smith had retired from the State Department and had become director of the Overseas Service Program at Bennett College in Millbrook, New York.

As ambassador to Laos, Horace Smith had accurately described some of the key problems in Laos that virtually no other US official was pre-pared to face squarely. His and Tobler's recommendation to either provide much more US aid or get out of Laos altogether was as unacceptable to the Eisenhower administration as similarly stark choices in Vietnam were later to the Kennedy and Johnson administrations. Ironically, within six months of Smith's departure from Vientiane, his enthusiasm for deposed Prime Minister Phoui Sananikone was commonplace among officials in Washington. Unfortunately for both Smith and the US government, his insights into Lao affairs were compromised by an inability to manage the US mission in Vientiane and a failure to inspire the confidence of his superiors in Washington.

Smith's successor as ambassador to Laos was Winthrop G. Brown, a trim and austere-looking New Englander who came to disagree with Washington almost as often as Smith had. Some Pentagon officials considered Brown's advice and recommendations virtually treasonous, and even his longtime friend Parsons sometimes disagreed with him about policy. But unlike Smith, Brown left Vientiane after two years of service with an enhanced reputation as a diplomat. Parsons concluded that Brown had "true qualities of leadership and, despite appalling, difficult circumstances, [had] brought unity to a country team long rent by emotion and schisms."[38]

Born in Seal Harbor, Maine, in 1908, Brown was raised in New York and graduated from Yale College and Yale Law School. He became a partner in a New York law firm and entered government service in 1941, working for the Lend-Lease Administration, which supplied military materiel to US allies. Brown spent most of World War II working out of the American embassy in London. After the war, he stayed on at the State Department as director of the Division of Commercial Policy. "I didn't know a tariff from a toothbrush at that point," he later recalled.[39]

Despite this limitation, Brown helped negotiate and later signed the landmark General Agreement on Tariffs and Trade. During the Korean War, Brown was named director of the Office of International Materials Policy, a federal agency that dealt with shortages of raw materials. In 1952 he returned to London as counselor of the American embassy in London, then served as director of the ICA mission in the United Kingdom. Immediately before his appointment as ambassador to Laos, Brown was the deputy chief of mission at the US embassy in India, a country that chaired the ICC in Indochina and played a leading role among nonaligned nations.

Before assuming his new post in Vientiane, Brown received briefings on Lao affairs from officials at the State Department, the Pentagon, and the CIA. Because of the conflict between Smith and Hecksher, his meetings with DCI Dulles and other top agency officials were an especially important part of his orientation. Brown later recalled that Dulles said: "You have my authority to send home any member of my staff at any time on twenty-four hours notice, without explanation and without damage to his career, if you feel that he is not loyally carrying out your instructions or working harmoniously in your country team."[40]

On July 12, ten days before his arrival in Vientiane, Brown met with Etienne Manac'h of the French Foreign Ministry, who reiterated his country's interest in resuming all military training in Laos. Despite its immediate importance, the training agreement that had loomed so large soon appeared insignificant to US policymakers, who were consumed by events in Laos that were more pressing, difficult, and dangerous. By the end of 1960, US Army Special Forces were not only training FAL units but also planning combat operations and participating in them. And, as the French had feared, the Soviet Union became more directly involved in Indochina, escalating the conflict in Laos into a superpower confrontation.

Chapter 8

Unacceptable Developments

AT APPROXIMATELY 3:00 A.M., August 9, 1960, Captain Kong Le, commander of the elite FAL Second Parachute Battalion, led a coup d'état against the two-month-old Somsanith government. Supported by armored units, his paratroopers seized control of Vientiane and its key installations, including the airport, the radio station, and the Chinaimo army base three miles downriver from the town. The coup was virtually bloodless, with much random shooting in the air, few casualties, and little property damage. Paratroopers wearing red berets established roadblocks, letting traffic into Vientiane but not out of it. One person stopped at a rebel roadblock was Francis J. Tatu, a young US embassy political officer who was riding to work, unaware of the coup. When the paratroopers "saw the diplomatic plates," he later recalled, "they passed us through, and I said, 'Gee, they're playing war games again.'"[1]

Whether "by accident or design," in the words of UK military attaché Lieutenant Colonel Hugh Toye, Kong Le launched his coup on a day when Prime Minister Somsanith and his cabinet were in Luang Prabang. The RLG ministers had traveled to the royal capital to help the king plan an elaborate state funeral for his late father, whose nine-month-old remains were "reposing in a very impressive gilded urn in the front hall of the palace," Ambassador Brown recalled. "It was a problem of finding the auspicious day and all that kind of thing." When news of the coup reached Lao officials in Luang Prabang, Defense Minister Phoumi Nosavan was instructed to end the rebellion.[2]

Although Kong Le controlled little beyond Vientiane, broadcasts in his name transmitted over Lao National Radio announced that the High

Revolutionary Command (HRC) had assumed all civil and military powers in the kingdom. Asking the population to remain calm, the HRC pledged to support the constitution and the king. It would also "struggle" against corruption and ask all "foreign troops" to leave the country. The new government would have a neutral foreign policy and seek to "maintain friendly relations and a good neighbor policy with all countries." To improve standards of living, Kong Le declared that Laos would accept "economic assistance from all countries without any reservation."[3]

Just twenty-six years old, Kong Le was considered one of the best officers in the FAL. US intelligence and military officials consistently assessed his Second Parachute Battalion as strongly opposed to the Pathet Lao. Born into a mixed Khmu-Lao family, Kong Le joined the army in 1951. Though slight of stature and soft-spoken, Kong Le quickly demonstrated an aptitude for military leadership. He received training in paramilitary operations and unconventional warfare at the CIA-sponsored scout and ranger school in the Philippines. Since October 1958, Kong Le and the battalion he led had received assistance from CIA paramilitary adviser Jack Mathews. Operating under USOM-PEO cover, Mathews was responsible for providing training and support for the battalion, and he worked closely with US Special Forces training teams.[4]

Before the coup, Kong Le had led his battalion effectively in operations in the rugged border areas of North Vietnam and other remote parts of the kingdom. Prior to the April 1960 election, General Phoumi had selected the Second Parachute Battalion to spearhead Clean Up operations in southern Laos. Despite the recognition of his fighting ability, Kong Le resented the contrast between the frequent, dangerous missions of his low-paid men and the physical and financial security of FAL leaders in Vientiane. He "was very fed up with the vast disparities in wealth" in the army and "the conspicuous spending of senior military officers," Ambassador Brown recalled. "And it was perhaps significant that the coup started by a mortar and machine gun attack on the very comfortable and elaborate home of the Chief of Staff of the Army."[5]

CIA officials judged Kong Le to be "highly competent" and "a born leader," according to a declassified history of agency operations in Laos. Sergeant Julius A. Wyngaerat, who served as a Special Forces medic on a Hotfoot training team, later recalled that Kong Le "had the best damn battalion in all of Laos." He added, "These guys were really professionals."

The judgment of Ambassador Brown and his country team was that Kong Le was a good paratroop captain who "was fed up with fighting, particularly fighting fellow Laotians." Brown recalled Kong Le's observation, "I have fought for many years, and I have killed many men, and I have never seen a foreigner die." To Brown, Kong Le represented the idealistic, perhaps naive view of Laotians who believed that "if they could establish a neutral position, if they could stop being involved with the Americans or with anybody else, that somehow or other, all these problems would go away."[6]

Unlike past and future coups in Laos, the security for Kong Le's rebellion was exceptionally tight, with planning for the operation concealed from Mathews. Although an excellent soldier, Kong Le appeared to recognize his limitations as a politician. After achieving the coup's initial objectives, he sought out the Lao statesman who personified a truly neutral Laos: former Prime Minister Souvanna Phouma. Kong Le asked Souvanna, then president of the National Assembly, to dissolve the legislature. He refused, saying he would not do so unless instructed by the king. Souvanna also declined to accept the post of prime minister unless asked by the king, and he initially dissociated himself from the HRC.

In his history *The Indochinese Experience of the French and the Americans,* Arthur Dommen provides evidence that Kong Le's coup may have initially involved a conspiracy with General Phoumi that would allow the habitual Lao army plotter to take over the kingdom. According to this "alternative version" of the coup, the original plan called for Kong Le to seize Vientiane and for Phoumi to return promptly to the town and take over from his presumably loyal subordinate. The French, in this version of events, had learned of the plot in advance, provided assistance to Kong Le, and blocked Phoumi's immediate return to Vientiane. In other words, France somehow managed to transform the Phoumi takeover into a coup that "put Prince Souvanna Phouma in power." In a monograph for the State Department, Dommen wrote: "Circumstantial evidence suggests that, rather than being a case of simple discontent on the part of Kong Le's soldiers, the action may have been planned between Phoumi and Kong Le as a way of Phoumi's seizing power. In that case, the plan went awry."[7]

Acknowledging the absence of "any definite proof," Dommen finds this speculative account of Kong Le's coup "a more satisfactory" explanation for many details "that emerge from a careful reading of the contemporary reports." A weakness of this hypothesis, however, is the ideological nimbleness required by Kong Le to shift allegiance so quickly from Phoumi to Souvanna, two men whose principles, politics, and goals for Laos were well known and completely opposite. And although Phoumi often had self-destructive impulses, it seems unlikely that even he would believe the US government would tolerate the coup described by Dommen. Only two months earlier, the United States had opposed Phoumi's selection as prime minister in a constitutional government. Though often stubborn, and the CIA's foremost protégé in Laos, Phoumi likely realized that a violent, unconstitutional power grab in Vientiane—particularly one toppling a government the United States favored—would likely trigger the withdrawal of all Western support from Laos until new leadership in the kingdom emerged.

Whatever its origins, the Kong Le coup caught the US government off guard. Officials in Washington had no idea who was behind the revolt, but they reflexively suspected their Lao bête noire: Souvanna Phouma. Kong Le was also a complete puzzle to policymakers. At Secretary of State Herter's August 9 staff meeting, Assistant Secretary Parsons reported that the Lao paratrooper was a good officer and "generally pro-American." But the content of leaflets distributed on behalf of the HRC appeared to have a distinctly anti-American tone.[8]

In the days immediately following the coup, US officials could find no connection between Kong Le and the Pathet Lao or North Vietnam. The State Department did, however, tell Ambassador Brown that the prospect of a "neutral government (under Souvanna Phouma or anyone else) dedicated to another fruitless round of negotiations with [the] Pathet Lao would be one fraught with [the] greatest danger to [the] independence of [the] country and its preservation in the free world." Because of this perceived danger, department officials informed American embassies in mainland Southeast Asia that it was "most important" to put down the rebellion as quickly as possible. Moreover, "snuffing out" the coup should be a strictly Lao affair—a pointed reference to possible intervention by Thailand, which, as the US embassy in Bangkok reported, was unlikely to accept passively "Phoumi's ouster" or a leftist threat on its border. The State Department warned the embassy in Bangkok that Thai intervention could transform a domestic Lao problem into an international conflict, involving North Vietnam and the PRC.[9]

A successful countercoup without foreign assistance was simply "not feasible," according to General Phoumi, who outlined a plan "to straighten things out" at a secret meeting in Bangkok on August 10. In attendance were Prime Minister Sarit and other Thai officials, as well as Leonard S. Unger, the American chargé d'affaires in Bangkok; Major General Briard P. Johnson, chief of the US military assistance command in Thailand; and Robert "Red" Jantzen, the CIA chief of station in Bangkok. Phoumi intended to deploy some five hundred paratroopers to retake the airfield in Vientiane, which would allow additional FAL forces to arrive by air. He also wanted Erawan forces—Lao paratroopers receiving training in unconventional warfare and antiguerrilla tactics from US Special Forces in Thailand—to participate in the operation. Phoumi planned to establish one headquarters in his hometown of Savannakhet and a second one in Luang Prabang. His plan required US and Thai support in such areas as air transportation, supplies, and radio equipment. Aircraft were of particular importance because the rainy season made most roads impassable. Unger told Phoumi that his request would require approval from Washington.[10]

Commenting on Unger's report of the meeting, Ambassador Brown opposed overt support to Phoumi from Thailand. There was not only historical animosity between Thailand and Laos to consider, but also contemporary Lao disapproval of Phoumi's closeness to Sarit. In Brown's view, Laotian awareness of Thai support could push the coup group further to the left, as well as provide a pretext for North Vietnamese intervention on behalf of the rebels. Brown recommended that CAT provide aircraft with clear Lao markings for any countercoup.[11] Such an approach would have the added advantage of exercising greater control over air operations—for example, by preventing overeager Thai pilots from entering combat areas.

Washington gave preliminary approval to aspects of Phoumi's request, including the use of US military assistance supplies in Thailand for RLG operations in Laos; the assignment of senior PEO officers to Savannakhet and Luang Prabang as advisers to review plans and requests for equipment; the establishment of secure communication between these officers and General Johnson's MAAG in Thailand; and the provision of a clandestine radio transmitter in north Thailand to broadcast on behalf of the RLG. There was, however, a problem associated with Phoumi's request. Because the US government had been unable to contact other leading members of the RLG, the ambitious defense minister was the only source of information on Lao policy. In other words, US officials could not be sure whether Phoumi was acting on his own behalf or that of government ministers in Luang Prabang.

The August 12 NSC meeting was likely a difficult one for CIA chief Allen Dulles. The agency he led had failed to anticipate Kong Le's coup, even though one of his case officers had been working closely with the paratroop captain for nearly two years. Perhaps reflecting his frustration at the inability of the US government to influence affairs in a poor country with an unusually large CIA presence, Dulles sprinkled his briefing on Laos with acerbic observations on events and individuals in the kingdom. Commenting on the limited number of CAT pilots in Laos, he said that those who were there "were not very dependable," a judgment many of his case officers in Laos would likely have questioned. The CIA chief said that unnamed "sinister elements" might have been behind the coup, and it seemed possible that Souvanna Phouma would form a neutral government, a development the French would look upon favorably.[12]

Rhetorically throwing up his hands, Dulles declared to President Eisenhower and his advisers "that anything might happen in Laos and that there were few people of any courage" in the kingdom. He reported that one of the US officials at the August 10 meeting with Sarit, presumably Bangkok chief of station Red Jantzen, was "disappointed" with the "performance" of General Phoumi. According to the minutes of the NSC meeting, Dulles summarized his views of the country with the comment "It would be almost a miracle if we can hold on there." Ending his observations on a more optimistic note, the DCI said "the situation was difficult but not hopeless."[13]

At the same meeting, Livingston T. Merchant, the State Department undersecretary for political affairs, reported that the movement of CAT aircraft to Bangkok was already under way. However, there had not been a US offer of planes to the RLG or a "firm request" for them from the Somsanith government. Merchant said that the State Department did not want to simply turn over aircraft to Phoumi and recommended that US planes only be used for "sensible military operations." President Eisenhower, who expressed concern about wasting airplanes, told his advisers "that the U.S. should provide aircraft only if the Laotians can develop a feasible plan."[14]

At a joint State Department–JCS conference following the NSC meeting, US officials discussed additional difficulties in supporting RLG efforts to restore control in Vientiane. Parsons reported indications that all Lao groups, with the possible exception of General Phoumi, wanted "to avoid bloodshed." This was a "very Lao" reaction, Parsons said. A related issue was the unity of rebels and loyalists in "their dislike" of Phoumi. A CIA source in the FAL speculated that if Phoumi attempted to use the First Parachute Battalion in a countercoup, it would "very likely join" Kong Le's battalion, as the two units had trained together and developed a mutual spirit of camaraderie.[15]

On August 13, 1960, a crowd in Vientiane responded to appeals from Kong Le to demonstrate in front of the National Assembly and demand the resignation of the Somsanith government. Some demonstrators carried anti–United States banners—for example, "American Imperialists Go Home"—but most of the crowd, according to a CIA report, "appeared friendly to United States observers." Inside the assembly, deputies were not permitted to leave the building. At 7:00 P.M., with Souvanna presiding over the legislature and Kong Le in attendance, the deputies unanimously adopted a resolution dissolving the Somsanith government.[16]

In Luang Prabang, Prime Minister Somsanith and Foreign Minister Khamphan Panya declared that the assembly resolution to dismiss the cabinet was illegal. Such a motion, the cabinet ministers said, required a twenty-four-hour period to provide the prime minister with an opportunity to debate the resolution. Despite occasional gestures of resolve, the RLG officials isolated in Luang Prabang "were dispirited and primarily concerned with [the] problem of reaching [a] solution which would preclude bloodshed," according to former prime minister Kou Abhay. Although Khamphan Panya and Phoumi were still prepared to use force in Vientiane, the rest of the cabinet concentrated more on reaching a "bloodless arrangement with Kong Le than taking measures to counter him."[17]

After a fruitless day of negotiations between RLG ministers in Luang Prabang and members of the HRC in Vientiane, the Somsanith government resigned on August 14, and the king asked Souvanna Phouma to form a government. Ambassador Brown reported to the State Department that some of the former ministers would likely return to Vientiane and others would travel to Savannakhet, "presumably" to join Phoumi. Brown feared that the general might "refuse [to] accept defeat and take [the] law into [his] own hands," either by attempting to take over the whole country or to "split off" the southern portion of the kingdom under his control. Brown believed that either course of action "would be disastrous."[18]

In the ambassador's view, it was important that further political changes in Laos follow the constitution. If Phoumi took control forcibly, the only beneficiaries would be the Pathet Lao and its communist supporters. His countercoup would be opposed not only by most Laotians, who exhibited "a genuine and growing popular feeling for a more centralist government," but also by the United Kingdom, France, and the United Nations. Neutral Cambodia "would be further aroused," and North Vietnam and the PRC would be handed "a major propaganda" victory and perhaps provoked into military intervention. Acknowledging the dangers of a centralist RLG, as well as "Phoumi's undoubted abilities and strong pro-Western attitude," Brown reported the unanimous view of his country team that the general be informed, in "unmistakably clear" language, of US opposition to any military action to regain control of the country or split it.[19]

The State Department agreed with Brown. Parsons had not been pleased to learn that Phoumi's immediate response to the resignation of the Somsanith government was to "march on [the] rebels in Vientiane." Such an operation, Parsons observed, could not be "mounted overnight," would require a US or Thai airlift and other forms of supports, and would probably trigger outside intervention in an internal dispute that had thus far remained "localized." In a cable to the American embassy in Bangkok, Parsons also appeared irritated that Sarit seemed to view immediate support for "Phoumi's apparent decision to go it alone" as a proxy for the US commitment to Thailand, a country that had received significant amounts of overt and covert military assistance for a decade.[20]

Like most US officials, Parsons viewed the quick capitulation of the Somsanith government as unfortunate. Nonetheless, the assistant secretary did not think that the US government should "intervene on behalf of Phoumi." The Lao defense minister's apparent refusal to accept the resignation of the Somsanith government likely diminished Phoumi's status among civilian leaders, and the loyalty of the FAL forces to him would be questionable. "Premature support of an individual who may be isolated politically could prejudice this and our common interest in SEA [Southeast Asia] as [a] whole," Parsons cabled Unger in Bangkok. Washington policymakers had a "high regard for Phoumi and his ability," Parsons reported. "If he does not make [a] misstep now, his position and influence will be preserved for [the] future when it may be needed even more."[21]

In an attempt to ensure that Phoumi's partisans within the CIA followed US policy, Parsons made a telephone call on August 15 to Desmond FitzGerald, chief of the agency's Far East Division. Drawing FitzGerald's attention to recent State Department cables sent to the embassy in Vientiane, Parsons told his bureaucratic counterpart that it would be "most unfortunate if any junior employee of the Agency were to encourage General Phoumi in any way to act against Vientiane." Although the agency was generally a highly disciplined organization, it seems likely that Parsons felt compelled to make this call because of the CIA's close relationship with the general and the CDNI. FitzGerald assured Parsons that the agency would do nothing "to encourage Phoumi either in the direction of separatism or military action against Vientiane."[22]

At 4:00 A.M. on August 16, CIA and PEO representatives assigned to Phoumi's headquarters in Savannakhet informed the general that the US government was not prepared, at this point, to support him in a forcible effort to retake Vientiane. According to Ambassador Brown's report to Washington, "Phoumi nodded politely but said that he would proceed with his original plan." Later that same day, only hours after Souvanna Phouma had proposed a new cabinet to the National Assembly, an FAL C-47 military transport aircraft flew over Vientiane at a low altitude, dropping leaflets in French and Lao announcing Phoumi's intention to retake Vientiane by force.[23]

PEO chief Heintges reported to CINCPAC and Washington that he had received a message from Phoumi, providing details of his planned countercoup. An FAL force eventually totaling five thousand troops would seize the city and attack the rebels in and around Vientiane. Phoumi said he had been infiltrating loyal troops and civilians into Vientiane for several days, and the operation would begin on either August 20 or 21. Heintges wrote that his staff thought Phoumi's plan was feasible if aircraft and the French airbase at Seno were available. The French, however, were determined to deny Seno to Phoumi and to defend it by force if necessary. "I am convinced Phoumi means business," Heintges wrote. Although he avoided an explicit policy recommendation, the PEO chief left little doubt that he wanted Washington to support Phoumi's plan: "I know he is in good graces with [the] king and [the] best friend [the] US has among the Lao."[24]

Policymakers in Washington faced an unappealing choice of which Lao leader to support. Under the best of circumstances, US officials considered Souvanna "occasionally tricky and weak." Exacerbating these traditional suspicions was Souvanna's new cabinet, whose ministers had little experience or international stature. "The assumption of power by the Souvanna Phouma cabinet may represent the beginning of a Lao slide into Communism," speculated Daniel V. Anderson, director of the State Department's Office of Southeast Asian Affairs.[25]

Yet all-out support for Phoumi would find international favor only with the governments of Thailand and South Vietnam. A violent counter-coup backed by the US government would be denounced by the United Kingdom and France, reduce the likelihood that the United Nations or SEATO would play a stabilizing role in Laos, and inevitably give rise to op-position forces who would probably overthrow Phoumi. Splitting the po-litical difference between Souvanna and Phoumi, Acting Secretary of State Dillon informed Ambassador Brown on August 17 that Phoumi's forces should be supported as a "counterpoise" to the weak new government and that the CIA had been authorized to give the Lao general financial assis-tance for supplies and troop pay. While working with Souvanna's cabinet in the short term, US officials wished to "preserve our assets" until the day "action might have to be taken to prevent unacceptable developments."[26]

Policymakers had quickly decided that Kong Le was a "bad actor." His neutralism was anathema to US officials, the new cabinet appeared to be under his control, and he seemed to have developed political ambi-tions. CIA reports indicated that Kong Le considered the current govern-ment provisional and that he would head the "only legal political group once order [was] restored." Kong Le had apparently rejected offers of Pathet Lao assistance, but the US government feared the possibility that he might change his mind. State Department officials considered Kong Le an "emotional and truculent paratroop captain" who was "dangerously immature and irrational." CIA headquarters warned: "We may eventually be faced with an Asian Castro." Ambassador Brown later said that the de-monization of the occasionally erratic Kong Le was a key misjudgment by the US government. The paratrooper was "a patriot, not a communist."[27]

While policymakers discussed the relative merits of various Lao lead-ers, Ambassador Brown was preparing for imminent anarchy in Vientiane. Even without US aircraft, some five hundred of General Phoumi's countercoup forces were on their way to Vientiane, traveling by boat on the Mekong River. Although Kong Le's fatigued paratroopers now had a sloppy, unmilitary appearance, they still possessed the means to provide formidable resistance to a countercoup. Brown, who had earlier requested and received authority to evacuate the six hundred American citizens in Vientiane and some five hundred Filipino contract employees of the US government, decided on August 18 to evacuate US dependents the following day. "Once peace had been made we would all come back," recalled Peggy Ann Brown, the ambassador's wife. "Well, it wasn't made. And it dragged on and on and on. So I lived in Bangkok for two years with the children."[28]

On August 18, 1960, President Eisenhower presided over an NSC meeting that revealed deep divisions within his administration over strategy and tactics in Laos. Allen Dulles described the situation there as "still confused" and reported differing US opinions about the susceptibility of Souvanna to Pathet Lao influence and the legality of his new government. The Lao National Assembly had unanimously approved Souvanna's latest government, but with paratroopers and armored cars stationed outside, the deputies had been voting under duress. "They had lived for some days in the Assembly chamber and would have done almost anything to get out," Dulles told the NSC.[29]

When Dulles reported that the US government had "strongly urged" Phoumi not to attack Vientiane, Secretary of Defense Thomas S. Gates spoke up on behalf of senior military and civilian officials at the Pentagon, who had grown uneasy with the lingering crisis and the absence of any action other than restraining the only strong anticommunist in Laos. Why, Gates asked, did we hope "that Phoumi would not take Vientiane?" The town was being held by one man and one battalion, the defense secretary declared, and "the sooner we knocked off Kong Le the better."

According to the minutes of the meeting, Dulles replied first to Gates, observing that "the Lao are not much given to fighting." Acting Secretary of State Dillon began his response to the defense secretary's comments by agreeing that the first US "objective should be to get rid of Kong Le." Once his troublesome presence was removed, it would be possible to establish an anti–Pathet Lao government that included both Souvanna and Phoumi. Dillon then pointed out the political risks of Phoumi's attacking

Vientiane. The only way his forces could arrive there in strength was with US aircraft. Overt US help for a bloody assault on Vientiane "would be highly adverse" to American interests and "strongly opposed" by Western allies. Even the Australians, who had been generally supportive of a "strong" US policy in Laos, had advised against an attack by Phoumi. Dillon and other State Department officials believed that the US government should keep Phoumi's forces strong and that Kong Le's paratroopers would possibly "cave in" in the face of "overwhelming force."[30]

Secretary Gates replied to Dillon's defense of current policy in Laos by saying that he would not argue the matter further in this particular venue. His did want to say, however, that the Pentagon "disagreed with the State position." Based on the minutes of the August 18 NSC meeting, President Eisenhower tried to find common ground among his divided advisers. Although he "agreed that it would be undesirable to cause a bloody fight" overtly supported by the United States, the president said it was important to stimulate "disaffection" in Vientiane. He suggested that psychological-warfare pamphlets be dropped on the town every night. Dulles replied that this had already been done. "We could help do it again," he said. When Eisenhower asked whether the Thais could institute a blockade, the DCI said that this, too, had already been accomplished and would eventually "cause Vientiane to be starved out."

General Lyman L. Lemnitzer, then chief of staff of the US Army, wondered how bloodshed in Vientiane could be prevented as long as Kong Le controlled the town. General Lemnitzer urged that Phoumi and his forces be brought to Vientiane as rapidly as possible, declaring that the plan for assaulting the town was a good one. When Dillon observed that this plan would require aircraft that were not Lao, Gates responded that the US government "would be acting in support of a freely elected government." President Eisenhower, however, pointed out that "there was now a new government in Laos."

The president then asked if there was any way for the United States to help transport Phoumi's forces part of the way to Vientiane. Dillon replied that there were no airports between the general's headquarters in Savannakhet and Vientiane. When Eisenhower asked about the possibility of an airdrop, Dillon said that this was the key issue. Should US aircraft be supplied to Phoumi? Dillon was willing to provide "aircraft as long as we continued to control them." Although no major decisions were made at this NSC meeting, Pentagon officials had almost certainly raised doubts in the president's mind about the efficacy of current State Department policy in Laos.[31]

The legality of Souvanna's government, a topic Dulles had raised at the August 18 NSC meeting, remained a lingering source of disagreement both in and outside of Laos. General Phoumi and his supporters dismissed the vote of the National Assembly as coercion and stressed the absence of a signed royal ordinance, which was required for the formal establishment of a new government. The United Kingdom, France, and Australia, in contrast, accepted the legality of the resignation of the Somsanith cabinet, the selection of Souvanna by the king to form a new government, and the unanimous National Assembly vote approving it. The "military force is largely on Phoumi's side," Ambassador Brown reported to the State Department, and the "apparent if not actual legal and international right [is] on Souvanna's side."[32]

Washington officials refused to recognize Souvanna's government, which exacerbated the political instability in Vientiane. In a top-secret, limited-distribution telegram to Brown, Parsons asked if there were some way to delay King Savang's formal investiture of Souvanna and his weak government. A delay, Parsons reasoned, would keep the political situation fluid and enable the United States "to appraise other possibilities," such as Phoumi's planned attack against Kong Le's forces.[33]

Phoumi and his allies, who were thinking along similar lines, did everything within their power to prevent the king's approval of the new government. Sympathetic to Phoumi's uncompromising anticommunism, the king was reportedly having second thoughts about Souvanna and, in particular, the members of his new cabinet. Savang's first loyalty, however, was preserving the monarchy. He had no intention of intervening in a dispute between rival factions of his army, which would likely create enemies on one or possibly both sides. The question of political leadership in Laos, in the king's view, could not be addressed until the military disagreement had been solved. To Ambassador Brown, Savang's attitude appeared "inert." Khamphan Panya, the former Lao foreign minister and Phoumi's top representative in Luang Prabang, told a CIA source that the king, "though reticent," was "firmly behind" the general.[34]

Souvanna attempted to confirm the legality of his government by sending an envoy to Luang Prabang with a royal ordinance for the king's signature. After landing there, Souvanna's representative was arrested and his papers confiscated. On August 19 Edouard Zellweger, the special representative of UN Secretary General Hammarskjöld, traveled to Luang Prabang to learn the king's views of the crisis and to deliver, at Souvanna's request, copies of the ordinance approving his government. An experienced Swiss diplomat, Zellweger was responsible for coordinating the UN's economic activities in Laos. Because of his seniority, he was authorized by Hammarskjöld to engage discreetly in political activities that might have a calming influence on the kingdom.

The primary mission of Zellweger's trip to Luang Prabang was to gather information from the palace for the benefit of the United Nations, as well as the French, UK, and US ambassadors in Vientiane. The Western diplomats were eager to "smoke out [the] King's true position" but reluctant to leave troubled Vientiane and descend on the palace en masse. At the airport in the royal capital, FAL officers prevented Zellweger from entering the town. After convincing the military officials of his authority and rights, the UN representative proceeded to the palace, where he was denied access to the king.[35]

When Zellweger asked why the royal ordinance appointing Souvanna's government had not been signed, he was informed that no such documents had been received at the palace. The diplomat offered the copies provided by Souvanna, but they were not accepted. The secretary-general of the royal palace said that the king must be kept out of the confrontation between two military groups, declaring: "Le roi n'est pas visible et ne le sera pas" (The king cannot be seen, nor will he be). Mervyn Brown, then a young British diplomat in Vientiane, recalled that the idea of "an invisible king" seemed amusingly appropriate to many of his colleagues, given Luang Prabang's fairytale atmosphere of palaces, princes, and ceremonies. The palace comment about the king's visibility, or lack thereof, Brown wrote in his memoirs, "brightened our lives" at a grim moment in Laotian history.[36]

Zellweger returned to Vientiane, frustrated by the reception he had received in Luang Prabang. His reaction was mild, however, compared to the fury of Khamphan Panya, who was angry with the UN representative for trying to present the king with the ordinance Souvanna had prepared. According to a CIA report from the royal capital, Khamphan "scathingly criticized" Zellweger, who he had assumed was merely carrying a message to the king from Hammarskjöld. The Lao official was reportedly "'stunned' by Zellweger's intervention in [the] internal affairs of Laos."[37]

To Pentagon officials, the absence of a signed royal ordinance formally establishing Souvanna's government was one more reason why the US government should consider Phoumi and his supporters as an interim Lao government "with sufficient residual authority to accept defense support funds and supplies." And regardless of legal niceties, Defense Department officials argued that funds and supplies for Phoumi's forces were essential to "the development of a stable, free, representative Laos government with the will and ability to resist Communism from within as well as without."[38]

A key Pentagon concern was supplying Phoumi with money to pay his troops. On August 15 the general had requested 10 million kip from the US government, which agreed to deliver 8 million kip if he did not attack Vientiane. The CIA, which was responsible for providing the funds covertly, faced difficulties gathering the requested cash. The only sizable stocks of kip were in the RLG treasury in Vientiane, which was still largely under Kong Le's control. Phoumi's urgent need for funds was emphasized by an August 21 CIA cable from Savannakhet, warning agency headquarters that "without immediate financial support his movement will collapse within one week." The author of this cable, which an agency historian later characterized as "apocalyptic," was case officer John Freeman "Jack" Hasey.[39]

Although many CIA operatives of the 1950s and 1960s, particularly those working in Southeast Asia, can safely be described as colorful, Jack Hasey likely led a more eventful life than the vast majority of his fellow case officers. Born in 1916 and raised in Bridgewater, Massachusetts, where his father was an executive and director of one of the world's largest shoe manufacturing firms, Hasey attended Phillips Exeter Academy and Columbia University. He achieved little academic distinction at either institution. Preferring sports and socializing to books, Hasey later wrote that by the end of his freshman, and only, year at Columbia, "I think I can truthfully say that I knew every night-club doorman and head waiter in New York."[40]

In 1936 Hasey sailed for Paris with vague aspirations of improving his French and attending the Sorbonne. He had spent a number of happy childhood summers abroad, and he particularly liked the people of France and their customs, including "their easy unhurried ways" and "agreeable tolerance for the odd." To Hasey, Paris seemed a city "either purposely or unintentionally planned for the complete satisfaction and enjoyment of men." Hasey's charm and social graces, not to mention his father's international business connections, led to an offer of employment with Cartier, specializing in jewelry sales to wealthy Americans. He was good at his job, and his more glamorous clients included Douglas Fairbanks Jr., Marlene Dietrich, Prince Ali Khan, and the duke and duchess of Windsor.

As war in Europe became increasingly likely, Hasey began taking a more serious interest in foreign affairs. After Nazi Germany invaded Poland on September 1, 1939, he attempted to the join the French Foreign Legion. US neutrality, however, prevented Hasey and other American citizens in France from serving as combatants. He helped form a volunteer ambulance company and commanded a small unit during the so-called Winter War between Finland and the Soviet Union. Assisting the outnumbered Finns in the arctic region near Lake Ladoga, he developed severe frostbite on his feet and was wounded during a Russian air raid in February 1940.

After the fall of France later that same year, Hasey traveled to London, where he met General Charles de Gaulle and was commissioned as a second lieutenant in the Free French forces. Finding himself underemployed as a member of the medical corps in England, Hasey began training with the infantry of the Free French Foreign Legion. After his request for a transfer to the infantry was approved, Hasey fought against Italians in Eritrea and Vichy-French in Syria. On June 20, 1941, while charging a machine-gun nest near Damascus, Hasey felt "a numbness in my throat and chest, a peculiar sensation of being pushed backed while going forward."[41]

He had been struck by machine-gun fire in his jaw, neck, chest, and hand. After six months of convalescence and reconstructive operations, Hasey returned to the United States for more plastic surgery to rebuild his jaw and chin. He recovered from his wounds, but his voice remained a raspy half-whisper for the rest of his life. On April 18, 1942, General De Gaulle named Hasey a Companion of the Order of the Liberation, the highest French honor for service in World War II. Only four Americans, one of whom was General Eisenhower, received this award. When he recovered from his wounds, Hasey served as a liaison officer between Eisenhower and De Gaulle.

After the war Hasey returned to work at Cartier as a sales manager in Paris and New York. Selling jewelry did not hold his interest for very long, and he reportedly sought career advice from Eisenhower, who suggested that the newly established CIA might have use for a man with his skills and experience. Overcoming an earlier aversion to spying as a "distasteful and deceitful business," Hasey joined the agency in 1950. He returned to France, where later in the decade the CIA directed him to become friends with Phoumi, an up-and-coming Lao officer who one day would likely hold a high position in the kingdom.

After the Kong Le coup, the agency sent Hasey to the general's head-quarters in Savannakhet, "expressly to capitalize on their friendship," according to a CIA historian. Operating under USOM-PEO cover, Hasey shared the "fervent pro-Phoumi bias" of the other US intelligence and military officials assigned there. Later, there were allegations that Hasey was too close to Phoumi to be an effective intelligence officer. One key official who disagreed with this assessment was Ambassador Brown. Like the new CIA chief of station in Vientiane, Gordon L. Jorgensen, Hasey earned Brown's confidence for performing his duties in a professional manner. The ambassador later recalled that Hasey's "sympathies were entirely with General Phoumi, but I think he was a good soldier, and I think he [carried] out his instructions."[42]

Phoumi eventually received the funds he had requested from the United States. Perhaps even more significant for the general's prospects was the growing support in the Eisenhower administration for the Pentagon's views on Laos. On August 22 Parsons drafted a cable to Brown, providing the ambassador with the latest policy guidance. The embassy had heretofore been "properly concerned with [the] avoidance of a pitched battle for Vientiane and in favor of [a] peaceful resolution which [the] Lao generally desire." Nevertheless, wrote Parsons, the objective of preventing an armed clash—which was likely an end in itself for the British, the French, and the United Nations—should "remain subordinate to our overall objectives in Laos." In a subsequent letter to Brown, Parsons wrote: "There is a general feeling that we must act strongly to preserve and use Phoumi and the army."[43]

The strength of that feeling was evident at a "special" meeting at the

Pentagon on August 23, 1960. Livingston Merchant and Parsons represented the State Department, and the Pentagon officials included the secretary of defense and most of the service chiefs. The purpose of the conference was to attempt to reconcile the two departments' differing views on resolving the crisis in Laos. After introductory pleasantries by Defense Secretary Gates and Undersecretary Merchant, Parsons provided a brief summary of recent developments in Laos, which included an encouraging report that Souvanna and Phoumi had reached a tentative agreement in Savannakhet "that would help restore complete order in the country." In a generally upbeat presentation, Parsons did note that Kong Le had distributed weapons to some three thousand villagers near Vientiane, including Pathet Lao forces, to bolster the town's defenses. Kong Le's representative in Savannakhet had agreed to Phoumi's request to retrieve the arms, apparently without acknowledging the difficulty of recovering them.[44]

It was Defense Secretary Gates who cut to the chase by summarizing the fundamental JCS concern: "Souvanna Phouma is weak," and "Phoumi is our only friend."

The impression of the JCS, said Gates, "was that Phoumi felt isolated and was in fact 'damned lonely.'" He added, "The Chiefs felt that we should be telling him we are on his side and that we want to maintain him in power." The JCS did not agree with the administration's policy of restraining Phoumi from attacking Vientiane and "would have preferred immediate and aggressive action" against Kong Le. The service chiefs had the impression, Gates said, that US agencies in Laos "were acting as negotiators rather than standing on Phoumi's side."[45]

Thomas S. Gates, then fifty-four, was a different breed of defense secretary from his two predecessors in the Eisenhower administration. "Engine Charlie" Wilson and Neil McElroy, who had established reputations as businessmen at General Motors and Procter & Gamble, respectively, focused primarily on efficient management of the Department of Defense. Gates, who had more experience in the military and the Pentagon, had a deeper interest in foreign policy. He respected and admired the late John Foster Dulles but took a dim view of the Department of State, finding it an undisciplined institution that "wandered around on its own."[46]

A graduate of the University of Pennsylvania and an investment banker by profession, Gates had served as a naval officer in World War II, earning one Bronze Star for operations against the Japanese on Luzon and a second one for his efforts in the Iwo Jima and Okinawa campaigns. Maintaining an interest in naval affairs after the war, Gates was appointed undersecretary of the navy in 1953 by President Eisenhower. His subsequent Pentagon appointments included secretary of the navy and undersecretary of defense. On December 2, 1959, President Eisenhower appointed Gates as secretary of defense.

Although no defense secretary could rival Eisenhower's primacy in national security policy, Gates took a more active role in military affairs than either Wilson or McElroy had. Unlike his immediate predecessors at the Department of Defense, Gates met regularly with the Joint Chiefs of Staff and encouraged them in fulfilling their statutory responsibilities as the president's principal military advisers. He helped enhance US strategic capabilities by leading the development of the Joint Strategic Target Planning Staff, which improved coordination and eliminated duplication in US Air Force and Navy nuclear targeting. To many, Gates seemed an impressive activist who would be on President-elect Kennedy's short list of possible holdovers from the Eisenhower administration.

At the Pentagon meeting with Merchant and Parsons, Gates stressed the importance of assuring Phoumi "of our complete support." The defense secretary said that General Lansdale—the Pentagon deputy assistant for special operations, a longtime covert operator in Southeast Asia, and the scourge of State Department officials almost everywhere—had told him, "We have to hit these things early or they grow into a dangerous compromise coalition." Remarking that the chiefs were after him daily about support for Phoumi, Gates challenged the State Department officials to point out the weakness of the Pentagon's views and to tell him why those views were considered "so impetuous."[47]

Merchant replied to Gates, "Of course we want to respond quickly to Phoumi," adding that CAT flights to pay, feed, and supply his troops were clear evidence of US support. Parsons said that the State Department realized Phoumi was "the only tough leader." But he added, "We must [also] recognize that he is not popular with the Lao people." Parsons also said that if the Souvanna-Phoumi agreement in Savannakhet failed to produce desirable results, he would favor the US government moving "farther and faster" on the Lao general's behalf.

The warnings about Phoumi's lack of popular support or the importance of establishing a broadly based, anticommunist government in Laos made no apparent impression on the Pentagon officials. General Curtis E. LeMay, the brooding, cigar-smoking air force vice chief of staff, "growled," according to the minutes of the meeting, "What's wrong with telling Phoumi we will give him everything he wants?" After listening to Merchant's opposition to providing "a blank check" to the Lao general and Parsons's explanation of CIA measures to inform Phoumi of US support, General LeMay declared: "Here we are battling to keep another country from going communist. It's going to be another situation of too little too late. We must tell him we support him."[48]

Merchant replied that perhaps the US government could communicate its support for Phoumi in more explicit terms. CNO Arleigh Burke, who was every bit as tough as LeMay, provided the civilians with an incongruous domestic analogy. Admiral Burke said, "It is just like telling your wife you love her. She knows it and you know it but you have to tell her quite frequently." In an earlier memorandum to Gates, Burke had stated his views on Lao politics in more direct terms: "It would be *wrong* to try to influence Phoumi to accept a compromise with Souvanna Phouma on any terms other than those Phoumi himself desires."[49]

Defense Secretary Gates told the State Department officials that "the $64 question" was: "Does [Phoumi] know he is our boy?" Whether in negotiations or combat operations, Gates said, this was what the US government wanted Phoumi to know. When the defense secretary asked Merchant if he agreed, the State Department official replied that a message "in these explicit terms" would be transmitted to Phoumi. Merchant added that the State Department and JCS should keep "awfully close" on the topic of support for the Lao general.

As in the late summer of 1959, State Department and Pentagon officials discussed the possibility of direct US military intervention in Laos to prevent a victory by the Pathet Lao. In a selective summary of recent history in Laos, Gates declared: "Here we have a country which through free elections has placed in power a government which has been temporarily overthrown. What better case could we get, assuming the King and Phoumi stand firm, for our direct intervention?" Without US forces, Gates added, the FAL "could not stand up to the Pathet Lao who are better led and probably better motivated."[50]

It is unclear whether the comment above was intended as a reference to North Vietnamese regulars, rather than the "Pathet Lao," as recorded in the minutes of the meeting. There had never been any doubt among US officials that PAVN invaders, unobstructed by outside forces, could roll through the Lao army from Sam Neua to the Mekong River in a matter of weeks, if not days. However, US assessments of the FAL had consistently stated that it was capable of dealing with the purely military dimensions of the local Pathet Lao threat. If Gates actually believed that the Pathet Lao were now militarily superior to the FAL, his assessment would not only be a new and troubling judgment about the capabilities of the Lao army but also an indictment of the training his department had been responsible for providing.

As the meeting at the Pentagon wound down, Assistant Secretary of Defense John N. Irwin asked about the attitudes of US allies. The British view of Laos, Merchant replied, was "generally" the same as that of the French, who sought a neutral Laos and wanted to avoid any military trouble there. Three days earlier, the American embassy in London had reported the views of the UK Foreign Office: Kong Le was a typical Asian nationalist who, once he "climbed down somewhat," should be tolerated by the US government; despite Kong Le's grip on Vientiane, "Souvanna was more of a free agent than the U.S. recognized and should be strengthened"; and the restoration of Phoumi to a position of power "would endanger the long-term stability of the country and invite another coup."[51]

Referring to the lack of UK enthusiasm for American policy in Laos, Defense Secretary Gates concluded the meeting by joking that the US government should threaten to use atomic weapons in Laos. "This would so frighten the British," Gates said, that they would provide conventional military support for the US effort as a less dangerous alternative. Parsons, however, found nothing humorous about the Pentagon conference. Convinced that the civilian and military officials there had "an over-simplified view of an extremely complex and ever-changing situation," Parsons wrote Brown: "I have attended quite a few such meetings but have never seen such strong and persistently expressed dissatisfaction with the State Department position."[52]

After the meeting, the State Department informed Brown of the agreement with the Pentagon that "Phoumi despite his lack [of] popularity was our best bet as [a] staunch anti-Communist." Therefore, he should receive explicit "assurances of our complete support" and "willingness to honor quickly any reasonable request." A joint State Department–Defense

Department–CIA cable to the US mission in Vientiane instructed the agency to deliver the message directly to Phoumi. This decision was a shock to Ambassador Brown, who neither agreed with the policy nor appreciated that a CIA officer, rather than an embassy official, was delivering this message to Phoumi.[53]

The explicit expression of US support for Phoumi deepened the divisions among the Western allies. The UK government had generally agreed with US policy in Laos—much more so than the French—but British ambassador John Addis told Ambassador Brown that he was "shocked" by the US assurances to Phoumi, which would only make the general more intransigent in negotiating with Souvanna. In Addis's view, a truly neutral government was in the best interests of Laos and the West, including the United States. Phoumi's methods had "demonstrably failed," said the British ambassador. Souvanna, he declared, was the best man to lead the Lao government.[54]

The preliminary agreement that Souvanna and Phoumi had reached on August 23 was devoted largely to military matters, particularly ways of defending Vientiane from the increasing Pathet Lao threat. The agreement called for a reorganization of the FAL, with the recently dismissed General Ouan resuming his duties as commander in chief, and the recovery of weapons Kong Le had distributed to villagers in the Vientiane area. Phoumi reportedly accepted Souvanna's cabinet as the "de facto" government, and the two men agreed to stop their competing propaganda broadcasts and leaflet drops. Political problems would be resolved by constitutional means in Luang Prabang, with Souvanna, Phoumi, and all of the deputies of the National Assembly reporting to the king.

Subsequent interpretations of the agreement's provisions differed among the Lao officials supposedly bound by them. After Souvanna and Phoumi spent several days jockeying for political and military advantage, the National Assembly convened in the royal capital on August 29. Former prime minister Somsanith resubmitted the resignation of his government, which the king accepted. Savang asked Souvanna to form a new government, which came as an unpleasant shock to Phoumi. He subsequently told Hasey and other US officials: "The only reason I agreed to go to Luang Prabang and enter into discussions with Souvanna Phouma was that I counted on the king to charge me with the responsibility for re-establishing order and security in Laos."[55]

Initially, Souvanna sought to reappoint the same cabinet that the king and the US government had found weak and inexperienced. Forced to compromise, Souvanna proposed a new, more internationally known cabinet. He kept the defense and foreign affairs portfolios for himself, and proposed Phoumi as minister of interior and the largely honorary role of vice premier. The interior ministry, a less important portfolio than defense, would limit Phoumi's involvement in military affairs. Approved by the National Assembly and the king on August 31, the new government was indisputably legal.

US policymakers were not, however, prepared to accept a Lao government that appeared to be under the thumb of Kong Le. The paratroop captain, who had initially opposed Souvanna's new cabinet, particularly the inclusion of Phoumi, dropped his opposition to the proposed government, but distrust lingered. The CIA reported "rumors of alleged plots against various leading Lao, especially Phoumi."[56]

On September 2 Souvanna and virtually all of his cabinet flew to Vientiane for the traditional swearing-in ceremony at Sisaket Wat, perhaps the oldest surviving Buddhist temple in the city. Phoumi, however, returned to his headquarters in Savannakhet. Later alleging that the prime minister intended to arrest him in Vientiane, Phoumi said: "The only reason I accepted the position in the cabinet at Luang Prabang was to be able to leave the city safely." Wearing a shoulder holster with a pistol in it the entire time he was in the royal capital, Phoumi said he told Souvanna that he was "staying very close to him." Phoumi continued, "If any attempt was made on my life he and I would die together."[57]

Phoumi's return to Vientiane was essential to achieving a broadly based Lao government, but neither his absence nor his presence deterred Souvanna from pressing ahead with policy objectives that had changed little since 1956. His first goal was the restoration of internal peace in the kingdom. Calling for a general amnesty and reconciliation among all Laotians, Souvanna appealed to Souphanouvong to meet with him in Vientiane or somewhere else. Souvanna's foreign policy sought "genuine" neutrality and friendly relations with the kingdom's neighbors and "all peace-loving" countries. He was also willing to accept economic aid from any country as long as it came without political preconditions.

A newer theme in Souvanna's political rhetoric was public criticism of the Lao government that had replaced his own in 1958. On Radio Vientiane, Souvanna declared that Prime Minister Phoui had made three major political and military errors that had compromised Lao neutrality and led to the country's current difficulties: First, he raised the status of the Lao mission in Saigon to an embassy, which suggested that the kingdom sought closer relations with the anticommunist Diem government. Second, Phoui had approved the establishment of a Nationalist Chinese consulate in Vientiane, which indicated a desire for closer relations with Chiang Kai-shek's anti-PRC government. And third, Phoui's government permitted the introduction of US military training teams in Laos, which both violated Geneva provisions Souvanna had pledged to obey and stirred up the communists.[58]

Privately, Souvanna told Ambassador Brown that he did not think that Laos should "renew [the] contract" for the US training teams. "It had been a mistake to bring [the] teams into Laos," the prime minister said. "It would have been much better" if the United States had expanded its longstanding training of Lao forces in Thailand, which had not produced an "adverse reaction" from the communists. Repeating an argument that had not persuaded American officials in the past, Souvanna said: "Westerners must recognize that [the] only way to save Laos and save [the] whole of SEA from communism is to allow [the] Lao to be genuinely neutral."[59]

Ambassador Brown was more receptive to Souvanna's appeal than any previous senior U.S official. Although he shared Washington's dim view of the prime minister's sometimes excessive self-confidence and his penchant for wishful thinking, Brown was impressed by Souvanna's leadership qualities and the sincerity of his convictions. The ambassador doubted that the communists would be "as gentle and accommodating" as Souvanna appeared to think, but the prime minister's insistence on some form of reconciliation with the Pathet Lao seemed to Brown "the only kind of approach that would have any chance of working."[60]

Brown was not alone in his appraisal. For example, Lewis E. Gleeck Jr., Parsons's special assistant for SEATO affairs, found the arguments of Souvanna and Brown "more compelling" than the rigid anticommunism of Sarit and U. Alexis Johnson, the American ambassador in Bangkok. "The core of the matter," in Gleeck's view, was that extreme right-wing leadership had "failed" in Laos: "Phoumi's [December 1959] coup forced out the Phoui government. The subsequent elections were rigged, and the Somsanith government with strong man Phoumi in the driver's seat, followed." Gleeck added: "If Phoumi hasn't any more real support that he has been able to generate (outside of Sarit, the PEO and [the CIA]) even when he stacks the deck, I don't see how we can continue to increase our support for him."[61]

But on the State Department's seventh floor, where the senior political appointees worked, the dim view of Souvanna remained unchanged. A telegram to Brown acknowledged that the prime minister appeared to have wide political support "at this time" and that his new cabinet represented an "exceptionally broad spectrum of Lao political life." Nonetheless, Brown was instructed to inform Souvanna: "While we understand his desire to restore peace to Laos we are convinced that [the] Pathet Lao leadership is controlled by [the] international Communist movement whose goal is enslavement not freedom of [the] country. This [is] even more clear to us in 1960 than it was in 1956."[62]

Phoumi, the department ordered, should be made "aware of our continued confidence in him as a staunch anti-Communist and our full support for [a] broadly based and constitutional cabinet which unifies responsible non-Communist elements." The Lao general, however, was unresponsive to such sentiments and in a "bitter mood," according to a report from Hasey. On September 2 Phoumi charged that the US government was "turning Laos over to [the] commies by its failure to support him." He admitted to Hasey that he had agreed to join the Souvanna government to "stall for time," indicating to the CIA officer that he "might launch a counter-coup." Phoumi also told Hasey what US policymakers most wanted to hear: he might be willing to assume his responsibilities as vice premier and minister of interior—if he could be sure of his physical safety in Vientiane.[63]

Phoumi's stated concern for his safety turned out to be a delaying tactic. US officials initially believed that the general had legitimate reasons for fear, particularly because of Kong Le's continued presence and influence in Vientiane. Souvanna, however, declared that the paratroop captain was under his control and offered several different proposals to ensure Phoumi's safety. Despite appeals from the prime minister and Ambassador Brown to return to Vientiane and participate in the government, Phoumi remained at his headquarters in Savannakhet. According to the CIA, Phoumi's attitude there was "a mixture of indecision, injured pride, and extreme bitterness over what he considers abandonment by the US."[64]

The Souvanna-Phoumi standoff presented the State Department with a policy choice that appeared to be a lose-lose proposition. The US government would not "support Phoumi in a separatist movement nor in [a] military attack against [the] legal government of Laos." Yet officials in Washington remained convinced of Souvanna's shiftiness and would not back "a government of Laos which appeared [to] be on [the] verge of yielding to impossible conditions imposed by Communist-led PL." In other words, the State Department was unwilling to take a chance either on Phoumi's takeover of the government or on Souvanna's policy of reconciliation with the Pathet Lao. "The Far Eastern Bureau," Parsons wrote later, "was caught in the middle and, without good alternatives to propose, still resisted radical moves."[65]

Clinging to the long-standing, but never realized, US goal of uniting the kingdom's anti- and noncommunist leaders, senior State Department officials returned to the Pentagon on September 9 for "another exchange of views on Laos."[66] In the absence of Defense Secretary Gates, John N. Irwin, assistant secretary of defense for international security affairs (ISA), led the charge against the State Department officials. Advising the Pentagon on foreign affairs, ISA has been described as "a buffer between the politically innocent views of the JCS and the militarily innocent views of State."[67] General Phoumi, Irwin declared, had received no "concrete" expressions of the US attitude toward him, no support for "any requests" he had made, and "no real reason to know that the U.S. Government" sympathized with him. Merchant and Parsons rebutted these assertions, citing the 8 million kip the CIA had provided, the explicit expressions of confidence in the general, and other tangible measures of US support. What Phoumi really wanted, Parsons said, "was support for civil war," something the United States refused to provide.[68]

Changing the topic, General Lemnitzer asked the State Department and CIA officials "who had made the estimate that Phoumi could return to Vientiane safely?" General Charles P. Cabell, deputy director of Central Intelligence, replied that it was the consensus of the embassy, the PEO, and the CIA station in Vientiane that "there was a reasonable expectation" for Phoumi's safety. (In a country where officials of every nationality faced varying degrees of risk, Ambassador Brown had earlier informed Washington that the embassy was "unable to guarantee [the] safety of any individual, including its own officers.") General Lemnitzer, unimpressed with Cabell's answer, said he "thought that only Phoumi could analyze the safety factor."[69]

When Admiral Burke asked Parsons whether he knew Phoumi personally, the State Department official said he did and summarized his view of the Lao general. He "was not the kind of fellow who could run Laos" for very long, said Parsons. "[The] best Lao government was under Phoui [Sananikone], but Phoumi had out-maneuvered him." He added that it was Phoumi who had rigged the 1960 elections, and it was his elite paratroop battalion that had overthrown the Somsanith government. At the end of his comments, Parsons expressed "grave doubts that in spite of all his good attributes Phoumi was the man to run Laos."[70]

Merchant, in his concluding remarks, reminded the assembled officials "that the only beneficiaries of a civil war would be the Pathet Lao and the Communists." Ironically, General Phoumi, perhaps the most vocal anticommunist in Laos, and his front man, Prince Boun Oum, announced a revolution against Souvanna's government the very next day. "From that time on," Ambassador Brown later recalled, "things began to deteriorate seriously."[71]

Chapter 9

Who the Hell Is Our Boy?

Phoumi's rebellion, though less shocking to the US government than Kong Le's coup, was still an unpleasant surprise for Americans in Vientiane and Washington. The Lao general informed US officials of his latest power grab on September 10, 1960, when embassy first secretary Julian P. Fromer traveled to Phoumi's headquarters in Savannakhet. The meeting was intended as one last attempt by Ambassador Brown to persuade the general to return to Vientiane and work with Souvanna, who had been frustrated by Phoumi's continued absence and was prepared to dismiss him from the cabinet. Phoumi had told the embassy that Fromer's visit would be pointless, but he did agree to see the ambassador's representative, who was joined by Jack Hasey, Phoumi's CIA case officer; Lieutenant Colonel John S. Wood Jr., the PEO adviser to Military Region IV; and Lieutenant Colonel Joel C. Hollis, the embassy's army attaché.[1]

Fromer, then forty-five years old and chief of the embassy political section, repeated the main themes of the US position. They included the importance of Phoumi's role in the government and his influence in negotiations with the Pathet Lao; the plans for protecting him, which included an FAL battalion loyal to him at the Vientiane airport and the presence of Kong Le hostages in Savannakhet; and the standard embassy warning: "The U.S. government cannot support you in any separatist movement or in any military attempt to overthrow the legal government."[2]

In a manner described as "polite and relaxed," Phoumi attempted to justify his behavior to the Americans. Returning to Vientiane would signify his acceptance of the Kong Le coup, which he said was "arranged by Souvanna Phouma." The general said that if he joined the government in Vientiane, it would only be a matter of time before Souvanna invited Pathet Lao representatives to join the cabinet; by then it would be "too late for me to get out and rally the country against the communists." Denouncing the prime minister for various acts of personal and political perfidy, Phoumi told Fromer: "I understand your point of view but you are not well informed of the situation in Vientiane. Souvanna wants to complete his coup and won't stop until I am destroyed."

When Colonel Hollis asked Phoumi what would happen if he continued to remain in Savannakhet, the general looked at his watch—it was 11:40 A.M.—saying: "I might as well tell you. At noon we will announce our revolution in the name of Boun Oum." The rebellion would include all of Laos. Vientiane would be placed under siege, but not under attack at the present time. Was the king aware of this action? Hasey asked. The king, Phoumi replied, was "not very well informed," but Prince Boun Oum would be sending him a message indicating respect for the monarchy and "the dissolution" of both the National Assembly and Souvanna's government. Fromer asked when the revolution would start. The general's reply suggested that he believed it was already under way: "Did you hear any explosions last night? Was there any damage around the airport?"[3]

Colonel Hollis, who had checked in with FAL leadership before flying to Savannakhet, said that he knew of no such reports. In fact, and likely unknown to Hollis and the others, two mortar rounds from Thailand had landed in Vientiane the previous night. One round exploded near the airport and the other close to a gasoline depot. Clearly expecting sabotage operations around the airport, Phoumi told the US officials, "Communications with Vientiane have been cut over the country."[4]

The broadcast by Boun Oum was an hour later than Phoumi had planned, but its content matched his remarks to Fromer. Additional communiqués that same day focused on maintaining control of information to and from Savannakhet. The revolutionary committee banned listening to radio broadcasts from Vientiane, the Pathet Lao, Hanoi, and Peking. Owners of radio and telegraphic equipment were ordered to inform Phoumi's headquarters of these possessions. And contact with Vientiane, the Pathet Lao, or anyone outside the kingdom required explicit approval from the revolutionary committee.

Prince Boun Oum led a family that not only was one of the wealthiest in the kingdom but also had ruled the separate principality of Champasak in southern Laos until 1946, when the French unified the country. In exchange for renouncing his sovereignty over Champasak, Boun Oum had been named inspector for political and administrative affairs of Laos, a largely honorific title that did, however, rank him just below the king and the crown prince in the royal hierarchy. By all accounts a courageous guerrilla fighter in World War II, Boun Oum served as prime minister of Laos from 1949 to 1950.

US officials had mixed opinions of the prince. L. Michael Rives, a young Foreign Service officer who had represented the United States in Vientiane until Charles Yost arrived in 1954, described Boun Oum as a "potential troublemaker" who disliked Crown Prince Savang and resented the royal family's treatment of him since he gave up his claim to rule southern Laos. Ambassador Smith considered him a "hedonistic playboy." In an intelligence summary, prepared for Allen Dulles to brief the NSC at its first meeting following Phoumi's revolution, the CIA characterized Boun Oum as "an earthy, practical man of action widely respected in southern Laos."[5]

According to the minutes of the NSC meeting, Dulles elaborated on the agency's institutional assessment of Boun Oum with the flattering observation that the prince had "a good reputation" and "a high standing in Laos." Dulles predicted that Boun Oum would "probably strengthen the Phoumi movement." Later in September, General Cabell, the agency's deputy director, provided a somewhat different assessment of the prince to top Pentagon and State Department officials. Boun Oum, he said, was a "crook and dope addict."[6]

The announcement of the revolution "gravely shocked" Souvanna Phouma, who particularly feared Thai support for Boun Oum and Phoumi. Without the general's return to Vientiane, Souvanna told Ambassador Brown, he would be unable to negotiate with the Pathet Lao from a position of strength and unity. "Under these circumstances," said Souvanna, "I have to stop all conversations with the PL." In his report to the State Department, Brown assessed the overall situation as "very Laotian." Phoumi did not intend to attack Vientiane in the immediate future, and Souvanna had not declared the general a rebel. As with Phoumi's initial plan for a countercoup against Kong Le, both the general and the prime minister were maneuvering for political and psychological advantage. Brown recommended that the US government "sit tight," at least until the prime minister had conferred with the king.[7]

Rejecting such a passive approach, Secretary of State Herter instructed the ambassador to seek an audience with the king as soon as possible. For the first time since Lao independence, State Department officials declared, the kingdom was "facing [a] real threat of dismemberment" because of regional and factional divisions. The only hope for peace, in the department's view, was the authority of the king to impose a royal reconciliation. To add force to the démarche, Brown should ask the other Western ambassadors in Vientiane to make similar representations to the king.[8]

Brown met with the king in Luang Prabang on September 13. After the ambassador presented the State Department's views, Savang said he was shocked, confused, and shamed by his country's political immaturity and the inability of its national institutions to operate effectively. He condemned the kingdom's lack of statesmen and men of decision but had no intention of forcing a reconciliation between Souvanna and Phoumi. In the king's view, the prime minister had full legal power to restore order. If he would not exercise that authority, then Souvanna should resign, and the king would select a new government. Savang told Brown that it was appropriate for Souvanna to seek advice from the king, but the prime minister "had no business ask[ing] him [to] make [a] decision or take action."[9]

When Brown asked who would be prime minister if Souvanna resigned, the king replied that it would "doubtless [be] Boun Oum." Savang described the prince as a "man of good will but not very well educated." The king added that there were also "some questions about his private life." In his report to the State Department, Brown wrote that the "king clearly distrusts and dislikes Souvanna and favors Phoumi." Remarking that Savang appeared "defensive," the ambassador predicted that the king would "do his best by inaction [to] force" Souvanna's resignation.[10]

To State Department officials, it seemed that Souvanna's resignation was the most likely outcome for the current political-military impasse in Laos. They informed Ambassador Brown that the "only available course" of action was to "work toward [the] formation of [a] government headed by a respected and non-controversial Lao which Phoumi can be persuaded to support." Brown disagreed, believing that it was time for the US government "to exercise its still considerable and perhaps decisive influence" by supporting "Souvanna wholeheartedly."[11]

In exchange for the prime minister's assurances in such areas as excluding Pathet Lao representation in the cabinet and granting amnesty for the Savannakhet group, Brown recommended that the United States "declare openly its complete support" for Souvanna and provide aid to Laos exclusively through his government. (In other words, no more backchannel aid to Phoumi and the forces loyal to him.) The ambassador concluded his recommendation to the department by stating that the CIA, PEO, and USOM chiefs in Vientiane concurred with his proposal.[12]

Brown's recommendation faced widespread opposition from other US officials. In Bangkok, Ambassador Johnson was "appalled" by the idea and by the "adverse effects such a policy would have on Thailand." Elbridge Durbrow, the American ambassador in Saigon, was "seriously concerned" that Brown's recommendation would "bring us into [a] direct clash" with the Diem government in South Vietnam. It was Durbrow's view that policymakers in Washington should "give greater weight" to the views of US allies in the region, rather than the United Kingdom or France, which bore "little direct responsibility for [the] security of [the] free world position in SEA."[13]

Policymakers in Washington agreed with Brown that full support for Boun Oum was undesirable and that continued inaction risked prolonging a "dangerous stalemate." But full support for Souvanna was simply "not acceptable." A joint state-defense message, dated September 16, proposed another alternative: If the crisis was not resolved in three days—that is, the resignation of Souvanna and the appointment of a new government—Brown should seek another audience with the king to convey the following message: unless the Lao resolved their internal divisions, Brown would have the authority "to suspend all aid to [the] government." The ambassador was further advised that such pressure would be applied gradually and that the US government did not "contemplate" abandoning Laos. But if the latest plan did not succeed, US officials would have to "consider any and all alternatives still open."[14]

Brown may have had this joint State Department–Defense Department message in mind when he later characterized some of his cables from Washington as "masterpieces of double-talk," largely unrelated to Laotian realities. In his September 18, 1960, reply to the department, he pointed out two significant and somewhat obvious problems with his instructions: the "king's unwillingness to take decisive action" and "Phoumi's obstinacy." The ambassador questioned the State Department assumption that there was a "respected figure" in Laos who could both control Kong Le and avoid the taint of being a "Phoumi/US stooge." And the most likely outcome of Souvanna's resignation, Brown predicted, would not be the orderly change in government that department officials envisioned but the immediate reoccupation of Vientiane by Kong Le with or without help from the Pathet Lao.[15]

Brown's disagreement with Washington initially triggered a mild rebuke from Parsons, who cabled that he was "a little disturbed by [the] lack of understanding which appears to be developing between us." In a follow-up letter and cable to Brown, however, senior State Department officials thanked Brown for his assessment, which was judged "particularly helpful" in making policy decisions. Although the ambassador disagreed frequently with his superiors at the State Department, they neither resented his views nor lost confidence in him as they had with Horace Smith. Parsons's long-standing relationship with Brown was undoubtedly one reason the embassy and the State Department maintained harmonious relations in the face of sharp policy differences. And unlike Ambassador Smith, who had a poisonous relationship with Henry Hecksher, Brown and his CIA chief of station worked together effectively. "Gordon Jorgensen was a man of exceptionally moral character, of very great professional ability, and a very wise person," Brown later recalled. The ambassador considered the CIA officers in Vientiane "top flight" and "relied on Jorgensen as my political advisor much more heavily than any member of my State Department section."[16]

As instructed by Washington, Ambassador Brown met with Souvanna to request an audience with the king. Brown officially informed the prime minister that the United States was "gravely concerned" by the deepening military and political divisions within Laos. The ambassador added that his comments did not imply a US belief that the current situation was Souvanna's fault. Nevertheless, all efforts at national reconciliation had failed, which made it difficult to imagine how US aid could be used effectively. Brown explained that he intended to ask the king to make further efforts to unify the country by "inviting, in fact ordering," Souvanna, Phoumi, and other leading Lao figures to meet under royal auspices and to agree on a government that "would command [the] support of all patriotic" Laotians.[17]

Souvanna replied that he was "fully in accord" with US policy. "Some reconciliation and agreement must be found," he said. "I hope you will succeed in this effort." When asked by Brown if he would be willing to have General Phoumi as commander-in-chief of the FAL, Souvanna replied that he was prepared to support any arrangement that "would bring [the] country together and stop [the] senseless fighting." Brown probed further, inquiring whether the prince would be willing to serve as a minister in a government led by someone else. Somewhat opaquely, Souvanna responded that it would depend on unnamed "conditions."[18]

Brown met with the king, whose mood appeared more decisive and confident. Savang told the ambassador that before the country's political divisions could be addressed, the FAL must be unified. The king said he had invited all his military commanders to Luang Prabang to build a consensus for an anticommunist policy and reestablish "some sense [of] harmony among" the FAL officers. Savang also expressed a willingness to retain Souvanna as prime minister if he changed his policy. It is all right to "be neutral," the king declared, "but [the government] must be anti-Communist."[19]

To force the resignation of the prime minister, General Phoumi and Prince Boun Oum engaged in a "war of nerves," in the words of CIA officials. Between September 10 and 20, there were four incidents in Vientiane of machine-gun fire, exploding mortar rounds, and detonation of planted explosives. Damage to the waterworks "considerably reduced" the town's "barely adequate" supply of water. The main theme of Phoumi's propaganda over Radio Savannakhet—the imminent attack of Vientiane by his force—was "beginning to affect [the] morale" of the population, the agency reported. Rumors of imminent or actual fighting had prompted some residents to build trenches around their homes.[20]

The contributions of Thailand's Prime Minister Sarit to Phoumi's psychological warfare included an embargo that prevented the delivery of virtually all imports to Vientiane. The embargo had been in effect since August, and by the end of September, Vientiane's supplies of diesel oil for the power plant, fuel for aircraft, and gasoline for cars were running low. On September 21 the RLG announced gas rationing in Vientiane. The following night an explosive charge detonated at the storage facilities of the Standard-Vacuum Oil Company outside of Vientiane. Plastic explosives were later found attached to a pump at a nearby civilian gas station.

Although Phoumi's psywar and sabotage tactics showed signs of success, his military forces appeared no match for Kong Le's. In a battalion-size engagement during the night of September 21–22, Kong Le's paratroopers routed Phoumi forces occupying Paksane, some ninety miles east of Vientiane. Phoumi's poorly led troops scattered into the bush or fled across the Mekong River into Thailand. Accounts of the fight were "extremely varied," according to the Vientiane CIA station, but it was clear that Kong Le had captured Paksane and that Phoumi had suffered "a major defeat, both militarily and psychologically."[21]

The debacle at Paksane prompted US military officials to question, at least momentarily, the leadership ability of General Phoumi. In a message to the JCS, Admiral Felt, commander of US forces in the Pacific, said that Phoumi had lost stature because of "his fear for his personal safety" and the "miserable performance of his forces at Paksane." Moreover, the general's sabotage and harassment activities in Vientiane had "done him no good." Maintaining the view that Souvanna was untrustworthy and naive, Admiral Felt wanted to ensure that Phoumi "accepted and followed" US advice "even if we have to ram it down his throat" by withholding aid. Observing that many of the US messages to Phoumi had been delivered by midlevel embassy, CIA, and military officials, Felt cabled that "no big US guns have been trained on him personally, with [an] unequivocal Dutch Uncle talk."[22]

Smart, short, and irascible, Admiral Harry D. "Don" Felt was a Naval Academy graduate who had led carrier strikes against the Japanese in World War II. His awards for heroism and extraordinary achievement included the Distinguished Flying Cross, the Navy Cross, and the Legion of Merit. His postwar career included a variety of increasingly responsible assignments, both ashore and at sea. CNO Arleigh Burke selected Felt as his deputy in 1956 because of his independence of thought and willingness to question his boss's decisions. Provoking fear and outrage in the halls of the Pentagon, the demanding Felt "would grab three-star officers by the lapels, literally shake them," according to Vice Admiral William P. Mack, "and say, 'Why don't you do so and so or such and such?' They'd be thirty or forty pounds heavier than he was, but that didn't bother him much at all." When the command assignment at CINCPAC opened up in 1958, Admiral Burke facilitated the transfer of his pugnacious deputy. "It isn't pleasant to fight continually with a good friend," Burke later recalled.[23]

Admiral Felt's September 30, 1960, assessment of the situation in Laos raised questions not only about Phoumi's leadership but also about the quality of intelligence from the kingdom. Foreshadowing similar

US concerns during the Vietnam War in the 1960s, Felt told officials in Washington that there was insufficient information for policymakers to make informed judgments about Laos. Intelligence on military activity, for example, was provided by FAL officers. This meant that the US government was relying on "inexpert" sources and information "subject to distortion."[24]

Felt's analysis was "disturbing" to General Nathan F. Twining, chairman of the Joint Chiefs of Staff. Defense Secretary Gates called the CINCPAC appraisal "a very bothersome message," according to the minutes of a September 30 where-do-we-go-from-here meeting of senior Pentagon and State Department officials. Gates admitted that "he continued to be mixed up about the situation" in Laos. The Defense Department "wanted support for 'our boy' [Phoumi]," he said, but this "opinion was not shared by the Ambassador. Then this recent dispatch from CINCPAC casts doubt not only on Souvanna Phouma but also on Phoumi. 'Who the hell *is* our boy?'"[25]

Admiral Burke acknowledged that he "was confused, too." Although Phoumi had lost stature, Burke said, he was "still the only anti-communist with a force in being. We have to use the assets we have." Declaring that Souvanna was "not even a weak reed but merely jelly," Burke repeated a common refrain among the US supporters of the Lao general: "Phoumi may be an SOB but he is our SOB."[26]

John Steeves, who substituted for Parsons at this meeting, later recalled: "Phoumi, we always knew, was either stupid, inept, corrupt—he was a bastard, but he was our bastard." The consensus view in Washington, said Steeves, was, "We must stick with the anti-communist group no matter how bad they were. Try to reform, try to control them, but you couldn't stop paying the troops. You couldn't stop aiding the country. All you could do was put up with their nonsense as best you could and try to control them."[27]

The problem for the US government was that Phoumi could not be controlled by anyone, with the possible exception of "Uncle" Sarit in Thailand. Despite repeated US references to the Lao general as "our boy," "our SOB," and "our bastard"—not to mention having full-time CIA and PEO officers at his headquarters—Phoumi was unwilling to subordinate his personal ambition to rule Laos to US policy goals. As the strongest anticommunist in the kingdom, the general appeared to be the one with leverage in US-Laos relations. "Phoumi was persuaded that when the chips were down we would back him, regardless," Brown later recalled. "Therefore he was in the position of running American foreign policy and not the United States."[28]

At the September 30 meeting with Pentagon officials, Livingston Merchant made the dubious declaration that the US government did "have one ace in the hole," former Prime Minister Phoui Sananikone. Steeves, according to the minutes of the meeting, informed the group that "Phoui hadn't been able to get along with the king," implying that the US government should not count on his return as prime minister. Steeves could have said more, as Ambassador Brown did later. Recalling Washington's "exasperating" requests to produce an alternative leader to Souvanna, Brown declared: "The only trouble with Phoui was that Souvanna hated him, Phoumi hated him, the King hated him, and Kong Le hated him, and he had no popular support. Otherwise, he was an admirable fellow for Prime Minister."[29]

It was at this meeting, just two months after Brown's arrival in Vientiane, when Pentagon officials made one of their earliest requests to recall the ambassador. Secretary Gates said what State Department officials knew well: "There was a basic conflict between Washington and the Ambassador." Merchant defended Brown, pointing out that his messages reflected the views of the PEO chief, the CIA station chief, and the military attachés. Steeves reminded the group that "in every instance Ambassador Brown had forcefully carried out his orders." This made no difference to Admiral Burke, who replied: "Brown appeared tied to Souvanna Phouma and what was needed was a new broom."[30]

The outcome of the State Department–JCS meeting was a cable to Ambassador Brown instructing him "to seek an immediate audience with the king." Brown should inform the monarch that the political situation in Laos had "disintegrated" to a point where he must "take authority into his hands." Savang should appoint a "caretaker" government under royal decree, which would be led either by him or by a prime minister "other than Souvanna Phouma." In an FYI postscript to the telegram, Brown was informed of Washington's increasing tilt toward Phoumi: "Believe you should know that there is strong and growing sentiment here to give exclusive and all-out support to those able and willing to salvage at least that portion of the country centered in Savannakhet if the King [is] unwilling or unable to take such leadership [as] suggested above."[31]

Brown agreed with the State Department that it was "imperative" to persuade the king to "force unity" among the Lao leaders. The ambassador, however, continued to believe that policymakers viewed Souvanna too negatively and Phoumi too positively. An immediate question from the embassy's point of view was whether the United States should insist upon the "removal of Souvanna at all costs." Brown thought it was "preferable" for the king to meet with all the principals and have that group agree on a government and prime minister. The ambassador, however, had an unequivocal view of Phoumi's revolutionary committee, declaring that it "must be dissolved."[32]

Brown acknowledged that Souvanna's current relative strength meant that he would be less inclined to compromise and that the king would have to exert more pressure on him "towards accommodation than [on] Phoumi." (The Lao general, according to a CIA assessment, appeared "to be nearing the end of his rope.") Souvanna had reportedly sent the king a draft royal ordinance dismissing from the army not only Phoumi but also some two dozen other officers loyal to the Savannakhet revolutionary group. The prime minister also pressed forward with his program of pursuing peace and neutrality, preparing for negotiations with the Pathet Lao, and accrediting the Soviet ambassador to Cambodia as ambassador to Laos. Souvanna's reputation as a peacemaker received a further boost from the Pathet Lao, which did not fight his troops but continued to attack Phoumi's.[33]

Despite his liabilities, Souvanna seemed to Brown the only alternative to chaos in Laos. The ambassador was sure that removing the prime minister would spark a resurgence of Pathet Lao activity that would be almost impossible to combat, given the current political and military divisions in the country. Policymakers, Brown urged, should decide to "make [the] best of Souvanna," who shared US worries about growing Pathet Lao strength. General Phoumi's cooperation would be welcome, but to Brown it appeared that Souvanna was the "only rallying point left" in the country.[34]

The ambassador took an especially dim view of Pentagon plans to provide arms and supplies to Phoumi and to airlift his forces as needed. Such support was required, in the view of the JCS, to prevent another defeat that would lead to the "complete demoralization" of Phoumi's forces. With the concurrence of the state and defense departments, the JCS authorized CINCPAC on October 3 to provide FAL forces loyal to Phoumi with "necessary arms and supplies." According to a Pentagon summary of logistic support to Phoumi, CINCPAC and the PEO requested (and later received) large amounts of weapons, ammunition, communications equipment, clothing, and money over a ten-day period beginning on October 4. The arms included carbines (4,000), .45 caliber submachine guns (1,000), M7 grenade launchers (300), 60 mm light mortars (25), 57 mm recoilless rifles (13), and 81 mm heavy mortars (10). The military cash requests in this period were $300,000 for rice and related supplies and $250,000 to pay for "airlift inside Laos."[35]

It seemed to Brown that the amount of military assistance required to make Phoumi's forces effective would be regarded within Laos as a "clear declaration" against the lawful government. Externally, US military aid to the Lao general would be viewed as intervention in the internal affairs of another country, equivalent to the Soviet Union's interference in the Congo, which President Eisenhower had recently criticized at the United Nations. As for US-RLG relations, massive amounts of support for Phoumi would "diminish, if not eliminate," US influence with Souvanna, who might ask the Americans to leave the country for supporting the "rebels."[36]

As instructed, Ambassador Brown met again with the king on October 6, 1960. Savang, who seemed disgusted with everyone, had called together his military commanders on September 28, and they in turn had agreed to a cease-fire. Kong Le, the most dynamic and arguably the most powerful military officer in the FAL, neither attended the king's meeting nor felt bound by the agreement reached there. He quickly resumed offensive operations against Phoumi's forces southeast of Paksane. "Kong Le was still [a] force in Vientiane," Savang said, adding that the "Pathet Lao were pulling [the] strings there."[37]

Brown appealed to the king as the only person in Laos with the power and influence to resolve the current crisis. The US government, Brown said, believed drastic measures were required, such as the king taking power and appointing a prime minister and army commander-in-chief who could restore order and unity. Brown said that if no action was taken, "all might be lost." The king replied that "perhaps all was already lost."

In his report to the State Department, Brown cabled: "At this point I thought he was going to cry."

The king refused Brown's appeal for action, saying he would appoint a new government only if Souvanna resigned or the National Assembly passed a vote of no confidence in the prime minister. The ambassador informed Savang that, as of October 1, US aid to Laos had been suspended, with the exception of urgent supplies for troops fighting the Pathet Lao. The US government was, however, prepared to provide aid to the FAL through the king or any other channel he might establish. The king again demurred, replying that the suspension of aid might teach his people to use such assistance as intended. The king, Brown reported, felt "rebuffed in his one effort at reconciliation and therefore [was] willing to let [the] situation further degenerate rather than commit Royal prestige in [an] effort which he inwardly fears might fail and thereby diminish Royal power and authority."[38]

Because of the king's "unwillingness to assume the responsibilities requested of him," Washington policymakers decided "to make [a] last desperate effort to work through and with Souvanna Phouma as the legal facade of legitimate government." The United States would support the prime minister if he took the following steps: (1) move his government, at least temporarily, from Vientiane to Luang Prabang, where Kong Le would exercise less influence; (2) take all feasible steps to prevent Kong Le from attacking any other FAL units; (3) preserve government assets, including the treasury, preferably by transferring cash to Luang Prabang; and (4) desist from current negotiations with the Pathet Lao. Souvanna's reaction to these conditions would be "a test of his intentions," in the words of Livingston Merchant.[39]

Although grudgingly conceding the absence of immediate alternatives to Souvanna, Washington policymakers continued their efforts to maintain Phoumi's morale and his forces' fighting ability. The CIA transported two hundred Lao paratroopers training in Thailand to southern Laos and provided the general's forces with rice and pay. The Pentagon assigned PEO operations and logistics officers to Phoumi's headquarters in Savannakhet. If the "last desperate ploy" of working through Souvanna failed, the State Department informed Brown, the US government must face the "difficult alternative" of providing exclusive support to Phoumi.[40]

Brown's instructions also informed him that a "special team" from Washington would be traveling to Laos to provide the ambassador and other mission officials with "the thinking" behind this latest approach. The members of the team would be Assistant Secretary of State Parsons, Assistant Secretary of Defense John Irwin, and Vice Admiral Herbert D. Riley, CINCPAC chief of staff. The primary objective of the visit, which was not mentioned in the message to Brown, was to reconcile differences between the ambassador and Washington. Any differences in views were to be isolated, but Undersecretary Dillon made it clear to State Department and Pentagon officials that he "hoped . . . there would be no differences."[41]

On October 9 Brown discussed with Souvanna the US conditions for support. The meeting, according to the ambassador's report to the State Department, went as well "as could reasonably be expected." The prime minister had no problem with the suggestions to control Kong Le and preserve the treasury's assets. Souvanna also indicated that moving the government to Luang Prabang could be arranged. US objections to negotiation with the Pathet Lao, however, "would be very difficult," as arrangements had been made and a quick settlement was "important." Souvanna promised to give all the US conditions serious thought, and Brown did not press him for an immediate reply.[42]

The ambassador informed Washington that Souvanna was "obviously deeply annoyed and clearly personally hurt" by reports of FAL paratroopers in Thailand transported to Phoumi's base in southern Laos. The prime minister, who had wanted to deploy these crack troops to Vientiane or the Plaine des Jarres, said this action showed that the United States "followed [the] wishes [of the] rebels rather than [the] legal government." In an October 8 letter to Brown, Souvanna had raised objections to the US condition that any further aid to Laos would have to be distributed to all provinces, including those controlled by Boun Oum and Phoumi. The prime minister wrote that no legal government "could finance [a] rebellion." Moreover, the imposition of such a condition would be an infringement of "Lao sovereignty."[43]

The Vientiane CIA station noted that this letter was the first time Souvanna had formally raised the issue of US interference in Lao affairs. In an October 10 summary of recent events in the kingdom for Undersecretary Dillon, John Steeves wrote: "A basic concern of the Department has been the possibility that Souvanna, if pressed too far, particularly in connection with our supplying and paying Phoumi's forces, while they are still in a state of revolt against his government, might lodge a complaint in the UN against US activities in Laos violating the sovereign wishes of the legal government."[44]

Undersecretary Dillon met with President Eisenhower on October 11 to brief him on Laos. He arranged the meeting because the president might soon have to decide among some "not very pleasant" alternatives facing the US government. The White House meeting was a relatively small one; the only other attendees were Merchant and Steeves from the State Department, Gates and General Lemnitzer from the Pentagon, DCI Allen Dulles, and General Goodpaster from the White House staff. The president's advisers began with grim military and political assessments of conditions in the country. General Lemnitzer said that the military situation with the Pathet Lao was "not at all satisfactory." Dulles reported that the Soviet ambassador was due in Vientiane the following day; that promises of Soviet aid were likely forthcoming; and that Souvanna was dealing with the Pathet Lao.[45]

Dillon informed the president of "the threat of being 'hailed into' the UN for aggressive intervention at any time," according to the minutes of the meeting. He also said that for some weeks there had been differing points of view about Laos between officials in Vientiane and Washington, with the former inclined to support Souvanna and the latter Phoumi. Assistant secretaries Parsons and Irwin, together with Admiral Riley, were in Southeast Asia now, Dillon said, in an attempt to resolve these differences and propose further actions "if the situation does not develop favorably."[46]

Defense Secretary Gates told the president that he was "very pessimistic" about "keeping the country for the free world, even if Souvanna does not make some kind of deal with the Communists. The prospects are not good." Although portions of his comments about providing covert supplies to Phoumi remain classified, Gates observed that simply paying the general's troops was complicated by the lack of Lao currency available to the US government.

On the diplomatic front, Merchant reported that Thailand and South Vietnam were "deeply disturbed" by an emerging communist threat on their borders. Dillon added that there was a split among the SEATO allies, with the British, the French, and the Australians reluctant to back "any vigorous action" in support of Phoumi. According to the minutes of the meeting, there was further discussion, followed by President Eisenhower's admission that he had little to suggest "beyond what is now being done." His one concrete proposal, according to General Goodpaster's minutes, was "to try to take special measures to win Souvanna Phouma to our side, such as placing funds in escrow for him in Bangkok."[47]

Although he was not called upon to make any decisions that day, Eisenhower exhibited little of the leadership that he had often demonstrated at other times and in other areas of foreign affairs. John Steeves, who attended the meeting in Parsons's absence, was particularly unimpressed with the president's suggestion of bribing the already wealthy Souvanna. Years later Steeves recalled that Eisenhower "was kind of looking out on the rose garden—he turned around and he said, 'Ah, that doesn't sound very serious to me.' He said, 'Why don't you give that guy Souvanna Phouma six thousand dollars and he'll forget it.'" To Steeves, who distrusted the prime minister and feared a communist takeover in Laos, it seemed that the president understood neither the issues nor the personalities involved. Steeves concluded that the US problems in the kingdom were "to some degree a reflection of the disinterest of the President himself and abysmal ignorance. Eisenhower just couldn't care less."[48]

This harsh view of Eisenhower's interest in Laos is likely overstated, but it does raise the question, Who was leading the formulation of Lao policy at the end of his presidency? The documentary record indicates that both Eisenhower and Herter paid little attention to Laos and demonstrated even less command of the issues when discussing the country. Undersecretary Dillon and Livingston Merchant, the undersecretary for political affairs, were more deeply involved in Lao affairs, but they lacked the authority to make policy. Years later Parsons observed that in the final months of 1960, the Eisenhower administration "found it difficult or impossible to make top-level action decisions on new or changing problems or crises, such as we were undergoing in Laos and Viet-Nam."[49]

In his history of the Eisenhower administration and Vietnam, David L. Anderson found a similar pattern of high-level inattention to a country that appeared relatively stable when compared to neighboring Laos. After the intense deliberations about united action, the Geneva conference, and support for Diem during Eisenhower's first term, there was "little evidence of the president's hand, hidden or otherwise, in Vietnam policy making." In the final months of 1960, when the unraveling of the "Diem miracle" in South Vietnam began to accelerate, "Eisenhower and Secretary of State Christian Herter provided inadequate leadership. Herter had not been involved in the extensive Indochina discussions of 1954–55 and was unfamiliar with Southeast Asian affairs."[50]

As with Laos, officials in the US national security bureaucracy held divided views about the most effective ways of combating the communist-led insurgency in South Vietnam. The State Department sought to press Diem to reform his authoritarian leadership, and the Pentagon urged a more empathetic approach to the South Vietnamese president. In the fall of 1960, a failed coup by South Vietnamese paratroopers increased tensions between the US government and Diem, who felt the Americans in Saigon had been too evenhanded during the battle. Possibly inspired by Kong Le's example, the attempt to overthrow Diem prompted Livingston Merchant to question facetiously "whether the U.S. should stop training paratroopers."[51]

Eisenhower biographer Stephen Ambrose wrote that the fall of 1960 was a "terrible" time for the president. He had hoped to improve US-Soviet relations by the end of his presidency, an aspiration doomed by the downing of a U-2 spy plane over Soviet territory the previous May and by Khrushchev's subsequent denunciation of the United States at an aborted summit meeting in Paris. These setbacks, "combined with Eisenhower's lame duck status, took much of the energy and vitality out of the President and his administration." He was also disappointed that presidential candidates John F. Kennedy and Richard M. Nixon adopted anticommunist rhetoric that criticized—directly in Kennedy's case and indirectly in Nixon's—Eisenhower's measured approach to national security and defense spending. The election of Kennedy, whom the president neither liked nor respected, seemed to Eisenhower a repudiation of his leadership. The day after the election, a visibly depressed Eisenhower told his son: "All I've been trying to do for eight years has gone down the drain."[52]

In his letters and his unpublished memoir, J. Graham Parsons frequently referred to the official symbol of Laos—three elephants under a parasol—whenever he mentioned his "tricephalous" trip to Laos with Assistant Secretary of Defense John Irwin and Vice Admiral Herbert Riley from CINCPAC. The other word Parsons invariably associated with the visit was "regret." Despite their instructions, the three officials did nothing to resolve the differing views of Vientiane and Washington, and Parsons later referred to the trip as "a virtual disaster."[53]

It was Friday evening, October 7, 1960, when Parsons learned of this particular assignment. He was just finishing up a week of long-delayed vacation at his family home in Stockbridge, Massachusetts, when a State Department official telephoned him, requesting his immediate return to Washington for a Saturday morning meeting with Undersecretary Dillon. Parsons later recalled "telling Doug that I was a poor choice for this mission, both because I was not privy to the State-Def[ense]-JCS discussion which triggered it and because Souvanna and I had so long had opposing views about his policies. He brushed this aside with just a few words."[54]

Perhaps the most unappealing aspect of the trip was that two assistant secretaries and a vice admiral were unlikely to resolve the institutional conflicts of the embassy in Vientiane, the State Department, and the Pentagon, not to mention the disagreements between the analytical and operational components of the CIA. On the same day Parsons was called back from vacation, Sherman Kent, the chief of CIA's Office of National Estimates, submitted to Allen Dulles an appraisal of Laos that was closer to the embassy's view of the situation than his agency's operational directorate. Kent's memorandum presciently concluded: "Phoumi's continuance as a political and military factor is likely to be more disruptive than constructive in the present situation."[55]

A key purpose of the Parsons-Irwin-Riley mission was to determine "a pattern and rhythm" for supplying General Phoumi that would not place the US government in an "unfavorable light should the Lao situation be brought into the UN." An October 15 cable from Parsons to Washington indicated that the group could not reach agreement on this point. He favored a minimalist form of support for Phoumi—a "holding action" aimed at maintaining his fighting capabilities rather than building them into a more effective force for offensive operations. The latter course of action would involve more US advisers and materiel, which would lead to "complications with [the] already suspicious French" and risk a request from Souvanna to withdraw the PEO from Laos. Ambassador Brown concurred with Parsons's analysis and recommendation.[56]

Assistant Secretary Irwin, however, emphasized the importance of an effective system of support and supply for Phoumi. He argued that the US government was already assuming some risk by assisting the general, and the only way to avoid it would be to "do nothing for Phoumi and little for other anti-Communist forces in Laos." Since the United States could "already be placed in an unfavorable light," Irwin proposed an "enlarged mechanism" for supporting the general's forces. Agreeing that US support should be provided in a way "least likely to disturb [the] political situation," Irwin recommended that Phoumi receive "sufficient personnel to carry out his operational and logistic responsibilities." Admiral Riley agreed with Irwin's analysis and recommendation.[57]

In a follow-up cable to the State Department, which he did not show to Irwin or Riley until after he sent it, Parsons brooded over the difficulty of "salvaging" the situation in Laos. One factor that had struck him powerfully since his arrival in the kingdom was Souvanna's "power to place us in [an] absolutely impossible situation." Until "events frustrate or defeat him and he leaves office," Souvanna had the legal right to demand that the US government cease interfering in Lao affairs. "He could easily be goaded into demanding that we remove the PEO," which would effectively end US support to Laos. Two critical needs, in Parsons's view, were resuming US military and civilian support for anticommunist elements throughout the country and ending the "present untenable and exposed position of giving support to [a] group of declared rebels by [the] legal government."[58]

A key Parsons recommendation was "seeking Souvanna's acceptance" of US support to Phoumi for operations against the Pathet Lao. Ambassador Brown, Parsons suggested, could tell the prime minister that the fragmented Lao supply system and the limited amounts of materiel and food in Vientiane precluded centralized military assistance to anticommunist forces in the kingdom. The United States would ensure that Phoumi did not use its aid against Souvanna and would, of course, cease such assistance should the general attack the RLG. Although Souvanna might not agree to this proposal, his acceptance would mean that strong US "support to all regions becomes possible and legitimate." And should reports of widespread FAL disillusionment with Souvanna prove true, the resumption of US aid would strengthen the hand of military leaders like FAL commander General Ouan in coercing the prime minister's resignation and the appointment of a new government by the king.[59]

On October 17 Parsons learned of an "abrupt turn in events" that suggested his proposed course of action with Souvanna might be feasible. Intelligence received by the American embassy in Bangkok indicated that the prime minister had directed his FAL commander in Luang Prabang to attack nearby Pathet Lao forces. Souvanna also planned to send a representative to meet with Phoumi in Thailand, "presumably with [a] view to achieving unity." Parsons agreed to a proposal by Ambassador Brown for an immediate meeting with the prime minister to discuss a resumption of US aid to all FAL forces. As part of this plan, Phoumi would be instructed to "respond constructively" to any Souvanna proposal for reconciliation. Parsons wrote Washington that he and the other senior officials in Laos had no "illusions" about the prime minister, but they agreed, "We would be derelict if we did not grasp [this] opportunity."[60]

Ambassador Brown met with Souvanna at 4:00 P.M., October 17, 1960. The prime minister reported that he had been in Luang Prabang the previous day and had found his military commanders "very uneasy" about the Pathet Lao. He instructed his officers to resist when attacked and to go on the offensive if he were unable to arrange a genuine ceasefire in the next day or two. Souvanna said that he had instructed General Ouan to make all necessary preparations and equip the FAL for combat. It is "necessary to be strong," the prime minister said, adding that he had "no intention [of] capitulating to [the] Pathet Lao or of yielding to unacceptable" demands.[61]

Brown replied that he was glad to hear this because US officials shared his view of the danger posed by the Pathet Lao. What was most essential, the ambassador said, was the unity of the army, which was rapidly disintegrating. The US government wanted to help rebuild the effectiveness of the FAL and to provide it with money and materiel. The only way to support the army throughout the country, however, was to provide supplies directly to the commanders of all Lao military regions. It "would be a great contribution" to FAL unity, Brown said, if the prime minister "would give his approval to such [a] course of action."

Reflecting on the implications of providing pay and weapons to Phoumi's forces, Souvanna said that the US proposal would be "very, very difficult" to accept. The army must be supported, said Souvanna, but any arms supplied to Phoumi would probably be turned against the government. The ambassador said he was sure that Phoumi "would give categorical assurances on this point." Moreover, the US government would use its influence to ensure the general's compliance. If necessary, Brown said, we would station men with Phoumi's forces to guarantee that US-supplied materiel would not be "used against Vientiane."

Souvanna said "he did not trust Phoumi on this point," nor was there any basis for such trust. Nonetheless, the prime minister said, he was sending an emissary to Bangkok to seek out Phoumi and ask him once again to dissolve his revolutionary committee and to acknowledge the authority of Souvanna's government. If the general had conditions for accepting his authority, the prime minister would consider them. "I am stretching forth a hand to him despite all that he has said and done to me," Souvanna said.[62]

On the same day, and at virtually the same hour, as Ambassador Brown's démarche to Souvanna in Vientiane, a meeting between Phoumi and US military and intelligence officials took place in Ubon, Thailand, just across the Mekong River from the Lao general's headquarters. In contrast to the ambassador's meeting, which suggested a modest degree of reconciliation between Souvanna and American officials, the conference in Ubon conveyed a message to Phoumi that the US government "fully and unequivocally supported his ambitions" to march on Vientiane and seize control of the government.[63]

The Americans present at the meeting in Ubon were Assistant Secretary Irwin and Admiral Riley; lieutenant colonels Albert R. Brownfield and John S. Wood, PEO officers who served as Phoumi's military adviser and deputy military adviser, respectively; and Bangkok CIA chief Red Jantzen and case officer Jack Hasey, who were political advisers to the general. Parsons was invited to attend the meeting, but he remained in Bangkok to discuss Thai affairs with Ambassador Johnson and attend to other Far East matters. His failure to travel to Ubon meant that every US official there was an ardent supporter of the general. There would be no balancing State Department voice to urge the general to dissolve his revolutionary committee or reconcile with Souvanna.[64]

According to a memorandum of conversation, Phoumi thanked Irwin for meeting with him and Boun Oum and for the generous US aid enabling "Free Laos" to fight communism. Phoumi, whose military fortunes had improved somewhat since the humiliating defeat at Paksane, reviewed his military and political plans for the Americans. The first item he mentioned was the importance of a coordinated attack on Vientiane. To control the country, Phoumi said, he "must retake Vientiane at [the] right time."

Irwin began his remarks by saying that Parsons, Riley, and he had traveled to Laos to consult with the leading figures in the kingdom and to express US concern with the situation. The trip to Ubon by the two Pentagon officials, Irwin said, "should show our confidence and support" for Phoumi. Irwin then explained the "two U.S. policies" for support to Laos. The first was "support for anti-communist forces." The second was an "attempt to unify them under [a] legal government."

Irwin told Phoumi that because of US relations with its allies, as well as "certain restrictions" imposed by the government in Vientiane, there were limits on how much support the United States could currently provide anticommunist forces in Laos. For the US government to provide Phoumi with pay and supplies, the general "must respect these restrictions," Irwin said. "Independent and uncoordinated actions will only jeopardize our aid." He emphasized that Phoumi must work closely with Colonel Brownfield and Jantzen in making his operational plans. Irwin "hoped" that the Lao general understood the US could not "presently" participate in certain actions. Phoumi replied that his views were "identical" to those of the United States. My "sole aim [is] Lao unity," he said, assuring the US officials of his "full cooperation."[65]

Admiral Riley then discussed the two phases envisioned by the US military. In the first, current phase, which he hoped would "soon change," the US government had to exercise restraint. Contrary to the natural tendency of a military man, offensive action must be delayed. Phoumi should consolidate his strength in the south and develop an impregnable defense against the Pathet Lao and Kong Le. Riley warned the Lao general that attacking Vientiane or Kong Le before "we can provide substantial help" would place the United States in a position where it would be unable to assist him. Once the "anti–Pathet Lao elements become legal"—that is, Boun Oum and Phoumi—the US government would be prepared to "openly support" them.

Irwin stressed to Phoumi, "We have [to] move cautiously. You must not move independently or we [will] have to consider stopping aid to you. None of us wish this but such action would place us in [a] difficult posture on [the] international scene." The Pentagon civilian added that Phoumi's "shelling" of Vientiane did much to harm his position internationally.

Thus far, according the minutes of the meeting, Irwin and Riley had attempted to exercise some degree of control over the headstrong general.

But Phoumi, despite his earlier assertions of complete agreement with American attitudes, quickly dismissed his visitor's concerns. The general declared that the establishment of a Soviet embassy in Vientiane provided an "idea [of] how little time [was] left." The Soviet Union, he said, wanted to "install Pathet Lao forces in Vientiane. Urgent action [was] needed." It was doubtful, he said, there was time for anything else but acting directly, installing a legal government, and reestablishing a "free country." He then laid out his plan for seizing Vientiane and establishing a new government.[66]

The record of the meeting indicates no objections to his plan by the Pentagon or intelligence officials present. In fact, the response to Phoumi was quite the contrary, according to a top-secret, eyes-only, no-distribution cable that Brown sent Parsons some three weeks later: "I am reliably informed that during [the] Irwin-Riley visit [to Ubon], after [the] formal conversation was finished, Riley took Phoumi aside and told him privately that [the] U.S. had completely lost confidence in Souvanna and was backing Phoumi to go back and clean up [the] situation."[67]

Parsons, who regretted not going to Ubon with Irwin and Riley, wrote in his memoir that his absence was "interpreted by Phoumi's enthusiastic [CIA] liaison," Jack Hasey, and "by Phoumi himself, as a green light to march on Vientiane." Parsons also wrote that he "was told"—the source was not identified—that Admiral Riley "interpreted my abstention as tacit approval of the Defense/JCS position, which it was not." What Assistant Secretary Irwin thought of Parsons's absence is unknown, but his overall conclusion from the trip to Laos was that "no improvement could be expected in the US position there so long as Souvanna remained Premier."[68]

The policy train wreck resulting from the three officials' trip to Laos should have been evident to anyone reading the cable traffic. In a memorandum to colleagues in Dillon's office, Foreign Service officer Seymour Weiss pointed out the contradictory messages and actions of Parsons, Irwin, and Riley. State Department officials had been generally satisfied with the diplomatic efforts of Brown and Parsons and the policy shift toward "support of the legitimate government under Souvanna," Weiss wrote. Yet the telegram from Irwin reporting on the meeting with Phoumi gave no indication that the military officials had even asked the general to cooperate with Souvanna or to dissolve his revolutionary committee.

In fact, it appeared to Weiss that "Phoumi intends to try and recapture control of the government displacing Souvanna in the process—precisely what Defense and CIA have consistently advocated." Hoping for further clarification of US policy, Weiss observed: "Heaven only knows where this leaves us."[69]

Most senior US officials appeared to ignore the divided opinions and actions of the Parsons-Irwin-Riley mission to Laos. After reviewing their "very helpful" reports and recommendations, the State Department informed Ambassador Brown of the latest Laos policy decision: "For reasons of expediency" the US government accepted "the inevitable of working with Souvanna Phouma as the constitutional and legally installed Prime Minister." Operating through Souvanna would be "expensive cover," in the words of Brown's instructions, particularly because it required paying Kong Le's troops. The costs, however, were "considered acceptable" to "buy time" for building up Phoumi's strength.[70]

This policy, according to the State Department, had "the additional merit of consistency and continuity in the eyes" of the British, the French, and the Australians. It was important to gain "the maximum support from them." The ambassador was instructed to continue "to press Souvanna Phouma to extricate himself from the influence of Kong Le." Furthermore, Brown should attempt to slow down and, if possible, "sabotage" the prime minister's negotiations with the Pathet Lao. A final task assigned to the US mission in Vientiane was to persuade Phoumi to dissolve "voluntarily" his revolutionary committee.[71]

On October 19 Souvanna agreed to the US proposal that all pay for the FAL would go through Vientiane, strengthening at least the appearance of RLG control over Phoumi's forces. The prime minister also consented to direct US delivery of munitions and other supplies to FAL forces in southern and northern Laos. Souvanna did, however, have two conditions. The first was that US aid should not be used against his government; the second was that US assistance should not support the secession of southern Laos. Brown replied that "those conditions would be acceptable."[72]

Ambassador Brown, whose three months of service in the kingdom had been among the most eventful in the history of US-Lao relations, allowed himself a moment of mild optimism in an October 21 cable to Washington: "For the first time in many weeks, the complicated pieces of the puzzle which is Laos seem to be grouping themselves into a pattern which is potentially manageable, at least for the short term." Even the French were being helpful, allowing the US government to supply Phoumi through their airfield at Seno. Brown wrote, "We should endeavor to exploit and fortify the presently developing set of tenuous relationships which enable us legally to support countrywide resistance to PL." State Department officials tended to agree with Brown, observing that there had been indications of "some forward progress" toward "stabilization" of the situation in Laos.[73]

The qualified optimism in Vientiane and Washington was a sharp contrast to the "marked state of worry and depression" in the UK Foreign Office in London. British officials responsible for Lao affairs were convinced that Souvanna and his plans for a negotiated settlement with the Pathet Lao were "the only possible and practical course for Laos." Unlike officers in the Pentagon and the CIA's operations directorate, UK diplomats had "little regard and even less confidence in Phoumi." Moreover, US-supplied evidence of the Pathet Lao's influence on Kong Le seemed unpersuasive. To UK officials, Kong Le appeared loyal to Souvanna, but he might not stay that way if Phoumi and his CDNI cohorts assumed positions of power in the government.[74]

On October 24 Phoumi received a detailed briefing on the latest agreements between Souvanna, the United States, and France from Thomas J. Corcoran, the deputy political adviser to CINCPAC. The US representative in Vientiane for eight months in 1950 and a former Lao desk officer, Corcoran was assigned by the State Department to be its special representative to the Savannakhet group. Accompanied by CIA officers Jantzen and Hasey, as well as Colonel Brownfield, Corcoran traveled to the general's headquarters to discuss payment of his troops through Vientiane; direct supply of materiel to forces in southern and northern Laos; and use of the French airfield in Seno for the delivery of munitions. The State Department official also informed Phoumi of Souvanna's growing recognition of the need to resist the Pathet Lao throughout the country. Corcoran then made, in his own words, a "low key suggestion" to the general that he might contribute to the anti–Pathet Lao cause by "publishing a message to the king announcing [the] dissolution of Revolutionary Committee."[75]

Corcoran reported that Phoumi's reaction to his presentation was "uniformly negative." The split between Vientiane and Savannakhet, the general said, was even "greater now." If his paymasters went to Vientiane, they would be arrested. Perhaps PEO officers could deliver the funds to him in Savannakhet. Phoumi said that dissolving the revolutionary committee would serve no purpose, as individuals might still be considered rebels by the government. He also told Corcoran of his concern about an imminent Pathet Lao attack in Thakhek, a provincial capital in the Lao panhandle north of Savannakhet. (The CIA station in Vientiane was skeptical of Phoumi's threat assessment. The previous day an agency situation report commented that it was "obvious" the general was "employing the 'communist behind every bush' technique in presenting [the] situation to U.S. representatives.")[76]

Corcoran met with the entire revolutionary committee on October 26. The atmosphere was friendly, "in typical Lao fashion," but members of the committee showed "flashes of irritation and frustration," according to Corcoran. They found the US attitude toward Laos "equivocal" and had been angered by a request from Souvanna to dissolve the committee in exchange for an overseas diplomatic post for Phoumi. They were "highly suspicious" of military support to FAL forces in northern Laos, fearing a US attempt to "play off" one anticommunist group against another.[77]

The rebel leaders, Corcoran reported, were "in no mood to heed my suggestion re dissolution." They also rejected Corcoran's proposal to send their paymasters to Vientiane and wondered what would happen at Seno if relations between France and the United States deteriorated. Corcoran reported to the State Department that the members of the committee believed that the US government intended to "make them knuckle under to Souvanna Phouma whom they consider at best [a] commie prisoner and at worst [a] commie collaborator. They are also convinced he is after their scalps."[78]

Although Brown almost certainly would have opposed literally scalping Phoumi, the ambassador was angered by the general's attitude with Corcoran and by his failure to honor his commitment to Irwin and Riley to follow US advice. "We cannot afford [to] allow ourselves [to] get in [a] position where he can disregard or hedge on our advice and still continue to get our support," Brown wrote the State Department. The ambassador warned, "Unless we display [the] utmost firmness in making Phoumi comply with his promises [to] be guided by our policy, we will completely lose control. The slightest give on our part will constitute surrender, given Phoumi's temperament."[79]

Attempting once again to bridge the differences between Phoumi and Souvanna, Brown met with the prime minister on October 26. Souvanna, whose mood appeared as "black as thunder," said that he had no intention of negotiating further with the general. The prime minister said that his several attempts to reach out to Phoumi had been "uniformly rebuffed" and that the matter would now "have to be handled by force." Souvanna said that US support for the general was the reason why Phoumi "was not going to be reasonable." The prime minister also expressed his frustration with the continuing Thai blockade, despite repeated assurances that it would soon be lifted. With diesel fuel for Vientiane's power plant about to run out, Souvanna said that if Laos could not secure its basic needs through "normal channels," he would request help from the Soviet Union.[80]

In his report to the State Department, Ambassador Brown wrote that the prime minister was "obviously discouraged" and feeling in a "corner and alone." Brown later reflected: "[The US government] simply pushed Souvanna into the arms of the Soviet Union and the Chinese and the Pathet Lao. We were always complaining that he was too weak, that he couldn't control his forces, he couldn't control the Pathet Lao, and yet we've always denied him the resources and the political support which would be necessary to enable him to do so."[81]

Chapter 10

Virtually a Traitor

ON OCTOBER 28, 1960, senior State Department officials met again with the Joint Chiefs and top Pentagon civilians to continue their efforts to reach a common understanding about events in Laos and the appropriate US response to them. Defense Secretary Gates said it was his "impression that we were holding Phoumi's feet to the fire while treating Souvanna Phouma rather gently." Assistant Secretary of State Parsons replied that the general's CIA adviser in Savannakhet, John Hasey, had said "time and again" that it was necessary to "keep Phoumi under firm control." Parsons added that in several instances the general had not kept his promises to the US government. In an apparent reference to Phoumi's ambition to attack Vientiane and lead a Lao military dictatorship, Livingston Merchant added, "We have to realize while Phoumi is someone we want to use, his objectives differ from ours."[1]

Noting Souvanna's failure to act on recent embassy suggestions, Parsons told the group that the prime minister's usefulness to the United States was declining. The problem, said Parsons, was how "to get a new free government in power" without triggering a military reaction by the Pathet Lao or Kong Le. Parsons proposed moving a quorum of National Assembly deputies from Vientiane to Luang Prabang, where they would feel more secure in casting a vote of no confidence in Souvanna. The US mission in Laos would then "try to get the King to appoint Phoui to form a new government."[2]

"Who the hell is Phoui?" Gates asked. Likely appalled by the defense secretary's ignorance of recent Lao history and one of the kingdom's leading political figures, Parsons replied: "Phoui was the best Prime Minister

Laos has ever had." What Parsons did not say was that the US government had, at the very least, silently acquiesced in General Phoumi's coup deposing Phoui in late December 1959. Despite his anticommunist credentials, Phoui had lost the confidence of US officials for his failure to get along with the younger, more dynamic military and civilian Lao in the CDNI. The former prime minister had been bitter about the lack of US support, but at a recent meeting with Parsons at the American embassy in Tokyo, Phoui had declared his eagerness to return to his homeland and his willingness to cooperate with his former rival General Phoumi.[3]

After the meeting at the Pentagon, the State Department instructed Ambassador Brown to "exfiltrate" National Assembly members from Vientiane to Luang Prabang and to encourage the formation of a Phoui-led government that included the country's leading noncommunists. Brown, who continued to believe that Washington officials were misreading the situation in Laos, saw many problems with this scheme. The king disliked Phoui "too much" to appoint him prime minister. Savang was "too indecisive" for the proposed action. Souvanna would not likely agree to serving in a Phoui-led government because the former prime minister had abandoned Souvanna's policy of neutrality and moved the RLG to the right. The British, the French, and the Australians would probably not find such a government acceptable. Overall, Brown thought his latest instruction "overestimates [the] U.S. ability [to] accomplish desired results." The ambassador urged continued pressure on both Phoumi and Souvanna to come to terms.[4]

Although they found Brown's analysis "very helpful," State Department officials repeated their belief that power was shifting "away from Souvanna" toward the Pathet Lao and instructed the ambassador to work toward "a Phoui solution." According to Parsons, Pentagon officials were "quite disturbed" by Brown's unenthusiastic reaction to that concept. More generally, they were troubled by the State Department's "failure to assure prompt implementation of top level decisions." Assistant Secretary of Defense Irwin believed that "U.S. influence and power [was] being stultified" by this failure and suggested a number of possible reasons for the problem, including a "hesitancy to *act* in the field" and an "acceptance of argumentation after a decision has been reached."[5]

Defense Secretary Gates, who found the administration and management of the State Department "shocking," was likely thinking of Laos when he later recalled: "You sent out an order—you'd finally agree on a

nder of the FAI. Third Infantry Battalion, led a bloodless
against Souvanna's "communist-controlled government" in
ng. Taking control of the town's military installations and
nthieng assigned an infantry company to guard the palace
, who was reportedly sympathetic to the coup. Declaring his
ieneral Phoumi, the major appealed to Savannakhet for rein-
At 8:15 A.M. on November 11, troops from the First Parachute
Savannakhet landed at Luang Prabang airport.[10]

ting with Ambassador Brown the following day, Souvanna
ded to retake Luang Prabang by force. Brown thought this
h an operation would weaken Vientiane's defenses, inviting
General Phoumi. The prime minister also made the improb-
ion that the king was a prisoner of the rebel group, cut off
l government. "This was an intolerable situation which could
ed [to] persist," said Souvanna, who asked Brown to cease
S supplies to Luang Prabang.[11]

mber 14 Souvanna repeated to Brown his intention to retake
ng by force. Because of the logistical, political, and military
is plan, the ambassador still did not accept Souvanna's dec-
ce value. Brown was, however, acutely aware of the "serious
ich an attack would raise for the US government. Inevitably,
be immediate requests from Phoumi for money, arms, and
ansport his troops to Luang Prabang or Vientiane. Yet un-
dissolved Souvanna's government, the United States would
harsh international consequences of supporting a rebellion
l government. Another worrisome comment from the prime
that Phoumi's intransigence was a consequence of his US
ording to Brown's report of the meeting, Souvanna said that
ave to reconsider the whole situation" concerning American

ic day Phoumi traveled to Luang Prabang to ask the king—
e prisoner of Major Bounthieng—to remove Souvanna from
ve the National Assembly, and authorize the formation of
ationary government. The king refused, insisting that any
vernment must be consistent with the constitution. The fol-
November 15, the general met with State Department rep-
Corcoran and CIA officer Hasey in Savannakhet. Corcoran

position with the State Department—a
sador, and he'd write a novel back to y
obey the order." Military unhappiness
yond mere irritation with his questionin
Pentagon considered Win Brown virtu:
recalled. "The senior levels of the State
support, although his old friend, Jeff P:

Ambassador Brown was the most
isfaction with the US response to the
officials also appeared unhappy with tl
directives from the highest levels of go
Gates to tell Secretary Herter that he p
President so that the two of them, plu
whole problem and secure a clear-cut na
onel Edwin F. Black, a military assista
such a meeting is held, and Presidentia
be established a specific mechanism to
necessary to see that the President's deci:

Neither Gates nor Herter seemed
disagreements over Laos to President E
secretaries of state and defense, togethe
hours to resolve their differences. Acc
analysis of decision making and policy
record of the meeting indicates that the:
Laos was an unacceptable goal, that So
(although several pointed out that the
did not agree), and that, partly by assu
coup to oust Souvanna, the King shoulc
government with a claim to legality."[8]

After the meeting, the personal ins:
Ambassador Brown were blunt. Obser·
"taken fully into account," Herter decla
in Souvanna." Ousting the prime mini:
a new government with Phoui playing
for [the] achievement [of] our policy." '
immediately to plan and act on this ba:

In the early evening of November 10, 1

may, comm
coup d'état
Luang Prab
airport, Bo
and the kin
support for
forcements.
Battalion in

At a me
said he inte
unlikely. Su
an attack by
able declara
from his leg
not be allov
delivery of l

On Nov
Luang Prab
hurdles to t.
laration at f
questions" s
there would
aircraft to t
less the kin;
still face the
against a leg
minister wa
support. Ac
"he might l
aid.[12]

That sa·
the ostensib
office, disso
a new revo
change in g
lowing day,
resentative

found that he and Phoumi appeared to be "talking at cross purposes" about ending the political crisis in Laos.[13]

Although "blandly" agreeing not to attack Vientiane, the general would not commit to cooperating with Phoui. He said that the US scheme to reach a political agreement in Luang Prabang among the leading noncommunists was worthwhile, but it would only be "a temporary" solution, followed by another crisis. Near the end of the conversation, Phoumi raised the contentious issue of paying his troops, saying he could not understand why the United States insisted that he send his paymasters to Vientiane to pick up the cash. Why not provide the pay directly to him as before? If he could not pay his troops, the general warned, there would be desertions in the near future. Corcoran, who sympathized with Phoumi on this issue, replied that pay for his troops should be discussed at a later date.[14]

To Ambassador Brown, the method of paying Phoumi's troops was both a legal issue and a test of the general's willingness to honor his commitments. Souvanna had conceded on the direct supply of US materiel to Phoumi's forces, Brown reasoned, and the general should fulfill his part of the bargain by sending his paymasters in a PEO plane to Vientiane with assurances of their safety. Moreover, continued covert financial support to Phoumi would quickly be discovered and used by enemies of the United States to demand the ouster of the PEO. "I beg of you not to allow us to be forced by one man's stubbornness into cutting our throats in Vientiane [and] in the UN," Brown wrote Parsons in an eyes-only, no-distribution telegram. If the US backed down in this matter, the ambassador warned, "Phoumi will be wholly out of our control."[15]

On November 17 Brown reported on progress toward the US-backed "Phoui solution." The "skids" were under Prime Minister Souvanna, and the principal question was "how best to administer [the] final push." There appeared to be mounting Lao pressure for Souvanna's resignation, which the US should encourage with "discreet assistance." The ambassador discussed problems with the plan to transport National Assembly deputies to Luang Prabang. Most deputies were reluctant to desert their families in Vientiane, where security measures were being tightened. "Considerable sums [of] money will be required," Brown reported, "though this, of course, [is] manageable." An even larger problem threatened the success of the "Phoui solution"—which few Lao leaders favored: "Phoumi, the

principal power factor, has not yet accepted it. Without his full cooperation, it cannot work."[16]

Phoumi's military and political prospects were strengthened by the
defections to the Savannakhet group by the provincial governors and battalion commanders in the first Military Region and by General Ouan,
whom Souvanna had recently replaced as commander of the FAL. With
his support weakening among conservative Lao, Souvanna turned increasingly to the left. He traveled to Sam Neua to meet with his brother
and Pathet Lao leader Prince Souphanouvong and returned to Vientiane
with an agreement to form a government of national union. The cabinet
would include representatives of the NLHS and the Savannakhet group.
Neither Boun Oum nor General Phoumi, however, would be allowed to
serve as a minister. The agreement also affirmed that Laos would accept
aid from the PRC and North Vietnam.

Despite the growing pressure on the prime minister, Ambassador
Brown found Souvanna in a relaxed and cheerful mood at a meeting with
him on November 21. Appearing greatly satisfied with the agreement he
had reached with Souphanouvong, the prime minister now intended to
advise the king of the accord and to ask him to call a meeting in Luang
Prabang of representatives from Vientiane, the Pathet Lao, and Savannakhet. Brown, who considered Souvanna's latest idea for a coalition government a "pipe dream," repeated US reservations about having NLHS
members in the cabinet and accepting aid from communist nations. The
ambassador did, however, agree that a meeting with the king would be
constructive. Unspoken was the US belief that such a gathering would
likely lead to the legal removal of Souvanna as prime minister. When
the ambassador "gently inquired" whether Souvanna still insisted that
Phoumi's paymasters travel to Vientiane, which Brown described as "an
obstacle to reconciliation," the prime minister replied: "I am going to have
to ask you to stop all aid to Savannakhet."[17]

Souvanna's apparent belief that the US would honor his request to
cease its assistance to General Phoumi might explain the prime minister's
high spirits. They may also have been buoyed by the diplomatic support
he continued to receive from the other Western allies. The French still
backed him as prime minister and the concept of a coalition government
that included the NLHS. UK officials thought that if the NLHS received
less important cabinet portfolios, a coalition government might prevent

a civil war. The Canadian ICC commissioner to Cambodia, d'Iberville Fortier, visited Vientiane in November 1960 and reported that he had met no one—excluding American and Thai officials—"who claimed to understand the logic" of the US position. Diplomats in the British, French, and Australian embassies, Fortier wrote, were "extremely critical" of American actions and convinced that the situation would "become hopeless" unless the US government altered its policy.[18]

Souvanna's relaxed mood may also have been influenced by an FAL plan to improve the military balance by threatening a government countercoup in Luang Prabang. On November 20, 1960, the CIA station in Vientiane learned that the FAL general staff had given orders "to prepare for an attack" on the royal capital. The previous evening, twenty trucks transporting three FAL companies had departed for Muong Kassy, some seventy-five miles south of the royal capital. Five hundred Pathet Lao troops were reportedly heading toward Luang Prabang "to aid in the attack," according to CIA sources. A follow-up agency message reported that the US military attaché in Vientiane had been asked by an FAL source to transmit this information covertly to Phoumi's forces in Luang Prabang and Savannakhet. Ambassador Brown reported to the State Department that "necessary warnings have been discreetly issued" to Phoumi and his supporters.[19]

In Washington, Secretary of State Herter informed General Goodpaster at the White House that FAL forces had left Vientiane to retake Luang Prabang and intended "to meet up with some Pathet Lao on the way." The president's senior advisers, Herter said, were drafting instructions to Brown "to back Phoumi's forces." Herter wanted Goodpaster to pass the message to the president, who was concluding a two-week vacation in Augusta, Georgia. Goodpaster replied that he could, of course, make arrangements to send the message to Eisenhower but recommended that the secretary telephone the president directly.[20]

Ten minutes later, Herter informed Eisenhower of "the move on" Luang Prabang. The president's advisers, Herter said, "felt we ought to take the wraps off Phoumi right away." When Eisenhower asked about the size of Phoumi's forces, Herter replied that it would depend on how many "stayed with him." The secretary mentioned the delicate issue of either paying Phoumi's troops directly or through Vientiane. The notes of this telephone conversation do not indicate the president's view of this matter.

What was recorded in the notes was the president's recommendation "to tell the troops they would get one-half pay now and the rest when they 'licked the other fellow.'" Another topic discussed was providing Phoumi with CAT planes to airlift his troops to Luang Prabang. Eisenhower sought assurances from Herter that "Phoumi was the nearest thing to representing a government." The secretary of state replied that "this was so, particularly since Souvanna Phouma was playing with the Pathet Lao."[21]

With the approval of the president, the State Department informed Brown that because of the threat to Luang Prabang, the US government would make direct, covert payments for Phoumi's troops; fulfill his requests for materiel and aircraft; and lift any US-imposed military restrictions on the general if the royal capital was attacked. According to Brown's instructions, State Department officials were "puzzled" by Souvanna's failure to mention the current military movements to the ambassador, which suggested that the prime minister was "either ignorant or deliberately misleading" the United States.[22]

As was often the case in Laos, the intelligence on Pathet Lao or government military operations was inconclusive about key policy-relevant facts. On November 22, 1960, PEO chief Heintges, Army attaché Hollis, and CIA chief of station Jorgensen provided Washington with a combined assessment of a "possible attack on Luang Prabang." Concluding there was "clear evidence" of four to six FAL companies moving toward the royal capital for "the reported purpose of [an] attack," the US officials wrote that the information available was "too fragmentary" for detailed analysis. There were "indications" that FAL troops would be joined by Pathet Lao reinforcements, but the evidence to identify the PL forces and the extent of their involvement was "less specific." Despite the signs of an impending government–Pathet Lao operation, the officials in Vientiane warned that there was "no evidence to date that a final decision to attack Luang Prabang has been made."[23]

The following day Souvanna assured Ambassador Brown that he had no intention of attacking Luang Prabang—unless, of course, General Phoumi's forces attacked him. The prime minister was, however, unwilling to remain idle in the face of intelligence reports of a planned Phoumi offensive assisted by Americans. It was the fear of such an attack that had prompted Souvanna to order his forces into the field and to request formally that the United States immediately cease all aid to the rebels in Savannakhet. A diplomatic note, dated November 22, declared that such assistance was contrary to US, UK, and French recognition of Souvanna's government as the only legal RLG and that Lao unity was endangered by a rebellion "encouraged" by the United States.[24]

Ambassador Brown forwarded the note to Washington and discussed options for responding to it. In Brown's view, there was "no alternative except to suspend aid to Gen[eral] Phoumi as requested by Souvanna." Ambassador Johnson disagreed, predicting that complying with the request would have "seriously adverse effects on Thai attitudes." Johnson recommended that the US government "avoid any answer" to the note, continue its aid to Phoumi, and concentrate "on getting Souvanna out of office." If Ambassador Brown insisted on a reply, it should be a "temporizing" response. Thomas Corcoran, the State Department representative to the Savannakhet group, held similar views: the "only way out of this impasse is to destroy the technical legality of Souvanna's regime by quick action in Luang Prabang."[25]

In Washington, Assistant Secretary Parsons summarized Souvanna's note at the secretary of state's November 23 staff meeting, remarking: "The 'moment of truth' in Laos may have arrived." The State Department informed Brown that the US government could neither "disregard" the RLG note nor "accede to virtual abandonment of anti-communist forces in Laos." Because of the "extremely precarious" US position in Laos and the plan to depose Souvanna, the department instructed Brown to "temporize" by such measures as seeking "clarification of [the] terms 'rebels' and 'all aid.'"[26]

Souvanna subsequently provided the obvious answer to the ambassador's query, explaining that these terms meant arms and ammunition for Phoumi's forces. The prime minister would allow the United States to provide food, medicine, and other supplies, but he would not permit the Americans to supply weapons that might be turned against him. Brown, temporizing further, said he would transmit Souvanna's clarification to Washington. A subsequent Pentagon analysis of the 1960 Laotian crisis observed: "It was always a question how long Souvanna could be kept turning the grindstone on which the axe intended for his own neck was being sharpened."[27]

While State Department officials stalled for time in hopes that Souvanna might be deposed politically, Admiral Felt, the commander of US forces in the Pacific, sought to strengthen Phoumi's military position. Convinced that "at least one Phoumi military victory" was a precondition to a political solution in Laos, Felt ordered PEO officers in Savannakhet to encourage offensive operations by Phoumi north of the Nam Ca Dinh River, the cease-fire line between the general's forces and Souvanna's. Although he chafed at State Department restrictions on military activity in Laos, the admiral was acting under authority granted to him when Souvanna appeared to be preparing to retake Luang Prabang. The view within Felt's headquarters was that if Phoumi could seize Paksane, while successfully holding Luang Prabang, "Vientiane might crack apart." If such pressure did not compel Souvanna's resignation, Phoumi's forces would be well positioned to attack Vientiane.[28]

Phoumi, who had been assembling a force of five battalions, launched a general offensive "to clean out" the area south of the Nam Ca Dinh on November 28, according to the Vientiane CIA station. If successful, Phoumi planned to cross the river and advance toward Paksane. Ambassador Brown objected strongly to military operations north of the river, which Souvanna would undoubtedly interpret as preparation for an attack on Vientiane. Brown wrote the State Department that it would be the "height [of] folly [to] encourage Phoumi [to] torpedo our plan for [a] political solution by [a] premature attack."[29]

Brown was also disturbed that CINCPAC was issuing orders directly to Colonel Brownfield at Phoumi's headquarters in Savannakhet, without seeking the views of either the ambassador or PEO chief Heintges. A CINCPAC order to Brownfield, instructing him to help Phoumi reinforce Luang Prabang, triggered a sharp response from the ambassador, who observed that there was no indication of Souvanna's intention to order an attack and that the defenders had expressed confidence in their ability to hold the royal capital. Brown cabled Washington that the incident illustrated the "extreme importance [of] routing important command decisions through [the] ambassador who is responsible in [the] last analysis for US policy and action in Laos subject [to] Washington's direction and who is necessarily more currently informed than persons at greater distances."[30]

Brown expressed himself more bluntly in two eyes-only, no-distribution cables to Parsons and Merchant, which sought clarification of the ambassador's authority in Laos. Independent CINCPAC orders to Savannakhet, some of which Brown viewed as "detrimental to US interests," placed him in an untenable position. Observing that he had responsibility without authority, Brown asked who was in charge of making decisions that require a "careful balance [of] fluid political and military factors?" The ambassador suggested to Parsons that he was prepared to resign over the issue: "Perhaps someone else can operate under these conditions. I cannot."[31]

Parsons, who was "deeply distressed" by the erosion of Brown's authority, assured the ambassador that the State Department had been fighting a "major battle" with the Pentagon about limiting Phoumi's offensive "in present circumstances" and referring CINCPAC directives about future operations "to Washington for prior approval." In a transparent reference to President Eisenhower, State Department officials had "threatened [to] go to [the] top" over the disagreement. Although largely sympathetic to the ambassador's protest, Parsons reminded Brown that, with civil war looming, the views of CINCPAC and the JCS could not be ignored "on matters on which they are best qualified." In fact, the State Department had already reluctantly agreed with the Pentagon that Phoumi should be authorized to retake Paksane. Reaffirming the "principle that major decisions" in Laos should be communicated through the ambassador and the PEO chief, Parsons stressed to Brown the necessity of reconciling the "civil and military sides" of the government, no matter how "difficult or perhaps intolerable" such an accommodation "may seem to you in [the] peculiar fragmented Lao circumstances."[32]

One consequence of the State Department's latest battle with the Pentagon was a new JCS directive restricting "Phoumi's military operations until further notice." The Lao general could, however, consolidate his positions north of the Nam Ca Dinh, and CINCPAC could, "as unobtrusively as possible," use CAT aircraft to provide supplies to Phoumi's troops at Luang Prabang. Ambassador Brown, who was gratified by the JCS directive and the State Department's "splendid support," had won a short-lived, largely irrelevant bureaucratic victory. A political settlement in Laos was highly unlikely, civil war was a near certainty, and Phoumi's forces were finally fighting well.[33]

The increased effectiveness of Phoumi's soldiers was attributable to the combined efforts of PEO officers, US Army Special Forces, and CIA paramilitary experts, whose assistance had expanded from training to operations. US Army Major Eleazer "Lee" Parmly IV, for example, wrote the plan for the attack on Paksane. Captain James E. Ipsen, leader of a Special Forces training team and an artillery officer, assisted an effective 105 mm howitzer battery at Nam Ca Dinh. "I was very proud of what our people did there in getting Phoumi's forces into the shape that they were in," General Heintges said later. "Of course, I was not allowed to have any of the people who were supposed to be civilian technicians accompany the battalions or anything in combat. Well, I didn't and couldn't abide by that."[34]

What the State Department did allow in Laos was the assignment of an elite, CIA-controlled Thai paramilitary team to each of General Phoumi's five battalions. Operating under the bland name of the Police Aerial Reinforcement Unit (PARU), the Thai warriors had undergone a rigorous selection process and received thorough training in small-group tactics, jungle fighting, and airborne operations. Organized in teams similar to US Army Special Forces, PARU was ideally suited for clandestine CIA operations in Laos. The Thai language is similar to Lao, which eliminated the need for inefficient English-French-Lao translations to communicate with Phoumi's soldiers. And because the Thai were indistinguishable from lowland Lao to most Westerners, the presence of this US-controlled combat force in the kingdom could be plausibly denied.

Directing PARU's operations was a soft-spoken Texan and World War II veteran named James W. "Bill" Lair, who arrived in Thailand in 1951. Operating out of the CIA cover organization in Bangkok, the Overseas Southeast Asia Supply Company, better known as Sea Supply, Lair had a broad mandate from the CIA to train guerrilla fighters to resist a possible invasion by China. He lacked the flamboyance of some agency operators in Southeast Asia, but his work with the Thai and later with Vang Pao's Hmong army led senior CIA operations officer James N. Glerum to conclude that "Lair enjoyed more respect from foreign counterparts than any other American he'd ever known."[35]

Immediately after the Kong Le coup, Lair sensed that if PARU was "ever going to go into big operations," Phoumi's countercoup would be the perfect opportunity. The CIA officer began spending more time at the embassy in Bangkok and less at his PARU training camp in Hua Hin. Lair volunteered to fly to Savannakhet to deliver one of the covert US payments for Phoumi's troops that Ambassador Brown found so disturbing. The trip seemed a low-risk assignment to Lair. "I figure if you arrive with a plane full of money, they are not going to do much to you," he said later. After delivering the funds, the CIA officer learned of Phoumi's intention to attack Vientiane. He informed the general of PARU capabilities, and the general welcomed the assistance. With approval from the US and Thai governments, Lair's PARU teams began arriving in Savannakhet to serve as advisers and "stiffeners" in Phoumi's battalions.[36]

After Phoumi's victory at Vientiane (but before Lair's fateful introduction to Hmong leader Vang Pao), the CIA operative experienced "one of the great moments in my life." Desmond FitzGerald, chief of the CIA's Far East Division, told Lair that the accomplishments of his PARU forces in just a few months was "worth far more" than all of the agency's support for other organizations in Laos.[37]

A prelude to Phoumi's assault on Vientiane was a coup d'état aimed at seizing control of the town from within. For some weeks, American officials had encouraged Phoumi to coordinate any attack against Vientiane with Colonel Kouprasith Abhay, commander of the FAL military region that included the Lao administrative capital. The US hope was that an "adequately integrated" military operation would ensure Souvanna's resignation and keep bloodshed to a minimum. On December 7, 1960, Colonel Kouprasith informed Lieutenant Colonel Joel Hollis, the embassy's army attaché, that the coup would begin the following day. Ostensibly loyal to Souvanna, Kouprasith was an opportunist who had agreed to a secret alliance with Phoumi to overthrow the prime minister. Kouprasith told Colonel Hollis that troops from Savannakhet would be airlifted to Vientiane to participate in the operation.[38]

The coup began on schedule at approximately 5:15 A.M., with shooting around Camp Chinaimo on the eastern outskirts of Vientiane and armored vehicles rolling into town. Troops wearing white armbands established roadblocks and seized the airport, the police station, and other key installations throughout the town. The timing of the coup had been influenced by the conspicuous absence of Kong Le's paratroopers, who were engaged in anti-Phoumi operations outside of Vientiane. The takeover was a typically Lao affair, with only sporadic shooting, little or no bloodshed, and few arrests. A distinguishing tactic of the operation was disinformation, which included leaflets proclaiming the coup's support for Souvanna and neutrality. An official Lao radio broadcast urged the citizens of Vientiane "to remain calm and to support [the] Government and this coup. We adhere to following: 'Do not bruise a lotus flower; do not muddy clear water; do not anger a frog; do not harm a small frog.'"[39]

Souvanna Phouma, who was taken in by the ruse, assured Ambassador Brown that the troops now controlling Vientiane were loyal to him. US officials, well aware of the contact between Phoumi and Kouprasith, were initially confused and disappointed by the coup's neutralist proclamations. According to a Pentagon history of the Kong Le coup and its aftermath, PEO chief Heintges "dispatched a message indicating serious fear that the Kouprasith coup had not panned out as expected." Hugh S. Cumming Jr., director of intelligence and research at the State Department, reported, "Colonel Kouprasith has shown no abiding loyalty to anyone." The CIA station in Vientiane declared that it was "impossible to determine what will happen next."[40]

Unlike Souvanna and US officials, Kong Le quickly saw through the Lao disinformation tactics—an insight undoubtedly strengthened by reports that elements of Phoumi's First Parachute Battalion were landing near Camp Chinaimo. Kong Le's paratroopers, reinforced by two armored companies, returned to Vientiane on December 9. Wearing red scarves or red armbands on their uniforms, they peacefully but firmly reestablished control of the town and its airfield. The government radio station now denounced Kouprasith and his alliance with Phoumi, as well as intervention in Lao affairs by the United States and Thailand.

Kouprasith's forces withdrew to Camp Chinaimo, where pro-Phoumi deputies of the National Assembly were gathering. After a quick trip across the Mekong into Thailand, CAT aircraft authorized by Ambassador Brown flew these deputies to Savannakhet to join other legislators prepared to withdraw their support from Souvanna. At a December 9 meeting of State Department and Pentagon officials, Parsons said that "the prospects for establishing a new legal government" were enhanced by the large numbers of deputies in Savannakhet. He commented later in the meeting that the Kouprasith coup "did not go so far as we might have hoped but did lead to an opportune situation."[41]

National Assembly deputies were not the only Lao officials leaving town. With Phoumi's forces approaching Vientiane, Souvanna concluded that he was powerless to stop the looming battle. Vainly declaring Vientiane an "open city," which under international law should provide it with immunity from attack, Souvanna flew to Phnom Penh on December 9 with most of his cabinet. Like Souvanna, Cambodian chief of state Prince Norodom Sihanouk had been a consistent advocate for neutrality, both for his country and for Laos. Before leaving for Phnom Penh, Souvanna delegated his authority to a committee of military officers led by the FAL commander General Sounthone Pathammavong.

Presumably under pressure from Kong Le, General Sounthone's committee promptly ceded its authority to the three remaining civilian ministers, all leftists, who were led by Quinim Pholsena. On December 10 Quinim, along with representatives of the Pathet Lao and Kong Le, flew to Hanoi to request North Vietnamese and Soviet military assistance. Since December 4 Soviet aircraft had been delivering fuel and food to Vientiane. In response to Quinim's appeal, Soviet Ilyushin-14 transports arrived in Vientiane on December 11 with ammunition, heavy mortars, and 105 mm howitzers. Accompanying the materiel were North Vietnamese artillery advisers and a member of the Central Committee of the Vietnamese Workers' Party. According to observers from the military attaché's office at the American embassy, twenty-five Soviet transport flights landed in Vientiane between December 11 and 13.[42]

A quorum of National Assembly deputies in Savannakhet passed a vote of no confidence in Souvanna on December 11 and endorsed Phoumi's revolutionary committee. To help secure royal approval of the assembly action, Ambassador Brown instructed the CIA station to canvass its contacts in Luang Prabang and urge them to encourage the king to sign the required ordinances. Stuart Methven, the CIA base chief in the royal capital, spoke to three anticommunist deputies about the matter's urgency. According to an agency history, the three Lao met with Methven again on December 12, "smiling at his palpable anxiety." Holding a copy of the royal decree authorizing the Savannakhet group to form a provisional government, the Lao asked Methven: "Is this fast enough and legal enough for you?"[43]

With the king's approval of a new provisional government and Souvanna's flight out of the country, US officials were somewhat relieved that the conflict in Laos had polarized into a more straightforward-appearing cold war struggle between the US-supported Boun Oum–Phoumi government and the combined forces of Kong Le and the Pathet Lao, backed by Moscow and Hanoi. Souvanna's unwillingness to resign as prime minister and his insistence that his government was the only legal one did raise questions about the legitimacy of the Savannakhet group's claim to power. Nonetheless, the US government could now overtly respond to requests from General Phoumi with less risk of UN condemnation, while publicly denouncing the Soviet airlift of weapons and ammunition "as a violation of every standard of legal conduct."[44]

The Battle of Vientiane, which a State Department review of US-Laos relations characterized "as almost entirely an artillery duel," began with errant rounds from 105 mm howitzers shortly after 1:00 P.M. on December 13, 1960. Lawrence R. Bailey Jr., a US Army major serving as an assistant military attaché in the embassy, was in a jeep on his way to lunch when he heard muffled explosions and saw "great gray and brown geysers of mud and water" exploding on the Mekong flats. Although it is unclear whether the initial shells were fired by Phoumi's or Kong Le's artillery, the rounds landed far from any "red" or "white" targets. Bailey, an artillery officer and pilot who had arrived in Laos only days before, later noted that the poor marksmanship of Lao gunners was a military failing with consequences borne mainly by the civilians of Vientiane.[45]

Phoumi's main attacking force, which included troopers of the FAL first and third parachute battalions who had marched from Paksane to link up with Colonel Kouprasith's "white" soldiers at Camp Chinaimo, advanced into Vientiane from the east on a dirt road that ran alongside the Mekong. Supported by US Special Forces and Thai PARU teams, Phoumi's forces brushed aside Kong Le's roadblocks and seized the ferry crossing to Thailand. As Kong Le's "red" paratroopers made an orderly retreat westward toward his airport headquarters, the volume of fire from small arms, tanks, and other weapons was impressive. Both sides, however, aimed high to minimize casualties. British diplomat Mervyn Brown, who was caught in a crossfire between Phoumi's and Kong Le's forces, later wrote of the "well-established tradition in Laos" awarding "victory in battle to the side that made the most noise."[46]

At the American embassy, Colonel Hollis observed to Ambassador Brown that "a great deal of ammunition is being wasted." Located a few blocks from the river, the embassy was somewhat removed from the initial action in the Battle of Vientiane. Brown characterized the atmosphere within the building as one of "cheerful uncertainty." With the nearby Lao Defense Ministry alternating as a haven and a target for Lao soldiers of both sides, the sound of small-arms fire grew louder, and exploding shells began to shake the embassy. Ambassador Brown and some thirty other members of the US mission spent the night of December 13–14 at the embassy, which had neither electricity nor telephone service. On a table stacked with military C-rations, a sign read "room service."[47]

After a relatively peaceful night disturbed only by sporadic gunfire and the occasional mortar round, PEO chief Heintges arrived at the embassy. Like many others who lived along the river, Heintges had been temporarily trapped in his home when it became an area of intense, indiscriminate fire. With machine-gun bullets penetrating the walls of his house, the combat veteran sought shelter under his bed, where he attempted to allay the fears of his terrified Chinese cook. Communications at Heintges's headquarters were knocked out, prompting CINCPAC to temporarily designate Colonel Brownfield in Savannakhet as acting PEO chief.[48]

Throughout December 14, control of the area around the embassy seesawed between Phoumi's and Kong Le's forces. The Lao Defense Ministry caught fire, and ammunition stored there exploded for some two hours. At the embassy, shrapnel from one side or the other blew holes in the walls of the offices of the deputy chief of mission and the CIA chief of station. The ambassador's office was sprayed with bullets of various sizes, but there were no embassy casualties.

After US mission members spent another night sleeping in embassy offices and halls, Ambassador Brown took advantage of a lull in the fighting to evacuate all nonessential personnel to Thailand. (Family members of mission personnel had been evacuated to Bangkok the previous August.) A convoy of embassy employees, cooks, and housekeepers took the ferry across the Mekong River and entered Thailand without incident. At the embassy, a fire from an adjacent building spread to the roof and prompted Brown "to set up headquarters" at his residence. Because of the temporary move from the embassy, the burning of classified documents was a required procedure. To political officer Daniel O. Newberry, "putting out a fire at one end of the building and setting a fire at the other end" seemed an apt symbol of "the absurdity of the situation."[49]

By 5:00 P.M., December 16, the Battle of Vientiane was over. Phoumi's forces controlled the town and the airport; Kong Le's outnumbered troops began a disciplined withdrawal north of the town. Approximately two dozen soldiers loyal to Kong Le were reportedly killed in a three-day battle. About fourteen of Phoumi's troops were killed in action. An estimated six hundred civilians died in the battle, most by artillery fire that also wounded hundreds more and left the city "in a panic and the population in full flight," according to Brown.[50]

The indiscriminate shelling of Vientiane, some Western observers claimed, was rooted in Buddhist religious convictions that prevented many lowland Lao from aiming a gun at a fellow human being and pulling the trigger with the intent to kill. (Hmong warriors, who were gaining a reputation among US officials for their will to fight, suffered no such inhibitions.) To the ethnic Lao, according to this theory, lobbing artillery rounds at an impersonal distance seemed less disturbing because the lives taken or deaths avoided when shells landed were matters for Buddha to decide. Such assessments of the fighting preferences of the lowland Lao, particularly by Westerners with a limited knowledge of the people and Buddhism, do not seem a complete explanation for the disproportionate ratio of civilian to military dead at Vientiane.

For example, it seems likely that Lao soldiers who trained together, particularly the elite paratroopers who served in both Kong Le's and Phoumi's forces, were not eager to kill one another over an internal political dispute, much less a dimly understood East-West ideological disagreement. It has also been noted that many of the dead civilians in Vientiane were Vietnamese and Chinese, the traditional merchant class in Laos. Unlike the generally impoverished lowland Lao, who had virtually nothing to lose by temporarily abandoning their homes when fighting started, the Vietnamese and Chinese stayed in town to protect their property. Perhaps the best explanation for the high number of civilian dead in the Battle of Vientiane was the introduction into Laos of US and North Vietnamese artillery that was more destructive than the lighter weapons typically employed by the FAL, Kong Le, and the Pathet Lao. Whatever interpretation may be correct, the judgment of US embassy assistant military attaché Bailey is hard to dispute. Bailey, who in March 1961 became the first American POW in Southeast Asia, concluded long after the second Indochina war had ended that during the Battle of Vientiane "only the innocents suffered."[51]

Officials in Washington were both pleased by reports of Phoumi's military success in Vientiane and concerned by the likelihood of a strong communist reaction to the battle. The estimated responses ranged from covert and semicovert strengthening of the Pathet Lao to overt intervention by North Vietnamese or PRC forces. On December 14 the National Security Agency ordered all of its intercept stations in the Far East to SIGINT Readiness Condition Bravo, a heightened state of alert to collect communications and electronic intelligence indicating communist military preparations. Admiral Felt ordered US forces in the Pacific to an increased state of readiness.

After meeting with officials from the State Department and the Pentagon, General Goodpaster telephoned President Eisenhower at about 7:00 P.M., December 14, to brief him on the situation in Laos and to seek policy guidance. The president, who was at Walter Reed Hospital for a physical examination, said that "he wanted to be as firm as we can be," according to Goodpaster's notes of the conversation. "He thought we should act vigorously, now that we have the cover of legality." Eisenhower was "completely in favor" of using Thai and US aircraft to transport military and other supplies into Laos. He suggested the possibility of high-altitude reconnaissance over North Vietnam by U-2 aircraft and proposed "giving a bonus to Phoumi's troops to reward their success and inspire further effort." In a subsequent memorandum, General Goodpaster noted that the president also approved a request by the Boun Oum–Phoumi government for twenty additional 105 mm howitzers.[52]

On the diplomatic front, Secretary of State Herter parried UK and French objections to US policy. At a Paris meeting of NATO ministers, Lord Home, the UK foreign secretary, told Herter that US support for Phoumi and Soviet assistance to the Pathet Lao put the two superpowers "in a box." According to minutes of the meeting, the British diplomat said "there would be danger of foreign intervention on both sides, the possibility of nuclear weapons, and general war." What really worried UK officials, he said, "was the probability of long-term guerrilla warfare by the Pathet Lao." Referring to the decade-long British experience in combating the Malayan insurgency, Lord Home declared: "There is the definite danger that endless forces will be committed and then a drift into endless war."[53]

French Foreign Minister Maurice Couve de Murville sharply criticized the US "policy of making Laos a Western Bastion." He reminded Herter that American support for Phoui Sananikone's pro-Western government had prompted the Pathet Lao's "return to guerrilla warfare" in 1959. The United States, said Couve, should have supported Souvanna after Kong Le's coup. Instead, US assistance to Phoumi had forced the Lao prime minister "to work with the Pathet Lao." A Phoumi-led government, "with Boun Oum as a figurehead" was an appalling prospect to the French. "Boun Oum was a fool," said Couve, and "Phoumi cannot succeed."[54]

Herter acknowledged an obvious "point of contention" between the United States and its principal Western allies: "the possibility of Pathet Lao participation in any Laos government." The United States, he said, "did not mind a neutral buffer" state in Southeast Asia, but it "did mind a Communist-infiltrated Laotian government." The Pathet Lao had no interest in a "legitimate neutral" government, Herter declared. The key question was whether the allies would recognize the Boun Oum–Phoumi government. Lord Home replied that "the British felt they have to but they hoped Phoumi would broaden it," which at a minimum meant including Souvanna Phouma in the cabinet. In a subsequent meeting of the three foreign ministers, Couve said that the French government had not taken a position on the legal claims of either the Boun Oum–Phoumi government or Souvanna's. The "equivocal attitude" of the French, Herter reported to Washington, was "extremely disturbing."[55]

Another troubling development was Phoumi's slow pursuit of Kong Le, whose 400–600 troops north of the city might counterattack Vientiane, continue on the road to Luang Prabang, or move toward the Pathet Lao strongholds in Sam Neua and Phong Saly. (An estimated 1,000–2,000 Pathet Lao guerrillas, some of whom were directly supporting Kong Le, were in the same general area north of Vientiane, but they sought to conserve their combat capabilities and leave the fighting to the paratrooper captain and his followers.) A CIA briefing prepared for Allen Dulles reported that Phoumi had "tended to be over optimistic with regard to [the] extent and significance of his victory at Vientiane." The briefing continued, "He is certainly ill informed as to the disposition and intention of the enemy."[56]

To strengthen Phoumi's limited reconnaissance capabilities, the State Department authorized intelligence-gathering flights over Laos by the US air attaché in Saigon, Lieutenant Colonel Butler B. Toland Jr. On December 20 Colonel Toland photographed Soviet parachutes on the ground and "heavy road traffic" some twenty-two miles north of Vientiane. The following day he maneuvered his aircraft, a twin-propeller VC-47 military transport mounted with K-17 and K-20 cameras, to within one hundred feet of a Soviet IL-14 flying over a Lao drop zone with an open door. Providing conclusive evidence of Soviet support for Kong Le and the Pathet Lao, Toland's detailed photographs included a legible serial number on the wing of the IL-14. The pictures were rushed to Washington policymakers and later distributed to newspapers and magazines.[57]

The Soviet airdrops to resupply the forces of Kong Le and the Pathet Lao were a "grave concern" to US military leaders. Because the Lao armed forces lacked a combat air capability, Admiral Felt proposed the transfer of armed T-6 training aircraft from the Thai Air Force to the FAL. Designed in 1937, the slow, single-engine T-6s could be configured with wing-mounted .30-caliber machine guns, five-inch rockets, and racks for bombs weighing up to one hundred pounds. Felt envisioned familiarizing a small number of Lao pilots with the aircraft's combat capabilities, followed by a public RLG announcement that violations of Lao air space would no longer be tolerated and that intruders would be shot down. Even an unsuccessful attempt "to bag a few birds," Felt reasoned, would "be enough to scare off any transport planes."[58]

Felt's recommendation was favorably received by the JCS and the State Department. Although Ambassador Brown agreed in principle to providing the FAL with T-6 aircraft, he sought a precondition for any such action: a vote by the National Assembly to legitimate the provisional revolutionary government. With Souvanna Phouma still claiming to be prime minister, a return to traditional Lao constitutional procedures was essential to building international support for the new government. Unfortunately for US diplomacy on behalf of Boun Oum and Phoumi, neither man had much use for the Lao constitution or the National Assembly. According to a December 28 intelligence summary for President Eisenhower, Phoumi "seems inclined toward establishing a military dictatorship."[59]

The failure to seek the approval of the National Assembly was just one of the problems the new government posed for the United States, according to a year-end message to the State Department from Ambassador Brown. Others included a threat by Phoumi to take control of the French military base at Seno and to oust the French Military Mission from Laos altogether; a declaration that the kingdom would no longer abide by the Geneva Accords; and withdrawals of large amounts of kip from the National Bank without adequate supervision or controls. Echoing his earlier warnings about the Lao general, Brown wrote: "It appears that [the] time is rapidly coming when we must decide if, when, and how we make a really firm stand with Phoumi and [the] RLG if we are ever to have a real influence with them."[60]

The biggest question for Washington policymakers was whether the communists would intervene militarily on a substantial scale. An apparent answer was received on December 30, when the Lao government announced that five regular PAVN battalions, totaling twenty-five hundred men or more, had attacked an FAL position in Xieng Khouang Province near the border with North Vietnam. An "emergency" assessment from the US mission in Vientiane reported: "Indication enemy advancing rapidly on the Plaine des Jarres," the strategically valuable plateau where the main north-south and east-west roads in Laos intersect. Acknowledging the fragmentary nature of the available information, the report concluded that the US "must accept [the] probability [that] this is sizeable aggression from [the] DRV."[61]

On Saturday, December 31, President Eisenhower and his senior national security advisers received a briefing on the latest intelligence from the deputy chief of the CIA, General Charles Cabell. Senior agency analysts had concluded that some 1,500 to 2,500 troops "were moving from the direction of North Viet-Nam into Laos." Cabell and General Lyman Lemnitzer, now chairman of the JCS, showed the president a map indicating Pathet Lao control of an area north of Vientiane, as well as Sam Neua and Phong Saly provinces. The officials reported that tree cover in the mountainous jungles made the identification of enemy forces difficult. According to a Pentagon situation report, there were "no positive reports" that the attacking troops were "in fact North Vietnamese military units."[62]

President Eisenhower told the assembled officials that more information was necessary before the United States could take any overt action. But, he said, "we cannot afford to stand by and allow Laos to fall to the Communists," according to minutes of the meeting prepared by John Eisenhower. "The time may soon come when we should employ the Sev-

enth Fleet, with its force of Marines." General Lemnitzer informed the
president that the status of US contingency forces for Laos was DEF-
CON-2, an alert condition just short of maximum military readiness and
imminent war. General Cabell said the CIA was carefully watching troop
movements to determine if the communists sought to "cut the neck of
Laos" south of Sam Neua and "take over the entire country."[63]

Livingston Merchant, the senior State Department official at the
meeting, reported the evacuation of additional USOM and third-country
personnel from the US mission in Vientiane. He said that the State Department and the Pentagon were in complete agreement "on the para-
mount necessity of identifying open intervention" in Laos. Merchant
also emphasized the diplomatic importance of both the approval of the
Boun Oum government by the National Assembly and the resignation of
Souvanna Phouma. Later in the meeting, Merchant observed that "unfortunately" Souvanna's wealth precluded "bribery" as an instrument of
persuasion. Parsons added that the French had the most influence with
Souvanna, but they were "unwilling to induce him to leave the scene at
this moment."

Eisenhower stressed the importance of detailed reconnaissance to determine "the exact nature of the military operations" in northwest Laos,
bordering China. He was informed that the aerial reconnaissance capabilities in the region included CAT C-46 aircraft, Thai T-33 jet trainers,
and high-altitude U-2s stationed at Subic Bay in the Philippines. General
Lemnitzer observed that the best reconnaissance had been obtained from
an air attaché's plane that had recently photographed Soviet transports
air-dropping supplies. In a humorous aside, the president said that "for
the first time in 50 years he had discovered the usefulness of an attache."
On a more serious note, Eisenhower approved the use of CAT and Thai
reconnaissance aircraft and raised no objections to using U-2s. He did
not, however, approve overflights of China.

At one point in the meeting, Eisenhower declared, "[If] war is necessary, we will do so with our allies or unilaterally, since we cannot sit by and
see Laos go down without a fight." In light of the historical debate about
the president's advice to John F. Kennedy concerning US military intervention in Laos, discussed later in the epilogue, the comment appears to be
a significant indication of Eisenhower's willingness to fight there without
allies. At the conclusion of the December 31 meeting, according to John

Eisenhower's minutes, the president reemphasized, "We must not allow Laos to fall to the Communists, even if it involves war in which the US acts with allies or unilaterally." Livingston Merchant, in his notes, summarized the president's conclusion this way: "We should make precautionary deployment of US forces in the area for possible use, unilaterally if this should prove necessary."[64]

At a White House meeting on January 2, 1961, President Eisenhower said that he thought "the big question" was the position of US allies—an observation more consistent with his longstanding refusal to introduce US combat troops in Southeast Asia without allies. Livingston Merchant reported that only the Thai, the Filipinos, and the South Vietnamese unreservedly supported US policy in Laos. The British, the Australians, and the New Zealanders "did not fully share our views," and the French "were being completely obstructive." Secretary of State Herter added that the "French were deplorably weak." According to Merchant's notes of the meeting, Eisenhower replied: "The French! The older I get, the more disgusted with them I am—not the French people but their governments. De Gaulle is as bad as any of the previous ones."[65]

When discussing possible SEATO military action, President Eisenhower asked General Lemnitzer if it was true that the planning called for SEATO forces to hold the principal population centers, allowing the FAL to pursue enemy forces in the countryside. When Lemnitzer replied that this was indeed the intent of the "initial stages" of the operation, Eisenhower observed that "the one thing he had learned in his life was that, if one finds it necessary to use force, one should use enough force to ensure that this situation is cured." He added, "It is important not to leave a running sore or to fight under self-imposed limitations as we had in Korea." The president "didn't see much sense in just trying to hold isolated points."[66]

To complement the administration's military contingency planning, President Eisenhower had agreed to a State Department proposal for "a sober warning" to Soviet Premier Nikita S. Khrushchev about the dangers of intervention in Laos. The president authorized Llewellyn Thompson, the American ambassador in Moscow, "to tell Khrushchev that we view the situation with grave concern, that we are moving the positions of our forces to assure, if necessary, that the legitimate government will not be destroyed, and that in the event of a major war we will not be caught napping."[67]

Translating the president's views into the patois of diplomacy, the State Department instructed Ambassador Thompson to protest the Soviet airlift in Laos, to urge the USSR to use its influence to stop North Vietnamese interference in Laos, and to inform Khrushchev of US determination to honor its SEATO commitments. On January 4 Thompson delivered the unpublicized message to Vasili V. Kuznetsov, the first deputy secretary of the Soviet Foreign Ministry, who agreed to transmit it to Khrushchev. During a calm debate of the two governments' conflicting views of the crisis in Laos, Kuznetsov characterized Thompson's statement about the US SEATO commitment as an attempt "to frighten" the Soviet Union. The remark, Ambassador Thompson replied, was included to ensure that "the Soviet Government would understand the seriousness of [the] situation." In a formal response to Thompson's démarche, the Soviet government declared that threats have "never proved successful in relations with the Soviet Union. Force can always be met by force."[68]

The likelihood of imminent US military action gradually subsided as it became clear that regular North Vietnamese forces had not invaded Laos. Between January 3 and January 18, seven U-2 reconnaissance missions photographed North Vietnamese and Chinese lines of communication into Laos, searching for signs of communist military units. "The photography did not substantiate the Laotian claims" of foreign intervention, according to a CIA history of cold war overhead reconnaissance. By January 7 CINCPAC had reduced the readiness condition of US forces planned for Laos to DEFCON-3, with the rest of the Pacific command at DEFCON-5, the lowest alert status. On January 26 the RLG withdrew its charge of a North Vietnamese invasion. According to a cabinet minister, the RLG had cried "wolf" to assure Laotians that the Boun Oum–Phoumi government "had friends abroad."[69]

Although there had been no invasion, the military position of the RLG remained grave. Kong Le, operating in concert with the Pathet Lao, had taken advantage of the communist troop movements east of the Plaine des Jarres to seize control of the plateau from the west. The FAL forces there provided little resistance, abandoning some two thousand small arms, two 57 mm recoilless rifles, and two 105 mm howitzers. The retreating government forces also left behind their radio equipment, enabling Kong Le and the Pathet Lao to monitor FAL communications.

By controlling the strategically located plateau, Kong Le and the Pathet Lao threatened to attack Vientiane, Luang Prabang, and Paksane and to sever the northern half of the kingdom from the south.[70]

The weak diplomatic position of the RLG mirrored its grim military prospects. Although the National Assembly formally invested the Boun Oum–Phoumi government on January 4, 1961, the Soviet Union still recognized Souvanna's claim as prime minister, and the United Kingdom and France continued to resist SEATO support for the RLG. To resolve the crisis, world leaders had proposed numerous diplomatic initiatives, including reactivating the ICC in Laos, reconvening the Geneva conference, referring the dispute to the United Nations, and establishing a mediation group of neutral nations. From the Eisenhower administration's perspective, these approaches all shared a fundamental deficiency—the Pathet Lao's current position of strength meant that the communist-led group would likely negotiate as an equal with the RLG. This would surely lead to the kind of coalition government the Eisenhower administration had long resisted and "the probable loss of the country peacefully instead of militarily."[71]

Ambassador Brown, whose personal views remained largely out of step with US policy, summarized the current situation in Laos and proposed remedial action in a January 18 cable clearly intended for the consideration of the new president and his advisers. Describing the kingdom's crisis as increasingly complex and dangerous, Brown predicted that the military struggle would, at best, be protracted, providing "little hope for [the] security and integrity of [the] country in [the] near future." The ambassador favored increased support to Phoumi for an attempt to retake the Plaine des Jarres and other areas of the country. But even if the FAL achieved this immediate military goal, it seemed to Brown "an illusion to hope" that the US government acting alone, providing money and materiel to the FAL, could "establish security in Laos."[72]

Any chance of defeating communism in Laos, the ambassador wrote, would require the "political strength" of Western allies and neutral governments. Some form of international political solution was "fundamental." To broaden political support for the RLG, both in Laos and internationally, a reorganization of the Boun Oum–Phoumi government was essential—"the earlier the better." Although he opposed Pathet Lao representation in the cabinet, Brown suggested a renewed effort to include

Souvanna in a reorganized government, recognizing the "immensely difficult" task of reconciling the political and military rivalries.[73]

On the day Eisenhower left office and Kennedy became president, a US-engineered rapprochement between Souvanna and Phoumi seemed an unlikely prospect. The January 20, 1961, edition of the *New York Times* published an interview with Souvanna, who called the Boun Oum government "a group of clowns." Still a guest of Prince Sihanouk in Phnom Penh, Souvanna said he would not resign as prime minister and had no intention of joining either the right-wing government or the Pathet Lao. He bitterly denounced the United States, which had thwarted his efforts to establish a coalition government and betrayed him by plotting with Phoumi. Souvanna reserved the harshest criticism for his longtime nemesis J. Graham Parsons. Characterizing the diplomat as "the most reprehensible and nefarious of men," Souvanna declared: "He understood nothing about Asia and nothing about Laos."[74]

Souvanna made similar comments about US policy and Parsons in a letter to Senator Mike Mansfield (D-MT), a Far East expert who had publicly questioned whether American aid to Laos had produced anything more than "chaos, discontent, and armies on the loose." Mansfield forwarded Souvanna's letter to President Kennedy, urging "a new approach to policy" in Laos. Parsons, commenting on the letter, observed to a State Department colleague: "While Souvanna Phouma singles out an individual, myself, as unqualified, he apparently forgets that our policy toward Laos, as elsewhere, is not the policy of any individual but rather of the Government."[75]

Epilogue
A Legacy of Strife and Confusion

THE DAY BEFORE HIS inauguration, President-elect Kennedy visited President Eisenhower at the White House to discuss a range of topics, with a primary focus on national security issues. In a private Oval Office meeting with Kennedy, Eisenhower reviewed such highly classified subjects as procedures for authorizing the use of nuclear weapons and presidential authority for covert intelligence operations. A larger group, which included each president's secretaries of state, defense, and treasury, as well as a staff aide, met with Eisenhower and Kennedy in the Cabinet Room to discuss Cuba, the US gold position, and other pressing topics. According to Kennedy's own notes, the new president had two main purposes for meeting with Eisenhower: The first was a symbolic gesture aimed at reassuring Americans of a harmonious presidential transition after Kennedy's narrow victory over Vice President Richard M. Nixon. The second, more substantive reason for the meeting, was to determine how Eisenhower and his advisers "would deal with Laos." Kennedy had a particular interest in learning "how prepared they were for military intervention."[1]

The discussion between the two presidents and their advisers was nothing if not well documented. The attendees wrote at least five independent records of a meeting characterized as "Rashomonesque" by researchers Fred Greenstein and Richard Immerman. Despite a rich volume of primary sources, the notes of the two presidents' conversation and the recollections of participants reveal conflicting perceptions of a fundamental question: What did Eisenhower say to Kennedy about unilateral US military intervention in Laos? The answer is significant because it informs speculation about how Eisenhower might have responded to the Southeast Asian crises faced by presidents Kennedy and Johnson.[2]

Wilton B. Persons, a retired army major general and Eisenhower's White House chief of staff, wrote that Kennedy wanted to discuss "the basic unconcluded decisions with respect to Laos and get the advice of the outgoing Administration on them." President Eisenhower began his response, according to Persons, with the uncontroversial observation that "unilateral action on the part of the United States would be very bad for our relations in that part of the world and would cause us to be 'tagged' as interventionists." This remark may have contributed to the sweeping first entry in the notes of the meeting by Robert S. McNamara, the new secretary of defense: "President Eisenhower advised against unilateral action by the United States in connection with Laos."[3]

At the invitation of President Eisenhower, Christian Herter reviewed the current military and political situation in Laos. The most disturbing military factor, according to Herter's notes, was "the unwillingness of the armed forces of the recognized Government to fight." Commenting on the US commitment to SEATO, he said that the RLG could request assistance to combat external aggression; the Soviet airlift constituted such aggression; and the United States must honor its "solemn obligation" under the treaty. Herter added that both England and France might not feel similarly bound by the agreement.[4]

Kennedy, according to his own notes, then turned to President Eisenhower, who confirmed that "we should intervene" in Laos, presumably under SEATO auspices. The president-elect then asked a question he repeatedly posed to his military advisers in the initial months of his presidency: Could North Vietnam and China bring reinforcements into Laos faster than the United States could? Kennedy wrote that Eisenhower responded that "it was a question of whether they would be willing to see the war spread," a comment that, at a minimum, likely referred to conventional air strikes against troop concentrations, lines of communication, and other targets in North Vietnam and southern China. To McNamara, Eisenhower's answer to Kennedy's question about escalation "was not completely clear." Secretary of Defense Gates observed that the United States could deploy twelve thousand troops to Laos within seventeen days and possibly within twelve.[5]

There is no doubt that President Eisenhower, Secretary Herter, and Secretary Gates warned the new administration that communist control of Laos would lead to the "loss" of all Southeast Asia. It was the "cork in the bottle," in Eisenhower's words. Whether Eisenhower specifically urged unilateral US military intervention in Laos is less certain. Clark Clifford, a lawyer who served as Kennedy's aide at the meeting, wrote: "President Eisenhower stated that he considered Laos of such importance that if it reached the stage where we could not persuade others to act with us, then he would be willing, *as a last desperate hope, to intervene unilaterally.*'" Kennedy's secretary of state, Dean Rusk, did not take notes at this meeting, but he later recalled that Eisenhower advised Kennedy to "put American troops in Laos, 'with others if possible, alone if necessary.'"[6]

Yet McNamara, as mentioned earlier, thought that Eisenhower explicitly advised against unilateral US military intervention. According to General Persons's notes, Eisenhower observed that such intervention "would be a last desperate effort to save Laos," without making a specific recommendation. Kennedy's own conclusion about Eisenhower's views, which was less definitive than the completely opposite assertions of Rusk and McNamara, seems reasonable: "I came away from that meeting feeling that the Eisenhower administration would support intervention—they felt it was preferable to a communist success in Laos."[7]

The differing perceptions of the president's advice that day reflected the ambivalence Eisenhower and his immediate successors experienced when facing the grim alternatives of either a communist victory in Indochina or the introduction of US combat forces in an Asian land war. When a third option was available, presidents Eisenhower, Kennedy, and Johnson seized it, usually at the cost of increasing the long-term US commitment to the former Indochinese states. President Eisenhower, for example, had refused to intervene in the French–Viet Minh war, but he did establish SEATO and begin providing direct US assistance to South Vietnam, Laos, and Cambodia. In the late summer of 1959, Eisenhower seemed ready to introduce US troops to prevent communist forces from overrunning Laos. When the crisis turned out to be less threatening than it initially appeared, Eisenhower reverted to his long-standing commitment to united military action if diplomacy failed. He also stepped up US support to the RLG.

In the two-volume memoir of his presidency, Eisenhower briefly mentioned his January 19 meeting with Kennedy but did not refer to their discussion about Laos. His memoir devoted relatively few pages to the kingdom; it focused primarily on the military crises of 1959 and 1960, while including little about the preceding actions that led to those crises. Defending the decision to support the Boun Oum–Phoumi government, the former president wrote: "We were ready to stand by it against aggression from the outside." He did not, however, specify whether such a stand would be unilateral or require allies.[8]

President Kennedy entered office deeply concerned by the unfavorable military situation in Laos, the kingdom's geographic proximity to powerful communist nations, and the political weakness of the Boun Oum–Phoumi government, both internally and internationally. At the first White House meeting on Laos, on January 23, 1961, Kennedy wondered aloud to his advisers "how specifically we planned to save Laos" in such unpromising circumstances. Two days later he told the Joint Chiefs of Staff of his determination to assist the RLG but admitted that he was "not too optimistic."[9]

The Kennedy administration supported Phoumi's planned offensive to retake the Plaine des Jarres. A successful operation would improve the RLG's negotiating posture in any political settlement of the civil war. Phoumi's forces, however, suffered an ignominious defeat in early March, prompting Kennedy and his advisers to consider more robust military measures to strengthen the RLG's bargaining position. Their plans included aerial attacks by "sanitized" CIA and USAF B-26 bombers, interdiction of communist lines of communications by the growing number of CIA-trained Hmong forces, and an airborne assault by FAL paratroopers, with CAT and the Defense Department providing transport aircraft. If necessary, overt US forces would intervene. At a March 21 White House meeting, Secretary of State Dean Rusk explained, "Even if we move in, the object is not to fight a big war but to lay a foundation for negotiation."[10]

In a nationally televised press conference two days later, President Kennedy introduced most Americans to the kingdom of Laos and to the "difficult and potentially dangerous problem" there. Standing before three large maps of the kingdom, he stressed US support for the neutrality and independence of Laos. Indirectly announcing a reversal of Eisenhower's policy, Kennedy said that "if in the past there has been any possible ground for misunderstanding our desire for a truly neutral Laos, there should be none now." The president supported a UK proposal for an immediate cease-fire and prompt negotiations. A "peaceful solution" to the crisis, however, required an end to Soviet and North Vietnamese intervention, as well as Pathet Lao attacks against the RLG. "If these attacks do not stop," Kennedy warned, "those who support a truly neutral Laos will have to consider their response. . . . No one should doubt our resolution on this point."[11]

Despite Kennedy's public appeal for negotiations and his thinly veiled threat of intervention, the military position of the RLG continued to deteriorate. On April 26 Brigadier General Andrew Jackson Boyle, who had replaced General Heintges as PEO chief the previous January, reported that the FAL was "on the ropes." Pathet Lao units, stiffened by North Vietnamese cadres, appeared capable of taking any town in the country. That same day Ambassador Brown, who had often opposed CINCPAC plans for combat aircraft, requested authority to employ B-26 medium bombers to stop the Pathet Lao advance, recognizing that such action would "blow [the] whole cease-fire negotiation wide open" and "most likely involve [the] immediate intervention [of] U.S.-SEATO forces."[12]

President Kennedy denied Brown's request for B-26s, although he approved moving naval forces into the Gulf of Siam and placing contingency ground forces on a heightened alert status. Chastened by the mid-April debacle at the Bay of Pigs, Kennedy had become increasingly skeptical of a military solution in Laos, a point of view strengthened by the conflicting advice for obtaining a cease-fire that he received from the Joint Chiefs and other senior defense advisers. The leading JCS proponent for intervening in Laos, Admiral Arleigh Burke, recommended landing US troops in Thailand and South Vietnam, who would then move into Laos to protect population and communication centers. If forces from North Vietnam or China intervened, the United States should "escalate immediately" and launch air strikes against the two countries. The Air Force chief of staff, General Thomas D. White, was, however, "most reluctant to commit US land forces to the mainland of Asia." He proposed initial air attacks against communist military and supply centers in Laos. If such strikes failed to bring about a cease-fire, White's follow-up actions included air attacks against Hanoi. Defense Secretary McNamara and JCS chairman Lemnitzer favored US intervention in Laos, while General Maxwell D. Taylor, a former army chief of staff whom Kennedy had appointed military representative to the president after the Bay of Pigs, "opposed" putting in American troops.[13]

Although military intervention was, at best, a dangerous alternative with an uncertain outcome, President Kennedy "explicitly refused" to rule out this option. Determined to prevent communists from overrunning Laos, Kennedy would have found it difficult to resist ordering an overt US military response to Pathet Lao attacks on Vientiane or a PL attempt to cut the country in half. Moreover, the possibility of a US military response was the only option likely to induce the Pathet Lao to agree to a cease-fire and negotiations. President Kennedy's posture on forestalling a communist victory in Laos, White House aide Theodore C. Sorensen later wrote, "combined bluff with real determination in proportions he made known to *no one*."[14]

On May 3 the Pathet Lao agreed to a cease-fire, followed by an international conference on the "Laotian question" in Geneva. In one of his earliest reports from Geneva, an eyes-only message to the president, Dean Rusk observed: "I had not fully appreciated [the] extent to which [the] US had become isolated on Laos by acts [of the] previous administration seen both by friends and neutrals as overplaying our hand." He further reported a "deep-seated" impression among allies and nonaligned nations that the United States "had 'earned' [the] Communist reaction" to the Boun Oum–Phoumi government.[15]

Fundamental to any international settlement in Laos was a political agreement among the three competing princes—Souvanna, Souphanouvong, and Boun Oum—each of whom controlled a separate military force. In a sharp break with Eisenhower's policy and a departure from his own initial position, President Kennedy concluded that the best alternative in Laos was a coalition government with Souvanna as prime minister. Phoumi stubbornly resisted this political solution, which posed a significant problem for the Kennedy administration. As the kingdom's sole source of anticommunist military strength, however feeble, the Lao general played a key role in Kennedy's conception of a balanced coalition government. The policy challenge was to apply enough pressure to encourage his cooperation, while making sure, in Kennedy's words, "that Phoumi does not collapse."[16]

After a year of on-and-off negotiations among the princes, as well as Western and communist powers, a negotiated solution in Laos seemed near. The diplomatic progress was threatened, however, in the first week of May 1962, when combined Pathet Lao–North Vietnamese forces attacked Nam Tha, a provincial capital in northwestern Laos near the border with

China. The communists routed some of the RLG's best troops—three parachute and five infantry battalions—triggering the panicky flight of some forty-five hundred soldiers, most of whom abandoned their weapons and other US-supplied equipment. "The boys have their track shoes on and they are moving southwest" toward Thailand, Undersecretary of State George Ball informed the White House.[17]

At a May 9 press conference, President Kennedy noted that the communists had committed a "clear breach of the cease-fire" at Nam Tha. Describing the current state of affairs in Laos as "not a satisfactory situation," he urged the major powers and the three princes to move forward with negotiations. Kennedy acknowledged that a political settlement was "a very hazardous course." But, he continued, "introducing American forces which is the other one—let's not think there is some great third course—that also is a hazardous course."[18]

At a White House meeting the next day, Kennedy reviewed a proposed State Department response to the attack at Nam Tha, which had eliminated almost all RLG control in northern Laos. State Department officials noted that the "fear of U.S. intervention" had been the principal means of deterring more aggressive communist military action in Laos. To "reinvigorate the deterrent," they proposed US naval movements in the Gulf of Siam and army deployments in Thailand. "Such steps," NSC staffer Michael V. Forrestal wrote to the president, "would be designed to impress the Russians and Chinese with our concern without at the same time threatening China's sensitive interest in the northern provinces."[19]

With Rusk, McNamara, and General Lemnitzer in Asia, the president deferred any important decisions until they returned to Washington. Kennedy did, however, dispatch Central Intelligence director John McCone and Forrestal to the Gettysburg farm of former president Eisenhower to inform him of the latest developments in Laos. Despite their differing worldviews and political affiliations, Kennedy and Eisenhower had maintained a polite relationship, with the former providing the latter with briefings on key topics in foreign affairs. President Kennedy's principal motive for such updates was maintaining Eisenhower's support for his foreign policy. McCone, a Republican who had served as AEC chairman during the Eisenhower administration, was a natural intermediary for the current and former presidents.

McCone described to Eisenhower the military situation in Laos, as well as Phoumi's military incompetence and political intransigence. The

CIA chief and Forrestal reported that the United States faced a fundamental choice: a Laotian government of national union led by Souvanna, with Phoumi's participation; or the introduction of "U.S. forces in Laos with possible assistance from the Thais but not others." Eisenhower's reaction was consistent with his presidential views. He opposed the idea of a government led by Souvanna, whom he believed "had turned Communist" when he fled to Cambodia in 1960. McCone, according to his notes of the meeting, replied that all US background checks "indicated Souvanna was not a Communist though he was a weak man."[20]

Eisenhower also maintained his opposition to a cabinet with Pathet Lao representation, observing that every government that had included communists was eventually taken over by them. Because a communist-dominated Laos would threaten South Vietnam and Thailand, Eisenhower declared that the "most extreme measures, including the commitment of U.S. forces to combat in Laos, were justified." According to Forrestal, the former president also said that he would follow up US troop deployments "with whatever support was necessary to achieve the objectives of their mission, including—if necessary—the use of tactical nuclear weapons." To secure constitutional authority for intervention in Laos, Eisenhower suggested that Kennedy seek a congressional resolution authorizing military action in Southeast Asia, similar to the Formosa and Middle East resolutions of the 1950s. Eisenhower "was sure that Congress and the people would support such a resolution and he personally would use his influence with his Party and the Congress to assist its passage."[21]

Eisenhower's militant views on Laos, Kennedy confided to aides, put the administration in "a tough position." Committed to seeking a negotiated settlement of the conflict, Kennedy feared a public statement by Eisenhower urging US intervention in Laos. Such a declaration—at a time when, in Kennedy's words, the administration's "problem is how to stay out of there"—would create unhelpful public pressure for war. In addition to the policy conflict, an Eisenhower proposal for intervention would pose serious political risks. If, as Kennedy hoped, Souvanna returned as prime minister, and was then overthrown by the Pathet Lao, a public statement by Eisenhower would fuel domestic recriminations similar to the partisan "Who lost China" debate in the early 1950s.[22]

The possibility of the former president taking a public position on Laos contrary to the current president's was the likely reason for Kennedy sending McCone right back to Gettysburg on Sunday, May 13, to brief

Eisenhower "on the rather grim situation in Southeast Asia." This time, however, the CIA chief was accompanied by McNamara and General Lemnitzer, who had just returned from the region. After a cordial meeting with Eisenhower, McCone reported to Kennedy that the former president "now understands the complexity of the situation, the difficulties we have encountered with Phoumi, the extent of the Communist penetration in Laos, and the alternative courses of action open to us." Despite McCone's declaration, it seems unlikely that Eisenhower had significantly changed his views. He did, however, honor his pledge to support the president in foreign affairs. According to McCone's notes, Eisenhower "made it quite clear he would not at this time privately or publicly urge moving U.S. combat troops into Laos."[23]

Complicating Kennedy's effort to manage the 1962 Laos crisis was an article in the *New York Times* reporting the president's plans to order a "show of force" in Southeast Asia. At a White House meeting, Kennedy was visibly upset by the article, which implied the president was bluffing. Although undoubtedly annoyed by the leak from his government, Kennedy was likely even more disturbed that the news report might lead to communist doubts about his determination to prevent a complete Pathet Lao victory. Well aware that many wars had started because of miscalculations about an adversary's intentions, Kennedy told his advisers that the proposed troop deployments were "extremely serious" matters. Declaring that any such action would not be a mere "show of force," the president said: "Whatever we do, we mean business."[24]

On May 15 the White House announced that US military forces had been ordered to Thailand. They included a Marine battalion landing team, an Air Force fighter squadron, and elements of an Army battle group, part of which was already in Thailand for a SEATO exercise. Referring to US obligations under the SEATO treaty, the announcement emphasized both the defensive nature of the US deployment and the policy goal of reestablishing the cease-fire and resuming negotiations among the three princes. As with the previous year's crisis, the threat of US military intervention prompted the Pathet Lao to honor the cease-fire. In June the three princes agreed to a Souvanna-led government of national union. This, in turn, led to the "Declaration on the Neutrality of Laos" and a protocol listing procedures for monitoring compliance, signed by representatives of fourteen nations on July 23, 1962.

The declaration called for the withdrawal of all foreign troops, with the exception of the largely irrelevant French Military Mission, and prohibited the use of Lao territory to interfere in the affairs of other countries, a reference to infiltration from North Vietnam to South Vietnam. Compliance with the agreement was uneven, at best, with the more egregious violations committed by North Vietnam, which withdrew only a small fraction of its estimated 6,000–9,000 troops in Laos and continued to use the infiltration trails into South Vietnam. The Soviet Union ended its airlift, but this caused little hardship for the Pathet Lao, which still received weapons and equipment by road from North Vietnam.

The US government withdrew 1,190 military advisers (although officially acknowledging only 666), some 200 Thai military "volunteers" assigned to MAAG (not to be confused with the CIA-controlled Thai PARU units that remained with the Hmong army), and more than 400 Filipino "technicians" who provided instruction to RLG forces in such areas as equipment maintenance and ordnance storage. MAAG moved across the Mekong River to Thailand, where the US military had been stocking ammunition, construction materials, and general supplies for Phoumi's forces. The primary mission of the secret "non-resident MAAG Laos" was to provide advisory support to the anticommunist forces by working with an expanded military attaché office in Vientiane and with a new Requirements Office (RO) in the economic aid mission. The RO, a logistic-support scheme similar to the original PEO concept, was staffed with retired military men who were responsible for the supply of materiel for the internal defense of Laos. All but two of the CIA officers training and equipping the "secret army" of Hmong irregulars withdrew to Thailand. To preserve its tribal "assets," however, the CIA continued to supply the Hmong, first with food and other nonmilitary supplies and later with ammunition and weapons.[25]

The 1962 Geneva declaration helped avoid a direct superpower confrontation over Laos, but the kingdom that emerged from the conference was far less stable than the wobbly state shaped by the 1954 accords. When the earlier agreement was signed, the Pathet Lao was a small, weak presence confined to two northern provinces. In 1962 it controlled about one-half of the country, including the border area with Vietnam. Although the US government no longer sought to undermine Souvanna as it had in the 1950s, the prime minister now faced a more polarized political environment, in which neither left- nor right-wing officials showed much interest in holding the new government together.

Souvanna's fragile coalition began falling apart in the autumn of 1962, when the Pathet Lao began a campaign to weaken the neutral forces of Kong Le. The alliance between the Pathet Lao and Kong Le, always an uneasy one, had been based on a mutual hatred for Phoumi, rather than the ideological affinity feared by the Eisenhower administration. North Vietnam sharply reduced its supplies to Kong Le, while the Pathet Lao sought defections from his troops, assassinated his field commander, and launched "nibbling" attacks against his positions on the Plaine des Jarres. Such pressure brought Laotian neutrals and conservatives closer together. Hmong irregulars supported Kong Le's efforts on the plain, and the US government began to supply him directly. The irony of assisting Kong Le, whom the United States had been fighting since the end of the Eisenhower administration, was not lost on Kennedy.[26]

As the Geneva agreement unraveled, Kennedy administration officials appealed to the Soviet Union to honor its commitment to ensure North Vietnamese compliance with the accord. President Kennedy believed that Khrushchev and he had reached an understanding about the neutralization of Laos at their 1961 Vienna summit meeting. W. Averell Harriman, the architect of the 1962 declaration and Kennedy's principal negotiator at Geneva, had received assurances from his counterpart, Georgi M. Pushkin, that the Soviet Union would "police the commitments made by the Communist signatories not to interfere in the internal affairs of Laos nor to use Laos as a corridor into South Viet-Nam."[27]

In April 1963 Harriman sought and gained authorization from Kennedy for a special trip to Moscow to point out to Khrushchev that the Pathet Lao attacks on neutral forces were "really serious." The Soviet premier, who wanted to speak with Harriman and other US officials about nuclear testing, Berlin, and other matters, dismissed Laos as an insignificant country, where the Soviet Union had little control. Harriman cabled the president that Khrushchev "is fed up with the subject and wishes it would go away." The question of whether the Soviet premier had the will or ability to influence the Pathet Lao was "unanswered," Harriman reported. Michael Forrestal, who traveled to Moscow with Harriman, told his colleagues on the NSC staff: "Khrushchev did not have the foggiest notion of the geography of Laos and, when Harriman mentioned a few Laotian personalities, Khrushchev impatiently exclaimed that he did not know all those silly Laotian names or the individuals to whom these names belonged."[28]

The ineffectiveness of the 1962 Geneva agreement was a disappointment to President Kennedy. Although reluctant to back the US commitment in Southeast Asia with American combat troops, Kennedy saw Laos as a cold war contest where he was prepared to settle for an apparent tie but not an obvious loss. Summarizing Kennedy's view of the global ideological struggle, historian Lawrence Freedman observed: "He did not expect to be able to roll back communism, but neither did he intend to preside over its expansion." Whatever course of action he might have followed in Vietnam had he lived longer, Kennedy apparently did not think the 1962 Geneva agreement was a model for settling that conflict. Two months before his assassination, Kennedy pointed out to his advisers "that neutralization was not working in Laos" and wondered why de Gaulle and the influential columnist Walter Lippmann believed "the Laotian case provided an illustration of what should be done in Vietnam."[29]

The failure of the Geneva agreement to provide a semblance of stability in Laos prompted Kennedy to start down a path of covert and overt military escalation in Southeast Asia that his successor followed and extended. During an April 20, 1963, discussion of US policy in Laos, Kennedy asked his advisers about "military action we could take against Hanoi" and requested a study from the Pentagon on feasible military steps. Three days later the JCS submitted military options that might "bring about stability in Laos." Warning of the probable need for additional US forces to cope with the likely communist military response, the chiefs proposed air attacks against ports, bridges, airfields, fuel storage facilities, and industrial plants in both Laos and North Vietnam.[30]

Planning for air strikes against North Vietnam was a topic of discussion during a restricted session of the May 6, 1963, secretary of defense conference at CINCPAC headquarters in Honolulu. The conference, the eighth of its kind since President Kennedy's 1961 decision to increase the US advisory effort in South Vietnam, provided an opportunity for officials in Washington and Saigon to review the administration's military and civilian programs. After a summary by CINCPAC staff of contingency plans "for overt, gradually escalating operations in North Vietnam,"

McNamara reported that the JCS had briefed President Kennedy on eight targets for air attacks because of the situation in Laos. The defense secretary directed Admiral Felt to incorporate these targets in his plans. Army chief of staff General Earle G. Wheeler, who was not optimistic about presidential approval of overt air strikes in North Vietnam, explained to the senior military and civilian officials in Honolulu that the JCS targeting was "designed to convince Ho Chi Minh he should desist from intervention" in Laos.[31]

The military deterioration in Laos, which in the spring of 1963 appeared more serious to Kennedy administration officials than the insurgency in South Vietnam, prompted Rusk and McNamara to propose a three-phase program of covert and overt military pressure against Hanoi, culminating "in the initiation of military action against North Vietnam." In a June 18, 1963, memorandum to Kennedy, the secretaries of state and defense made it clear that their proposal was not a "contingency" plan but "a method of influencing the overall situation." Foreshadowing the flawed thinking behind President Lyndon Johnson's slowly escalating air attacks in the Vietnam War, the Laos program assumed that a gradual increase in political and military pressure would be controllable, avoiding "irreversible" escalation, and would achieve the administration's minimum objective: "the facade of a neutralist government presiding over a stabilized de facto partition" of the kingdom. Kennedy authorized the program's modest first steps, which included expanding clandestine military support to tribal groups in Laos, providing armed T-28 aircraft for reprisal strikes against the Pathet Lao, and stepping up the delivery of 105 mm howitzers and other heavy weapons to Phoumi and Kong Le.[32]

Kennedy kept tight control of this program. Like Eisenhower, he was more comfortable approving covert, rather than overt, action in Southeast Asia. According to the minutes of a June 19, 1963, meeting to discuss next steps in Laos, Kennedy was skeptical about air strikes against North Vietnam. How much damage would they really do? Wouldn't China intervene immediately? Would the threat of air attacks be more influential with the North Vietnamese than the actual operations? Declaring that options for overt military action in Southeast Asia required more study, Kennedy warned: "We are not likely to receive Congressional or public support of U.S. intervention in Laos and we should not kid ourselves about this too much."[33]

During the final five months of Kennedy's life, the tempo and intensity of Pathet Lao attacks decreased sharply, as the annual monsoons hampered military operations throughout the kingdom. At a time when the Buddhist crisis in South Vietnam was evolving into a military coup to overthrow Ngo Dinh Diem, President Kennedy continued his efforts to hold Khrushchev accountable for North Vietnamese compliance with the 1962 Geneva declaration. On August 2, 1963, Kennedy told Secretary of State Dean Rusk to warn the Soviets that if the situation in Laos continued to deteriorate, the US government would "have to take some action" to preserve the neutral government. The Soviets' "hands-off attitude" toward their Lao obligation, Kennedy declared, "removed any right they have to react to that action."[34]

Three weeks before Kennedy's assassination, analysts in the CIA's Office of Current Intelligence assessed the situation in Laos. Reunification of the country, they concluded, "appears more remote than ever." The previous spring NLHS cabinet ministers had withdrawn from Vientiane to remote regions of Laos controlled by the Pathet Lao. Phoumi, who firmly controlled the right-wing forces, believed that the coalition would "ultimately collapse" under communist pressure and that the United States would then likely decide to support him exclusively. With the rainy season coming to end, the Pathet Lao and Phoumi were "strengthening their positions in strategically important areas."[35]

How Kennedy might have responded to the problems in Laos faced by Lyndon Johnson in 1964 and beyond is as unknowable as the steps the slain president might have taken in Vietnam. Persuasive evidence can be cited for either a Kennedy decision to withdraw or a decision to escalate in Southeast Asia. But confident conclusions about either course of action are precluded by President Kennedy's ambivalence about the US commitments in Laos and South Vietnam and his unwillingness to make difficult policy decisions any earlier than necessary. What can be said is that his support for Souvanna Phouma and a coalition government was no more successful than Eisenhower's efforts to undermine the Lao prime minister in favor of right-wing leaders. Exemplifying the lose-lose quality of many US choices in Southeast Asia, the two presidents pursued different strategies in Laos, but the policy outcome for each was the same: a deeper, more dangerous US commitment to the region for his successor. In fairness to Kennedy, however, an observation White House aide Michael Forrestal made to the president in 1962 seems apt: "Laos is a chess game which was more than half played out before you sat down to the board."[36]

Acknowledgments

While conducting research for *Before the Quagmire,* I received valuable assistance from archivists at the National Archives and Records Administration, College Park, Maryland; the Dwight D. Eisenhower Library, Abilene, Kansas; the John F. Kennedy Library, Boston; the U.S. Army Military History Institute, Carlisle, Pennsylvania; the Seeley G. Mudd Manuscript Library, at Princeton University; and the Special Collections Division of the Georgetown University Library. I am particularly grateful for the help provided by Stanley Fanaras at the National Archives, Herb Pankratz at the Eisenhower Library, and Scott Taylor at Georgetown University. Kristin Coffey provided substantial research and editing assistance that made *Before the Quagmire* a better book.

Cold war historian Richard Immerman was kind enough to read a draft of the entire manuscript and made many useful suggestions for strengthening it. Historian George Herring, whose Vietnam War scholarship I have admired for decades, pointed me in the direction of the University Press of Kentucky and its director, Stephen Wrinn. Two anonymous readers selected by the UPK provided constructive criticism that I found helpful in revising the manuscript.

The observations about Laos of two men who served there some fifty-five years ago also benefited *Before the Quagmire:* Rufus Phillips, who provided unpublished portions of his book *Why Vietnam Matters;* and Joel Halpern, who spent time with me reviewing some of his papers at the John F. Kennedy and University of Massachusetts libraries.

Of course, I bear sole responsibility for the book's conclusions and any factual errors of commission or omission. Finally, I am grateful for the efforts of John Ware, a literary agent who has believed in this project from its earliest chapter drafts.

Notes

Abbreviations Used in the Notes and the Bibliography

APP	The American Presidency Project
CF	Central Files
CREST	CIA Research Tool, U.S. National Archives and Records Administration
CWYP	Charles W. Yost Papers
DDEL	Dwight D. Eisenhower Presidential Library
DDEOHP	Dwight D. Eisenhower Oral History Program, Dwight D. Eisenhower Presidential Library
DDEP	Dwight D. Eisenhower, *The Papers of Dwight David Eisenhower*
FAOHC	Foreign Affairs Oral History Collection
FRUS	U.S. Department of State, *Foreign Relations of the United States*
HSTOHP	Harry S. Truman Oral History Program, Harry S. Truman Presidential Library
JFDOHP	John Foster Dulles Oral History Program, Seeley G. Mudd Manuscript Library. Princeton Univ., Princeton, NJ.
JFDP	John Foster Dulles Papers
JFKL	John F. Kennedy Presidential Library
JFKOHP	John F. Kennedy Oral History Program, John F. Kennedy Presidential Library
JGPP	J. Graham Parsons Papers
JMHP	Joel M. Halpern Papers
KARC	Kennedy Assassination Records Collection
NARA	U.S. National Archives and Records Administration
NSF	National Security Files
POF	President's Office Files
RG 59	General Records of the Department of State
RG 84	Records of the Foreign Service Posts of the Department of State

RG 218   Records of the U.S. Joint Chiefs of Staff
RG 469   Records of U.S. Foreign Assistance Agencies
RHBP   Rothwell H. Brown Papers
RHP   Roger Hilsman Papers
SEA   Office of Southeast Asian Affairs
USAMHI   U.S. Army Military History Institute, Carlisle, PA

Introduction

1. Hoover to Dulles, March 1, 1956, DDEL, JFDP, Personnel Series; Parsons, unpublished memoir, JGPP, box 13, folder 17.

2. Robertson to Parsons, August 2, 1957, NARA, RG 59, CF, lot 59D19, box 2.

3. JGPP, box 12, folder 37; Taubman, *Khrushchev,* p. 487.

4. Brown to Parsons, July 26, 1965, JGPP, box 2, folder 55.

5. Schlesinger, *Thousand Days,* pp. 415–16.

6. Parsons, February 11, 1966, JGPP, box 2, folder 55.

7. JGPP, box 13, folder 17.

8. Eric Pace, *New York Times,* October 22, 1991.

9. Eisenhower, *Waging Peace,* p. 612.

10. Memorandum, May 29, 1958, NARA, RG 59, CF, box 3365.

11. NSC 5429/5, December 22, 1954, quoted in U.S. Dept. of Defense, "Chronological Summary"; State Dept. to Smith, July 30, 1958, *FRUS, XVI,* p. 471; Bissell, *Reflections of a Cold Warrior,* p. 147.

12. Brown to State Dept., December 12, 1960, *FRUS, XVI,* MFS; Parsons to State Dept., October 16, 1960, *FRUS, XVI,* p. 911.

13. National Intelligence Estimate (NIE) 63–5–54, August 3, 1954, www.cia.gov.

14. Boyle, interview by Frank Walton, February 28, 1971, USAMHI.

15. Because of the absence of census data in this period, the margin of error for the Lao population estimate could exceed plus or minus 500,000.

16. Halpern, "Lao Elite," p. 11; "America and Laos," p. 2.

17. Halpern, "Some Reflections," p. 4.

18. Dommen, *Indochinese Experience,* p. 255; Dulles to Smith, May 12, 1954, *FRUS, XVI,* p. 788; Dulles, July 23, 1954, JFDP, box 83, reel 32.

19. Excerpt of minutes of Zhou Enlai's meeting with Mendes-France, July 17, 1954, in Ostermann, "Inside China's Cold War"; Dulles to US delegation, June 23, 1954, *FRUS, XVI,* p. 1226.

20. For the sake of consistency with quoted documents, I use the name Sam Neua for the province that is more properly called Houa Phan. US documents from this period almost invariably call it Sam Neua, the name of the provincial capital.

21. Laos agreement, July 20, 1954, *FRUS, XVI,* p. 1521.

22. US delegation to State Dept., July 21, 1954, ibid., p. 1498.

23. Dulles to State Dept., April 27, 1954, ibid., p. 577.

24. Memorandum, July 30, 1954, DDEL, NSC Staff Papers, OCB Central File Series, box 79.

25. NIE 63–5–54, August 3, 1954, www.cia.gov.

26. Dulles, July 23, 1954, JFDP, box 83, reel 32.

27. Memorandum, August 17, 1954, *FRUS, XIII,* p. 1953.

28. Memorandum, October 26, 1954, ibid., pp. 2185–86.

29. Ibid.

30. Chapman, interview by Charles Stuart Kennedy, March 3, 1990, FAOHC.

31. Eisenhower to Churchill, March 29, 1955, *DDEP,* p. 16:1642.

32. Dillon, interview by Robert D. Schulzinger, April 28, 1987, FAOHC.

33. Lyon, *Eisenhower,* p. 904; Rabe, "Eisenhower Revisionism," p. 99.

34. Ambrose, *Eisenhower,* p. 626.

1. The Most Difficult Post in the Entire Foreign Service

1. Yost, interview by Richard D. Challener, December 13, 1966, JFDOHP.

2. Young to Yost, February 20, 1955, CWYP, box 15, folder 4; Ted M.G. Tanen, interview by Charles Stuart Kennedy, September 21, 2000, FAOHC.

3. Memorandum, September 1, 1954, NARA, RG 84, Laos, U.S. Embassy Vientiane, Classified General Records, 1954–1963, box 1A.

4. Halpern, "Lao Elite," p. 46.

5. Crosswell, *Beetle,* p. 16; Smith, July 23, 1954, *FRUS, XVI,* p. 1552; Yost, interview.

6. Yost, interview.

7. Yost to Robertson, September 2, 1954, NARA, RG 59, SEA, Subject Files Relating to Laos, 1952–58, box 1.

8. Finger, *Inside the World of Diplomacy,* p. 23.

9. Yost to State Dept., September 18, 1956, NARA, RG 59, CF, box 3364.

10. Yost to State Dept., December 14, 1954, ibid.

11. W. Wendell Blancké to State Dept., July 24, 1956, ibid.

12. *Current Intelligence Bulletin,* October 9, 1954, NARA, CREST; Yost to State Dept., January 12, 1956, CWYP, box 14, folder 1.

13. Yost to State Dept., October 8, 1954, *FRUS, XII,* p. 2121.

14. Yost to State Dept., November 30, 1954, ibid., p. 2322.

15. Yost to State Dept., November 16, 1954, CWYP, box 7, folder 10.

16. NSC 5429/2, August 20, 1954, NARA, RG 273.

17. Memorandum, December 19, 1954, NARA, RG 84, entry 2850, box 1A.

18. Gordon to ACS, G-2, March 15, 1955, NARA, RG 59, General Files, lot file no. 68 D 77; Yost to State Dept., February 28, 1955, CWYP, box 13, folder 13.

19. Wilson to Dulles, February 16, 1955, *FRUS, XXI,* p. 607; Memorandum, March 21, 1955, DDEL, White House Office, NSC Staff: Papers, 1948–61, OCB Central File Series, box 39.

20. Yost to State Dept., January 29, 1955, *FRUS, XXI,* p. 595.

21. Goscha, "Vietnam and the World Outside," pp. 170–71.

22. Yost to State Dept., January 11, 1955, *FRUS, XXI,* pp. 581–82.

23. State Dept. to Yost, January 19, 1955, ibid., p. 584; Draft memorandum, January 19, 1955; memorandum, February 2, 1955, NARA, RG 59, Executive Secretariat, Regional and Country Operations Files, 1953–1961, box 29.

24. Biographic Sketch, September 20, 1956, NARA, RG 59, SEA, Subject Files Relating to Laos, 1952–58, box 1; Biographic Sketch, February 18, 1963, NARA, RG 59, entry 5415-B, box 9.

25. Yost to State Dept., February 13, 1955, *FRUS, XXI,* p. 602.

26. Yost to State Dept., February 14, 1955, ibid., p. 604.

27. Robert Alden, *New York Times,* February 28, 1955; Parsons, JGPP, box 13, folder 17.

28. Immerman, *John Foster Dulles,* p. xiii.

29. Eisenhower, diary, May 14, 1953, *DDEP,* p. 14:224; Eisenhower to Guenther, December 22, 1954, *DDEP,* p. 15:1461; Immerman, *John Foster Dulles,* p. 46.

30. "The Threat of Red Asia," March 29, 1954, reprinted in *Department of State Bulletin,* April 5, 1954.

31. Gaddis, *Strategies of Containment,* pp. 138–39.

32. Johnson, interview by Philip A. Crowl, May 28, 1966, JFDOHP.

33. Memorandum, August 18, 1954, *FRUS, XII,* p. 752.

34. Memorandum, September 30, 1958, *FRUS, XVI,* pp. 254–55.

35. Mendenhall, interview by Horace Torbert, February 11, 1991, FAOHC.

36. Dulles, February 23, 1955, JFDP, series 5, box 333.

37. Yost to State Dept., February 21, 1955, *FRUS, XXI,* p. 610n.

38. Dulles to State Dept., February 28, 1955, ibid., p. 619.

39. Memorandum, February 27, 1955, ibid., pp. 611–12.

40. Ibid., pp. 615–16.

41. Dulles to Eisenhower, March 1, 1955, *FRUS, I,* p. 96.

42. Memorandum, February 27, 1955, *FRUS, XXI,* p. 618.

43. Yost, interview.

44. Yost to State Dept., March 6, 1955, NARA, RG 59, CF, box 3370.

45. Yost to State Dept., March 15, 1955, *FRUS, XXI,* p. 625.

46. Halpern, "Some Reflections," p. 7; Yost to State Dept., March 13, 1955, CWYP, box 13, folder 13.

47. Eisenhower to Churchill, March 29, 1955, *DDEP,* 16:1640–41.

48. Ibid., p. 16:1643; *FRUS, XXI,* p. 633n.

49. State Dept. to Yost, March 17, 1955, *FRUS, XXI,* p. 628.

50. Secretary of State for Foreign Affairs, *Second Interim Report,* p. 13; Yost to State Dept., May 3, 1955, *FRUS, XXI,* p. 641.

51. Yost to Young, May 6, 1955, *FRUS, XXI,* pp. 644–46.

52. Yost to State Dept., April 23, 1955, NARA, RG 59, CF, box 3362.

53. Yost to State Dept., January 13, 1955, *FRUS, XXI,* p. 578

54. Yost to State Dept., April 23, 1955.

55. Yost to Young, June 4, 1955, *FRUS, XXI,* p. 659; Yost to State Dept., May 30, 1955, CWYP, box 13, folder 13.

56. Yost to State Dept., July 8, 1955, CWYP, folder 14.

57. Memorandum, July 12, 1955, *FRUS, XXI,* p. 665.

58. State Dept. to Bangkok, July 11, 14, 27, 1955, ibid., pp. 112–21.

59. Memorandum, July 13, 1955, ibid., p. 667.

60. NIE 63.3–55, July 26, 1955, www.cia.gov.

61. Ibid.

62. Ibid.; Finger, *Inside the World of Diplomacy*, p. 24.

63. Yost to State Dept., May 30, 1955, CWYP, box 13, folder 13; Yost to Young, June 4, 1955, *FRUS, XXI*, p. 658.

64. In the years covered by this book, the US government referred to the Hmong as "the Meo" and the Khmu and other minorities living at middle altitudes as "the Kha." Both terms—particularly *Kha*, which means "slave"—are found offensive by many, though not intended as such by US officials in the 1950s and 1960s. In addition, *Hmong* is a term more familiar to audiences today than *Meo*. For these reasons, I will use the more contemporary terms *Hmong* and *Khmu* to describe these two tribal groups.

65. Helms, *A Look over My Shoulder*, chapter 25, "The War We Won."

66. Yost to State Dept., September 14, 1955, NARA, RG 59, CF, box 3363.

67. Ibid.

68. Yost to State Dept., December 31, 1955, *FRUS, XXI*, pp. 728–29.

69. Yost to State Dept., March 9, 1956, NARA, RG 59, CF, box 3363.

70. Embassy to State Dept., March 30, 1956; Yost to State Dept., March 14, 1956, NARA, RG 59, CF, box 3363.

71. W. Wendell Blancké to State Dept., July 24, 1956; Parsons to State Dept., November 7, 1956, NARA, RG 59, CF, box 3364.

72. Yost to State Dept., March 31, 1956, *FRUS, XXI*, p. 747.

73. Joel Halpern, interview by A. M. Halpern, August 24, 1959. JMHP, JFKL; see also "Travels with Phetsarath, 1959," in Evans, *Last Century of Lao Royalty*, pp. 129–33; and Ivarsson and Goscha, "Prince Phetsarath."

74. NIE 63.3–55, July 26, 1955, www.cia.gov.

75. Yost to State Dept., March 31, 1956, *FRUS, XXI*, p. 748.

76. Morris to Miller, September 29, 1955, CWYP, box 10, folder 3.

77. Yost to State Dept., April 6, 1956, NARA, RG 59, CF, box 3363.

78. Yost to State Dept., April 6, 1956, *FRUS, XXI*, pp. 754.

79. Ibid., pp. 753–55.

80. Ibid., p. 750n.

2. A Frontier Country in the Cold War

1. Parsons, JGPP, box 12, folder 37; Margaret Parsons to Adelaide Parsons, August 1, 1956, JGPP, box 10, folder 35.

2. JGPP, box 12, folder 33.

3. Parsons to Brown, November 19, 1932, JGPP, box 8, folder 36.

4. Parsons to Adelaide, Margot, and Jane Parsons, March 24, 1956, JGPP, box 10, folder 21; Parsons, JGPP, box 13, folder 17.

5. Parsons, JGPP, box 13, folder 17; memorandum, undated (ca. 1959), NARA, CREST.

6. Memorandum, June 8, 1956, *FRUS, I*, pp. 700–701; Parsons, JGPP, box 13, folder 17.

7. W. Wendell Blancké to State Dept., June 1, 1956, NARA, RG 59, CF, box 3363; State Dept. to Blancké, June 9, 1956, *FRUS, XXI,* pp. 774–75.

8. Memorandum, July 18, 1954, in Ostermann, "Inside China's Cold War," p. 70; Blancké to State Dept., June 12, 1956, CWYP, box 13, folder 4.

9. Memorandum, July 28, 1956, NARA, RG 59, SEA, Subject Files Relating to Laos, 1952–58, box 1.

10. Parsons to State Dept., March 15, 1957, *FRUS, XXI,* p. 904; Brown and Zasloff, *Apprentice Revolutionaries,* p. 43.

11. Langer and Zasloff, *North Vietnam and the Pathet Lao,* p. 37.

12. Memorandum, August 9, 1956, *FRUS, XXI,* p. 790.

13. Parsons to State Dept., August 6, 1956, ibid., pp. 785–86.

14. Ibid.

15. Chapman, interview.

16. Parsons to Robertson, August 7, 1956, JGPP, box 2, folder 25.

17. Ibid.

18. Ibid.

19. Clark to Parsons, September 26, 1956, JGPP, box 2, folder 25.

20. Trinquier, *Modern Warfare;* also see Trinquier's introduction by Bernard B. Fall.

21. Young to Sebald, February 20, 1956, CWYP, box 13, folder 4; Erskine to Dulles, February 13, 1956, *FRUS, XXI,* p. 743.

22. CIA to Secretary of Defense, March 3, 1956, *FRUS, XXI,* p. 749.

23. Memorandum, November 9, 1956, JGPP, box 2, folder 25.

24. Memorandum, September 24, 1956, *FRUS, XXI,* p. 822.

25. NSC Briefing, August 29, 1956, NARA, CREST.

26. Memorandum, September 24, 1956, *FRUS, XXI,* p. 818.

27. Ibid.

28. Memorandum, September 21, 1956, *FRUS, XXI,* p. 816; Young to Parsons, October 5, 1956, NARA, RG 59, SEA, Subject Files Relating to Laos, 1952–58, box 1.

29. Young to Robertson, November 7, 1956, *FRUS, XXI,* p. 834; State Dept. to Parsons, November 8, 1956, ibid., p. 837.

30. Parsons to State Dept., November 20, 1956, *FRUS, XXI,* p. 841.

31. State Dept. to Parsons, November 22, 1956, ibid., p. 845.

32. Parsons to State Dept., November 27, 1956, ibid., pp. 848–49.

33. Secretary of State for Foreign Affairs, *Third Interim Report,* p. 67.

34. Parsons to State Dept., December 28, 1956, *FRUS, XXI,* p. 866.

35. Ambassador to U.S. to secretary of state for external affairs, January 3, 1957, www.dfait-maeci.gc.ca.

36. Mendenhall, interview.

37. Robertson, interview by Ed Edwin, April 18–19, 1967, DDEOHP.

38. *Time,* April 13, 1959, www.time.com.

39. Robertson, interview by Philip A. Crowl, July 23–24, 1965, JFDOHP.

40. Baldwin, interview by Dennis J. O'Brien, March 13, 14, 1969, JFKOHP.

41. Erickson, interview by Charles Stuart Kennedy, June 25, 1992, FAOHC.

42. Memorandum, January 12, 1957, NARA, RG 59, SEA, entry 3121.

43. Parsons to State Dept., January 10, 1957, *FRUS, XXI,* p. 876.

44. Ibid., p. 855n.

45. Ibid., p. 871n.

46. Parsons to State Dept., January 4, 1957, *FRUS, XXI,* p. 872.

47. Parsons to Allen Dulles, March 21, 1957, JGPP, box 2, folder 8.

48. Ibid.

49. Phillips, unpublished manuscript excerpt from his book *Why Vietnam Matters,* n.d. (The published version of the book made deep cuts in the Laos section, primarily to maintain the book's focus on Vietnam.)

50. Parsons to Clark, April 5, 1957, JGPP, box 2, folder 7.

51. Ibid.

52. Erickson, interview.

53. NSC 5412/2, undated (ca. December 28, 1955), *FRUS: The Intelligence Community,* p. 748; Methven, *Laughter in the Shadows,* p. 49.

54. PEO to Defense Dept., August 10, 1956, USAMHI.

55. PEO to Defense Dept., January 10, 1957, USAMHI.

56. Brown, unpublished manuscript, ca. 1962, RHBP, box 4, folder, Laos 1956–1962, USAMHI.

57. PEO to Defense Dept., August 20, 1957, USAMHI.

58. Ibid.; Roy Wehrle to Charles Mann, September 24, 1962, NARA, RG 84, General Records, Laos, Box 4.

59. Chapman, interview.

60. Parsons to Young, June 25, 1957, *FRUS, XXI,* p. 939; JGPP, box 12, folder 37.

61. Parsons to Hall, December 17, 1957, JGPP, box 2, folder 21; U.S. House, *U.S. Aid Operations in Laos,* p. 25.

62. De Paul to Parsons, December 10, 1956, JGPP, box 2, folder 25.

63. U.S. House, *U.S. Aid Operations in Laos,* p. 16.

64. Ibid., pp. 2–3.

65. JGPP, box 12, folder 37.

66. Ibid.

3. Behind the Scenes

1. Dean to Parsons, April 17, 1957, NARA, RG 59, SEA, entry 3121.

2. JGPP, box 12, folder 37.

3. Ibid.

4. Parsons to State Dept., June 6, 1957, *FRUS, XXI,* p. 932.

5. State Dept. to Parsons, May 28, 1957, *FRUS, XXI,* p. 920; Parsons to Robertson, February 8, 1957, NARA, RG 59, CF, box 3364.

6. Newberry, interview by Charles Stuart Kennedy, December 1, 1997, FAOHC.

7. NSC Briefing, May 9, 1957, NARA, CREST.

8. Parsons to State Dept., May 13, 1957, NARA, RG 59, CF, box 3371.

9. Parsons to State Dept., May 29, 1957, ibid., box 3365.

10. Ibid.

11. Parsons to State Dept., June 3, 1957, NARA, RG 59, CF, box 3365.

12. Parsons to State Dept., July 17, 1957, *FRUS, XXI,* p. 951; Parsons to State Dept., June 3, 1957, ibid., p. 925.

13. Memorandum, March 7, 1958, NARA, RG 59, SEA, entry 3121.

14. Robertson to Dulles, June 28, 1957, *FRUS, XXI,* p. 943; embassy in France to State Dept., July 14, 1957, ibid., p. 950.

15. Souvanna Phouma, August 8, 1957, in Secretary of State for Foreign Affairs, *Fourth Interim Report,* pp. 44–47.

16. State Dept. to Parsons, August 6, 1957, *FRUS, XXI,* p. 955.

17. Parsons to State Dept., August 9, 1957, ibid., p. 961.

18. Parsons to State Dept., August 20, 1957, ibid., p. 974.

19. NIE 68–57, August 20, 1957, www.cia.gov.

20. Ibid.

21. Robertson to Parsons, October 23, 1957, *FRUS, XXI,* p. 997; Parsons to State Dept., October 24, 1957, ibid., pp. 1000–1003.

22. Parsons to State Dept., October 24, 1957.

23. Parsons to State Dept., October 29, 1957, *FRUS, XXI,* p. 1011; Robertson to Parsons, October 26, 1957, ibid., p. 1009.

24. Parsons to State Dept., November 1, 1957, *FRUS, XXI,* p. 1012.

25. Ibid.

26. Parsons to State Dept., November 19, 1957, NARA, RG 59, CF, box 3365.

27. Robertson to Dulles, November 18, 1957, *FRUS, XXI,* p. 1043; State Dept. to Parsons, November 27, 1957, ibid., p. 1050.

28. CINCPAC to CNO, January 7, 1958, NARA, RG 59, General Files, lot file no. 68 D 77.

29. Ibid.

30. JGPP, box 12, folder 37; Parsons to Stump, January 11, 1958, NARA, RG 59, SEA, Subject Files Relating to Laos, 1952–58, box 1.

31. JGPP, box 13, folder 17.

32. Parsons to State Dept., December 5, 1957, NARA, RG 59, CF, box 3365.

33. Robertson to Dulles, January 11, 1958, NARA, RG 59, SEA, entry 3121, box 1.

34. Memorandum, January 13, 1958, *FRUS, XVI,* pp. 411–19.

35. Ibid.

36. Ibid.

37. Memorandum, January 15, 1958, *FRUS, XVI,* p. 423.

38. Cooper, *In the Shadows of History,* p. 107; memorandum, October 19, 1954, *FRUS: The Intelligence Community,* p. 562; Killian, *Sputnik, Scientists, and Eisenhower,* p. 222.

39. Killian, *Sputnik, Scientists, and Eisenhower,* p. 223, emphasis in original.

40. *FRUS: The Intelligence Community,* p. 563.

41. J. Patrick Coyne, memorandum, May 9, 1961, www.cia.gov; memorandum, January 5, 1961, *FRUS, XXV,* p. 152.

42. Souvanna Phouma Visit folder, NARA RG 59, SEA, entry 3121, box 1. See also JGPP.

43. Press conference, January 15, 1958, APP.

44. Memorandum, January 14, 1958, *FRUS, XVI,* MFS.

45. Robertson to Dillon, January 24, 1958, ibid.

46. Dean, memorandum, February 11, 1958, *FRUS, XVI,* pp. 425–26.

47. Dean, interview by Charles Stuart Kennedy, September 6, 2000, FAOHC, part 1, p. 58.

48. Dillon to Allen Dulles, February 10, 1958, RG 59, SEA, entry 3121, box 5.

49. Ibid.

50. Conein, interview by William Rust, November 3, 1982.

51. Lansdale to Draper Committee, March 13, 1959, George C. McGhee Papers, series 16, box 1, folder 6, Georgetown Univ. Library.

52. Memorandum, July 23, 1958, NARA, RG 469, Laos Desk Subject Files, 1956–1962, box 5.

53. Parsons to State Dept., September 24, 1957, NARA, RG 59, CF, box 3365.

54. Memorandum, April 2, 1957, DDEL, NSC Staff: Papers, 1948–61, OCB Central File Series, box 40.

55. Ibid.

56. Phillips to Parsons, February 10, 1958, RG 59, SEA, entry 3121, box 1.

57. Phillips, interview by William Rust, October 21, 2009.

58. Parsons, interview by Dennis J. O'Brien, August 22, 1969, JFKOHP.

4. Dangerously Unstable

1. Smith, "Significant Developments in Laos," p. 31.

2. Little, interview by Hope Meyers and Patricia Squire, November 17, 1986, FAOHC.

3. Dean, interview, September 6, 2000.

4. Smith, "Significant Developments in Laos," p. 20; notes, September 6, 1969, JGPP, box 4, folder 9. Although Parsons and Smith were amiable colleagues before the latter's appointment as ambassador to Laos, subsequent policy conflicts poisoned the relationship.

5. Frank Wisner to Parsons, June 2, 1958; memorandum, March 7, 1958, NARA, RG 59, SEA, entry 3121.

6. Smith, "Significant Developments in Laos," p. 18; Parsons, September 6, 1969, JGPP, box 4, folder 9.

7. Phillips, interview.

8. Phillips, *Why Vietnam Matters,* p. 96.

9. Anthony and Sexton, *United States Air Force in Southeast Asia,* p. 17.

10. Smith to State Dept., April 5, 6, 1958, NARA, RG 59, CF, box 3365.

11. State Dept. to Smith, April 16, 1958, *FRUS, XVI,* MFS.

12. Smith to State Dept., April 17, 1958, NARA, RG 59, CF, box 3365.

13. State Dept. to Smith, April 18, 1958, *FRUS, XVI,* MFS.

14. Leonard Bacon to State Dept., March 11, 1958; Smith to State Dept., April 19, 1958, NARA, RG 59, CF, box 3365.

15. NSC Briefing, May 20, 1958, NARA, CREST.

16. Editorial Note, *FRUS, XVI,* p. 450.

17. State Dept. to Smith, May 15, 1958, ibid., pp. 441–42; Eric Kocher to Smith, May 19, 1958, *FRUS, XVI,* MFS.

18. Kocher to Robertson, May 29, 1958, NARA, RG 59, SEA, entry 3121.

19. Brown to Stump, May 12, 1958, *FRUS, XVI,* MFS.

20. Herter to Sprague, May 22, 1958, NARA, RG 59, SEA, entry 3121.

21. Smith to State Dept., May 29, 1958, NARA, RG 59, General Records, lot file no. 68 D 77; Smith to Parsons, July 29, 1958, JGPP, box 2, folder 56.

22. Smith, JGPP, box 2, folder 56.

23. Methven, *Laughter in the Shadows,* p. 54; Phillips, unpublished manuscript excerpt from *Why Vietnam Matters;* Thomas, *Very Best Men,* p. 279.

24. Phillips, unpublished manuscript; Methven, *Laughter in the Shadows,* p. 57.

25. Phillips, interview.

26. Chapman to State Dept., June 19, 1958, *FRUS, XVI,* MFS.

27. Smith to State Dept., July 10, 1958, *FRUS, XVI,* pp. 457–58.

28. Memorandum, May 29, 1958, NARA, RG 59, CF, box 3365.

29. State Dept. to Smith, July 17, 1958, *FRUS, XVI,* pp. 460–61.

30. NSC Briefing, July 23, 1958, NARA, CREST; State Dept. to Smith, July 30, 1958, *FRUS, XVI,* p. 471.

31. Editorial Note, *FRUS, XVI,* p. 472.

32. Smith to State Dept., August 5, 1958, NARA, RG 59, CF, box 3366.

33. State Dept. to Smith, August 6, 1958, *FRUS, XVI,* pp. 472–73.

34. Smith to State Dept., August 7, 1958, NARA, RG 59, CF, box 3366; Smith, "Significant Developments in Laos," p. 22.

35. Ahern, *Undercover Armies,* p. 6, emphasis added.

36. Brown, unpublished manuscript, ca. 1962, RHBP, box 4, folder, Laos 1956–1962, USAMHI; "President's Talking Paper," July 23, 1962, NARA, RG 59, entry 5415-B, box 8.

37. Dean, interview, September 6, 2000.

38. Chapman, interview; Smith to State Dept., July 29, 1958, *FRUS, XVI,* p. 469.

39. Smith, "Significant Developments in Laos," pp. 23–24.

40. Editorial Note, *FRUS, XVI,* p. 474.

41. Smith to State Dept., October 4, 1958, ibid., pp. 482–83.

42. CIA evaluation, October 3, 1958, *FRUS, XVI,* MFS.

43. Memorandum, February 19, 1963, NARA, RG 59, Country Director for Laos and Cambodia, 1955–1975, box 9.

44. Stuart-Fox and Bucknell, "Politicization of the Buddhist Sangha," pp. 61–62.

45. Notes, October 8, 1958, JGPP, box 2, folder 26; OCB meeting minutes, October 8, 1958, *FRUS, XVI,* pp. 484–85.

46. *Current Intelligence Weekly Review,* November 6, 1958, www.cia.gov.

47. Smith, "Significant Developments in Laos," p. 25.

48. Winthrop Brown to State Dept., January 25, 1961, *FRUS, XXII–XXIV,* MFS.

49. McNamara, Blight, and Brigham, *Argument without End,* p. 104; Karnow, interview by William Rust, September 23, 2010.

50. Smith, "Significant Developments in Laos," p. 11; Holt to Chapman, January 12, 1960, *FRUS, XVI,* MFS.

51. Smith, "Significant Developments in Laos," p. 26; Phillips, unpublished manuscript excerpt.

52. Smith to State Dept., January 12, 1959, NARA, RG 59, CF, box 3366.

53. Memorandum, January 15, 1959, DDEL, Records of White House Office of the Staff Secretary, Subject Series, Alphabetical Subseries, box 14. See also Smith, "Significant Developments in Laos."

54. News release, February 13, 1959, DDEL, International File, box 9.

55. Dillon to Sprague, August 20, 1958, *FRUS, XVI,* p. 475.

56. Smith to State Dept., February 19, 1959; Phoui to Smith, February 20, 1959, NARA, RG 59, CF, box 3366.

57. Smith to State Dept., February 23, 1959, ibid.

5. Drawing the Line

1. Felt, interview by John T. Mason, March 8–12, 1972, U.S. Naval Institute, Annapolis, MD, p. 510; Heintges, interview by Jack A. Pellicci, April 2, 1974, US-AMHI, pp. 500–504.

2. Heintges, interview, p. 505.

3. Ibid., p. 1.

4. Ibid., pp. 494–95.

5. Ibid., p. 498.

6. Ibid., p. 499.

7. Ibid., p. 532.

8. Heintges, December 12, 1958, NARA, RG 59, SEA, entry 3121.

9. Heintges, interview, p. 505.

10. Sidney Bingham to Heintges, January 26, 1959, *FRUS, XVI,* MFS.

11. Lansdale to Shuff, December 17, 1958, ibid.

12. Randolph Kidder to Matthew Looram, February 11, 1959, NARA, RG 59, SEA, entry 3121.

13. Memorandum, April 23, 1959, ibid.

14. Heintges, interview, p. 507.

15. Paris to State Dept., May 27, 1959, NARA, RG 59, CF, box 3372; Wing et al., *Case Study of U.S. Counterinsurgency,* p. C14.

16. Paris to State Dept., May 27, 1959, NARA, RG 59, CF, box 3372.

17. Heintges, interview, p. 524.

18. Smith to State Dept., October 5, 1959, NARA, RG 59, CF, box 3374.

19. Parsons to Robertson, April 27, 1959, NARA, RG 59, SEA, box 2511.

20. U.S. Dept. of State, "Comments by the Department of State," June 15, 1959.

21. Robertson, interview by Ed Edwin, April 18–19, 1967, DDEOHP.

22. Memorandum, November 30, 1958, JFDP, series 3, box 7.

23. Ambrose, *Eisenhower,* p. 525.

24. Parsons, JGPP, box 12, folder 30; memorandum of conversation with Eisenhower, December 29, 1960, Merchant Papers, Series I, box 6.

25. Young to Parsons, June 4, 1957, *FRUS, XXI,* p. 930; Herter to Sprague, May 31, 1958, NARA, RG 59, SEA, box 2511.

26. Herter, interview by Richard D. Challener, August 31, 1964, JFDOHP; Gates, interview by Richard D. Challener, July 13, 1965, JFDOHP; John Eisenhower, *Strictly Personal,* p. 234.

27. Parsons to Brown, August 5, 1965, JGPP, box 2, folder 55.

28. PEO, September 15, 1959, USAMHI; United Nations, "Report of the Security Council Sub-Committee," annex 5, p. 7.

29. Holt to State Dept., June 3, 1959, *FRUS, XVI,* p. 549.

30. PEO, September 15, 1959, USAMHI, p. 14.

31. Goscha, "Vietnam and the World Outside," p. 176; Hanyok, "Spartans in Darkness," p. 89.

32. Memorandum of conversation, May 20, 1959, NARA, RG 59, CF, box 3366.

33. *Central Intelligence Bulletin,* July 8, 1959, NARA, CREST.

34. Smith to State Dept., August 9, 1959, *FRUS, XVI,* pp. 555–56.

35. Memorandum, August 13, 1959, NARA, RG 59, SEA, entry 3121.

36. Ibid.

37. Editorial Note, *FRUS, XVI,* p. 559.

38. United Nations, "Report of the Security Council Sub-Committee," annex 6, p. 1.

39. State Dept. to Smith, September 3, 1959, *FRUS, XVI,* p. 583.

40. Smith to State Dept., September 3, 1959, ibid., pp. 585–87.

41. JCS to the secretary of defense, September 4, 1959, ibid., pp. 588–89.

42. Daniel Anderson, memorandum, September 10, 1959, ibid., p. 613.

43. Dillon, interview.

44. Alsop, interview by Elsbeth Rostow, JFKOHP.

45. Dillon to Eisenhower, September 5, 1959, *FRUS, XVI,* pp. 598–600.

46. Ibid.

47. Ibid.

48. Goodpaster to State Dept., September 5, 1959, DDEL, Office of the Staff Secretary, International File, box 9.

49. Dillon to Eisenhower, September 6, 1959, *FRUS, XVI,* p. 603; Beakley to Burke, September 7, 1959, *FRUS, XVI,* MFS.

50. Dillon to Eisenhower, September 6, 1959, *FRUS, XVI,* pp. 604–5.

51. United Nations, "847th Meeting." Also see Urquhart, *Hammarskjold,* pp. 329–67.

52. Memorandum, September 8, 1959; Gray to James Lay, September 14, 1959, *FRUS, XVI,* MFS.

53. Parsons, memorandum, September 11, 1959, *FRUS, XVI,* pp. 620–22.

54. Goodpaster, memorandum, September 11, 1959, *FRUS, XVI,* MFS.

55. Parsons, memorandum, September 11, 1959, *FRUS, XVI,* pp. 620–22.

56. Langer and Zasloff, *North Vietnam and the Pathet Lao,* p. 70.

57. Brown and Zasloff, *Apprentice Revolutionaries,* p. 96; Gaiduk, *Confronting Vietnam,* p. 166.

58. NSC Briefing, September 29, 1959, NARA, CREST.

59. Parsons to Dillon, September 23, 1959, NARA, RG 59, SEA, entry 3121.

60. Charles Shuff to Robert Murphy, October 20, 1959, ibid.

61. Parsons to Dillon, September 23, 1959; Murphy to John Irwin, October 2, 1959, NARA, RG 59, SEA, entry 3121.

62. United Nations, "Report of the Security Council Sub-Committee."

63. *Central Intelligence Bulletin,* October 16, 1959, NARA, CREST.

64. United Nations, "Report of the Security Council Sub-Committee," p. 31.

65. Lodge to State Dept., October 16, 1959, NARA, RG 59, SEA, entry 3121.

66. Memorandum, October 24, 1959, ibid.

67. Chapman, memorandum, October 29, 1959, NARA, RG 59, CF, box 3374.

68. Sidney Bingham to CINCPAC, October 28, 1959, RG 59, SEA, entry 3121.

69. Smith to State Dept., November 7, 1959, *FRUS, XVI,* MFS.

70. Ibid.

71. "Vientiane From-Repa [*sic*]," November 6, 1959, *FRUS, XVI,* p. 649.

72. Daniel DeBardeleben to Bissell, May 16, 1960, JGPP, box 4, folder 8.

6. Dichotomy

1. Smith to State Dept., December 1, 1959, *FRUS, XVI,* p. 685.

2. Smith and Tobler to State Dept. and ICA, November 8, 1959, *FRUS, XVI,* MFS.

3. Leonard Saccio to Dillon, memorandum, November 20, 1959, NARA, RG 469, Office of the Deputy Director, Subject Files 1958–60, Laos. The unexpurgated version of this document in the National Archives contains a summary of the still-classified portions of Embtel 1300 dealing with the CIA. See also Ahern, *Undercover Armies,* p. 9.

4. Smith and Tobler to State Dept. and ICA, November 8, 1959.

5. Ibid.

6. Smith to State Dept., November 9, 1959, NARA, RG 469, Office of the Deputy Director, Subject Files 1958–60, Laos.

7. Smith and Tobler to State Dept. and ICA, November 8, 1959.

8. Ibid.

9. Tobler to Riddleberger, December 3, 1960, NARA, RG 59, CF, box 3374.

10. Smith and Tobler to State Dept. and ICA, November 8, 1959.

11. Parsons to Herter, November 10, 1959, *FRUS, XVI,* p. 656n.

12. Memorandum, November 17, 1959, NARA, RG 59, SEA, entry 3121; memorandum, November 16, 1959, *FRUS, XVI,* p. 667.

13. Saccio to Dillon, November 20, 1959, *FRUS, XVI,* p. 674.

14. Ibid., p. 671.

15. Parsons to Smith, November 21, 1959, *FRUS, XVI,* pp. 675–77.

16. Ibid.

17. Smith to State Dept., November 9, 1959.

18. Parsons to Smith, November 21, 1959.

19. Ibid.

20. Parsons to Smith, December 1, 1959, *FRUS, XVI,* pp. 683–84.

21. Ibid.

22. Ibid.

23. Smith to State Dept., November 30, 1959, *FRUS, XVI,* pp. 680–83.

24. Ibid.

25. Ibid.

26. Ibid.

27. Smith to State Dept., December 1, 1959, *FRUS, XVI,* pp. 685–87.

28. Ibid.

29. Smith to State Dept., November 30, 1959, *FRUS, XVI,* MFS.

30. Ibid.

31. Ibid.

32. State Dept. to Smith, December 4, 1959, *FRUS, XVI,* MFS.

33. Parsons to Merchant, December 5, 1959, NARA, RG 59, SEA, entry 3121.

34. Parsons to Henderson, December 8, 1959, JGPP, box 2, folder 56.

35. Smith to Parsons, December 15, 1959, *FRUS, XVI,* p. 690; Daniel De-Bardeleben to Bissell, March 8, 1960, JGPP, box 4, folder 8.

36. Saccio, interview by Melbourne Spector, September 30, 1990, FAOHC.

37. State-ICA-CIA message to Smith, January 15, 1960, NARA, RG 469, Office of the Deputy Director for Operations, Laos Desk Subject Files 1956–62, Laos.

38. Holt to Chapman, January 12, 1960, *FRUS, XVI,* MFS.

39. DeBardeleben to Bissell, March 8, 1960; Steeves to Parsons, March 4, 1960, JGPP, box 2, folder 56.

40. DeBardeleben to Bissell, March 8, 1960.

41. DeBardeleben to Bissell, May 16, 1960, JGPP, box 4, folder 8.

42. DeBardeleben to Bissell, March 8, May 16, 1960.

43. Ibid.

44. Ibid.

45. State Dept. to Smith, December 19, 1959, *FRUS, XVI,* p. 701.

46. Smith to State Dept., December 21, 1959, ibid., pp. 702–3.

47. State Dept. to Smith, December 21, 1959; Smith to State Dept., December 22, 1959, *FRUS, XVI,* MFS.

48. Smith to State Dept., December 22, 1959, ibid.

49. State Dept. to Smith, December 22, 1959, *FRUS, XVI,* pp. 707–8; Smith, "Significant Developments in Laos," p. 1.

50. State Dept. to Smith, December 22, 1959.

51. Parsons, memorandum, December 23, 1959, *FRUS, XVI,* p. 708; memorandum, December 22, 1959, *FRUS, XVI,* MFS.

52. Goodpaster, memorandum, December 23, 1959, DDEL, DDE Diary Series, box 46, "Staff Notes December 1959."

53. Ibid.

54. Smith to State Dept., December 24, 1959, *FRUS, XVI,* p. 714.

55. State Dept. to Smith, December 28, 1959, ibid., pp. 717–19.

56. Ibid., emphasis added.

57. Holt to Chapman, January 12, 1960, *FRUS, XVI,* MFS.

58. Ibid.

59. Henry Koren to Edward Rice, May 4, 1962, RG 59, Office of the Country

Director for Laos, Records Relating to Laos, 1962–1966, box 1; Smith, "Significant Developments in Laos," p. 29.

60. Smith to State Dept., December 27, 1959, *FRUS, XVI*, MFS.

61. Smith to State Dept., December 29, 1959, ibid.

62. Ibid.

63. Smith to State Dept., December 30, 1959, *FRUS, XVI*, MFS.

64. Smith, "Significant Developments in Laos," p. 30. Also see Julian Fromer, memorandum, January 19, 1960, NARA, RG 59, SEA, entry 3121.

65. Smith to State Dept., January 2, 1960, *FRUS, XVI*, pp. 723–24; "The Laos Story," June 1962, JFKL, RHP, box 2.

66. State Dept. to Smith, December 30, 1959, *FRUS, XVI*, MFS.

67. Smith to State Dept., January 4, 1960; January 8, 1959 [1960], ibid.

68. State Dept. to Smith, January 7, 1960, ibid.

69. Smith to State Dept., January 9, 1960, *FRUS, XVI*, p. 728; Holt to Chapman, January 12, 1960.

70. Bissell, *Reflections of a Cold Warrior*, pp. 145–47.

7. Normal Dishonesty

1. The five statutory members of the NSC were the president, the vice president, the secretary of state, the secretary of defense, and the director of defense mobilization. Among the officials Eisenhower invited to participate in NSC deliberations were the director of Central Intelligence, the chairman of the JCS, and the secretary of the treasury. With the addition of other cabinet members and NSC staff, approximately twenty officials attended each meeting.

2. Memorandum, March 17, 1960, DDEL, Ann Whitman File, NSC Series, box 12; NSC Briefing, March 17, 1960, NARA, CREST.

3. Memorandum, March 17, 1960.

4. Ibid.

5. At a more restricted Oval Office meeting later that same day, President Eisenhower approved the CIA plan "A Program of Covert Action against the Castro Regime," which evolved into the Bay of Pigs fiasco in the Kennedy administration.

6. Memorandum, March 17, 1960.

7. Tobler to Saccio, January 21, 1960, RG 469, Office of the Deputy Director, Subject Files 1958–60, Laos.

8. Heintges to Defense Dept., March 12, 1960, *FRUS, XVI*, MFS.

9. State Dept. to Vientiane, March 26, 1960, ibid.

10. Holt to State Dept., March 19, 1960, ibid.

11. Parsons to Smith, April 15, 1960, *FRUS, XVI*, p. 750.

12. Paris to State Dept., April 12, 1960, *FRUS, XVI*, MFS.

13. CIA Information Report, April 19, 1960, ibid.

14. Memorandum, April 22, 1964, *FRUS, XXVIII*, p. 65; Methven, *Laughter in the Shadows*, pp. 76–77.

15. State Dept. to Smith, April 26, 1960, *FRUS, XVI*, p. 751; *Time*, May 9, 1960, www.time.com.

16. Henry Koren to Edward Rice, May 4, 1962, RG 59, Office of the Country Director for Laos, Records Relating to Laos, 1962–1966; State Dept. to Smith, May 5, 1960, *FRUS, XVI*, p. 751.

17. Smith to State Dept., May 5, 1960, *FRUS, XVI*, MFS.

18. Smith to State Dept., May 14, 1960, *FRUS, XVI*, pp. 768–71.

19. Ibid.

20. Brown and Zasloff, *Apprentice Revolutionaries*, p. 74.

21. *Central Intelligence Bulletin*, May 25, 1960, p. 4, NARA, CREST; Smith to State Dept., May 24, 1960, *FRUS, XVI*, MFS; memorandum, May 24, 1960, DDEL, Ann Whitman File, NSC Series, box 12.

22. Koren to Rice, May 4, 1962.

23. Smith to State Dept., May 30, 1960, *FRUS, XVI*, MFS.

24. Ibid.

25. Ibid.

26. Smith to State Dept., June 4, 1960, *FRUS, XVI*, MFS.

27. Memorandum, June 2, 1960, ibid.

28. Memorandum, March 31, 1960, NARA, RG 59, SEA, entry 3121.

29. Memorandum, June 2, 1960, *FRUS, XVI*, MFS.

30. Heintges to CINCPAC, June 7, 1960, ibid.

31. Felt to JCS, June 8, 1960, ibid.

32. Steeves to Felt, July 6, 1960, ibid.; State Dept.–Defense Dept. to Vientiane, June 14, 1960, ibid.; Memorandum, June 30, 1960, *FRUS, XVI*, p. 778.

33. Memorandum, July 21, 1960, *FRUS, XVI*, MFS.

34. Kraemer and Stewart, "Cross-Cultural Problems," p. 6; Wing et al., *Case Study of U.S. Counterinsurgency*, p. D72.

35. Kraemer and Stewart, "Cross-Cultural Problems," p. 5.

36. Heintges, interview, pp. 611, 557.

37. Steeves to Parsons, March 4, 1960, JGPP, box 2, folder 56.

38. Parsons to Henderson, November 28, 1960, JGPP, box 2, folder 57.

39. Winthrop Brown, interview by Richard D. McKinzie, May 25, 1973, HSTOHP.

40. Winthrop Brown, interview by Larry J. Hackman, February 1, 1968, JFKOHP.

8. Unacceptable Developments

1. Tatu, interview by Susan Klingaman, October 4, 2000, FAOHC.

2. Toye, *Laos*, p. 143; Brown, interview, February 1, 1968.

3. Brown to State Dept., August 9, 1960, *FRUS, XVI*, MFS.

4. Mathews to William Leary, March 23, 1993, McDermott Library, Univ. of Texas at Dallas.

5. Brown, interview, February 1, 1968.

6. Ahern, *Undercover Armies*, p. 49n; Blessing, *Warrior Healers*, pp. 98–99; Brown, interview, February 1, 1968.

7. Dommen, *The Indochinese Experience*, pp. 390–91; Dommen, "Laos," p. 18.

8. Editorial Note, *FRUS, XVI*, p. 782.

9. State Dept. to Brown, August 9, 1960 (140, 141); Leonard Unger to State Dept., August 9, 1960, *FRUS, XVI*, MFS.

10. Unger to State Dept., August 11, 1960, *FRUS, XVI*, p. 783.

11. Although the CIA-owned Civil Air Transport officially changed its name to Air America in March 1959, foreign affairs officials in the Eisenhower administration continued to use the acronym CAT when referring to the airline.

12. Memorandum, August 16, 1960, *FRUS, XVI*, pp. 787–89.

13. Ibid.

14. Ibid.

15. Memorandum, August 12, 1960, *FRUS, XVI*, MFS.

16. Situation report, August 13, 1960, ibid.

17. Unger to State Dept., August 14, 1960, ibid.

18. Brown to State Dept., August 15, 1960, ibid.

19. Ibid.

20. Parsons to Unger, August 15, 1960, *FRUS, XVI*, pp. 794–95.

21. Ibid.

22. Memorandum, August 15, 1960, NARA, RG 59, SEA, entry 3121.

23. Brown to State Dept., August 16, 1960, *FRUS, XVI*, MFS.

24. CINCPAC to State Dept., August 17, 1960, ibid.

25. Parsons to Brown, August 15, 1960; Anderson to Parsons, August 17, 1970, *FRUS, XVI*, pp. 797, 804.

26. State Dept. to Brown, August 17, 1960, ibid., pp. 807–8.

27. Memorandum, August 25, 1960, ibid., p. 810; situation report, August 16, 1960; State Dept. to Brown, August 17, 1960, *FRUS, XVI*, MFS; NSC Briefing, August 18, 1960, NARA, CREST; Brown, interview, February 1, 1968.

28. Peggy Ann Brown, FAOHC.

29. Memorandum, August 25, 1960, *FRUS, XVI*, pp. 808–11.

30. Ibid.

31. Ibid.

32. Brown to State Dept., August 17, 1960, *FRUS, XVI*, MFS.

33. Parsons to Brown, August 17, 1960, ibid.

34. Brown to State Dept., August 17, 1960; situation report, August 27, 1960, DDEL, International File, box 10: Laos.

35. Brown to State Dept., August 18, 1960, *FRUS, XVI*, MFS.

36. Brown, *War in Shangri-La*, p. 48.

37. Situation report, August 22, 1960, DDEL, International File, box 10: Laos.

38. John Irwin to Dillon, August 22, 1960, *FRUS, XVI*, MFS.

39. Ahern, *Undercover Armies*, p. 14.

40. Hasey, *Yankee Fighter*, p. 31.

41. Ibid., p. 275.

42. Ahern, *Undercover Armies*, p. 14; Brown, interview, February 1, 1968.

43. State Dept. to Brown, August 22, 1960, *FRUS, XVI*, p. 818; Parsons to Brown, August 26, 1960, *FRUS, XVI*, MFS.

44. Memorandum, August 23, 1960, *FRUS, XVI*, MFS.

45. Ibid.

46. Gates, interview.

47. Memorandum, August 23, 1960.

48. Ibid.

49. Burke to Gates, August 20, 1960, *FRUS, XVI,* MFS, emphasis in original.

50. Memorandum, August 23, 1960.

51. U.S. Dept. of Defense, "Chronological Summary," p. 7.

52. Parsons to Brown, August 26, 1960.

53. U.S. Dept. of Defense, "Chronological Summary," p. 7.

54. Brown to State Dept., August 25, 1960, *FRUS, XVI,* MFS.

55. Despatch, September 27, 1960, ibid.

56. Situation report, September 4, 1960, DDEL, International File, box 10: Laos.

57. Despatch, September 27, 1960.

58. Situation report, September 4, 1960.

59. Brown to State Dept., September 5, 1960, *FRUS, XVI,* MFS.

60. Ibid.

61. Gleeck to Parsons, September 7, 1960, NARA, RG 59, SEA, entry 3121.

62. State Dept. to Brown, September 2, 1960, *FRUS, XVI,* MFS.

63. Situation report, September 5, 1960, DDEL, International File, box 10: Laos.

64. NSC Briefing, September 6, 1960, NARA, CREST.

65. State Dept. to Brown, September 7, 1960, *FRUS, XVI,* MFS; Parsons, JGPP, box 13, folder 17.

66. Memorandum, September 9, 1960, *FRUS, XVI,* MFS.

67. U.S. Dept. of Defense, "Summary and Historical Analysis," p. 52.

68. Memorandum, September 9, 1960.

69. Ibid.; Brown to State Dept., September 6, 1960, *FRUS, XVI,* MFS.

70. Memorandum, September 9, 1960.

71. Brown, interview, February 1, 1968.

9. Who the Hell Is Our Boy?

1. Despatch, September 27, 1960, *FRUS, XVI,* MFS.

2. Ibid.

3. Ibid.

4. Ibid.

5. Saigon to State Dept., June 19, 1954, *FRUS, XIII,* p. 1722; Smith, "Significant Developments in Laos," p. 8; NSC Briefing, September 14, 1960, NARA, CREST.

6. Memorandum, September 30, 1960, *FRUS, XVI,* MFS.

7. Brown to State Dept., September 10, 1960, ibid..

8. State Dept. to Brown, September 10, 1960, *FRUS, XVI,* p. 839.

9. Brown to State Dept., September 13, 1960, *FRUS, XVI,* MFS.

10. Ibid.

11. State Dept. to Brown, September 14, 1960, *FRUS, XVI,* MFS; Brown to State Dept., September 15, *FRUS, XVI,* pp. 842–43.

12. Ibid.

13. Bangkok to State Dept., September 16, 1960; Saigon to State Dept., September 16, 1960, *FRUS, XVI,* MFS.

14. State Dept.–Defense Dept. to Brown, September 16, 1960, *FRUS, XVI,* pp. 848–50.

15. Brown, interview, February 1, 1968; Brown to State Dept., September 18, 1960, *FRUS, XVI,* pp. 850–51.

16. State Dept. to Brown, September 18, 19, 1960, ibid., pp. 852–53; Brown, interview, February 1, 1968.

17. Brown to State Dept., September 21, 1960, *FRUS, XVI,* MFS.

18. Ibid.

19. Brown to State Dept., September 22, 1960, *FRUS, XVI,* pp. 860–61.

20. NSC Briefing, September 20, 1960, NARA, CREST.

21. Situation report, September 23, 1960, DDEL, International File, box 10: Laos.

22. CINCPAC to JCS, September 30, 1960, *FRUS, XVI,* MFS.

23. Potter, *Admiral Arleigh Burke,* p. 407.

24. CINCPAC to JCS, September 30, 1960.

25. Memorandum, September 30, 1960, *FRUS, XVI,* MFS, emphasis in original.

26. Ibid.

27. Steeves, interview by Dennis J. O'Brien, September 5, 1969, JFKOHP.

28. Brown, interview, February 1, 1968.

29. Memorandum, September 30, 1960; Brown, interview, February 1, 1968.

30. Memorandum, September 30, 1960.

31. State Dept. to Brown, October 1, 1960, *FRUS, XVI,* MFS.

32. Brown to State Dept., October 3, 1960, ibid.

33. Brown to State Dept., October 4, 1960, ibid; NSC Briefing, October 5, 1960, NARA, CREST.

34. Brown to State Dept., October 5, 1960, *FRUS, XVI,* p. 877.

35. JCS to CINCPAC, October 3, 1960, ibid., p. 876; Operations Directorate, Joint Staff, to JCS, January 10, 1961, DDEL, International File, box 11: Laos.

36. Brown to State Dept., October 5, 1960.

37. Brown to State Dept., October 6, 1960, *FRUS, XVI,* pp. 883–85.

38. Ibid.

39. State Dept. to Brown, October 8, 1960, *FRUS, XVI,* pp. 886–88; memorandum, October 8, 1960, NARA, RG 59, lot file no. 68 D 77.

40. State Dept. to Brown, October 8, 1960.

41. Memorandum, October 8, 1960, *FRUS, XVI,* p. 889.

42. Brown to State Dept., October 9, 1960, *FRUS, XVI,* MFS.

43. Ibid.; situation report, October 9, 1960, DDEL, International File, box 10: Laos.

44. Steeves to Dillon, October 10, 1960, *FRUS, XVI,* MFS.

45. October 8, 1960, *FRUS, XVI,* p. 893n.

46. Memorandum, October 12, 1960, ibid., pp. 893–94.

47. Ibid.

48. Steeves, interview.

49. JGPP, box 2, folder 55.

50. Anderson, *Trapped by Success,* pp. 202–4.

51. Memorandum, November 21, 1960, DDEL, Ann Whitman File, NSC Series, box 13.

52. Ambrose, *Eisenhower,* p. 581; John Eisenhower, *Strictly Personal,* p. 285.

53. JGPP, box 13, folder 17.

54. JGPP, box 12, folder 30.

55. Kent to Dulles, October 7, 1960, NARA, CREST.

56. Parsons to State Dept., October 15, 1960, *FRUS, XVI,* pp. 904–8.

57. Ibid.

58. Parsons to State Dept., October 16, 1960, *FRUS, XVI,* pp. 908–12.

59. Ibid.

60. Parsons to State Dept., October 16, 1960, *FRUS, XVI,* MFS.

61. Brown to State Dept., October 17, 1960, ibid.

62. Ibid.

63. Seymour Weiss to Bell, October 19, 1960, *FRUS, XVI,* MFS.

64. Irwin to State Dept., October 18, 1960, ibid.

65. Ibid.

66. Ibid.

67. Brown to Parsons, November 8, 1960, *FRUS, XVI,* p. 908.

68. JGPP, box 12, folder 30; U.S. Dept. of Defense, "Chronological Summary," p. 534.

69. Weiss to Bell, October 19, 1960, *FRUS, XVI,* MFS.

70. State Dept. to Brown, October 18, 1960, *FRUS, XVI,* pp. 915–17.

71. Ibid.

72. Brown to State Dept., October 19, 1960, *FRUS, XVI,* MFS.

73. Brown to State Dept., October 21, 1960, ibid.; State Dept. to Brown, October 22, 1960, *FRUS, XVI,* p. 922.

74. London to State Dept., October 21, 1960, *FRUS, XVI,* MFS.

75. Corcoran to State Dept., October 25, 1960, ibid.

76. Situation report, October 23, 1960, DDEL, International File, box 10: Laos.

77. Corcoran to State Dept., October 26, 1960, *FRUS, XVI,* MFS.

78. Ibid.

79. Brown to State Dept., October 27, 1960, *FRUS, XVI,* p. 930.

80. Brown to State Dept., October 26, 1960, *FRUS, XVI,* MFS.

81. Brown, interview, February 1, 1968.

10. *Virtually a Traitor*

1. Memorandum, October 28, 1960, *FRUS, XVI,* MFS.

2. Ibid.

3. Ibid.; memorandum, October 25, 1960, NARA, RG 59, SEA, entry 3121.

4. Brown to State Dept., November 1, 1960, *FRUS, XVI,* MFS.

5. State Dept. to Brown, November 4, 1960; Parsons to Herter, November 9, 1960; Irwin to Gates, November 10, 1960, *FRUS, XVI,* MFS, emphasis in original.

6. Gates, interview; Chapman, interview.

7. Black to James Douglas, November 8, 1960, in U.S. Dept. of Defense, "Summary and Historical Analysis," p. 155.

8. Ibid, p. 156.

9. Herter to Brown, November 10, 1960, *FRUS, XVI,* p. 948.

10. Parsons to Herter, November 10, 1960, NARA, RG 59, SEA, entry 3121.

11. Brown to State Dept., November 12, 1960, *FRUS, XVI,* MFS.

12. Brown to State Dept., November 14, 1960, ibid.

13. Corcoran to State Dept., November 15, 1960, *FRUS, XVI,* pp. 959–62.

14. Ibid.

15. Brown to State Dept. (939), November 17, 1960, *FRUS, XVI,* p. 970.

16. Brown to State Dept. (938), November 17, 1960, ibid., pp. 966–69.

17. Brown to State Dept., November 21, 1960, *FRUS, XVI,* MFS.

18. Fortier to secretary of state for external affairs, December 1, 1960, www.dfait-maeci.gc.ca.

19. Situation report, November 21, 1960, *FRUS, XVI,* MFS; November 21, 1960, *FRUS, XVI,* p. 974n.

20. Herter, memoranda, November 21, 1960, *FRUS, XVI,* p. 973.

21. Ibid.

22. State Dept. to Brown, November 21, 1960, *FRUS, XVI,* p. 975.

23. Vientiane to State Dept., November 22, 1960, *FRUS, XVI,* MFS.

24. Brown to State Dept., November 23, 1960, ibid.

25. Brown to State Dept., November 24, 1960, *FRUS, XVI,* p. 979; Johnson to State Dept., November 25, 1960; Corcoran to State Dept., November 25, 1960, *FRUS, XVI,* MFS.

26. November 24, 1960, *FRUS, XVI,* p. 979n; State Dept. to Brown, November 26, 1960, *FRUS, XVI,* MFS.

27. U.S. Dept. of Defense, "Summary and Historical Analysis," p. 160.

28. CINCPAC to JCS, November 23, 1960, in U.S. Dept. of Defense, "Chronological Summary," p. 45; Sterling Cottrell to Parsons, December 1, 1960, *FRUS, XVI,* MFS.

29. Situation report, November 29, 1960, DDEL, International File, box 11: Laos; Brown to State Dept., November 29, 1960, *FRUS, XVI,* MFS.

30. Brown to State Dept., November 29, 1960.

31. Brown to Parsons (1042, 1043), December 2, 1960, *FRUS, XVI,* pp. 986–87.

32. Parsons to Brown, December 2, 1960, ibid., pp. 987–88.

33. JCS to CINCPAC, December 2, 1960, in U.S. Dept. of Defense, "Chronological Summary," p. 49; Brown to State Dept., December 3, 1960, *FRUS, XVI,* MFS.

34. Heintges, interview, pp. 578–79.

35. Ahern, *Undercover Armies,* p. 301.

36. Bill Lair, interview by Steve Maxner, December 11–13, 2001, Vietnam Center and Archive, Texas Tech Univ., p. 94; Lair, "Thai PARU."

37. Lair, interview, p. 85.

38. Brown to State Dept., November 17, 1960; situation report, December 7, 1960, DDEL, International File, box 11: Laos.

39. Editorial Note, *FRUS, XVI,* p. 998.

40. U.S. Dept. of Defense, "Summary and Historical Analysis," p. 179; Cumming to Herter, December 8, 1960, *FRUS, XVI,* MFS; situation report, December 9, 1960, DDEL, International File, box 11: Laos.

41. Memorandum, December 9, 1960, *FRUS, XVI,* MFS.

42. Anthony and Sexton, *United States Air Force in Southeast Asia,* p. 33; Goscha, "Vietnam and the World Outside," p. 179.

43. Ahern, *Undercover Armies,* p. 22.

44. Press release, December 17, 1960, *Department of State Bulletin,* vol. 44, no. 1123, January 2, 1961, p. 15.

45. "The Laos Story," June 1962, JFK Library, RHP, box 2; Bailey, *Solitary Survivor,* p. 59.

46. Brown, *War in Shangri-La,* p. 63.

47. Brown, notes, December 13, 1960, *FRUS, XVI,* MFS.

48. Ibid.; Heintges, interview, pp. 566–68.

49. Brown, notes, December 13, 1960; Newberry, interview.

50. Brown, notes, December 13, 1960.

51. Bailey, *Solitary Survivor,* p. 61.

52. Memorandum, December 16, 1960, *FRUS, XVI,* pp. 1008–9; memorandum, December 21, 1960, DDEL, International File, box 11: Laos.

53. Memorandum, December 15, 1960, *FRUS, XVI,* MFS.

54. Ibid.

55. Herter to State Dept., December 18, 1960, *FRUS, XVI,* MFS.

56. NSC Briefing, December 20, 1960, NARA, CREST.

57. Anthony and Sexton, *United States Air Force in Southeast Asia,* p. 34; for pictures of the IL-14, see NARA, RG 59, SEA, entry 3121.

58. CINCPAC to JCS, December 23, 1960, *FRUS, XVI,* p. 1017.

59. Memorandum, December 28, 1960, DDEL, DDE Diary Series, box 55.

60. Brown to State Dept., December 29, 1960, *FRUS, XVI,* MFS.

61. Embassy–Army Attache–PEO–CAS to State Dept., undated (ca. December 31, 1960), DDEL, International File, box 11: Laos.

62. J. Eisenhower, memorandum, December 31, 1960, *FRUS, XVI,* p. 1025; Operations Directorate, Joint Staff, to JCS, December 31, 1960, DDEL, International File, box 11: Laos.

63. Eisenhower, memorandum, December 31, 1960.

64. Ibid; Merchant, memorandum, December 31, 1960, *FRUS, XVI,* MFS.

65. Goodpaster, memorandum, January 2, 1961, *FRUS, XXIV,* p. 1; Merchant, memorandum, January 2, 1961, *FRUS, XXIV,* MFS.

66. Merchant, memorandum, January 2, 1961.

67. Merchant, memorandum, December 31, 1960; Eisenhower, memorandum, December 31, 1960.

68. Moscow to State Dept., January 4, 1961, DDEL, International File, box 9: Laos; memorandum, January 10, 1961, ibid.

69. Pedlow and Welzenbach, "Central Intelligence Agency," p. 221; Jac Nevard, *New York Times,* January 27, 1961.

70. Operations Directorate, Joint Staff, to JCS, January 13, 1961, DDEI ternational File, box 11: Laos.

71. Memorandum, January 17, 1961, *FRUS, XXIV,* p. 16.

72. Brown to State Dept., January 18, 1961, JFK Library, NSF, Countries 130.

73. Ibid.

74. *New York Times,* January 20, 1961.

75. *New York Times,* December 29, 1960; Mansfield to Kennedy, Janua 1961, JFKL, POF, Laos, General, 1961; Parsons to William Macomber, Janua 1961, NARA, RG 59, SEA, entry 3121.

Epilogue

1. Memorandum, January 17, 1961, JFKL, POF, Special Correspon Eisenhower; Kennedy, memorandum, January 19, 1961, *FRUS, XXIV,* p. 19.

2. Greenstein and Immerman, "What Did Eisenhower Tell Kennedy,"

3. Persons, memorandum, January 19, 1961, *FRUS, XXIV,* pp. McNamara, memorandum, January 24, 1961, ibid., p. 41.

4. Herter, memorandum, January 19, 1961, ibid., pp. 22–25.

5. Kennedy, memorandum, January 19, 1961; McNamara, memora January 24, 1961.

6. Kennedy, memorandum, January 19, 1961; Clifford, memorandum ary 24, 1961, JFKL, POF, Special Correspondence, Eisenhower, emphasis i nal; Rusk, *As I Saw It,* p. 428.

7. Persons, memorandum, January 19, 1961; Kennedy, memorandum, J 19, 1961.

8. Eisenhower, *Waging Peace,* p. 612.

9. Memorandum, January 23, 1961, *FRUS, XXIV,* MFS; memorandun ary 25, 1961, *FRUS, XXIV,* p. 43.

10. "Concept for the Recapture of the Plaine Des Jarres," March 9, 1961, KARC, RG 218, box 5; memorandum, March 21, 1961, *FRUS, XXIV,* p. 95.

11. Press conference, March 23, 1961, APP.

12. Boyle to CINCPAC, April 26, 1961, *FRUS, XXIV,* p. 142n; Brown Dept., April 26, 1961, ibid., pp. 139–40.

13. Burke, memorandum, May 2, 1961, *FRUS, XXIV,* MFS; White, m dum, May 2, 1961, ibid.; McNamara, memorandum, May 1, 1961, *FRUS,* 163.

14. Memorandum, April 26, 1961, *FRUS, XXIV,* p. 143; Sorensen, *Ker* 646, emphasis in original.

15. Rusk to Kennedy, May 19, 1961, *FRUS, XXIV,* p. 203.

16. Memorandum, February 21, 1962, ibid., p. 630.

17. Memorandum, May 6, 1962, ibid., p. 718.

18. Press conference, May 9, 1962, APP.

19. Memorandum, May 10, 1962, *FRUS, XXIV,* pp. 730–31.

20. McCone, memorandum, May 10, 1962, www.cia.gov.

21. Ibid.

22. Ball, memorandum, May 11, 1962; Roger Hilsman, memorandum, May, 10, 1962, *FRUS, XXIV,* MFS.

23. John Eisenhower, memorandum, May 14, 1962, DDEL, Post-Presidential Papers, Augusta-Walter Reed Series, Box 2; McCone, memorandum, May 13, 1962, *FRUS, XXIV,* pp. 760–61.

24. Max Frankel, *New York Times,* May 12, 1962; Marshall Carter, memorandum, May 13, 1962, www.cia.gov.

25. CHMAAG to CINCPAC, October 3, 1962, cited in Wing et al., *Case Study of U.S. Counterinsurgency,* p. B-28; Vientiane to Dept. of State, August 23, 1962, Dept. of State to Vientiane, September 30, 1962, and CHMAAG to CINCPAC, October 5, 1962, JFKL, NSF, Box 136; Vientiane to Dept. of State, August 11, 1962, and CINCPAC to JCS, July 15, 1962, NARA, RG 59, CF, 1960-63, Box 1773.

26. Memorandum, April 22, 1963, *FRUS, XXIV,* p. 992.

27. Harriman to Bundy, January 11, 1962, ibid., p. 577.

28. Kennedy-Harriman phone call, April 10, 1963, Dictabelt F, JFKL; Harriman to State Dept., April 27, 1963, JFKL, NSF, Countries, box 137; memorandum, April 30, 1963, *FRUS, XXIV,* p. 1006.

29. Freedman, *Kennedy's Wars,* p. 340; memorandum, September 3, 1963, *FRUS, IV,* p. 100.

30. Memorandum, April 20, 1963, *FRUS, XXIV,* p. 977; JCS to McNamara, April 23, 1963, *FRUS, XXIV,* MFS.

31. JCS, memorandum, May 9, 1963; CINCPAC, "Record of the Secretary of Defense Conference," May 8, 1963, NARA, KARC, RG 218, box 5.

32. Memorandum, June 18, 1963, *FRUS, XXIV,* p. 1023.

33. Memorandum, June 19, 1963, ibid., p. 1034.

34. Meeting with the president, August 2, 1963, Tape 103, JFKL.

35. Memorandum, November 1, 1963, *FRUS, XXIV,* p. 1054.

36. Forrestal to Kennedy, May 23, 1962, *FRUS, XXIV,* MFS.

Bibliography

Archival Sources

The American Presidency Project (APP). Univ. of California, Santa Barbara, www.presidency.ucsb.edu.

Brown, Rothwell H. Papers (RHBP). U.S. Army Military History Institute, Carlisle Barracks, PA.

Documents on Canadian External Relations, Foreign Affairs, and International Trade Canada, www.dfait-maeci.gc.ca.

Dulles, John Foster. Papers (JFDP). Seeley G. Mudd Manuscript Library. Princeton Univ., Princeton, NJ.

Dwight D. Eisenhower Presidential Library (DDEL), Abilene, KS.

FOIA Electronic Reading Room. Central Intelligence Agency, www.foia.cia.gov.

Foreign Affairs Oral History Collection of the Association for Diplomatic Studies and Training, Library of Congress (FAOHC), http://memory.loc.gov/ammem/collections/diplomacy/index.html.

Harry S. Truman Library, Independence, MO.

Heintges, John. Papers. U.S. Army Military History Institute, Carlisle Barracks, PA.

John F. Kennedy Presidential Library (JFKL), Boston, MA.

Lyndon Baines Johnson Library, Austin, TX.

Merchant, Livingston T. Papers. Seeley G. Mudd Manuscript Library. Princeton Univ., Princeton, NJ.

National Security Archive. George Washington Univ., www.gwu.edu/~nsarchiv.

Office of the Historian. U.S. Department of State, http://history.state.gov/historicaldocuments.

Office of the Secretary of Defense and Joint Staff Reading Room, www.dod.mil/pubs/foi.

Parsons, J. Graham. Papers (JGPP). Special Collections Division. Georgetown University Library, Washington, DC.

University of Wisconsin Digital Collections, http://digicoll.library.wisc.edu.

U.S. National Archives and Records Administration (NARA), College Park, MD.
Vietnam Center and Archive. Texas Tech Univ. www.vietnam.ttu.edu.
Yost, Charles W. Papers (CWYP). Seeley G. Mudd Manuscript Library. Princeton
    Univ., Princeton, NJ.

Oral Histories and Interviews

Alsop, Joseph. Interview by Elsbeth Rostow, June 18, 1964. JFKOHP.
Amory, Robert, Jr. Interview by Joseph E. O'Connor, February 9, 1966. JFKOHP.
Baldwin, Charles F. Interview by Dennis J. O'Brien, March 13 and 14, 1969.
    JFKOHP.
Bissell, Richard M. Interview by Joseph E. O'Connor, April 25, 1967. JFKOHP.
Boyle, Andrew J. Interview by Frank Walton, February 28 and March 27, 1971.
    USAMHI.
Brown, Mervyn. Interview by Malcolm McBain, October 24, 1996. British Diplo-
    matic Oral History Project. Churchill College, Cambridge, UK.
Brown, Peggy Ann. Interview by Monique Wong, October 25, 1992. FAOHC.
Brown, Winthrop G. Interview by Larry J. Hackman, February 1, 1968. JFKOHP.
———. Interview by Richard D. McKinzie, May 25, 1973. HSTOHP.
Chapman, Christian A. Interview by Charles Stuart Kennedy, March 3, 1990.
    FAOHC.
Conein, Lucien E. Interview by William Rust, November 3, 1982.
Corcoran, Thomas C. Interview by Charles Stuart Kennedy, June 21, 1988. FAOHC.
Dean, John Gunther. Interview by Charles Stuart Kennedy, September 6, 2000.
    FAOHC, Jimmy Carter Library. Atlanta, GA.
———. Interview by William Rust, March 25, 2010.
Dillon, C. Douglas. Interview by Robert D. Schulzinger, April 28, 1987. FAOHC.
Erickson, Elden B. Interview by Charles Stuart Kennedy, June 25, 1992. FAOHC.
Felt, Harry D. Interview by John T. Mason, March 8–12, 1972. U.S. Naval Insti-
    tute, Annapolis, MD.
Gates, Thomas S. Interview by Richard D. Challener, July 13, 1965. JFDOHP.
Goodpaster, Andrew J. Interview by Maclyn P. Burg, June 26, 1975. DDEOHP.
Green, Marshall. Interview by Charles Stuart Kennedy, March 17, 1995. FAOHC.
Halpern, Joel M. Interview by A.M. Halpern, August 24, 1959. JMHP, JFKL.
———. Interview by William Rust, May 25, 2011.
Heintges, John A. Interview by Jack A. Pellicci, April 2, 1974. USAMHI.
Herter, Christian A. Interview by Richard D. Challener, August 31, 1964. JFDOHP.
Johnson, U. Alexis. Interview by Philip A. Crowl, May 28, 1966. JFDOHP.
Karnow, Stanley. Interview by William Rust, September 23, 2010.
Lair, Bill. Interview by Steve Maxner, December 11–13, 2001. Vietnam Center and
    Archive, Texas Tech Univ.
Little, Ruth. Interview by Hope Meyers and Patricia Squire, November 17, 1986.
    FAOHC.
Mendenhall, Joseph. Interview by Horace Torbert, February 11, 1991. FAOHC.
Methven, Stuart. Interview by William Rust, November 1, 2009.

Newberry, Daniel Oliver. Interview by Charles Stuart Kennedy, December 1, 1997. FAOHC.

Parsons, J. Graham. Interview by Richard D. McKinzie, July 1, 1974. HSTOHP.

———. Interview by Dennis J. O'Brien, August 22, 1969. JFKOHP.

Phillips, Rufus C. Interview by William Rust, October 21, 2009.

Richmond, Yale. Interview by Charles Stuart Kennedy, June 9, 2003. FAOHC.

Rives, L. Michael. Interview by Charles Stuart Kennedy, July 25, 1995. FAOHC.

Robertson, Walter S. Interview by Philip A. Crowl, July 23–24, 1965. JFDOHP.

———. Interview by Ed Edwin, April 18–19, 1967. DDEOHP.

Saccio, Leonard J. Interview by Melbourne Spector, September 30, 1990. FAOHC.

Steeves, John M. Interview by Dennis J. O'Brien, September 5, 1969. JFKOHP.

Tanen, Ted M.G. Interview by Charles Stuart Kennedy, September 21, 2000. FAOHC.

Tatu, Francis J. Interview by Susan Klingaman, October 4, 2000. FAOHC.

Wheeler, Earle G. Interview by Chester V. Clifton, July 11, 1964. JFKOHP.

Yost, Charles W. Interview by Richard D. Challener, December 13, 1966. JFDOHP.

Books, Monographs, Unpublished Manuscripts, and Articles

Ahern, Thomas L., Jr. *Undercover Armies: CIA and Surrogate Warfare in Laos, 1961–1973*. Washington, DC: Central Intelligence Agency, 2006.

Ambrose, Stephen E. *Eisenhower: The President*. New York: Simon and Schuster, 1984.

Anderson, David L. *Trapped by Success: The Eisenhower Administration and Vietnam, 1953–61*. New York: Columbia Univ. Press, 1991.

Anthony, Victor B., and Richard R. Sexton. *The United States Air Force in Southeast Asia: The War in Northern Laos*. Washington, DC: Center for Air Force History, 1993.

Askew, Mark, William S. Logan, and Colin Long. *Vientiane: Transformations of a Lao Landscape*. New York: Routledge, 2007.

Bailey, Lawrence R., Jr. *Solitary Survivor: The First American POW in Southeast Asia*. Washington, DC: Brassey's, 1995.

Birtle, Andrew J. *U.S. Army Counterinsurgency and Contingency Operations Doctrine, 1942–1976*. Washington DC: Center for Military History, U.S. Army, 2006.

Bissell, Richard M. *Reflections of a Cold Warrior: From Yalta to the Bay of Pigs*. New Haven, CT: Yale Univ. Press, 1996.

Blaufarb, Douglas S. *The Counterinsurgency Era: U.S. Doctrine and Performance, 1950 to the Present*. New York: Free Press, 1977.

Blessing, Leonard D. *Warrior Healers: The Untold Story of the Special Forces Medic*. Lincoln, NE: iUniverse, 2006.

Brinkley, Alan. "A President for Certain Seasons." *Wilson Quarterly*, Spring 1990.

Brown, MacAlister, and Joseph J. Zasloff. *Apprentice Revolutionaries: The Communist Movement in Laos, 1930–1985*. Stanford, CA: Hoover Institution Press, 1986.

Brown, Mervyn. *War in Shangri-La: A Memoir of Civil War in Laos*. London: Radcliffe Press, 2001.

Brugioni, Dino A. *Eyes in the Sky: Eisenhower, the CIA, and Cold War Aerial Espionage.* Annapolis: Naval Institute Press, 2010.

Castle, Timothy N. *At War in the Shadow of Vietnam: U.S. Military Aid to the Royal Government, 1955–1975.* New York: Columbia Univ. Press, 1993.

Conboy, Kenneth. *Shadow War: The CIA's Secret War in Laos.* Boulder, CO: Paladin Press, 1995.

Cooper, Chester L. *In the Shadows of History: 50 Years Behind the Scenes of Cold War Diplomacy.* Amherst, NY: Prometheus Books, 2005.

Crosswell, D.K.R. *Beetle: The Life of General Walter Bedell Smith.* Lexington: Univ. Press of Kentucky, 2010.

Daalder, Ivo H., and I.M. Destler, moderators. "China Policy and the National Security Council," November 4, 1999. Center for International and Security Studies at Maryland and the Brookings Institution.

Dalley, George W. "The United States Response to the Kong Le Coup of August 9th, 1960, and Its Impact on Future U.S. Policy toward Laos during the Vietnam War." A paper presented at the Univ. of California, 2003.

Dean, John Gunther. *Danger Zones: A Diplomat's Fight for America's Interest.* Washington, DC: New Academia, 2009.

Dommen, Arthur J. *The Indochinese Experience of the French and the Americans: Nationalism and Communism in Cambodia, Laos, and Vietnam.* Bloomington: Indiana Univ. Press, 2001.

———. "Laos: A Self-Study Guide," 2004. School of Professional and Area Studies, Foreign Service Institute, U.S. Department of State.

Eisenhower, Dwight D. *The Papers of Dwight David Eisenhower: The Presidency: Keeping the Peace.* Vols. 18–21. Baltimore: Johns Hopkins Univ. Press (online edition), 2003.

———. *The Papers of Dwight David Eisenhower: The Presidency: The Middle Way.* Vols. 14–17. Baltimore: Johns Hopkins Univ. Press (online edition), 2003.

———. *The White House Years: Mandate for Change, 1953–1956.* New York: Doubleday, 1963.

———. *The White House Years: Waging Peace, 1956–1961.* New York: Doubleday, 1965.

Eisenhower, John S.D. *Strictly Personal.* Garden City, NY: Doubleday, 1974.

Evans, Grant. *The Last Century of Lao Royalty: A Documentary History.* Chiang Mai, Thailand: Silkworm Books, 2009.

Fall, Bernard B. *Anatomy of a Crisis: The Laotian Crisis of 1960–1961.* New York: Doubleday, 1969.

Fineman, Daniel. *A Special Relationship: The United States and Military Government in Thailand, 1947–1958.* Honolulu: Univ. of Hawaii Press, 1997.

Finger, Seymour M. *Inside the World of Diplomacy: The U.S. Foreign Service in a Changing World.* Westport, CT: Praeger, 2002.

Finlayson, Kenn. "Operation White Star: Prelude to Vietnam." *Special Warfare,* June 2002.

Freedman, Lawrence. *Kennedy's Wars: Berlin, Cuba, Laos, and Vietnam.* New York: Oxford Univ. Press, 2000.

Gaddis, John Lewis. *The Cold War: A New History.* New York: Penguin Press, 2005.

———. *Strategies of Containment: A Critical Appraisal of Postwar American National Security Policy.* Rev. ed. New York: Oxford Univ. Press, 2005.

Gaiduk, Ilya V. *Confronting Vietnam: Soviet Policy toward the Indochina Conflict, 1954–1963.* Washington, DC: Woodrow Wilson Center Press, 2003.

Goldstein, Martin E. *American Policy toward Laos.* Rutherford, NJ: Associated Univ. Presses, 1973.

Goscha, Christopher E. "Vietnam and the World Outside: The Case of Vietnamese Communist Advisers in Laos (1948–62)." *South East Asia Research,* July 1, 2004.

Greenstein, Fred I. *The Hidden-Hand Presidency: Eisenhower as Leader.* Baltimore: Johns Hopkins Univ. Press, 1994.

Greenstein, Fred I., and Richard H. Immerman. "What Did Eisenhower Tell Kennedy about Indochina? The Politics of Misperception." *Journal of American History,* September 1992.

Grose, Peter. *Gentleman Spy: The Life and Times of Allen Dulles.* Boston: Houghton Mifflin, 1994.

Gruenther, Richard L., and David W. Parmly. "The Crusade of a Green Beret: Eleazar Parmly IV in Southeast Asia." *Special Warfare,* March 1992.

Halpern, Barbara and Joel Halpern. "Laos and America: A Retrospective View." *South Atlantic Quarterly,* Spring 1964. http://scholarworks.umass.edu/anthro_faculty_pubs/32.

Halpern, Joel M. "America and Laos: Two Views of Political Strategy and Technical Assistance," 1959. RAND. http://scholarworks.umass.edu/anthro_faculty_pubs/11.

———. "The Lao Elite: A Study of Tradition and Innovation," 1960. RAND Research Memorandum, JFKL, JMHP.

———. "Some Reflections on the War in Laos, Anthropological and Otherwise," 1970. Univ. of Massachusetts, www.vietnam.ttu.edu.

Hanyok, Robert J. "Spartans in Darkness. American SIGINT and the Indochina War, 1945–1975," 2002. Center for Cryptologic History, National Security Agency.

Hasey, John F. *Yankee Fighter: The Story of an American in the Free French Foreign Legion.* New York: Little, Brown, 1942.

Helms, Richard. *A Look over My Shoulder: A Life in the Central Intelligence Agency.* New York: Random House, 2003.

Hilsman, Roger. *To Move a Nation: The Politics of Foreign Policy in the Administration of John F. Kennedy.* Garden City, NY: Doubleday, 1967.

Immerman, Richard H. *John Foster Dulles: Piety, Pragmatism, and Power in U.S. Foreign Policy.* Wilmington, DE: Scholarly Resources, 1999.

Ivarsson, Søren, and Christopher E. Goscha. "Prince Phetsarath (1890–1959): Nationalism and Royalty in the Making of Modern Laos." *Journal of Southeast Asian Studies,* February 2007.

Johnson, U. Alexis. *The Right Hand of Power: The Memoirs of an American Diplomat.* Englewood Cliffs, NJ: Prentice-Hall, 1984.

Killian, James R. *Sputnik, Scientists, and Eisenhower: A Memoir of the First Special*

Assistant to the President for Science and Technology. Cambridge, MA: MIT Press, 1977.

Kraemer, Alfred J., and Edward C. Stewart. "Cross-Cultural Problems of U.S. Army Personnel in Laos and Their Implications for Area Training," September 1964. George Washington University Human Resources Research Office.

Krebs, Ronald R. *Dueling Visions: U.S. Strategy toward Eastern Europe under Eisenhower.* College Station: Texas A&M Univ. Press, 2001.

Lair, Bill. "The Thai PARU and the War in Laos," October 21, 2006. Vietnam Center and Archive, Texas Tech Univ.

Langer, Paul F. "The Soviet Union, China, and the Pathet Lao: Analysis and Chronology," 1972. RAND Corporation.

Langer, Paul F., and Joseph J. Zasloff. *North Vietnam and the Pathet Lao: Partners in the Struggle for Laos.* Cambridge, MA: Harvard Univ. Press, 1970.

Leary, William M. "CIA Air Operations in Laos, 1955–1974." Center for the Study of Intelligence, www.cia.gov.

Lyon, Peter. *Eisenhower: Portrait of the Hero.* New York: Little Brown, 1974.

McNamara, Robert S. *In Retrospect: The Tragedy and Lessons of Vietnam.* New York: Times Books, 1995.

McNamara, Robert S., James G. Blight, and Robert Brigham. *Argument without End: In Search of Answers to the Vietnam Tragedy.* New York: Public Affairs, 1999.

Meeker, Oden. *The Little World of Laos.* New York: Charles Scribner's, 1959.

Methven, Stuart. *Laughter in the Shadows: A CIA Memoir.* Annapolis: Naval Institute Press, 2008.

Moise, Edwin E. "JFK and the Myth of Withdrawal." In *A Companion to the Vietnam War,* edited by Marilyn B. Young and Robert Buzzanco, 162–73 Oxford: Blackwell, 2002.

Morgan, Ted. *Valley of Death: The Tragedy at Dien Bien Phu That Led America into the Vietnam War.* New York: Random House, 2010.

Noble, G. Bernard. *The American Secretaries of State and Their Diplomacy.* Vol. 18, *Christian A. Herter.* New York: Cooper Square, 1970.

Osornprasop, Sutayut. "Amidst the Heat of the Cold War in Asia: Thailand and the American Secret War in Indochina (1960–74)." *Cold War History,* August 2007.

Ostermann, Christian F., ed. "Inside China's Cold War." *Cold War International History Project Bulletin,* Fall 2007–Winter 2008.

Paddock, Alfred H., Jr. *U.S. Army Special Warfare: Its Origins.* Rev. ed. Lawrence: Univ. Press of Kansas, 2002.

Paterson, Thomas G. *Contesting Castro: The United States and the Triumph of the Cuban Revolution.* New York: Oxford Univ. Press, 1994.

Pedlow, Gregory W., and Donald E. Welzenbach. "The Central Intelligence Agency and Overhead Reconnaissance: The U-2 and OXCART Programs, 1954–1974," 1992. CIA History Staff Monograph, www.cia.gov.

Phillips, Rufus. *Why Vietnam Matters: An Eyewitness Account of Lessons Not Learned.* Annapolis: Naval Institute Press, 2008.

Phraxayavong, Vilam. *History of Aid to Laos: Motivations and Impacts.* Chiang Mai, Thailand: Mekong Press, 2009.

Potter, Elmer B. *Admiral Arleigh Burke*. Annapolis: Naval Institute Press, 1990.

Prados, John. *The Blood Road: The Ho Chi Minh Trail and the Vietnam War*. New York: John Wiley, 1998.

Rabe, Stephen G. "Eisenhower Revisionism: A Decade of Scholarship." *Diplomatic History*, January 1993.

Richmond, Yale. *Practicing Public Diplomacy: A Cold War Odyssey*. New York: Berghahn Books, 2008.

———. "Some Left on Stretchers, Others in Straightjackets." *Foreign Service Journal*, May 1988.

Rusk, Dean. *As I Saw It*. New York: W. W. Norton, 1990.

Rust, William J. *Kennedy in Vietnam*. New York: Charles Scribner's, 1985.

Sander, Alfred Dick. *Eisenhower's Executive Office*. Westport, CT: Green Wood Press, 1999.

Savada, Andrea Matles, ed. "Laos: A Country Study," 1994. Federal Research Division, Library of Congress, http://memory.loc.gov.

Schlesinger, Arthur M., Jr. *A Thousand Days: John F. Kennedy in the White House*. New York: Houghton Mifflin, 1965.

Secretary of State for Foreign Affairs. *Fourth Interim Report of the International Commission for Supervision and Control in Laos*. London: Her Majesty's Stationary Office, 1958.

———. *Second Interim Report of the International Commission for Supervision and Control in Laos*. London: Her Majesty's Stationary Office, 1955.

———. *Third Interim Report of the International Commission for Supervision and Control in Laos*. London: Her Majesty's Stationary Office, 1957.

Sherman, Stephen. *Who's Who from HOTFOOT/WHITESTAR*. Houston, TX: RADIX Press, 2004.

Smith, Horace H. "Significant Developments in Laos, 1958–1960." LBJ Library, National Security File, Country File for Laos, "Laos Memos Volume 16 2/66–1/67," box 271.

Sorensen, Theodore C. *Kennedy*. New York: Harper and Row, 1965.

Stanton, Shelby L. *Green Berets at War: U.S. Forces in Southeast Asia, 1956–1975*. Novato, CA: Presidio Press, 1985.

Statler, Kathryn N. *Replacing France: The Origins of American Intervention in Vietnam*. Lexington: Univ. Press of Kentucky, 2007.

Stieglitz, Perry. *In a Little Kingdom*. Armonk, NY: M. E. Sharpe, 1990.

Stuart-Fox, Martin. *A History of Laos*. New York: Cambridge Univ. Press, 1997.

Stuart-Fox, Martin, and Rod Bucknell. "Politicization of the Buddhist Sangha in Laos." *Journal of Southeast Asian Studies*, March 1982.

Taubman, William. *Khrushchev: The Man and His Era*. New York: W. W. Norton, 2003.

Thomas, Evan. *The Very Best Men: The Daring Early Years of the CIA*. New York: Simon and Schuster Paperbacks, 2006.

Toye, Hugh. *Laos: Buffer State or Battleground*. London: Oxford University Press, 1968.

Trinquier, Roger. *Modern Warfare: A French View of Counterinsurgency*. Fort Leavenworth, KS: U.S. Army Command and General Staff College, 1985, www .cgsc.edu.

Tucker, Nancy Bernkopf, ed. *China Confidential: American Diplomats and Sino-American Relations, 1945–1996.* New York: Columbia Univ. Press, 2001.

Tuuainen, Pasi. *The Role of Presidential Advisory Systems in US Foreign Policy-Making: The Case of the National Security Council and Vietnam, 1953–1961.* Helsinki: SKS, 2001.

United Nations. "847th Meeting: 7 September 1959." 1959. Security Council Records, www.un.org.

———. "Report of the Security Council Sub-Committee under Resolution of 7 September 1959," November 5, 1959, S/4236, www.un.org.

Urquhart, Brian. *Hammarskjold.* New York: W. W. Norton, 1972.

U.S. Department of Defense. 1961. "Chronological Summary of Significant Events concerning the Laotian Crisis," April 21, 1961. Rev. version. Historical Division, Joint Secretariat, Joint Chiefs of Staff, www.dod.mil/pubs/foi.

———. "Summary and Historical Analysis of the Lao Incident, August 1960 to May 1961, Part I." Weapons Systems Evaluation Group, October 17, 1962, www.dod.mil/pubs/foi.

———. "Historical Analysis of the Lao Incident, August 1960 to May 1961, Part II," Weapons Systems Evaluation Group, October 1, 1963, www.dod.mil/pubs/foi.

———. *The Pentagon Papers: The Defense Department History of United States Decisionmaking on Vietnam.* Gravel Edition. Boston: Beacon Press, 1971.

———. *United States–Vietnam Relations, 1945–1967: Study Prepared by the Department of Defense.* Washington, DC: Government Printing Office, 1971.

U.S. Department of State. "Comments by the Department of State and ICA on the Report of the House Committee on Government Operations." Washington, DC: Government Printing Office, 1959. Reprinted by Dalley Book Service, Christiansburg, VA.

———. *Foreign Relations of the United States, 1952–1954. Vol. XII, East Asia and Pacific.* Washington, DC: Government Printing Office, 1984.

———. *Foreign Relations of the United States, 1952–1954. Vol. XIII, Indochina.* Washington, DC: Government Printing Office, 1982.

———. *Foreign Relations of the United States, 1952–1954. Vol. XVI, The Geneva Conference: Korea and Indochina.* Washington, DC: Government Printing Office, 1981.

———. *Foreign Relations of the United States, 1955–1957. Vol. I, Vietnam.* Washington, DC: Government Printing Office, 1985.

———. *Foreign Relations of the United States, 1955–1957. Vol. XXI, East Asian Security; Laos; Cambodia.* Washington, DC: Government Printing Office, 1990.

———. *Foreign Relations of the United States, 1958–1960. Vol. I, Vietnam.* Washington, DC: Government Printing Office, 1986.

———. *Foreign Relations of the United States, 1958–1960. Vol. XVI, East Asia-Pacific Region, Cambodia; Laos.* Washington, DC: Government Printing Office, 1992.

———. *Foreign Relations of the United States, 1958–1960. Vol. XVI, East Asia-Pacific Region, Cambodia; Laos.* Microfiche Supplement (MFS), 1992.

———. *Foreign Relations of the United States, 1961–1963. Vol. IV, Vietnam.* Washington, DC: Government Printing Office, 1991.

———. *Foreign Relations of the United States, 1961–1963. Vol. V, The Soviet Union.* Washington, DC: Government Printing Office, 1998.

———. *Foreign Relations of the United States, 1961–1963. Vols. XXII–XXIV, Northeast Asia; Laos.* MFS, 1997.

———. *Foreign Relations of the United States, 1961–1963. Vol. XXIII, Southeast Asia.* Washington, DC: Government Printing Office, 1994.

———. *Foreign Relations of the United States, 1961–1963. Vol. XXIV, Laos Crisis.* Washington, DC: Government Printing Office, 1994.

———. *Foreign Relations of the United States, 1961–1963. Vol. XXV, Organization of Foreign Policy; Information Policy; United Nations; Scientific Matters.* Washington, DC: Government Printing Office, 2001.

———. *Foreign Relations of the United States, 1964–1968. Vol. XXVIII, Laos.* Washington, DC: Government Printing Office, 1998.

———. *Foreign Relations of the United States: The Intelligence Community, 1950–1955,* Washington, DC: Government Printing Office, 2007.

U.S. House of Representatives, Government Operations Committee. *U.S. Aid Operations in Laos.* Washington, DC: Government Printing Office, 1959.

U.S. Senate, Select Committee to Study Governmental Operations. *Alleged Assassination Plots Involving Foreign Leaders.* Washington, DC: Government Printing Office, 1975.

———. *Supplementary Detailed Staff Reports on Foreign and Military Intelligence, Book IV.* Washington, DC: Government Printing Office, 1976.

Warner, Roger. *Shooting at the Moon: The Story of America's Clandestine War in Laos.* South Royalton, VT: Steerforth Press, 1996.

Wing, Roswell B., et al. *Case Study of U.S. Counterinsurgency Operations In Laos, 1955–1962.* McLean, VA: Research Analysis Corporation, 1964.

Zasloff, Joseph J. *The Pathet Lao: Leadership and Organization.* Lexington, MA: Lexington Books, 1973.

Zhai, Qiang. *China and the Vietnam Wars, 1950–1975.* Chapel Hill: Univ. of North Carolina Press, 2000.

Index